THE LIFE OF
DAVID BELASCO

VOLUME TWO

*"I will not be slack to play
my part in Fortune's pageant!"*
—Shakespeare

DAVID BELASCO

*"The natural successor of Lester Wallack, Edwin Booth and Augustin Daly, as
the leading theatrical manager of America."*—**W. W.**

THE LIFE
OF
DAVID BELASCO

BY

WILLIAM WINTER

(1836–1917)

"He, being dead, yet speaketh."

VOLUME TWO

BOOKS FOR LIBRARIES PRESS
FREEPORT, NEW YORK

First Published 1918
Reprinted 1970

March, 1970

STANDARD BOOK NUMBER:
8369-5202-2

LIBRARY OF CONGRESS CATALOG CARD NUMBER:
72-107837

PRINTED IN THE UNITED STATES OF AMERICA

CONTENTS

THE LIFE OF DAVID BELASCO—VOLUME TWO

CONTENTS

CONTENTS

CONTENTS

CONTENTS

ILLUSTRATIONS.

VOLUME TWO.

In Photogravure.

In Halftone.

"To him the laurels and the lyre belong:
He won them well, and may he wear them long!"

THE LIFE OF DAVID BELASCO

The London engagement of "Zaza" ended,
Belasco, Mrs. Carter, and the members of the
"Zaza" company returned to America, sailing from
Southampton, on board the steamship New York,
August 18, 1900. Mrs. Carter's tour in that play
began at the Criterion Theatre, New York, on
October 1, and Belasco turned his attention to
launching Blanche Bates as a star. The histrionic
vehicle which he selected for this purpose was a
revamped dramatization of Ouida's "Under Two
Flags." He had hoped to obtain a drama on a
fresh subject for her use and he had asked
Charles Frohman to assist in finding such a one.
But, after waiting a considerable time without
any suitable play coming to light and it being
essential to bring her forward in something, Belasco
determined to turn to an old subject and revivify
it. "I decided, in desperation," he writes, "to revive
'Under Two Flags,' which I had long been familiar
with, of which I had made at least two versions,

1

and which, in the old days, I had directed for Lotta. Her version of it, however, seemed very old-fashioned, and I employed Mr. Paul M. Potter to make a new adaptation of the book. I introduced a novel effect in that production in the sand-storm in the Fourth Act; it was simple in its mechanism, but it required much work to perfect it: it has since come into general use."

Ouida's novel is so well known to the public of the Library and, in one form or another, histrionic adaptations of it are so well known to the public of the Theatre, that the subject is, in every point of view, familiar, and minutely detailed consideration of it in this place would, therefore, be superfluous. The new theatrical epitome of that novel was made known, for the first time, at the Garden Theatre, New York, February 5, 1901. It was, in every detail, supervised and made practical by Belasco, and it owed its success to his ingenious and expert manipulation and to the embodiment of *Cigarette* given in it under his direction by Miss Bates. The story of that ardent, picturesque, adventurous girl is a story of amatory infatuation, brave exploits, and pathetic self-sacrifice, under romantic circumstances. The representative of *Cigarette* must be handsome, passionate, expeditious, magnanimous, resolute, full of resource, sparkling with energy,

BLANCHE BATES AS *CIGARETTE*, IN "UNDER TWO FLAGS"

potent in fiery conflicts of feeling, and, above all, capable of covering grief with a smile. That is the essence of her character. Blanche Bates, possessing rare personal distinction and a temperament equally attuned to the extreme moods of mirth and grief, was easily proficient in the assumption of that personality and in the pictorial and effective exposition of it. Without the presence of that actress the play (if it had ever been produced at all) would have passed as a populous, tumultuous stage pageant,—a spectacle of Moorish scenery and military bustle. Animated by her power, sensibility, and spirited, various, incessant action, it was lifted to dramatic importance and Belasco's "desperate" venture—as he calls it—proved brilliantly successful.

The employment of *Cigarette* is the salvation from various dangers of *Bertie Cecil,* a man whom she loves and whose love is bestowed on another woman, and her diligence in that employment is attended by risk and rewarded by ruin. Many persons appear to think that it is beatific to be loved by other persons and grievous not to be loved, and, accordingly, love-tales exemplary of the joy, on the one hand, and the sorrow, on the other, that are sequent from those antipodal conditions of experience are perennially popular. *Pygmalion* worships a stone; *Titania* caresses the ears of an ass, and the populace is thrilled. *Cigarette's* passion for *Bertie Cecil* is of the old, familiar kind, and, the scene being Algeria, her adventures are, theatrically, shown across a background of singular beauty,—because that country is remarkable for flowers, cedar forests, Oriental palms, Roman remains, stony deserts contrasted with smiling villages, and luxuriant gardens not distant from mountains covered with snow.

Taste, thought, ingenuity, and sedulous care were expended on every feature of the pageant by Belasco, and the result was a magnificent spectacle,—one of the richest and most impressive ever seen on our Stage. Had it been brought here by Henry Irving or Herbert Beerbohm-Tree, it would have been hailed as a transcendent exploit in stagecraft. Every scene was a picture, every picture was harmonious with the phase of the story to be illustrated, and in the transitions from the luxurious villa, with its prospect of the tranquil ocean faintly rippling beneath the moon, to the desolate, rocky, weird, and ominous mountain gorge a climax of solemn grandeur seemed to take shape, color, and charm, slowly rising out of a dream of romantic beauty. The drift of whirling mist over the darkening waves of sand on the bleak seacoast would have seemed the most consummate of illusions had it not

been excelled by the blinding terrors of a mountain
tempest. Those effects were wrought by simple
means, but they were not less splendid because of
the simplicity of their management.

The *dramatic* victory was not won, however, by
either the pageantry or the play. Mr. Potter's
variant version of "Under Two Flags" is hackneyed
in expedients, abrupt in movement, drastic in
method, coarse in character, shady in morals, florid
in style, and it was made silly, in some of the col-
loquies, by the infusion of contemporary slang and
reference. The listener heard of "rot" and also of
"the Klondike,"—unknown in the period of the
story. But the old novel had been made to yield
telling situations, and the strong and splendid acting of Miss Bates vitalized them, brilliantly animated the whole structure, and vindicated Belasco's
faith in the ability of the actress. The revelation
of jealousy working in an unsophisticated, half-
savage nature, the elemental passion expressed in
the fantastic dance, the prayer of the breaking heart
for her lover's fidelity, the supplication for his pardon, the agony when repulsed, the ecstasy when
triumphant, the tremendous conflict of emotions in
the wild ride for rescue,—they were all displayed
with more of human nature and more of a competent artist's power to control feelings and to shape

the effect of situation than had been seen on our
Stage for many a long day.—This was the original
cast of "Under Two Flags" at the Garden Theatre:

Bertie Cecil	Francis Carlyle.
John	Maclyn Arbuckle.
Rake	Edward S. Abeles.
Countess of Westminster	Rose Snyder.
Venetia Lyonnesse	Margaret Robinson.
Marquis of Chateauroy	Campbell Gollan.
Lord Constantia	Arthur Bruce.
Pierre Baroni	Albert Bruning.
Renée Baroni	Grace Elliston.
General Lamoricière	Matt. Snyder.
Paul Lamoricière	Madge West.
Captain de Chanrellon	Beresford Webb.
En-ta-Maboull	Frank Leyden.
Beau Bruno	Tefft Johnson.
Amineh	Mrs. F. M. Bates.
Cigarette	Blanche Bates.

BELASCO AND DAVID WARFIELD:—THEIR FIRST MEETING.

"Under Two Flags" was acted at the Garden
Theatre until June 3, 1901, when that house was
closed for the season and Belasco turned his attention to preparations for the appearance of Mrs.
Carter in a new play and for the bringing forward
of David Warfield as a star in the legitimate

A SCENE IN BELASCO'S "UNDER TWO FLAGS"

Theatre. That actor, then a popular variety hall performer and a member of the burlesque and travesty company maintained by Messrs. Weber & Fields at their theatre in New York,—in Broadway, between Twenty-ninth and Thirtieth streets,—had negotiated with Belasco, about August-September, 1900, relative to acting under his management and on November 2, that year, they entered into a formal agreement whereby Belasco undertook the direction of Warfield's professional career. Their contract was made to cover a first period of three years: it provided that Warfield should be presented as a star, beginning about September or October, 1901, and that he should be paid a weekly salary of $300 and should receive, further, 20 per cent. of the net profits of his professional exploitation during the first year, 25 per cent. during the second year, 30 per cent. during the third year, and 50 per cent. thereafter, if the contract should be renewed. This engagement also expressly required Belasco "personally to supervise the performances to be given" by Warfield as well as to provide a play for him to act in. The professional alliance thus begun between Belasco and Warfield has proved, for both parties to it, one of the most fortunate ever made in the Theatre. The personal friend-

ship between them began many years earlier:
Belasco has given the following glimpse of its
beginning:

"There was an usher at the Bush Street Theatre—a
bright little fellow with a most luminous smile. He is still
small, and his smile is still luminous. I did not then know
his name, but I had heard that among his family and
friends he was quite an entertainer, being able to sing, to
mimic and to recite. One day I was at home, in my front
room on the top floor, when I heard a voice in the street
below. I leaned out, and there on the corner, standing on
a box which scarcely raised him above the gaping onlookers,
was the little usher from the Bush Street Theatre, reciting
to a curious crowd. I went down and stood near until he
had finished. Then I went up to him and asked him his
name. 'Dave Warfield,' said he, giving me the smile that
lived long afterwards in *Herr von Barwig*, during all the
rehearsals of 'The Music Master,' and that was our first
meeting."

David Warfield was born in San Francisco on
November 28, 1866. He began theatrical life as
a programme boy, in the Standard Theatre of that
city. Later he became an usher in the Bush Street
Theatre there. His first professional appearance
was made as a member of a travelling theatrical
company at Napa, California, in 1888, as the
specious, rascally Jew, *Melter Moss,* in "The
Ticket-of-Leave Man." That company was disbanded at the end of one week, and thereafter

Warfield appeared at several San Francisco variety halls, and in a piece called "About Town," and gave imitations of actors whom he had seen,— among them Tommaso Salvini and Sarah Bernhardt,—and of "types" that he had observed in the streets of his native city. In 1890 he removed to New York and obtained professional employment, for a short time, in Paine's Concert Hall, in Eighth Avenue. His next engagement was to act *Hiram Joskins,* in a play called "The Inspector," produced by Mr. William A. Brady: that employment lasted two months. In March, 1891, he performed as *Honora,* in "O'Dowd's Neighbors," in a company led by Mark Murphy. In the season of 1891-'92 he acted with Russell's Comedians, under the management of John H. Russell, appearing as *John Smith,* in "The City Directory." In 1892-'93 he was seen as *Washington Littlehales,* in "A Nutmeg Match." In September, 1895, he became associated with the New York Casino Theatre, where he remained for three years, acting in "About Town," "The Merry Whirl," "In Gay New York," and "The Belle of New York,"—pieces which are correctly described as medleys of tinkling music and nonsense. In those "entertainments," frivolous and often vulgar, Warfield presented several variations of substantially the same identity,—an expert semblance of the New York East Side Jew. In 1898 he joined the company of Messrs. Weber & Fields, and at their theatre, where he remained for three seasons, he appeared in various rough and commonplace travesties of contemporary theatrical successes, generally presenting, in different lights, his photographic copy of the huckstering, acquisitive, pusillanimous Jew of low life. One notable variation of that type was his assumption of *The Old Man,* in a burlesque of the offensive play of "Catherine." Among the salient characteristics of his acting, in whatever parts he played, were fidelity to minute detail of appearance and demeanor and consistent and continuous preservation of the spirit of burlesque,—a spirit which combines imperturbable gravity of aspect with apparently profound sincerity in preposterous situations and while delivering extravagant, ludicrous speeches. True burlesque acting is a fine art and admirable as such, and Warfield was heartily approved in that field; but at the time when Belasco undertook to make him a star in the regular Theatre nobody, I believe, except the shrewd and prescient manager,—not even Warfield,—foresaw that within a few years he would have become one of the most popular serio-comic actors of the modern American Stage.

WARFIELD AND "THE AUCTIONEER."

The play in which Belasco elected to launch
Warfield was entitled "The Auctioneer." He had,
at first, intended to write this play himself, calling
it "The Only Levi." But his time and energy
were so preoccupied by labor in connection with
the establishment of Miss Bates and the direction
of Mrs. Carter's career that he was unable to
do so. He, therefore, employed a playwright
known as Lee Arthur (Arthur Lee Kahn) to
take his ideas and suggestions and weld them into
dramatic form. The fabric which Arthur, in fulfilment of this employment, delivered to him was
so wholly unfit for use ("an impossible thing,
unworthy of production," Belasco designated it)
that he subsequently engaged the late Charles Klein
to rewrite it in collaboration with Arthur, and,
finally, was compelled himself to rehash and partly
rectify it during rehearsals and early performances.
It was first acted at the Hyperion Theatre, New
Haven, Connecticut, September 9, 1901. Warfield,
testifying on the subject in court, several years
later, made a statement,—which, surely, may be
accepted as authoritative,—regarding this piece, as
originally produced, which is terse and informing:
"When we began to rehearse," he said, "we had a

book filled with words. The play was a frost. *It was the biggest failure you ever heard of,* the opening night. . . . Mr. Belasco worked day and night upon the reconstruction of that play, from the time that he started with the rehearsals the week before we left New York [preliminary rehearsals had been conducted by Messrs. Klein and Arthur] until we came to New York and played, three weeks later." The first performance of "The Auctioneer" in the metropolis occurred September 23, at the old Bijou Theatre, in Broadway, between Thirtieth and Thirty-first streets. The piece, as then made known, is a superficial, insubstantial one, which, however, contrives to illustrate some vicissitudes of fortune, and, in the main part, exemplifies the idea of a right philosophy in bearing them. That main part is a Jewish auctioneer, named *Simon Levi,* resident in Baxter Street, New York, and conducting an auction-room in the Five Points region. *Levi,* having inherited a modest but competent fortune, purchases a residence in a fashionable part of the city and invests the balance of his money in a Trust Company. Then, at a festival in celebration of the betrothal of his adopted daughter, a girl named *Helga,* he is apprized that his stock certificates in the Trust Company are bogus and that *Richard Eagan,* the affianced husband of

DAVID WARFIELD AS *SIMON LEVI*, IN "THE AUCTIONEER"

Helga, for whom he has bought a partnership in a Wall Street brokerage firm, is to be arrested, charged with fraud in issuing them. Forced, with his dearly loved and cherished wife, to leave his new home in ignominious circumstances, *Levi,* though feeble in body and hurt in spirit, bravely begins anew the strife of living,—peddling toys in the streets. He discovers, ultimately, that the actual swindler who has ruined him is one *Groode,* the partner of his prospective son-in-law, from whom he recovers his wealth, delivering the culprit up to justice and relieving the distress of his own loved ones. This story, notwithstanding Belasco's strenuous labor, lost little of its trite conventionality in its histrionic relation; but his capital stage management and the highly meritorious performance given by Warfield under his direction made of a flimsy, trivial play a notable and substantial success.

It was a shrewd device, when inducting Warfield into the regular Theatre, to do so not abruptly, but, as it were, by gentle actuation,—to provide for his first essay a character which was little more than an elaboration of his Jewish "specialty," in which his early success had been gained, with an element of pathetic experience and feeling superadded to it. "I had been watching Warfield for years," said Belasco, "and I felt sure that, if he

would only study, I could make a great character
[*sic*—meaning "eccentric"] actor of him; I told him
so, and when I thought he was ready I engaged
him." While I cannot altogether agree with
Belasco in his opinion, often and warmly declared,
that David Warfield is "a unique and great actor,"
—not, that is, in the same sense that, for example,
Henry Placide, William Warren, Joseph Jefferson
and John Hare were great actors,—there is no
question of his rare and fine talent nor of his
steady growth in artistic stature. He has revealed
in his acting an engaging personality, a genial
disposition, a gentle manner, quick sympathy with
right ideals, and capability of fervid emotion and
simple pathos. Of all the many players, male and
female, whom Belasco has guided and helped to
develop none, in my judgment, owes more to his
fostering care and assistance than Warfield does:
it is extremely probable that, without Belasco's
aid, he would have remained to the end of his
career a denizen of the music-halls, instead of
becoming, as he has become, one of the most loved
and admired actors of our Stage. As *Simon Levi*
he presented a genuine, consistent impersonation in
the vein of eccentric low comedy, at places touched
with tender feeling and momentarily irradiated with
pathos. His assumption of the physical attributes

of this particular Jew of low life,—the sallow
complexion; the thin, wiry hair; the splayfooted,
shambling gait; the voluble gestures, the singular
dialect; the manner, now aggressive, now fawning,
—was quite perfect; but his significant achievement
was his success in denoting a steadfast, affectionate,
patient nature beneath the mean outside of a
petty huckster subjected to cruel disappointment
and hardship.—This was the original cast of "The
Auctioneer":

Simon Levi	David Warfield.
Mrs. Levi	Maria Davis.
Mrs. Eagan	Marie Bates.
Callahan	Odell Williams.
Jacob Sampson	Harry Rodgers.
Richard Eagan	Brandon Tynan.
Mo Fininski	Eugene Canfield.
Minnie	Nellie Lynch.
Groode	William Boag.
Mrs. Sampson	Helena Phillips.
Helga	Maude Winter.
Dawkins	Horace James.
Critch	H. S. Millward.
Miss Manning	Nina Lyn.
Miss Crompton	Elizabeth Berkeley.
Miss Finch	Corah Adams.
Zeke	Cyril Vezina.
Mandy	Ruth Dennis.
Policeman	Harry Rawlins.
Chestnut Vender	Richard Bevan.

IN THE GRIP OF THE OCTOPUS.—ANCIENT
METHODS IN MODERN BUSINESS.

"The Auctioneer" played at the Bijou Theatre
until December 21,—105 consecutive performances
being given there. On December 23 Warfield
began a "road tour" in that play which lasted for
twenty weeks, ending at the Illinois Theatre, Chicago, May 10, 1902. The net profit from this
tour was $80,000,—certainly an amazing sum to
be gained by presentation in the regular Theatre
of an unknown star, fresh from the music halls,
who, all told, had appeared in perhaps a score of
productions! But Belasco's actual profit from the
fruits of his perspicacious judgment and enterprise
was far less than that great sum. The reason of
this seemingly strange fact is that in his professional exploitation of Warfield he had fallen
into the ruthless grip of an iniquitous "booking-
monopoly" which, practically, dominated for many
years what are known as "the first-class theatres"
of America and which is still perniciously active.
Belasco's conflict with that monopoly was long and
bitter; thousands of columns have been devoted to
it in the newspaper press of the country, and it
has, at various times, occupied a prominent place
in public attention. That conflict grew directly out

DAVID BELASCO
About 1885

of his undertaking the management of Warfield. Several actions at law have been incident to it. Testifying under oath in one of them, in 1905, Belasco gave an account of his experience in relation to "The Auctioneer" which I believe to be true in all essentials and of which I make the following abstract and brief chronicle:

After Belasco had undertaken to bring forward Warfield as a star he applied to Mr. Abraham Lincoln Erlanger, junior member of the firm of Klaw & Erlanger, theatrical managers and booking agents (i.e., "agents" who arbitrarily arranged tours by theatrical companies through American cities), for the purpose of making advantageous arrangements for Warfield to appear in New York and other cities. He applied to Mr. Erlanger because he was aware that it was, at the time, practically speaking, impossible for him to make such arrangements, except through the firm of Klaw & Erlanger, and that the junior member attended to such business for that firm. He called on Mr. Erlanger at his residence, No. 262 West Seventieth Street, New York, on Sunday, December 9, 1900, and stated his wish. Mr. Erlanger, in response, stated that "We [K. & E.] are not in this business for our health" and inquired "Where do we [K. & E.] come in?" Belasco replied that Klaw & Erlanger would receive their customary commission, $300 to $400, for "booking" the play. To this Mr. Erlanger rejoined "Hell, about that: we got to get something more." Belasco, after protesting that he was not, in any way, soliciting a favor; that he assumed all risk and liability in the venture, and that he felt it to be "a sort of blackmail" (and a very obvious sort, I should say!) to exact from him a share in whatever gains might accrue to him from presentation of Warfield, offered to surrender to Klaw & Erlanger 20 per cent. of such gains, in return for "a route." This offer, swore Belasco, Mr. Erlanger rejected, demanding that, instead he (his firm) should receive *50* per cent. of any profits from the exploitation of Warfield. To Belasco's inquiry as to why he should receive this unearned remuneration Mr. Erlanger rejoined "None of your damn' business; I want half, and *if I don't get half* out of Warfield *you can't have a route for him.* I will crush you out; sit upon you; jump upon you, and push you out; *crush you out of this theatrical business!"* He further admonished Belasco thus: "Understand me, Belasco; hereafter, I want 50 per cent. of every damn' thing you do!" Belasco, after taking several days to consider this extortionate proposal, decided that he could not avoid accepting it, if he was successfully to present

Warfield. He went, in company with his business manager, Benjamin F. Roeder, to Mr. Erlanger's office and there communicated his decision to him, saying: "Mr. Erlanger, I can't see any escape for me. I want it understood that you are *compelling* me to give up 50 per cent. I don't think it is right, but, if you insist, there is nothing else for me to do." The agreement was then made, the late Joseph Brooks, an associate of Klaw & Erlanger, being put forward, according to Belasco's testimony, as a "dummy" in the written contract, in order that the partnership of Klaw & Erlanger might be concealed from their partners in the Theatrical Syndicate,—Messrs. Charles Frohman, Al. Hayman, Samuel F. Nirdlinger (known as S. F. Nixon) and J. Fred. Zimmermann,—this concealment being desired in order that Klaw & Erlanger, as booking agents, might be able to exact more profitable terms from their Syndicate partners than would be possible if that firm were generally known to possess "an interest" in the presentation of Warfield in "The Auctioneer." Belasco, to substantiate his assertion that, actually, he was in partnership with Klaw & Erlanger, not with Brooks, in the said presentation, produced a number of paid cheques drawn to the order of that firm, to a total amount of more than $30,000,—which, he swore, represented its 50 per cent. of profits from "The Auctioneer" during the period while that play was "booked" by Klaw & Erlanger,—a period which, from the record, seems to have ended on January 31, 1902, at Duluth, Minnesota. Brooks, by way of explaining those cheques, testified that he had directed Belasco's business agent, Roeder, to make them payable to the order of Klaw & Erlanger because he, Brooks, was frequently absent from New York! Brooks *admitted* that he "made them [Klaw & Erlanger] a present of" two-thirds of the half-interest in presentation of "The Auctioneer" which he asserted was his.

TESTIMONY UNDER OATH:—BELASCO *VERSUS* ERLANGER.

If we accept Belasco's sworn testimony as true, then it must appear that in the matter of arranging a tour for Warfield in "The Auctioneer" he was the victim of as brazen and shameful an instance of blackmail as has ever been perpetrated. It must, however, in justice be specified that Mr. Erlanger, also testifying under oath, *flatly denied every material statement* made by Belasco bearing on this matter: the effect of Mr. Erlanger's sworn testimony, if it be accepted as true, must be to exhibit Belasco as a villain and a liar. The eminent

lawyer Samuel Untermyer, Esq., who appeared
for Belasco in the legal actions from the records
of which this conflictive testimony is cited, seems to
have been strongly impressed by its mutually exclu-
sive nature: in reading certain affidavits in the cases
he remarked that they were "so contradictory that
they reveal a most flagrant and rank perjury on
one side or the other." But every man's testimony
should receive the degree of respect and credence
to which his known character and reputation entitle
it. I have known Belasco for more than thirty
years and, though he is (as I know and in this
Memoir have shown) often inaccurate and heedless
in regard to chronologic sequence, I know him to
be trustworthy as to substance in the statement of
material facts; in short, *his* known character and
reputation are good. Erlanger, on the contrary, is
a person whose public record, as known to me, is
wholly consistent with Belasco's account of his conduct,—a cowardly, hectoring bully, of violent temper and unsavory repute. Apart from this, since
Erlanger has testified relative to certain affidavits made by him "The things I *swear to* I only
look at casually" (! ! !) I see no reason to believe
that the things he "swears to," derogatory of others,
are worthy of any respect or credence. It would
be pleasant to me to avoid any mention of this

person, his character and proceedings; but it is impossible to do so when writing an authentic account of the life of Belasco or of the American Stage since about 1896. "He [Erlanger]," Belasco has declared, "told me that if I refused his terms he would compel me to go into the streets and blacken my face to earn a living. He said that I spoiled the public instead of compelling them to take what the Trust chose to give, and that a man with ideals in the theatrical business wound up with a benefit within three years." There is, therefore, I believe, ample ground for the feeling toward and opinion about Erlanger which Belasco expressed in his testimony: "I detest the man and his methods. I detest him to-day. I think he is the most abhorred man in the country, because he strikes hard bargains, and he makes people give up more than any other man in the country."—The suits at law referred to in the foregoing passage (suits brought by Joseph Brooks against David Belasco and David Belasco Company, and by David Belasco Company against Marc Klaw, Abraham L. Erlanger and Joseph Brooks, the purposes of which were to establish whether Belasco and Brooks or Belasco and Klaw & Erlanger were partners in the presentation of David Warfield in "The Auctioneer" and to secure an accounting under the partnership agreement) were tried before the Hon. James J. Fitzgerald, J., sitting in equity, at Special Session of Part V., Supreme Court, State of New York, April 6 to 26, 1905. The decision and judgment were against Belasco, and his case was carried on appeal to the Appellate Division, First Department, of the Supreme Court, April 20, 1906.

LAW *VERSUS* JUSTICE.

That adverse decision and judgment were based on a technicality,—on a point of law, not on a point of fact. The learned Justice who rendered decision and pronounced judgment did not find that Belasco had failed to prove his contention that, actually, he was in partnership with Klaw & Erlanger, not with Brooks, in presentation of "The Auctioneer." He found that "parol evidence" could not be held to alter the effect of a written and sealed instrument of engagement. "The rule," he declared, "allowing parol *proof* of an undisclosed principal *is limited to simple contracts,* for if the agreement be *a sealed* one, *only the parties thereto subscribing* can be held bound." The question of prime public interest in this case (and it *is* of prime public interest, because the

veracity, reputation and standing of one of the
most eminent and influential men in our Theatre
are affected by it) is not whether Belasco could, in
law, under a strict rule of evidence, *enforce* against
Klaw & Erlanger the contract actually signed by
Brooks: the question is whether or not that contract
was, *in fact,* signed by Brooks as "a man of straw"
for Klaw & Erlanger, and by Belasco under duress.
I cannot conceive that any intelligent and judicious
person could read the testimony adduced and reach
any other conclusion but that Belasco had proved
his allegations as to fact.   And it seems clear to
me that the learned Justice must have felt satisfied
that Belasco had proved his case, *as to fact,*—
otherwise he would not have been at such pains
to argue *in extenso* the *incompetency* of such *proof*
under the rule.

A FAITHFUL FRIEND:—WARFIELD FOR BELASCO. THE END OF "THE AUCTIONEER."

Warfield's second season in "The Auctioneer"
began, September 8, 1902, at the Hollis Street
Theatre, Boston, and lasted for 39 weeks,—closing
at the Victoria Theatre, New York, May 30, 1903.
315 performances were given and the net profits were
$70,000.   His third season began at the Harlem
Opera House, New York, September 28.   It was in

December, 1903, that Brooks applied to Judge
David Leventritt for a receiver for "The Auctioneer." Warfield, then acting in New Orleans,
being apprised of this application, declared that he
would "not play under the management of Klaw &
Erlanger's representative, a receiver, or any one but
David Belasco." That declaration, being published
in the newspaper press, was construed by Judge
Leventritt as an attempt on the part of Warfield
to coerce the court in the matter of appointing a
receiver and,—remarking that if it had not been
for what he deemed to be an attempt at coercion
he would have been inclined to appoint Belasco as
the receiver,—he named W. M. K. Olcott. Warfield thereupon refused to continue acting, his tour
was summarily closed, January 10, 1904,—two
weeks' salary being paid by Belasco to the
members of the company, in lieu of notice,—and
Warfield returned to New York. Before leaving
New Orleans he published this statement:

"When I stated I would not play under the management
of any one but Mr. Belasco, I meant just what I said. It
was not a threat—simply expression of my honest conviction as to what was just and due to the man who has
made me a successful star. 'The Auctioneer' was Mr.
Belasco's own investment, every penny of it. It was he
who conceived the idea of starring me in a play of this

character. From this man Brooks I have received nothing, nor have I from Klaw & Erlanger, who are Mr. Belasco's partners in 'The Auctioneer.' The manner in which they became partners will be shown and proved when this case comes into court for trial. They refused to give Mr. Belasco bookings until he had surrendered 50 per cent. of the concern. I was an unmade star then, and Mr. Belasco was not in the position of power which he holds to-day. We had to divide. But of the profits which Klaw & Erlanger have made from the managers with whom they have booked the attraction, neither Mr. Belasco nor I have received one penny from our partners. As for Brooks, he has never had even carfare, unless Klaw & Erlanger have been more liberal to him than to us.

"The trouble and annoyance which this whole affair has caused me have made me ill. But, sick or well, I absolutely refuse to play in 'The Auctioneer' for any one but my own manager, Mr. David Belasco. I defy Mr. Erlanger to deny that he and Mr. Klaw, and not Mr. Brooks, are the real partners of Mr. Belasco in my tour. He told me so with his own lips, when the New Amsterdam Theatre was building last summer. He asked me to come and see how the foundations were getting on. And when I funked, before crossing a rather rickety looking plank, he said 'I won't let you get hurt, old man. Remember, I own 50 per cent. of you.' When Klaw & Erlanger hand over our share of the profits they have made on the side, through booking my play, I will go on with the tour, if my health permits."

After his arrival in New York, having read the remarks of the judge in appointing a receiver, Warfield made this further statement:

DAVID WARFIELD

"I must disclaim any intention of having attempted to coerce the court into appointing the receiver I desired. Realizing as I did the enormous amount of labor and energy expended by Mr. Belasco in making the tours of 'The Auctioneer' a success, and appreciating as I did that without me in the cast it was a grave question whether the success of 'The Auctioneer' could continue, I thought it but proper for me to inform the court that conscientiously I could not continue to act unless Mr. Belasco was appointed receiver. I am very sorry that my statement had the effect it did have, but it is pleasing for me to learn that the charges made by Mr. Brooks against Mr. Belasco were unfounded and not believed by the court, because the court in its opinion says that were it not from a desire to rebuke *me* it might have felt inclined to have appointed Mr. Belasco receiver. That is sufficient satisfaction to us who know Mr. Belasco's character, because it is certainly fair to assume that the court would not have felt inclined to appoint Mr. Belasco receiver if it believed the charges brought against him.

"I am forced to continue the stand I originally took. I have closed the season of 'The Auctioneer,' nor will I continue to act in that play under the management of any person but Mr. Belasco."

Brooks applied for a mandatory injunction to compel Warfield to continue acting in "The Auctioneer," under the receivership direction of Mr. Olcott, and arguments supporting and opposing that application were heard before Justice Leventritt in the Supreme Court on January 26, 1904. Counsel for Warfield contended that while the court

might enjoin Warfield from acting for any persons
outside of his contract, it had no jurisdiction to
compel him to act if he declined to do so. Justice
Leventritt agreed with that view of the matter and
held that a mandatory injunction as prayed for
could not issue. Warfield did not act again for
eight months.

TEMPERAMENTAL SYMPATHY.—EARLY READING: "THE LOW SUN MAKES THE COLOR."

In his youth Belasco was an omnivorous reader
(as he continues to be), but his favorite reading was
that of History, and among historical characters
that specially enthralled his imagination was Mary,
Queen o' Scots. Indeed, he has, in conversation,
given me the impression that, from an early age, his
mind has been deeply interested in the study of those
famous women of history whose conduct of life is
shown to have been governed by their appetites and
passions. That taste seems morbid, but it is readily
explicable. Such women have been, are, and always
will be a direct spring of tense, dramatic, romantic
situations and tragic events, and sometimes their
experience involves incidents and culminates in
catastrophes which make a strong appeal to persons
who possess, as Belasco does, a highly emotional

temperament. *Queen Guinevere,* in Tennyson's
pathetic "Idyl," remarks that "the low sun makes
the color." Such women as Malcolm's Queen
Margaret of Scotland or Mme. Roland, probably,
would be viewed by Belasco with merely languid
respect or indifference. Such a woman as Navarre's
Marguerite de Valois, or Queen Catherine the
Second of Russia, or the irresistible siren Barbara
Villiers, or that all-conquering captivator Arabella
Stuart,—whose image lives, perpetual, in sculp-
ture and, as Brittania, on the coins of Great
Britain,—would, on the contrary, provide for him
an exceedingly interesting study. It is not,
therefore, altogether surprising that when Belasco
had established Mrs. Leslie Carter as a successful star it pleased him to select for public illus-
tration in a drama one of the most depraved and
dissolute feminine characters that hang on the
fringes of history,—the shameless hussy who, about
145 years ago, was picked out of the streets of
Paris, and under the auspices of the most notorious
titled blackguard of his time wedded to a com-
plaisant degenerate, in order that she might succeed
Mme. Pompadour as the mistress of King Louis the
Fifteenth of France. Marie Jeanne Becu (1746-
1793), who began life in Paris as a milliner, became
a courtesan, under the name of Mlle. Lange, was

later a lure for a gambling house, then, ennobled as
the "Countess du Barry," was installed as the mistress of the corrupt King Louis the Fifteenth,—
whom practically she ruled for five years,—and
finally was slaughtered in the Reign of Terror, is
the theme of one of the most pictorial, popular,
and successful of Belasco's plays. His selection of
a story of that remarkable female's adventures for
dramatic exploitation was not, however, wholly
spontaneous. In 1899, aware that a successor to
the torrid termagant of the Paris music-halls would
presently be required for Mrs. Carter's use, he
began to cast about for a play with a central character suited to her personality and method. Not
finding anything which he deemed satisfactory in
the numerous dramas, old as well as new, by many
authors, which he examined, he began, regretfully,
to contemplate the necessity of writing one to fit
his star,—regretfully, because he was weary and
would have been glad to avoid adding the labor of
authorship to that of business and stage management. His election had practically fallen on Queen
Elizabeth as the central figure to be shown, when he
abruptly determined to visit England, partly in
faint hope of finding there a drama which would
serve his end; more with intent to refresh his mind
by change and travel and to stimulate himself to

his new task by visiting all the places associated
with the life and reign of Elizabeth. He sailed
from New York on June 14, 1899. Soon after he
arrived in London an American playbroker, Miss
Elisabeth Marbury, communicated to him that "she
had a great idea for a part for Mrs. Carter."
Belasco, entertaining a high opinion of Miss Marbury's judgment and rejoiced at the sudden prospect of escaping the labor of authorship, immediately went to see her, at Versailles, in France, and
there was informed that the French poet M. Jean
Richepin "proposed to write a play founded on
the life of du Barry." The appended account of
what followed has been written by Belasco, and it
provides explicit information on a subject that at
one time was disputed with acrimony in the newspaper press and occupied much of the attention of
the theatre-going public:

GENESIS OF BELASCO'S *DU BARRY.*—CHARACTER OF
THE HISTORIC ORIGINAL.

"Miss Marbury outlined the plot as told to her by the
dramatist, and, as she repeated it to me, the story seemed
to possess great possibilities. I had produced Revolutionary plays with much success and the period was
dramatic. No manager in search of a woman's play could
have resisted the fascinating little milliner of history! Not

long after our first interview I made arrangements with
M. Richepin. I smile at the recollection of my conversation with the French author! He spoke very little English
and I no French at all; yet I seemed to know what he said,
and he grew most enthusiastic over my pantomime. The
contracts were arranged, the advance royalties paid, the
costume plates begun, and before I left for London the
scene models were ordered from the scenic artist of the
Comédie Française. Carried away by the enthusiasm of
M. Richepin, I bought yards and yards of old du Barry
velvets, antique silks, and furniture of the period. When
I left for home I had made all arrangements to produce a
play not a line of which was written. I returned to New
York elated, feeling certain that in a few weeks M. Richepin would have the piece ready for rehearsals. When the
manuscript of 'Du Barry' arrived, I could scarcely wait to
open the package. Alas! I was doomed to disappointment. 'Du Barry,' in the literary flesh, was episodic. It
was poetic and beautifully written, but deadly dull. It
differed entirely from the story I had heard in Versailles.
My company was practically engaged, my models done—
and no play! I wrote to M. Richepin, and gave him my
opinion of the manuscript. I did not utterly condemn his
first draft, for I hoped that with some suggestions, he
might be able to reshape his material; but the longer he
worked the more impossible the manuscript became, until
at last I lost all faith in it. It possessed a certain charm,
but—it was not a play. By this time I had paid M.
Richepin something like $3,000 in advance royalties, and
the properties and scenes were almost all delivered. I was
so deeply involved that I saw no way out of it. As du
Barry was free to any dramatist, I decided it was time to
have a hand in dramatizing the lady myself. I knew

exactly what I wanted and what was best suited to Mrs. Carter. Under the circumstances, it seemed to me that I could save time and cablegrams by taking my own suggestions instead of sending them to Paris. I arrived at this decision only when I found that M. Richepin was a far greater poet than playwright. So I threw out his play and set to work on my own."

Speaking of the character of "the little French milliner," Belasco has said: "History paints du Barry as the most despised woman of her time. She is said to have been the most evil creature antedating the French Revolution. I had a vast number of books relating to du Barry, and ransacked them all for one redeeming trait in her character: not one kind word. Alas! Not *one!* For the first time in my life I found myself in the hands of a really bad woman. I had never met one before (bad men I *have* met, but women,—never!). I felt a desire to rush to her defence. . . . But— I need not have troubled myself to defend the lady, for, good or bad, from the first night until the close of the play three years later the public liked the French milliner and the houses were sold out."

A little more careful ransacking of his vast du Barry library might have revealed some of the kind words about "the lady" which Belasco sought. Voltaire, in 1773, signified his appreciation of du

Barry's charms in the following couplet, which certainly carries adulation to an extreme limit:

"C'est aux mortels d'adorer votre image;
L'original était fait pour les dieux."

The following description of this handsome female explains, at least partially, the influence that she exerted. It was written by the Comte de Belleval, one of her many admirers:

"Madame du Barry was one of the prettiest women at the Court, where there were so many, and assuredly the most bewitching, on account of the perfections of her whole person. Her hair, which she often wore without powder, was fair and of a most beautiful color, and she had such a profusion that she was at a loss to know what to do with it. Her blue eyes, widely open, had a kind and frank expression, and she fixed them upon those persons to whom she spoke and seemed to follow in their faces the effect of her words. She had a tiny nose, a very small mouth, and a skin of dazzling whiteness. In short, she quickly fascinated every one."

A FANCIFUL FABRIC.—"DU BARRY" FIRST PRODUCED.

The play which Belasco fabricated and produced under the name of "Du Barry" is radically fanciful: its uses historic names, but it is not, in any sense, history. As in many precedent cases so in this one,

MRS. LESLIE CARTER AS *DU BARRY*

authentic records were ignored and an arbitrary, gilt-edged, rosy ideal took the place of truth. *Nell Gwynn,* in the person of Miss Henrietta Crosman, had worn the halo but a little time before (Bijou Theatre, New York, October 9, 1900), and if *Nell Gwynn* could wear it, why not *Marie Jeanne?* This burnishing process, to be sure, is diffusive of vast and general misinformation, but for most persons that seems to be quite as useful as accurate knowledge, and, after all, if the Stage is to present imperial wantons in any fashion it may as well present them in a decent one. The gay *du Barry* as seen by the dramatist,—or, at least, as shown by him,—was abundantly frail, but she was also fond, and while she did not scruple to pick up the royal pocket-handkerchief she nevertheless, in her woman's heart, remained true to her first love: that is the story of the play. The adventurous actual du Barry became the paramour of Cossé-Brissac, after King Louis the Fifteenth had died and after she had been exiled from the French Court. In the play the lady hides that lover in her bed (he has been wounded, and she persuades him to seek this retirement by pounding on his wounds with a heavy candlestick, until he becomes insensible), so that the jealous *King,* committing the blunder of Byron's *Don Alfonso,* in "Don Juan," cannot find him: she

also wields the convenient candlestick with which
to smash the sconce of an interloping relative who
otherwise would betray him; she defies, for his sake,
the gracious Majesty of France and every appur-
tenance thereunto belonging; and, at the last, she
goes pathetically to the guillotine, still loving him
and still deploring her innocent, youthful past, when
they were happy lovers together, when all was peace,
joy, and hope,—because as the old poet Rogers
prettily phrases it, "Life was new and the heart
promised what the fancy drew." As a matter of
fact, the amiable countrymen of du Barry sent her
to the guillotine, in the winter of 1793, because they
had ascertained that she was too rich to be a patriot
and also, probably, had entered on a secret cor-
respondence with their enemies in England.

As an epigraph to his play the dramatist selected
a remark by Oliver Wendell Holmes, that "not the
great historical events but the personal incidents that
call up sharp pictures of some human being in its
pang or struggle reach us more nearly." That
statement sounds well, but it labors under the disadvantage of not being true. The play, however,
exemplifies it to the extent of showing its heroine
chiefly in her "pang"—a condition which, seemingly,
ensues upon her being a feather-brained fool, but
which she loquaciously ascribes to Fate and a ruth-

less appetite for "pretty things." There is some lightness at the start, when *Jeanne* is a milliner, but the opening act proves to be practically needless, since the play does not actually begin till after the second curtain has been raised. Then the volatile girl is tempted by the offer of the *King's* love, and in order that she may accept it her honest lover is made to misunderstand her, in an incredible manner, such as is possible only on the stage. In the Third Act she has become a great personage, almost a queen, and that act, which is interesting, various, and dramatic, terminates with a highly effective scene, possible in a play, but impossible in life,—when *du Barry's* wounded lover, falling insensible on that lady's bed and being carelessly covered with drapery, remains there, sufficiently visible to a crowd of eager and suspicious pursuers who are searching for him—but do not find him. The rest of the piece shows the *King's* efforts to capture the fugitive and *du Barry's* schemes and pleadings to save him, and it terminates with a pathetic farewell between the lovers as *Jeanne,* deserted and forlorn, is being conveyed to the guillotine.

Mrs. Carter, adept in coquetry, displayed, as *du Barry,* her abundant physical fascination, but if she had refrained from removing her shoes and showing her feet at brief intervals during the performance she would have been considerably more pleasing in that easy vein of bewitchment:—they were not even pretty feet. In serious business the method of Mrs. Carter as *du Barry* was to work herself into a state of violent excitement, to weep, vociferate, shriek, rant, become hoarse with passion, and finally to flop and beat the floor. That method has many votaries and by them is thought to be "acting" and is much admired, but to judicious observers it is merely the facile expedient of transparent artifice and the ready resource of a febrile, unstable nature. An actor who loses self-control can never really control an audience. There were, nevertheless, executive force and skill in Mrs. Carter's performance, after it had been often repeated under the guiding government of her sagacious and able manager.

Belasco's "Du Barry" was first produced at the New National Theatre, Washington, D. C., December 12, 1901. The first performance of it in New York occurred December 25, that year, at the Criterion Theatre, where it was continuously acted till the close of the season, May 31, 1902, receiving 165 consecutive performances. The play is comprehended in five acts and eight scenes and it implicates fifty-five persons,—of whom five are conspicuous characters by whom the burden of the action is sustained,—and a host of supernumeraries. It was set on the stage in a scenic investiture of extreme costliness and ostentation, being, indeed, almost overwhelmed in the profusion of its accessories of spectacle. Referring to this extreme opulence of environment and attire, Belasco has said: "I offered Charles Frohman a half-interest in my 'Du Barry,' but he declined to come in with me because of the immense expense. His judgment was logical, too. 'Du Barry' might easily have ruined any manager. The expenses of the production were such that there was little profit to be made. When the curtain rose it afforded the public an opportunity to see how a manager's hands were forced by the very prodigality of the subject he had chosen. My production was lavish because the play was laid in a lavish time. The mere 'suggestion' of luxury would not do,—or so I thought. Were I to do it again, it would be from an entirely different standpoint." I much doubt whether, if the venture were to be made anew, Belasco would make it in a different way. At any rate, the purpose he had in mind was fully accomplished: the immense prodigality of his presentment profoundly impressed and greatly delighted his audiences, and the Criterion was densely crowded at every performance. The two most striking scenes were those of Act Three, which showed a room in the Palace of Versailles, and the Last Scene of Act Five, in front of a milliner's shop. The latter portrayed a street in Paris, shadowed by strange, "high-shouldered" houses, through which the wretched *du Barry,* abject and terrified, was dragged to execution, —huddled in a tumbril, attended only by a priest, the *Papal Nuncio,* and followed by a fierce, hooting rabble, while other men and women appeared at various house-windows, to jeer and curse her. It was an afflictingly pathetic scene, conceived and executed with perfect sense of dramatic effect and perfect mastery of the means of creating it.

This was the original cast of "Du Barry":

King Louis the Fifteenth of France..Charles A. Stevenson.
Comte Jean du Barry.................Campbell Gollan.
Comte Guillaume du Barry.............Beresford Webb.
Duc de Brissac.....................Henry Weaver, Sr.
Cossé-Brissac........................Hamilton Revelle.
The Papal Nuncio.....................H. R. Roberts.
Duc de Richelieu....................Frederick Perry.
Terray, Minister of Finance.............C. P. Flockton.
Maupeou, Lord Chancellor..............H. G. Carlton.
Duc d'Aiguillon.......................Leonard Cooper.
Denys............................Claude Gillingwater.
Lebel...............................Herbert Millward.
M. Labille............................Gilmore Scott.
Vaubernier...........................Walter Belasco.

CHARLES A. STEVENSON AS *KING LOUIS THE FIFTEENTH*,
IN BELASCO'S "DU BARRY"

Scario.................................J. D. Jones.
Zamore..............................Master Sams.
Jeweller.............................B. L. Clinton.
Perfumer..........................Edward Redford.
Glover.............................Thomas Thorne.
Flute Player..............................A. Joly.
A Turk.............................Albert Sanford.
Valroy..............................Douglas Wood.
D'Altaire................................Louis Myll.
De Courcel..........................Harold Howard.
La Garde...............................W. T. Bune.
Fontenelle............................Warren Bevin.
Renard..............................Arthur Pearson.
Citizen Grieve........................Gaston Mervale.
Marac..............................Walter Belasco.
Benisot...............................H. G. Carlton.
Tavernier.............................John Ingram.
Gomard..............................Charles Hayne.
Hortense............................Eleanor Carey.
Lolotte..................................Nina Lyn.
Manon........................Florence St. Leonard.
Julie................................Corah Adams.
Leonie............................Blanche Sherwood.
Nichette...............................Ann Archer.
Juliette...............................May Lyn.
Marquise de Quesnoy.....................Blanche Rice.
Sophie Arnauld.....................Helen Robertson.
The Gypsy Hag.......................C. P. Flockton.
Mlle. Le Grand........................Ruth Dennis.
Mlle. Guinard.......................Eleanor Stuart.
Mme. le Dauphine { Marie Antoinette } .....Helen Hale.
{ at sixteen }
Marquise de Crenay.................Dora Goldthwaite.

Duchesse d'Aiguillon........................Miss Lyn.
Princesse Alixe..........................Miss Leonard.
Duchesse de Choisy....................Louise Morewin.
Marquise de Langers....................May Montford.
Comtesse de Marsen..............Edith Van Benthuysen.
Sophia......................................Irma Perry.
Rosalie.............................Helen Robertson.
Cerisette................................Julie Lindsey.
Jeannette Vaubernier, { afterward "La du Barry" } Mrs. Leslie Carter.

RICHEPIN AND THE "DU BARRY" LAWSUIT.

After Belasco had rejected Richepin's play about
du Barry, returned the manuscript of it to him, and
announced that he would produce a play about that
celebrated favorite of royalty, written by himself,
there was much pother in theatrical circles and much
newspaper parade of warnings and threats, by
Richepin and various of his agents, of the dire
consequences which would fall upon him for so
doing. The once widely known firm of lawyers,
Howe & Hummel, were the American representatives of the French Authors' Society, which supported Richepin, and Mr. A. Hummel,—who,
1905, was convicted of subornation of perjury,
imprisoned for one year on Blackwells Island, and
debarred,—who was the active member of that firm,
on January 25, 1902, brought suit against Belasco,

MRS. LESLIE CARTER AS *DU BARRY*

on behalf of the French author, alleging, substantially, that Belasco's "Du Barry" was, in fact, Richepin's drama of similar name ("La du Barry") and demanding an accounting for the receipts from representations of it. Belasco's reply to the complaint in that suit was served on March 4, 1902, and it was explicit and conclusive. In that answer he specifies that on July 22, 1899, he entered into a contract with M. Richepin, which that author obtained "by false and fraudulent representations," wherein he agreed to write for Belasco a "new and original" play about du Barry, which was to be "entirely satisfactory to this defendant [Belasco]," —failing which he was at liberty to reject the work and return it to Richepin. Belasco, "relying upon the said representations, statements, and promises. and not otherwise, and believing the same to be true, paid to the plaintiff, on the signing and execution of the agreement, the sum of $1,000"; and, on or about July 1, 1901, upon receiving from Richepin (in London, during the run of "Zaza") the manuscript, in French, of "La du Barry," he paid $1,500 more. Of his own play, "Du Barry," Belasco swore that it is "wholly composed and originated by this defendant, without any aid or assistance whatever from the play alleged to have been written by" Richepin. The latter's play, Belasco pointed out, was "not new and original," as required by the contract between them, but was "taken, plagiarized, pirated, and copied, by the plaintiff, from public sources and publications, common and open to the public, and that the said play was wholly unsatisfactory to him [Belasco], of which fact he notified the plaintiff, and that the said manuscript was thereafter returned to, and accepted by, the plaintiff." A motion on behalf of Richepin to strike out these damaging clauses from Belasco's answer was made and argued before Justice Freeman, in the Supreme Court, March 13,—Mr. Hummel maintaining that the allegations of fraud and plagiarism by Richepin were "irrelevant and redundant." The motion was peremptorily denied,—after which the legal ardor of the French poet and his agents cooled and his suit languished: Richepin never proceeded in the case (which appears to have been an effort to extort money from Belasco), and it was formally discontinued in January, 1908.

Richepin's play (called "Du Barri") was produced by Mrs. Cora Urquhart Potter, March 18, 1905, at the Savoy Theatre, London, and it was a complete failure. "I had planned to take Mrs. Carter to London, in 'Du Barry,' " Belasco has told me, "but Mrs. Potter's failure was so decisive that I gave up all thought of attempting to do so."

Writing about the "Du Barry" lawsuit, Belasco
says: "Our quarrel was long and heated, but eventually all was 'forgotten and forgiven,' and I could
once more read Richepin's mellow poetry without
tearing my hair, and Richepin said publicly, 'The
rest is silence,' or something as nearly like it as
the Frenchman *can* say,"—which, truly, was most
generous on the part of " the Frenchman," in view
of the fact that, altogether, Belasco had paid him
$3,500 in a venture toward making which he had,
at most, contributed merely the suggestion of a
subject.

A GRACIOUS TRIBUTE:—"REMEMBER THAT WE LOVED
YOU."

On the first day of the new year, 1902, Belasco
was the recipient of a gracious tribute which, as he
feelingly said to me, is one of his most cherished
memories. The performance ended about half-past
eleven on the night of December 31, 1901, and a
little before midnight all the members of the company concerned in representation of his drama
assembled on the stage about Belasco, Mrs. Carter,
and Charles A. Stevenson, ostensibly to greet the
new year. Just at midnight beautiful silver chimes
slowly rang out the hour, and as Belasco turned to

wish the assembled company a happy New Year
Mr. Stevenson stepped forward before he could
speak and, uncovering a massive and beautiful loving-cup of silver set upon an ebony pedestal, presented it to Belasco "as a token of the great esteem
and true affection with which, during the long and
arduous preparation of 'Du Barry,' every member
of your organization has learned to regard you."
Belasco, always warm-hearted and peculiarly sus-
ceptible to even casual acts of courtesy and kindness, was so much affected by the cordial feeling
displayed by all about him in the conveyance of
this rich gift that for several moments he was
unable to make any acknowledgment. Then, speaking with difficulty and almost in a whisper, he said:
"I—I thank you, all—all—from my heart. It is
very lovely. You have worked so hard, with me and
for me—all of you—so nobly and so unselfishly that
I feel it is *I* who should give a loving-cup to you
—to every member of the company. In all my
experience I have not received a more generous,
touching tribute—anything which I have appreciated more. I am poor in words—I can only say
to all of you thank you, thank you, thank you—a
thousand thousand times."

As Belasco ceased speaking the orchestra began
to play the air of "Maryland, My Maryland," pass-

BELASCO, ABOUT 1902

ing from that into other melodies associated with his successful plays and closing with a plaintive tune written specially for use in "Du Barry."

On the "Du Barry" loving-cup there are three inscriptions. The first is

Washington, D. C.
December 12, 1901
Mrs. Leslie Carter in David Belasco's Play "Du Barry"

The second is

Presented to
Mr. David Belasco by the Members of His Company
New Year's, 1902

The third is a line from the play of "Du Barry":

"Remember that we loved you; we loved you
through it all"

THE THEATRIC *RICHMOND* "LOOKS PROUDLY O'ER THE CROWN."

The upward progress which Belasco made in the Theatre within a period of six years is amazing. When the curtain was raised for the first performance of his "The Heart of Maryland," at the Herald Square, in October, 1895, he possessed almost nothing except his reputation as one of the

most skilful of stage managers and a copious crop
of debts. When the curtain fell on the last performance in 1901 of "Du Barry," at the Criterion,
he was, as dramatist, director, and theatrical manager, known, esteemed, and recognized throughout
the English-speaking world: his debts were all discharged: he possessed a competent fortune, hosts
of admirers, troops of friends: within less than three
years he had made three memorably successful presentments in the British capital (where American
ventures are supposed always to fail!): three of the
most accomplished and popular actors of the American Stage, Mrs. Carter, Blanche Bates, and David
Warfield, were under his direction and closely bound
to him. The whirligig of Time had indeed brought
striking changes. Lester Wallack, Edwin Booth,
Lawrence Barrett, John McCullough—they were
but names in theatrical management. Augustin
Daly, the great representative manager of the
Theatre in America, was dead. Albert M. Palmer,
once Daly's rival, was obscurely employed as a
"business agent" for Richard Mansfield, while
Mansfield's own ambitious but ill-fated essay in
theatre management (at the Garrick, New York,
in 1895) was completely forgotten; Mansfield was
definitely committed to the policy of a "travelling
star," and the Theatre in New York was Charles

Frohman's much vaunted Department Store. Mr.
and Mrs. Harrison Grey Fiske, at the Manhattan,
were indeed maintaining an admirable dramatic
company and making an earnest endeavor in
authentic theatrical management. But, in general,
the mean spirit of the petty huckster and the
sordid, selfish policy of trade monopoly dominated
the American Stage; the chair of artistic managerial sovereignty was empty, "the sword unswayed,
the empire unpossessed," and Belasco, ambitiously
emulative of great exemplars in his vocation, like
a theatric *Richmond,* looked "proudly o'er the
crown." He was, unquestionably, the natural successor to Wallack, Booth, and Daly; but in order
to seize their pre-eminence, to win and wear their
laurel crown of leadership, he required to have what
they had each possessed,—namely, a theatre of his
own in the capital. There seemed no chance of his
obtaining one: yet, without such a citadel, notwithstanding all his labor and achievement, he might
easily be crushed: the oppressive hand of the
Theatrical Syndicate (in his estimation veritably a
"wretched, bloody, and usurping boar") had already
been laid heavily on Belasco: a half-interest in his
presentment of Warfield in "The Auctioneer" had
been extorted from him and an equal share in his
exploitations of Mrs. Carter and Miss Bates had

been demanded, though not yielded up. What if
he should be denied "routes" for those players? He
had brought out Mrs. Carter in "Du Barry" at the
Criterion not because he wished to do so,—that
house, which accommodated only 932 persons, being
far too small for an advantageous season,—but
because it was the only theatre in New York which
he could secure. Charles Frohman was its manager
and Charles Frohman was a member of the Syndicate: the Criterion might be closed to him at the
end of his current contract. If shut off from
the "first class theatres" of the leading cities "on the
road" and shut out of New York he would practically be ruined. These and similar considerations
gave grounds for grave uneasiness to Belasco. On
the afternoon of January 7, 1902, he was alone in
his office, a little room in Carnegie Hall, as he had
been every afternoon for more than a week, seeking
to devise some means of obtaining control of a New
York theatre for a term of years. Toward evening
he was disturbed by a knocking at the office door.
His visitor, when admitted, proved to be the theatrical manager Oscar Hammerstein, between whom
and himself there existed merely a casual acquaintance. "Mr. Belasco," said Hammerstein, without
any preliminaries, "the Theatrical Syndicate is trying to crush me out of business. Valuable attrac-

tions have been prevented from patronizing my
houses this season. I must have attractions. You
must have a New York theatre, or you will find
yourself helpless. I have one in Forty-second
Street, the Republic, which I am willing to turn
over to you. I have come up here on an impulse,
on the chance that you may be willing to take over
control of the Republic." Belasco instantly replied:
"Mr. Hammerstein, I shall be very glad to take
over your theatre." In less than a week all details
of agreement had been arranged between the two
managers, and on January 14, in the office of Judge
A. J. Dittenhoefer, they signed a contract whereby
Belasco undertook the management of the Republic
Theatre. That contract was for a period of five years,
with an option of renewal by Belasco for another five
years, and under it he assumed full government of
the theatre,—engaging himself to pay to Hammerstein a rental of $30,000 a year and 10 per cent.
of the gross receipts from all performances given
there. It was also stipulated that neither Mrs.
Carter, Blanche Bates, David Warfield, nor any
other "star or attraction" under Belasco's management should play at any other New York theatre,
"except for one week each at the Harlem Opera
House and the Grand Opera House." "That
lease," Belasco has declared to me, "was a great

thing for Hammerstein,—but it was a greater thing for me, and I did not forget that afterward, when I was paying him from $60,000 to $72,000 a year for his theatre. When some of my friends used to say to me, 'Don't you realize that you are paying Hammerstein an *unheard-of* rent for his house?' I used to answer, 'And don't *you* realize how very lucky I am *to be in a position* to pay him an unheard-of rent?' "

A DANGEROUS ACCIDENT.—ALTERING THE REPUBLIC.

A few weeks subsequent to signing the lease of the Republic Theatre with Hammerstein Belasco met with an accident which came near to putting an end to all his projects by causing his death. On the night of March 16 he witnessed a performance of his "Du Barry," at the Criterion. While the setting was being placed for the last scene—a cumbrous, intricate setting, in which he took special interest—he left his box in the auditorium and went upon the stage to direct the work. As he did so a large and heavy cornice which was being swung into position high in air broke and fell, striking him full upon the head. Another piece of scenery, thrown out of balance by the falling cornice, collapsed, and in a moment Belasco was buried beneath a mass of tangled wreckage. He was with difficulty extricated, unconscious and profusely bleeding. A physician was called, who, after a quarter of an hour, having stanched the bleeding, succeeded in restoring the injured manager to consciousness. It was at first feared that he had sustained a fracture of the skull, but happily he was found to be suffering only from shock and loss of blood due to a severe scalp wound. He was removed to his home and within a few days he had regained his usual health.

After carefully examining the interior of the Republic Theatre Belasco became convinced that it required to be altered for his use. "The stage was wrong, the house was wrong, and the colors set my teeth on edge," he has told me. Hammerstein was willing that he should make any changes he desired. Belasco, accordingly, took possession of the theatre at about the end of March and, on April 19, 1902, the work of altering it so as to make it conform to his wishes was begun. He started that work intending to spend from $15,000 to $20,000 on improvements. When it was finished he had expended more than $150,000. The whole interior of the building was torn out, leaving nothing but four walls and part of the roof. Toward the front of the property a space was blasted out of solid rock wherein, beneath the auditorium, were built a retiring-room for women and a smoking-room for men. A sub-stage chamber, more than twenty-five feet deep, was also blasted out of the rock,—incidental to which excavation a perpetual spring of water was tapped. Talking with me about his experience in remodelling the Republic Theatre, Belasco, in his characteristically cheery and philosophical way, said: "I remember your telling me about the trouble Edwin Booth got into, blasting out a ledge of rock when he was building his theatre [Booth's Theatre, Twenty-third Street and Sixth Avenue, 1868-'69], but I don't believe he had half as bad a time as we did when that spring broke loose! I was so crazy about having my own theatre I wanted to have a hand in everything and I used to go down and fire some of the blasts, in spite of the protests of my family and staff, who expected I'd blow myself to Kingdom Come. And it was *I* who fired the charge that started that spring! My boys in the theatre used to call me 'Moses' after that, for that I did smite the rock and there came water out of it. We *damned* it, heartily, I can tell you, but it was a long time before we could get it *dammed,* and it cost me a small fortune to have the stage cavity cemented in."

BELASCO'S "STUDIO" IN THE FIRST BELASCO THEATRE

One day, during the work of alteration, a stranger presented himself to Belasco, demanding that he be permitted to inspect the property and explaining that he held a mortgage on it. "I had nothing to do with the mortgage," Belasco told me; "that was Mr. Hammerstein's business; but I let him come in. He surveyed the scene of devastation with horror, standing on a scaffold, high up, and gazing into the black pit. 'God above me!' he exclaimed, after a little while, 'I've got a mortgage on four walls and a hole in the ground!'—and he fled. I never saw him again."

THE FIRST BELASCO THEATRE.

The work of demolishing and rebuilding the Republic for Belasco was performed in five months. When it was completed he possessed one of the handsomest and best equipped playhouses in the world. "The theatre," Belasco has often said, "is, first of all, a place for the *acting of plays*." That simple statement might be deemed a platitude, were it not for the striking fact that its maker is the *only* theatrical manager of the present day who practically recognizes its truth: to the majority of other managers the theatre, it seems, is, primarily, a place for almost anything rather than *acting*,—is, in fact, first of all, a place for the exploitation of their tedious conceit and the making of money by any means. The stage of the Belasco Theatre was designed and built with the purpose of obviating the disadvantages of restricted space and of affording every possible mechanical aid to the acting of plays. The entire "acting surface" of that stage —the entire surface, that is, which could be revealed to the view of the spectators,—was a mosaic of close-fitting trapdoors, so that on occasion it might be opened at any place desired. In the centre of the stage was "an elevator,"—that is, in fact, a movable platform,—fifteen feet wide and thirty feet long. Upon this platform, when it had been lowered into the cellar cavity, were placed the paraphernalia required in the setting of the scenes,— articles technically designated as "properties" (furniture, etc.), and "set pieces" (solid, heavy parts of scenic rooms, houses, etc.)—which were then raised to the stage level for use: when done with, these paraphernalia were sunk again into the cellarage, where the platform bearing them was shifted aside and another similar one, loaded with material for the next setting, replaced it and was in turn raised to the stage.

The drops (painted cloths), ceilings, etc., were all arranged for hoisting into the flies, as in most

modern theatres; but Belasco had the ropes by
which these articles were raised from his stage so
attached to counterweights and cranks that one
man could, with ease, raise pieces which, in former
times, it had required from three to six men to
hoist.

The footlights were so arranged that the light
from them was diffused upon the stage and players
without the spectators, even those in the upper
stage boxes, being able to perceive whence it came.
The electric lamps in the footlights, borders, etc.,
were placed in small, individual compartments,
so that no unintentional blending of lights could
occur: but every necessary different color of lamp
was provided and all the lamps in the house, whether
upon the stage or in the auditorium, were connected
"on resistance,"—that is, so connected with the electric current feed wires that the lights could be (as
invariably they were) turned up or down, as
required, gently, by degrees. In short, every
arrangement that knowledge, experience, and pre-
vision could suggest as necessary and that liberality,
ingenuity, and care could devise was provided. "I
have an even better electrical equipment in my
present theatre than I had in my first house,"
Belasco has said to me, "and I am proud of it.
But in my first house I had the very best there

was in the world at the time. I had a plant that would have lit a palace: in fact, I very much doubt whether there was a palace anywhere in all the world as well equipped in the matter of lighting."

Belasco's first theatre contained seating accommodation for 950 persons,—300 in the gallery, 200 in the balcony, and 450 on the orchestra, or main, floor. No effort or expense was spared to make the house in every way comfortable and delightful to all who visited it. Outside, in front, a massive iron marquee-awning shadowed the main entrance, overhanging the street-walk out to the curb. The doors of the theatre were of heavy wrought iron and opened into a lobby which was, in fact, a sort of reception hall. The walls and ceilings of this lobby were sheathed in oak panelling of antique finish, and large, luxurious seats of heavy oak, upholstered in leather, were placed at each end of it. Across the rear of the auditorium, on the orchestra floor, close to the hindermost row of seats, extended a massive screen built of rosewood, with heavy crystal lights, to protect the audience within from drafts of air and to exclude street sounds. The colors of the decorations were reds, greens, and deep golden browns,—all used in warm, subdued shades. The rear and side walls were hung with rich tapestries, depicting an autumnal forest. The

BELASCO IN HIS STUDIO AT THE FIRST
BELASCO THEATRE

floors were covered with heavy, soft, dark-green velvet carpets. The seats were upholstered in silk tapestry of a complementary shade of silver-green color, and on the back of each of them was embroidered the semblance of a bee,—fit emblem of Belasco's energetic, ceaseless toil. The ceiling and dome were handsomely decorated in dull gold, sparingly used, with soft grays and rose. There were two drop curtains,—one of heavy, rose-colored velvet; the other an old-fashioned one of plain green baize. Every detail of the architecture and decorations was delicate and harmonious, and the general effect was at once opulent and restful. The architects employed by Belasco were Messrs. Bigelow, Wallis & Cotton, of New York: the director was Mr. Rudolph Allen. But the active inspiration of all this beauty and luxury provided for the public enjoyment, the conglutinating and executive force which in the face of manifold dissensions and difficulties held all the associate laborers together and drove through to successful completion all the varied work of invention and reconstruction, was Belasco himself. At last he had carried bricks for himself to some lasting purpose! When he opened his playhouse it was in every detail as well as in every essential a new theatre, veritably the creation of *his* mind and will, and he very appro-

priately dropped the name of the Republic and
called it The Belasco Theatre.

**"AFTER THIRTY YEARS OF LABOR."—BELASCO IN HIS
OWN THEATRE:—THE OPENING NIGHT.**

The first Belasco Theatre was opened on Monday
night, September 29, 1902, with a revival of "Du
Barry." The night was sultry, but the house was
crowded, in every part, far beyond its normal
capacity; the performance was one of remarkable
fluency, vigor, and intensity, and it was received by
the audience with well-nigh frantic manifestations
of enthusiasm. After the Third Act there were
more than twenty curtain calls, and finally, in
response to vociferous crying for him by name,
Belasco came upon the stage, dishevelled, pale, and
weary, but very happy, and addressed the audience,
saying:

"Ladies and Gentlemen: It is so hard for me to speak to
you as I would wish. There is so much to say, yet so
little that I can say. It is your kind sympathy and
approval that have made this little playhouse possible. I
owe you—the public—far, far more than I can tell. You
all know that it has been my life-work, my greatest ambition, to give you the best I could. In this I can honestly
say I have not faltered since I first knocked at your door,

DAVID BELASCO

many years ago. And in that endeavor I stand firm
to-night. I thank the friends who have upheld me so
loyally all these many years. I thank the press for the
encouragement I have received. There are some very
beautiful things in the lives of those I have followed, and
one of these is the fellowship of brother workers. I am
always inspired, I always shall be inspired, by the memory
and example of three inimitable comrades of the Theatre,—
one the late Lester Wallack, another the late, lamented
Augustin Daly, and yet another who is still with us, who
has given the best years of his life to advance the art which
both you and I love so well: I refer to Mr. A. M. Palmer.
They fought the good fight, these three; they kept the
faith. They gave us glorious traditions to remember and
live up to. They gave all to advance the highest. This is
something we must never forget.

"Ladies and gentlemen, there is another of whom I must
make some mention—one whose sympathy and help have
contributed to my being here to-night. I mean my friend
and companion in work, Mrs. Leslie Carter. Here and now
I wish gratefully to acknowledge the debt of her services,
her unselfishness and loyalty in time of many struggles.

"I have many plans for this little theatre, ladies and gentlemen. Let me say just a word to you about the managerial
policy. I am anxious to make my patrons feel at home
when they honor me by coming, and so I have tried to make
your surroundings in front of the curtain those of a comfortable, home-like drawing-room. I intend that the productions and casts shall be the best that work and care can
provide. In all ways I desire to make this new dramatic
home of ours a dwelling of refinement, good taste, good
entertainment, and good art. No stone shall be left
unturned, no effort unmade, to accomplish that end. You

cannot know what it means to me to speak to you, at last, after thirty years of labor in the dramatic calling, from the stage of my own theatre. Ladies and gentlemen, I thank you—I thank you—I can say no more."

THE FIRST PROGRAMME.

The following is the programme, in detail, of the first performance given in Belasco's Theatre on what was, in many ways, the happiest and proudest night of all his life:

BELASCO THEATRE

BROADWAY AND FORTY-SECOND STREET

Under the Sole Management of David Belasco

Evenings at 8 precisely   *Matinées Saturdays at 2*

DAVID BELASCO

PRESENTS

Mrs. Leslie Carter

IN HIS NEW PLAY

"DU BARRY"

"Not the great historical events, but the personal incidents that call up single, sharp pictures of some human being in its pang or struggle, reach us more nearly."—Oliver Wendell Holmes.

CAST

King Louis the Fifteenth of France......C. A. Stevenson.
Comte Jean du Barry, eventually brother-in-law
  of *La du Barry*....................Campbell Gollan.
Comte Guillaume du Barry, his brother....Beresford Webb.
Duc de Brissac, Capt. of King's Guard..Henry Weaver, Sr.
Cossé-Brissac, his son (of the King's Guard),
  known as *"Cossé"*..................Hamilton Revelle.
The Papal Nuncio......................H. R. Roberts.

Duc de Richelieu, Marshal of France	Under King Louis the Fifteenth	..Geo. Barnum.
Maupeou, Lord Chancellor		C. P. Flockton.
Terray, Minister of Finance		H. G. Carlton.

Duc D'Aiguillon......................Leonard Cooper.
Denys, porter at the milliner shop....Claude Gillingwater.
Lebel, confidential valet to His Majesty..Herbert Millward.
M. Labille, proprietor of the milliner shop...Gilmore Scott.
Vaubernier, father of *Jeannette*.........Charles Campbell.
Scarlo, one of "*La du Barry's*" Nubian servants.J. D. Jones.
Zamore, a plaything of "*La du Barry's*"....Master Sams.
Flute Player................................A. Joly.

Valroy	Of the King's Guard	.Douglas J. Wood.
D'Altaire		......Louis Myll.
De Courcel		...Harold Howard.

La Garde	Two Tavern Roysterers	....W. T. Bune.
Fontenelle		..Thomas Boone.

Benard, one of the "Hundred Swiss"......Warren Deven.
Citizen Grieve, of the Committee of Public
  Safety.............................Gaston Mervale.
Marac, one of the Sans-Culottes.........James Sargeant.
Denisot, Judge of the Revolutionary Court..H. G. Carlton.
Tavernier, clerk of the court..............John Ingram.

Gomard...............................Charles Hayne.

Hortense, Manageress for Labille the milliner

Eleanor Carey.

Lolotte		...........Nina Lyn.
Manon	Girls	...Florence St. Leonard.
Julie	at the	........Corah Adams.
Leonie	Milliner's	....Blanche Sherwood.
Nichette	Shop	.........Ann Archer.
Juliette		...........May Lyn.

Marquise du Quesnoy, known as "La Gourdan,"
   keeper of a gambling house.............Blanche Rice.

Sophie Arnauld, queen of the opera.......Miss Robertson.

The Gypsy Hag, a fortune-teller..........C. P. Flockton.

Mlle. Le Grand..	Dancers from the	....Ruth Dennis.
Mlle. Guimard...	Grand Opera	..Eleanor Stuart.

Mme. La Dauphine—Marie Antoinette at sixteen

Helen Hale.

Marquise de Crenay.		.....Helen Robertson.
Duchesse D'Aiguillon	Ladies	...........Miss Lyn.
Princesse Alixe.....	of	.......Miss Leonard.
Duchesse de Choisy..	King Louis	.....Louise Morewin.
Marquise de Langers	Court	......May Montford.
Comtesse de Marsen.		Grace Van Benthuysen.

Sophie, a maid...........................Irma Perry.

Rosalie, of the Concièrgerie...........Helen Robertson.

Cerisette................................Julie Lindsey.

AND

JEANNETTE VAUBERNIER, afterwards La du
   Barry...................MRS. LESLIE CARTER.

Guests of the Fête, Dancers from the Opera, King's Guardsmen, Monks, Clowns, Pages, Milliners, Sentries, Lackeys, Footmen, King's Secret Police, Sans-Culottes, a Mock King, a Mock Herald, a Drunken Patriot, a Cocoa Vender, Federals, National Guards, Tricoteuses.

SYNOPSIS OF SCENES.

Act I.—The Milliner's Shop in the Rue St. Honoré, Paris.
JEANNETTE TRIMS HATS.

Act II.—(One month later.) *Jeannette's* Apartments, adjoining the Gambling Rooms of the *Marquise de Quesnoy* ("La Gourdan").
"THE GAME CALLED DESTINY."

Act III.—(A year later.) *Du Barry* holds a Petit-Lever in the Palace of Versailles—at noon.
"THE DOLL OF THE WORLD."

Act IV.—Scene 1. In the Royal Gardens. Before the dawn of the following morning.
"FOLLY, QUEEN OF FRANCE."
Scene 2. Within the Tent.
"THE HEART OF THE WOMAN."

Act V.—(A lapse of years.) During the Revolution.
Scene 1. The Retreat in the Woods of Louveciennes.
"FATE CREEPS IN AT THE DOOR."
Scene 2. (Five days later.) In Paris again.
"A REED SHAKEN IN THE WIND."
Scene 3. In Front of the Milliner's Shop on the same day.

"Once more we pass this way again,
Once more! 'T is where at first we met."

Time: Period of King Louis the Fifteenth and after the reign of his Successor.

Place: Paris, Versailles, and Louveciennes.

Mr. Belasco wishes to state that, as the traditional parting of Madame du Barry and the King of France is impossible for dramatic use, he has departed entirely from historical accuracy in this instance. He also begs to acknowledge his indebtedness to M. Arsène Houssaye for his sequence of scenes. ("Nouvelle à la main, sur la Comtesse du Barry.")

Between Acts I, II, and III there will be intervals of 12 minutes; between Acts IV and V an interval of 15 minutes.

The entire production under the personal supervision of Mr. Belasco.

Stage Manager . . . . H. S. MILLWARD.

Scenery by Mr. Ernest Gros.

Incidental Music by Mr. William Furst.

Stage decorations and accessories after designs by Mr. Wilfred Buckland.

General Manager for Mr. Belasco . . . . MR. B. F. ROEDER.

As an epigraph for the first performance given in his theatre, and also for a souvenir book then distributed,—a richly printed volume called "The Story of Du Barry," written by James L. Ford and issued in a limited edition,—Belasco used, under the caption "Before the Curtain," the appended fourteen lines from Francis Bret Harte's versified address written for the dedication of the California Theatre, San Francisco, January 18, 1869, on which occasion (when Belasco was among the spectators) it was read by Lawrence Barrett:

> "Brief words, when actions wait, are well;
> The prompter's hand is on his bell;
> The coming heroes, lovers, kings,
> Are idly lounging at the wings;
> Behind the curtain's mystic fold
> The glowing future lies unrolled.

. . . . .

"One moment more: if here we raise
The oft-sung hymn of local praise,
Before the curtain facts must sway;
Here waits the moral of your play.
Glassed in the poet's thought, you view
What money can, yet can not do;
The faith that soars, the deeds that shine,
Above the gold that builds the shrine."

A STUPID DISPARAGEMENT.—INCEPTION OF "THE DARLING OF THE GODS."

Among the meanest and most stupid disparagements of Belasco which I have chanced to notice in recent years is one made by Mr. Albert Bigelow Paine, the adulatory biographer of Samuel L. Clemens (Mark Twain). In recording a conversation which he says he had with Clemens Mr. Paine writes: " 'I suppose,' I said, 'the literary man should have a collaborator with a genius for stage mechanism. John Luther Long's *exquisite plays* would hardly have been successful without David Belasco to stage them. *Belasco cannot write a play himself,* but in the matter of acting construction his genius is supreme.' " (The italics are mine.—W. W.) Remembering that Belasco is, among many other things, the author of "May Blossom," "The Heart of Maryland," "The Girl of the Golden West," "Peter Grimm," and "Van der Decken," it seems to me that Mr. Paine has, in that sapient comment, provided for thoughtful persons a useful measure of his intelligence. Furthermore, his disparagement of Belasco as a writer of plays suggests that it is competent, in this Memoir, to inquire as to what, precisely, are the "exquisite plays" of John Luther Long, one of Belasco's collaborators in authorship. Mr. Long is a fiction writer of talent, which has been widely and generously recognized. His name is associated with six plays and no more, —namely, "Madame Butterfly," "The Darling of the Gods," "Dolce," "Adrea," "The Dragon Fly," and "Kassa." "Madame Butterfly," as a play, is, exclusively, the work of Belasco: it was written and produced before he and Long met. "Kassa" is a commonplace farrago of theatrical absurdity, rant, and miscellaneous trash, tangled into a mesh of sacerdotal trappings and fantastic, complex, and dubious Hungarian embellishments and is as devoid of literary merit as it is of dramatic vitality. It was produced by Mrs. Leslie Carter, in 1909, after she had ceased to act under the direction of Belasco, and it was a failure. "The Dragon Fly" was written by Long in association with Mr. E. C. Carpenter, was produced in Philadelphia, in 1905, and was a failure. "Dolce" has not been acted or published and I know nothing about it. As to

"The Darling of the Gods" and "Adrea,"—not only did Belasco "stage" those plays (that is, produce them), but he is at least as much *their author* as Mr. Long is; a fact which I venture to assume that Mr. Long would be the last to deny.

"The Darling of the Gods" owes its existence wholly to Belasco. When he had leased the Republic Theatre and while he was preparing to undertake its renovation he also began to plan his managerial campaign there. In a letter he writes:

(*David Belasco to William Winter.*)

". . . It was a strenuous, anxious time for me. I had so many things to think of and so much to do that sometimes I felt like that man in Dickens who tries to lift himself out of his difficulties by his own hair! I saw that I was to be forced to fight for my professional life—and I wasn't ready. The public had been taught, season by season, to expect always more and more from the actor, the author, and, especially, the producer. The standard of production was so high that the theatre-goer looked not only for great acting but also for artistic perfection and beauty in the stage settings. The progressive manager was forced to invest immense sums in his stars and productions, and it was because I did this without hesitation that I was so unpopular with some of my contemporaries. According to them I "spoiled the public" because I looked *first* to the artistic instead of to the commercial result."

Belasco had for several years prior to 1902 desired to present Mrs. Carter in a series of

Shakespearean and classical plays which, as he wrote to me in that year, "have long been in her repertory but in which I have never yet had the opportunity of bringing her out." Mrs. Carter was then the principal player under his management: it was both justice to her and sound business judgment for him to open his new theatre with a performance in which she was the star. It would indeed have been a brilliant achievement for him to have opened it with a superb revival of one of Shakespeare's great plays. But, on the other hand, theatrical management,—although, rightly understood, it entails, first of all, a moral and intellectual obligation to the public,—is a venturesome business, not an altruistic amusement: Belasco had invested more than $98,000 in making his presentment of "Du Barry": it, plainly, was necessary to earn with that drama at least the cost of producing it before he could bring forth Mrs. Carter in another play. And it was obvious that while he could impressively open his new theatre with a sumptuous revival of that popular success it could not advantageously hold the stage there for more than a month or two and that he must have another striking dramatic novelty ready in hand with which to follow the revival. Among the many plays which Belasco wrote and rewrote during the strolling days of his youth is a melodrama entitled "Il Carabiniere," which he called "The Carbineer." The scenes and characters of that old play are Italian. Belasco resolved to refashion it for the use of Blanche Bates. But the multifarious demands on his time and strength made it necessary for him to have assistance in performing this task, and remembering the success of Miss Bates in his Japanese tragedy of "Madame Butterfly" he altered his purpose and determined to base on the old Italian tale a romance of Japan, and he proposed to John Luther Long,— well versed in Japanese customs,—that he should help him in the work. This proposal was accepted; the manuscript of "The Carbineer" was turned over to Long, and, about February, 1902, the collaborators began their work on the play which afterward became famous under the name of "The Darling of the Gods." That play is practically a new one, not an adaptation: the labor of writing it was finished in June, and it was produced for the first time anywhere, November 17, 1902, at the New National Theatre, Washington, D. C.: on December 3, following, it was acted for the first time in New York, at the Belasco Theatre, where it succeeded "Du Barry," which had been acted there for the last time on November 29. This was the original cast of "The Darling of the Gods":

Prince Saigon	....	Charles Walcot.
Zakkuri, Minister of War	....	George Arliss.
Kara	....	Robert T. Haines.
Tonda-Tanji	....	Albert Bruning.
Sir Yuke-Yume	....	James W. Shaw.
Lord Chi-Chi	....	Edward Talford.
Admiral Tano	....	Cooper Leonard.
Hassebe Soyemon	....	Warren Milford.
Kato	....	J. Harry Benrimo.
Shusshoo	....	F. Andrews.
Inu, a Corean Giant	....	Harrison Armstrong.
Yoban	....	Carleton Webster.
Crier of the Night Hours	....	Charles Ingram.

Kugo		........Maurice Pike.
Shiba		.........E. P. Wilks.
Migaku	The seven spies	........Rankin Duvall.
Kojin	of *Zakkuri*	........Arthur Garnell.
Ato		........Joseph Tuohy.
Tcho		Winthrop Chamberlain.
Taro		........John Dunton.

Man in the Lantern	....	Westropp Saunders.
The Imperial Messenger	....	F. A. Thomson.
First Secretary	....	Legrand Howland.
Second Secretary	....	A. D. Richards.

Banza		......Gaston Mervale.
Nagoya		......Albert Bruning.
Tori		..Fred'k A. Thomson.
Korin		......Rankin Duvall.
Bento	*Kara's* "Two-sword	...J. Harry Benrimo.
Kosa	Men"	.....Richard Warner.
Takoro		........John Dunton.
Kaye		.......Arthur Garnell.
Nagoji		.......A. D. Richards.
Jutso		........Dexter Smith.

A SCENE FROM "THE DARLING OF THE GODS"

"The Feast of a Thousand Welcomes"

Little Sano.............................Madge West.
Chidori........................Mrs. Charles Walcot.
Rosy Sky...........................Eleanor Moretti.
Setsu......................................Ada Lewis.
Kaede..............................Dorothy Revell.
Madame Asani.....................France Hamilton.
The Fox Woman....................Mrs. F. M. Bates.
Isamu..............................May Montford.
Niji-Onna............................Helen Russell.
Nu............................Madeleine Livingston.
Princess Yo-San.......................Blanche Bates.

Gentlemen of Rank, Messrs. Redmund, Stevens, Dunton, Smith, Meehan, Richards, Shaw, Chamberlain and Shaw.

Geisha Girls, Misses Winard, Karle, Vista, Mardell, Coleman and Ellis.

Singing Girls, Misses Livingston, Mirien and Earle.

Heralds from the Emperor, maids-in-waiting to the Princess, screen bearers, Kago men, coolies, retainers, runners, servants, geisha, musume, priests, lantern bearers, banner bearers, incense bearers, gong bearers, jugglers, acrobats, torturers, carp flyers, Imperial soldiers and Zakkuri's musket-men.

THE PLAY AND THE PERFORMANCE OF "THE DARLING OF THE GODS."

The tragic drama of "The Darling of the Gods" is an excellent play, one of exceptional power and ethical significance. It is a unique fabric of fancy, wildly romantic, rich and strange with unusual characters, lively with incident, occasionally mystical with implication of Japanese customs and religious beliefs, opulent with an Oriental splendor of atmosphere and detail, like that of Beckford's romance of "Vathek,"—fragrant with sweetness,—like Moore's "Lalla Rookh,"—busy with movement, effective by reason of situation, and communicative of a love story of enchaining interest and melancholy beauty. That story is told in continuous, cumulative action, —each successive dramatic event being stronger than its predecessors in the element of suspense; and at the climax there is a weird picture of supernatural environment, a thrilling suggestion of the eternity of spiritual life and personal identity,—a poetic symbolism, at once pathetic and sublime, of the glory and ecstasy, the supreme triumph, of faithful love.

The story of *Yo-San,* the heroine of that play, who is designated "the darling of the gods," separated from all adjuncts and accessories, is simple. She is a princess in Japan, betrothed to a Japanese courtier whom she does not wish to wed. She has stipulated, as a·preliminary condition of their marriage, that the courtier must prove his valor by capturing a certain formidable outlaw, *Prince Kara,* who, on being captured, will be put to death. She has been saved from fatal dishonor through the expeditious courage and promptitude of that outlaw (unrecognized by her as such), and on seeing each other they become lovers. *Kara* pledges himself to appear at the palace of her father, at a "feast of a thousand welcomes" to be held in his honor, there to receive that parent's thanks. Thither he comes, passing through the guards of *Zakkuri,* the dreaded *War Minister of Japan,* but sustaining a desperate hurt in doing so. *Yo-San,* when her lover, wounded and almost dying, has failed to make his escape from the precincts of the palace through a cordon of enemies, conceals him in her dwelling, and for many days she tends him, till his wounds are healed, and then, for a time, those lovers are happy in their secret love. The girl is, however, compromised by this indiscretion, and when presently her father, *Prince Saigon,* discovers her secret,—and, as he thinks, her dishonor,—she is declared an outcast; and her lover (taken prisoner while attempting to fight his way to freedom) is doomed to torture and death. She is compelled to gaze upon him as, stupefied with opium, he is led down into a chamber of infernal torment. Then she is apprised that she can secure his life and liberty by betraying the hiding place of her lover's outlaw followers, and in desperate agony she does betray them: but she gains nothing by that action except an access of misery. *Prince Kara,* surprised with his band by soldiers

of the *War Minister,* having, with a few of his followers, fought his way through the lines of his
enemies and discovered that the secret of their
hiding place, confided by him to *Yo-San,* has been
by her revealed, commits suicide in the honorable
Japanese manner, and she is left alone, with only
his forgiveness as a comfort, and with the hope that,
—after a thousand years of loneliness and grief, in
the underworld of shadows,—she will be again
united with him in the eternal happiness of heaven.
The play shows *Yo-San* as an innocent, confiding,
pathetic figure, a child-woman, passing amid stormy
vicissitude, cruel temptation, and afflicting trials to
a forlorn and agonized death by suicide, and leaves
her at the last, redeemed and transfigured, on the
verge of Paradise, where *Kara* stretches out his
arms to embrace her, and where there is neither
trouble nor parting nor sorrow any more.

The experience of this Japanese girl is the old
ordeal over again, of woman's sacrifice and anguish,
when giving all for love. Something of Shakespeare's *Juliet* is in that heroine, something of
Goethe's *Margaret,* something of the many passionate, wayward, mournfully beautiful ideals of
woman's sacrifice that are immortal in story and
song. She is a loving and sorrowing woman, true,
tender, faithful forever, and celestial alike in her

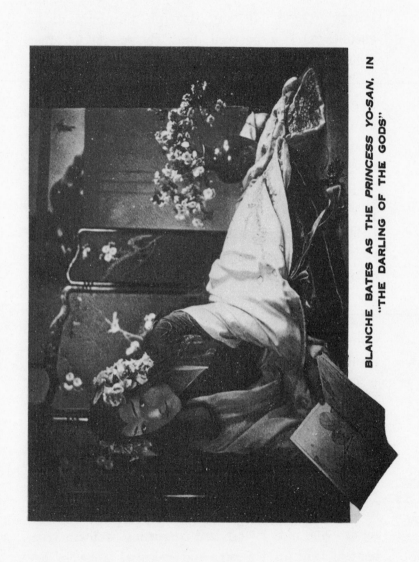

BLANCHE BATES AS THE *PRINCESS YO-SAN*, IN "THE DARLING OF THE GODS"

love, her temptation, and her grief. The character of *Yo-San* combines some of the finest components of womanhood and, indeed, exemplifies virtues such as redeem the frailty of human nature—purity of heart and life, true love, endurance, heroism of conduct, and devoted integrity of spiritual faith. Blanche Bates gained the greatest success of her professional career by her impersonation of *Yo-San*. She was an entirely lovely image of ardent, innocent, ingenuous, noble womanhood—such an image as irresistibly allured by piquant simplicity, thrilled the imagination by an impartment of passionate vitality, and by its exemplification of eternal constancy in love,—the immortal fidelity of the spirit, —captured the heart. Her facility of action and fluency of expression were continuously spontaneous, and she was delightful both to see and to hear. Indeed, the acting of Miss Bates, which, from the first of her performances on the New York Stage, had shown a charming wildness and freedom, was, in the character of *Yo-San,* more unconventional than ever. Her appearance was beautiful, her action graceful, alert, vigorous, and free from all restraint of self-consciousness and finical prudery. The clear, keen, healthful north wind was suggested by it, the reckless dash of a mid-ocean wave, the happy sea-bird's flight. There was no ostentation about it, no parade, no assumption of the moral mentor. Her personation of Belasco's *Juliet* of Japan came in a time of dreary "problems," "sermons," "lessons," "arguments," "symbols," and the flatulent nonsense of siccorized novels and dirty farces, and it came as a relief and a blessing—the authentic representative of youth, health, strength, love, and hope.

There is one moment in "The Darling of the Gods" when suspense is wrought to a point of intense tension, and when the inherent, essential faculty of an actor, the power to reveal almost in a flash the feeling of the heart and the working of the mind, is imperatively required. It is when *Kara,* wounded, exhausted, desperate, has sought refuge in the dwelling of the *Princess Yo-San* and, by her, has been succored and concealed. *Migaku, the Shadow,* a spy of the terrible *War Minister, Zakkuri,* has traced him to that refuge, but a devoted guardian of *Yo-San, Inu,* a Corean giant, has detected the presence of the spy, has seized and slain him, and has hidden the body in a stream. *Zakkuri* and the father of *Yo-San* follow the spy, and come to the dwelling of *Yo-San. Zakkuri* wishes that it be searched, but he agrees to accept her oath, if she will give it, that she knows nothing of the whereabouts of *Kara.* The *Princess* is summoned and, denying the presence of *Kara,* is required by her father to swear that she has spoken the truth. Words can faintly indicate the beauty of the picture and action which follow, as the girl seeks to protect her lover. The time is night. The scene is a strange, fantastic, fairy-like garden of old Japan, a bower of flowers with twining wistaria wreathing the trees and houses, and, far, far off, visible in the silver moonlight, a great snow-capped volcano, the peak of which is touched with ruddy light. The father and the dreaded *Minister of War* stand before the door. Miss Bates, as *Yo-San,* stood a little above them, dressed in soft, flowing white garments, open at the throat, her black hair loose about her face and shoulders, her beautiful dark eyes suffused with a fascinating expression of innocence, tranquillity, and tenderness. Without a moment of hesitation, on being required to take the most solemn of oaths, she, with sweetly reverential dignity, raised a bowl of burning incense and, holding it before her, spoke, in a voice of perfect music: "Before Shaka, God of Life and Death,—to whom my word goes up on this incense, —I swear, hanging my life on the answer, I have not seen this Kara!" Then, as the discomfited searchers withdrew, she stood a moment, in the soft light streaming upon her from within the house, and, gazing after them, added, looking upward, "It is better to lie a little than to be unhappy much!" If she had done nothing else,—though the remainder of her professional life should be barren,—that single moment stamped her as a great actress.

It is, in any time, a noble achievement—one too much praised in words, too little sought in deeds— to bring home and make vital to the human heart the sanctity and beauty of love. The actor who does this can do no more. Pictorial art upon the stage attains to a marvellous height when it presents such a scene as that of the River of Souls and the reunion of long-sundered souls, in this romantic, imaginative, and beautiful play. Such an achievement in the dramatic art as the setting before the public of such a play and such a performance as Blanche Bates gave of its heroine vindicate the beneficent utility of the Theatre, because it cheers and ennobles, and thus practically helps society, through the ministration of beauty. This is a hard world. Almost everybody in it struggles beneath burdens of care and sorrow. Multitudes of human beings dwell in trouble and suffering. An imperative need of our race is the strength of patience and the light of hope. Dramatic art, or any art, which satisfies that need, or even remotely helps to satisfy it, is a blessing. The rest is little, if at all, better than a curse.

There was fine acting in "The Darling of the Gods" besides that of Miss Bates. The part of *Zakkuri*, the *War Minister*,—a callous, remorseless, cold villain, of the Duke of Alva type,—is the main source of action in the drama, and it is elaborately and vividly drawn. It was played by George Arliss, who gave in it a thrilling incarnation of dangerous force and inveterate wickedness, almost humorous in its icy depravity: he had an exceptional success, even for an actor who always acts well.

And there are many splendid imaginative and dramatic passages in this play besides those which have been particularly examined. As set upon the stage by Belasco it was a spectacle of superb opulence, surpassing all its predecessors in wealth of color and beauty of detail. In the Scene of the Night Watch at the gates; in that of the stealthy, nocturnal search for *Kara*, outside the lodge of the *Princess*, and in that of *Yo-San's* supplication for her lover's life there is the very poetry of terror. Some of the expedients employed had been used in earlier dramas,—such as "Patrie" and "Tosca,"—but they were so freshly handled that they were made newly terrible with an atmosphere of grisly dread. Belasco, in short, offered to his public in this production a true dramatic work of novelty, variety, and scenic splendor, extraordinarily rich in the element of histrionic art; an offering that was symmetrical and magnificent, prompting a memory of the old days of "Pizarro," "The Ganges," and "The Bronze Horse," but proving that his day also was golden and that Aladdin's Lamp had not been lost.

THE CREATION OF DRAMATIC EFFECTS.— DIFFICULTIES WITH THE RIVER OF SOULS.

Supreme dramatic effects are, as a rule, produced in the Theatre as results of patient, prescient labor, using known, definite means to definite foreordained ends,—as, for example, in such perfect histrionic epitomes as *Shylock's* return through the lonely midnight streets to his deserted dwelling, as arranged by Irving; the momentary shuddering horror of Mansfield's *King Richard the Third,* when, alone, in the dusk, seated upon the throne to which he has made his way by murder, he sees his hand bathed blood-red in a seemingly chance-thrown beam of light; the exquisitely poetic and lovely scene of the serenade, in "Twelfth Night," invented by Daly, in which the theme of the comedy is pictured without a word; or the long, dreary vigil of *Madame Butterfly,* waiting

GEORGE ARLISS AS *ZAKKURI, THE MINISTER OF WAR,*
IN "THE DARLING OF THE GODS"

through the night for her recreant lover, devised by Belasco. Sometimes, however, even the most resourceful of stage managers, though possessed of perfectly clear purpose, find themselves baffled and balked in every endeavor to embody a picture in action and create a designed effect: it is with them as it is with a painter who, while knowing exactly what he desires to depict and, theoretically, exactly how to paint it, nevertheless fails again and again in his attempts to do so, until, as sometimes happens, chance seems to point a way to achievement. Such an experience came to Belasco, in his execution of the imaginative and lovely scene of the River of Souls, in this Oriental tragedy. Writing of it, he records the following interesting recollection:

"There was one scene in 'The Darling of the Gods,' called the River of Souls, which drove me almost mad and very nearly beat me. It was a sort of purgatory between the Japanese Heaven and the Japanese Hell. I engaged twenty young girls who were supposed to represent the floating bodies of the dead, but they wouldn't float. No matter how hard I tried, the twenty souls looked like twenty chorus girls. Night after night, I kept the young ladies and a number of carpenters at work, but the illusion could not be carried out. The play was produced in Washington, and during the last rehearsal the River of Souls was the blot on the production; in fact, I had postponed the opening for three nights because of this scene. At last I made up my mind to give it one more trial and if it could not be

improved to cut it out. Dawn found Miss Bates asleep in a
stage-box, the company curled up on properties, the carpenters and electricians ready to drop, and the River of
Souls as bad as ever. So I threw up my hands. 'Thank
you, ladies and gentlemen,' I said, 'out goes the River of
Souls.' I gave the order to strike [to clear the stage of
scenery]. At that moment all set-pieces were pulled apart,
the gauze curtain was down, and two calcium lights were
at the back of the stage. As the scene-shifters drew up the
back drop a carpenter walked across. His shadow was
thrown several times on the shifting gauze in a most spec-
tral fashion. 'Stop!' I called out. 'Stop where you are!
Don't move! Don't move!' The poor carpenter halted in
his tracks: he must have thought me mad. 'We've got it!'
I exclaimed. I sent out for coffee and rolls, and called
another rehearsal at six in the morning. I must say
everyone rejoiced with me. When we finished breakfast I
had the gauze so arranged as to catch the shadows of the
young ladies whose souls were supposed to be floating between heaven and hell. I threw away the expensive paraphernalia, and instead of permitting the young women to
be suspended in the air they walked behind the gauze,
stretching out their arms as though floating through the
strong rays of light. I have shown many different scenes,
but none so baffling as this and none more impressively
effective. . . . When I met Sir Herbert Beerbohm-Tree,
who produced 'The Darling of the Gods' in London, he
said that as he read the description of this effect in the
manuscript he had not believed it could be carried out."

"The Darling of the Gods" was one of the most
costly and least profitable of all Belasco's many

lavish productions: the original investment exceeded $78,000 and the expenses of presentment were so great that, notwithstanding it was acted to immense audiences, at the end of two years he had gained with it only $5,000.

AN OPERATIC PROJECT.—PETTY PERSECUTIONS.— AN ARREST FOR LIBEL.

While demolition of the Republic Theatre and construction of its successor were in progress Belasco made an unsuccessful attempt to fulfil a purpose which he had cherished for several years,—the purpose, namely, to cause the writing of, and to produce, a series of true comic operas, American in theme but similar in character to the brilliant and delightful combinations of satire, melody, and fun which made famous the names of Gilbert and Sullivan. "I hoped," he said, "to find a pair of American authors that could be developed into at least something like such a team as Gilbert and Sullivan, and for a while I thought I should succeed,—but it was too much to hope for." As part of his plan for this operatic enterprise Belasco engaged the well-known singer Miss Lillian Russell, for whose talents he entertained high respect: "I *know*," he has said to me, "that Lillian Russell could have done far finer things than ever she has done—and I wanted her to do them under my management." Inability to obtain any musical play for Miss Russell's use which was satisfactory to him finally compelled Belasco to release her from engagement and to abandon a project which, adequately performed, would have been of great benefit to our Stage.

From the time when it became publicly known that Belasco had assumed the management of a theatre of his own, in New York, until 1909, when self-interest at last reopened to him the long closed theatres dominated by the Theatrical Syndicate, he was made the object of an almost continuous series of attacks, annoyances, and persecutions, often merely petty, sometimes extremely serious, the origin of which is not always demonstrable but the motive of which, unmistakably, was to defame, hamper, and injure him in his professional vocation. Thus, a few days before the opening of his new theatre he was accused in several newspaper diatribes of having "stolen" the services of three prominent actors,—namely Lillian Russell, Blanche Bates, and David Warfield,—then under engagement to him, from other theatrical managers, regardless of prior contracts. The dispute on this subject has been top-loftically described as a tempest in a teapot, but as the accusation is, in fact, one of most

dishonorable and illegal conduct the entire refutation
of it should be recorded. Miss Russell wrote about
the matter as follows:

"I am very proud to have it known that Mr. Belasco is
to be my future manager, but it is doing him a great injustice to assert that he tried to get me away from other
managers with whom I was under contract. He, emphatically, did nothing of the kind. Everything was done in the
most amiable spirit among all concerned, and, as a matter
of fact, he and I were brought together, in a business relation, entirely by outside parties."

From Miss Bates came a letter in which she said:

"I was entirely free from all contract obligations when
Mr. Belasco first made me an offer to come under his
management. I left Liebler & Company quite voluntarily,
as I did not care to go to London with 'The Children of
the Ghetto.' I was therefore out of an engagement when
Mr. Belasco sent for me to create the leading part in a
new comedy. . . . I was given the greatest opportunity
of my life in 'Madame Butterfly,' and I have grown from
leading woman to a star under his management. And
because I know that my artistic future is safer in his
hands than with anyone else I would not for a moment
consider an offer from another manager."

And Mr. Warfield sent to Belasco by telegraph
from Boston this request and statement:

"Please deny for me that I had one more year [of service under contract] at Weber & Fields'. I came to you
having always had an idea you could better my position."

A week before the first presentment of "The Darling of the Gods" in New York an allegation even more injurious was made against Belasco when several newspapers of the metropolis published affirmations by a female author, known as Onoto Watanna, to the effect that characters and incidents from two stories by her, "The Wooing of Wistaria" and "A Japanese Nightingale," had been appropriated by Belasco and incorporated in "The Darling of the Gods" and that two acts of that play were pirated from a dramatization of one of those stories.

To these aspersions Belasco made prompt rejoinder by institution of a suit against Mrs. Bertrand W. Babcock, asking $20,000 damages for malicious libel. Mrs. Babcock was arrested, December 3, 1902, on a warrant issued in this action and held in $500 bail. At the time of her arrest Belasco made a statement as to his motives and feelings in bringing suit in which he said:

"My purpose in causing the arrest of Mrs. Babcock (Onoto Watanna) is to stop, once and for all, the groundless persecution to which I am subjected whenever I dare to present a new play. That my productions are thorns in the sides of several managers I am perfectly aware, but through Mrs. Babcock, who will now have to give an account of her claims against me in court, I hope to reach the real instigators of this attack against my integrity as a manager and a man. I have never met Mrs. Babcock in my life nor have I read either of her books, to one of which Klaw & Erlanger have announced that they have purchased the dramatic rights. The first I heard of Mrs. Babcock was about two months ago, at which time my play had neither been put in rehearsal nor read to any one who could possibly have told her of its plot, characters, or incidents. At that time she informed a prominent morning newspaper man that the firm of Klaw & Erlanger were very anxious to have her bring a suit against me for plagiarism. I laughed at the whole matter, for, knowing that 'The Darling of the Gods' was entirely original with Mr. John Luther Long and myself, I could not conceive of any person being foolish enough to make such a charge. But it was the last shot in my enemies' locker. From the day I started work on this production I have been harassed in every direction. I am almost as anxious to get this case into court and settled at once and for all as I am to have the 'Du Barry' controversy clinched. All I claim is the right of any citizen to pursue his business unmolested.

"This whole affair from start to finish is a conspiracy to throw a nasty slur on my name as a playwright and manager on the eve of a new production in which I have invested a great deal of money: and with the courts to help me I intend to unmask a few of the real culprits. Furthermore, I find now that Mrs. Babcock's story 'The Wooing of Wistaria' was not published until last September. Our play was finished early in June. By causing the arrest of this woman I hope, in addition to justifying myself, to establish a precedent whereby other playwrights, when they happen to be successful, may be able to take drastic means to protect themselves against similar persecutions."

On February 6, 1903, at a hearing in this libel suit of Belasco's, before Justice Leventritt, of the Supreme Court, Mrs. Babcock, in effect, withdrew the libel complained of (denying that she had made the defamatory allegations ascribed to her), and the order of arrest previously issued against her was, in consequence, vacated. The purpose of the aspersions made was, undoubtedly, that stated by Belasco.—A dramatization of Mrs. Babcock's story of "A Japanese Nightingale" was produced by Klaw & Erlanger, at Daly's Theatre, New York, November 19, 1903, with Miss Margaret Illington as *Yuki,* its chief female personage: the production of that play, it was generally understood in theatrical circles at the time when it was made, was designed to exhibit the authentic investiture and interpretation of a tragedy of Japan and thus to display the artistic and managerial superiority of Messrs. Klaw and Erlanger to Belasco: it was acted at Daly's forty-four times and then withdrawn.

On May 30, 1903, the 186th performance of "The Darling of the Gods" occurred at Belasco's Theatre, which was then closed for the season. On June 6, at Minneapolis, Minnesota, Belasco brought to an end a tour by Mrs. Leslie Carter and a theatrical company of 147 other players, presenting his "Du Barry," which began at Brooklyn, New York,

DAVID BELASCO
About 1889 - '90

December 2, 1902, which comprehended forty-two
cities (extending as far south as Galveston, Texas,
and as far west as San Francisco), and which
involved travel of more than 10,000 miles, during
most of which the company was luxuriously trans-
ported on special trains.

SECOND SEASON AT THE BELASCO.—A
CONTEMPTIBLE OUTRAGE.

The Belasco Theatre was reopened for its second
season, that of 1903-'04, September 16, with a
revival of "The Darling of the Gods,"—acted by the
original company,—which held the stage there until
November 14, sixty-four performances being given.
On November 16 Mrs. Carter emerged there in
"Zaza," which was acted for one week and was followed, on the 23rd, by "Du Barry," of which sixteen
performances were given. A peculiarly contemptible outrage, incidental to the protracted campaign
of persecution waged against Belasco, was perpetrated on the first night of the "Zaza" revival
when a process server, employed and instructed by
the disreputable Abraham Hummel, leaped upon
the stage during the performance and served upon
Mrs. Carter (who had nothing to do with the matter) notice of an action at law brought by Miss

Eugenie Blair and Mr. Henry Gressit against Belasco, in which, alleging rights of ownership in the play by Charles Frohman (who at the time was also represented by Hummel), they prayed for an injunction to stop his presenting "Zaza" in New York. "Few things," Belasco has said, "could have distressed me more than the thought that Charles Frohman could be in any way a party to such conduct." Among the many miscellaneous papers which Belasco has permitted me to examine, in compiling material for this Memoir, is a hurried note from Frohman which indeed reads strangely in the light of this incident:

(Charles Frohman To David Belasco.)

"New York, Friday,
"(August 30?), 1899.

"Dear Dave :—

"Don't fail me on 'Shenandoah.' This is *my chance*, and you can do much for me. *You know how I depend on you!* After our engagement the tour is arranged as you have asked it. 11 A.M., Tuesday, Star Theatre. All details I have people to look after.

"CHARLES."

The great success of "Shenandoah," which made possible the career of Charles Frohman, was in large part due to the sagacious and practical help of

Belasco, given in response to this appeal,—and the
latter manager, it seems to me, changing a single
word, might well have exclaimed with the betrayed
monarch in Wills's play about the Martyred King,
"Charles Murray, hast thou waited all these years
to pay me—*thus!*" Frohman, Belasco has informed
me, assured him, long afterward, when Gentle Peace
had enfolded all their contentions, that he was not
priorly cognizant of Hummel's outrageous instructions: well,—perhaps he was not: but, if he was not,
it is a pity he did not so declare at the time of his
quondam friend's persecution and so shield himself
from contempt. Belasco's lawyer, the Hon. A. J.
Dittenhoefer, commenting on this needless and
shameful interruption of a public performance,
observed that "The case has remarkable features.
As Mr. [Charles] Frohman is half-owner of the
play with Mr. Belasco, he is really being served with
papers by his own lawyers; moreover, Mrs. Carter
is not named in the papers, and it is against all
precedent and decency to serve them on her in such
a way. They should have been served on Mr.
Belasco, or on the box-office, which stood open.
There has been plenty of time and ample opportunity for that." Of course there had been "plenty
of time and ample opportunity"!—but such orderly
and decent service would not have annoyed and

distressed a nervous, impulsive, sensitive man, whom it was desired to harass and injure.—The injunction asked for was denied by Justice Scott, December 11, 1903.

HENRIETTA CROSMAN AND "SWEET KITTY BELLAIRS."

On June 15, 1900, Belasco entered into an agreement with the English fiction writer Egerton Castle by which he obtained optional rights of producing dramatizations of five novels by that author and his wife and collaborator, Agnes Castle. He relinquished his rights in four of those novels, "Young April," "The Pride of Jennico," "The Star Dreamer," and "The Secret Orchard," but he exercised them with regard to a fifth, "The Bath Comedy," upon which he based a play. His purpose, originally, was to bring forth Blanche Bates in its central character, when "The Darling of the Gods" should have ceased to hold public interest. Many reasons, however,—chief among them desire to please Mr. Castle 'by an early production,—caused him to change his plan. He, accordingly, in January, 1903, engaged the accomplished actress Miss Henrietta Crosman to assume the principal part in the play which he had founded on Mr. Castle's story, and, on November 23, of the same year, at the Lafayette Square Opera House, Washington, D. C., he produced it for the first time, under the title of "Sweet Kitty Bellairs." Pursuant of what was, I am convinced, a deliberate plan to harass Belasco and hinder him in his managerial enterprises, the lawsuit instituted by Joseph Brooks (incidents of which have already been recounted) was brought almost in the moment of that first performance. Belasco, however, had grown accustomed to persecution and remained unperturbed by it. On being notified, November 24, of Brooks's allegation in the matter and asked for a statement, he dismissed the subject in two sentences: "It is," he said, "a pack of lies, and I am too busy with this production ["Bellairs"] to make any answer to these persons [meaning Brooks and his associates] now. When I am disengaged I will make a reply."

Belasco's presentment of his "Sweet Kitty Bellairs,"—made for the first time in New York, December 9, 1903, at the Belasco Theatre,—revealed a comedy as well as a spectacle, because, while it satiated the vision with luxuriance of ornament and color, it set a truthful and piquant picture of manners in the jewelled framework of a story generally credible and always romantic as well as at once humorous and tender, merry and grave. The central purpose of it is the display of a study in womanhood, an exceptional female character, a peculiar and fascinating type; and the predominant attribute of it, accordingly, is sexuality. The dashing coquette of old English fiction lives again in his *Kitty Bellairs,*—not precisely *Lady Froth, Lady Bellaston, Mrs. Rackett,* or *Mrs. Delmaine,* but a purified, glorified ideal of those gay, tantalizing, roguish dames, a creature of sensuous beauty and reckless behavior, whose whole occupation in life is the bewitchment of man; and, in a silver fabric of gossamer comedy, this siren and all her associates are engaged in adjusting their amatory relations. In other words, this is a play of intrigue. "The Bath Comedy" is an extravagant and flimsy novel, and the dramatist derived but little material from it,—that little, however, comprising the jealous, peppery, belligerent, irrational husband; the silly, pretty wife, with her saccharine endearments and ever-ready tears; the ingenuous young nobleman, *Lord Verney,* so readily dazzled; and the burly, genial, blundering ardent Irish soldier, *O'Hara,* so fond and faithful, so rich in desert, and, at the last, so completely forlorn. Expert use is made, likewise, of the diverted love-letter, inclosing the tress of red hair. No spectacle, indeed, could, intrinsically, be funnier than that presented by the enraged, suspicious, tumultuous husband, intent on fighting

with every red-haired man in Bath, in order to be
avenged on the unknown epistolary suitor of his
absolutely innocent wife.   Taking this bull-headed
mistake as a pretext for action, and taking as a basis
Kitty's wicked scheme for the relief of *Lady Standish,*—who has temporarily wearied her husband by
her dulness and who will be taught to win and hold
him by gay indifference and the piquant allurement
of coquetry,—Belasco built a structure of story and
action practically original and certainly brilliant.
Writing on this subject, he modestly says: "The
dramatization was not easy: I was obliged to add
to the plot, but I used the atmosphere and characters of the book,"—and, it may be added, contrived to fashion a charming and effective comedy
where, perhaps, any other dramatist of the time
would have failed.

After an insipid Prologue, in crude rhyme, the
old English city of Bath is shown, in a beautiful
picture, and therein is displayed a populous, animated scene, constructed to exhibit as a background
the raiment, manners, morals, and pursuits of Bath
society, in the butterfly days that Smollett and
Sheridan have made immortal.   Then the story,—
slender and frail but amply adequate for its light
purpose,—is rapidly disclosed. *Kitty Bellairs* will
help *Lady Standish* to bewitch her indifferent hus-

band by making him jealous; and when, through
Kitty's artful roguery, his dangerous wrath is
directed against *Lord Verney*, whom she would like
to have for her own sweetheart, she will intervene
to prevent the impending duel and will implicate
herself in a most disastrous and distressing tangle
of comic trouble. Two situations ensue that are
essentially dramatic and that also involve affecting
and enjoyable elements of pathos and humor.
Kitty and *Lady Standish,* having proceeded to
Lord Verney's lodging, in hope to avert a catas-
trophe that their mischief has invoked, are in peril
of compromising discovery there, and at the climax
Kitty takes upon herself the apparent disgrace and
shame by coming forward to shield her friend.
Later, in the thronged assembly-room,—in a pageant
of almost unprecedented magnificence,—the brilliant *Bellairs,* ostracized by the ladies of Bath,
appeals to *Lady Standish* for vindication and finds
that spineless comrade too weak and too timid to
speak the truth. The latter incident provides the
supreme moment of the comedy, and, however much
its probability may be questioned, no spectator of
it, adequately acted, will for an instant doubt its
theatrical effect. The preparations for it are made
with extraordinary skill. The scenic adjuncts to it
provided by Belasco were of royal opulence. It is

fraught with emotional suspense; it is a sharp surprise, and it has the decisive potentiality of a dramatic act. Later the scene shifts to a Bristol tavern, where *Lady Betty* makes a tardy explanation, retrieving the wrong, while *Verney* and *O'Hara* and the rest of the soldiers march away,—in a storm, most deftly managed (as Belasco showed it), of wind and pouring rain,—and *Sweet Kitty Bellairs* is left in possession of the field, a little rueful, perhaps, but rehabilitated and triumphant. This close seemed somewhat tame, as a sequel to the ballroom effulgence, but it was inevitable: after the clock has struck twelve it must necessarily strike one. There is no thirteen.

The antique moralist, while gazing on that gorgeous spectacle,—"the teacup time of hood and hoop, or when the patch was worn,"—might, perhaps, be moved to inquire whether women, in their traffic with the impulses of love, the caprices of their own sex and the follies of the other, do really think and act as they are made to think and act in this play of Belasco's: but, as the antique moralist knows nothing whatever about women, he would only bewilder himself by such interrogatory. Enough to know, in gazing on that spectacle, that it dazzles his vision and that the story pleases his fancy. He sees a woman to whom humdrum conventionality is intolerable; a woman who is fearless alike of vindictive feminine spite and insolent masculine tolerance; a woman who can be magnanimous; a woman who is nothing if not brilliant: and all this ought to content even a cynic. The dramatist has made *Kitty Bellairs* much more of a woman and *Lord Verney* much more of a man than they were in the Castle novel,—where, indeed, *Bellairs* is unprincipled and heartless and *Verney* foolish: a coarse flirt and a callow milksop. Evil influence may be incarnate, without evil deed. In the play this heroine is a thoroughly noble, gentle, and tender woman, underneath her panoply of mirth and mischief, and she acts from a good heart, and not from mere vanity and sensuous caprice. Miss Crosman entered into this character with absolute sympathy, and, as to the glittering side of it, so embodied it as to create a cogent effect of nature. There is an appeal made by *Kitty* to her Irish and other military friends, when they behold her in apparent disgrace, that strikes the true note of pathos, and, in the speaking of this, Miss Crosman eloquently and nobly expressed the dignity of conscious virtue, while in the denotement of tenderness she much exceeded expectation,—because tenderness is not characteristic of her acting in general, the drift of her temperament and style setting toward pert assurance, skit-

HENRIETTA CROSMAN AS *MISTRESS KITTY BELLAIRS*,
IN "SWEET KITTY BELLAIRS"

tish sport, sparkling raillery, and sprightly banter. *Kitty's* attitude, during most of the comedy, is that of a maker of innocent mischief,—with a spice of wickedness in it,—and she complicates everything from pure love of drollery. This Miss Crosman made perfectly and delightfully clear. The dilemma in Act Second, when *Kitty* and *Lady Betty* are surprised in the bedroom at *Verney's,* and the exaction of an hysterical outburst at the end of Act Third a little overtaxed the strength of the actress; but her impersonation of *Kitty Bellairs* lives in memory and is treasured for unity of purpose and consistency of method, blithe spirit and buoyant action, sentiment sweetly denoted beneath arch pleasantry and many winning graces of manner, inflection, and playful prettiness. Belasco gained a new and lasting laurel of success with this production, in which all points had been well considered and nothing left to chance. The first performance in New York was given in the presence of a brilliant and delighted multitude. The final curtain did not fall till after midnight,—but

> "Noiseless falls the foot of Time
> That only falls on flowers."

This is the original cast of "Sweet Kitty Bellairs":

"They lived in that past Georgian day
When men were less inclined to say
That 'Time is gold' and overlay
With toil their pleasures."

IN THE PROLOGUE.

Master of Ceremonies....................Mark Smith, Jr.
The Prologue will be spoken by........Antoinette Walker.

IN THE PLAY.

Sir Jasper Standish....................John E. Kellerd.
Col. the Hon. Henry Villiers..............Edwin Stevens.
Captain Spicer..........⎤ ⎡Frank H. Westerton.
Lord Verney, Lieut......⎥ Of the ⎢..Charles Hammond.
Mr. Tom Stafford, Lieut.⎥ 51st ⎢......James Carew.
Mr. Bob Chichester, Lieut.⎥ Regiment. ⎢.......Clyde Fogel.
Gandy, Private..........⎥ ⎢......Addison Pitt.
Fenwick, Private........⎦ ⎣......Shelley Hull.
The Bishop of Bath and Wells...........H. Rees Davies.
Col. Kimby McFiontan................R. Peyton Carter.
Capt. Denis O'Hara.........⎤ ⎡J. Malcolm Dunn.
Major Owen MacTeague.....⎥ Of the ⎢...Alfred Cahill.
Mr. Lanty MacLusky, Lieut..⎥ "Innis- ⎢..Douglas Wood.
Mr. Darby O'Donovan, Cornet.⎦ killings." ⎣..Emmet Lennon.
Mallow................................Stanley Drewitt.
The Innkeeper of the Bear Inn..........Harold Watts.
First Courier...........................Howard Hull.
Second Courier...........................S. K. Blair.
Post Boy..........................William Whitney.
Mistress Kitty Bellairs..............Henrietta Crosman.
Lady Standish (Julia)............Katharine Florence.
Lady Marie Prideaux.................Louise Moodie.

Lady Bab Flyte........................Edith Crane.
Mistress Bate-Coome...............Genevieve Reynolds.
Hon. Mrs. Beaufort...........Charlotte Nicoll Weston.
Miss Prue...........................Bernice Golden.
Miss Doll...............................Sybil Klein.
Miss Debby..............................Jane Cowl.
Miss Sally..........................Lydia Winters.
Selina...............................Lillian Coffin.
Lydie.................................∴...Estelle Coffin.
Barmaid of the Bear Inn.................Mignon Hardt.

Clorinde ......⎫   ⎧Mrs. Irvin Chapman.
Dorothea .....⎪   ⎪.Gertrude Dorrance.
Arabella ......⎬ Mrs. Bate-Coome's ⎨....Edith Rowland.
Angela ....⎪   daughters.   ⎪.......Helen Hale.
Marjorie.......⎭   ⎩......Edna Griffen.
Mistress Tilney...........................Sara Delaro.

SIDE-LIGHT AND COMMENTARY ON "SWEET KITTY."

"Sweet Kitty Bellairs" was acted at the Belasco Theatre until June 4, 1904, when the season ended and that house was closed. It was revived there in the fall, September 3, and, with Miss Crosman in its chief part, was subsequently acted in many other cities. In the season of 1905-'06, Miss Crosman having retired from Belasco's management, it was again revived, with Miss Bertha Galland as Kitty, and on October 5, 1907, with Miss Eva Moore in that part, it was played at the Haymarket Theatre, London. On February 3, 1904, while this comedy was in the full tide of its first success, one of the many groundless suits against Belasco, accusing him of plagiarism, was brought by Grace B. Hughes, otherwise known as Mary Montagu, who asserted that Belasco's play was an infringement of one by her, entitled "Sweet Jasmine," and applied for an injunction to stop him from further presentment of it. Her application was argued before Justice E. Henry Lacombe, March 18, and on March 26 was denied. One of the most vicious propensities of newspaper journalism was sharply illustrated in connection with Miss Montagu's wanton aspersion on Belasco's honesty: when it was *made,* her charge of plagiarism was generally and conspicuously published by the press; when it was *disproved,* it ceased to be "live news" and merely curt and, in general, obscure record was made of the issue. Minor "resemblances" between the two plays, adduced by the complainant in this action by way of substantiating her charge of literary theft, were such as the facts that in both a military band played music; in both "green" is mentioned as the color of grass, and in both a lover states the nature of his feeling toward the woman he loves. Yet, without any possibility of redress, Belasco was compelled to expend energy, time, and money on making

a serious defence against the preposterous accusations of irresponsible frivolity! To oppose and
defeat the suit of Miss Montagu cost him a
large sum. There is no reasonable doubt that,
in the majority of cases, such accusations of plagiarism as those which have been brought against
Belasco are made in hope that the person accused
will buy off the accuser as the quickest and cheapest
way of ending annoyance. Belasco, however, has
never gratified such hope; and he assured me: "I
never will—for I prefer to lose a thousand dollars
in money and ten thousand in time and trouble
rather than to submit to blackmail." In denying the
writ applied for by this impudent defamer the court
declared that "No direct evidence of copying, either
of language or dramatic situation, is shown. A
comparison of the two plays shows that *they are
wholly dissimilar in plot, in characters, in text, and
in dramatic situations.* The climax of one act in
each piece was principally relied upon in argument
—where the unexpected discovery of the leading
character in a place where she should not be makes
a dramatic situation. . . . This is an old device;
it was common property to all playwrights since
Sheridan used it in 'The School for Scandal' [And
since long before that time!—W. W.]. Analyz-
ing the details of the situations as presented in these

two plays, the points of *essential difference* so far outnumber the points of similarity that it is difficult to understand how anyone could persuade himself that one was taken from the other."—The following letters provide an interesting side-light and commentary on the history of "Bellairs":

(*David Belasco to Egerton Castle, in London.*)
"Cartwright Cottage,
"Manhanset Manor, New York,
"August 29, 1904.

"My dear Mr. Castle:—

"You must pardon me for not replying to your letter. I am much run down by overwork, and as I had to finish Mrs. Carter's new play for the coming season besides much other work my doctor ordered me to the Adirondack Mountains, and before going I gave orders to my secretary to keep all mail for me until my return. Thank you for the story you sent. It is charming, but as it so closely follows the line of 'Sweet Kitty Bellairs,' and as that play has made such a success, I am afraid that another on the same subject and in the same period would fall flat in this country. So if anyone applies to you for the rights you will understand that I relinquish them.

"Next week 'Sweet Kitty' opens at my theatre for a few weeks, then it will be started off on tour. I need not tell you the condition of things theatrical in America. The Syndicate has brought nothing but disgrace and humiliation to the profession. Things artistic are at their lowest ebb. Last season was the worst financially the theatres ever experienced. Many fortunes were lost. Outside of 'Sweet Kitty Bellairs' I don't think any manager produced a success. Of course I lost money on the production. A play of that period is expensive, and as I make my productions perfect it invariably takes me a year to get back the original cost. This coming season is the year of the Presidential Election, which always hurts the theatres, but I think we shall do well on tour because of our New York success. I think it inadvisable to attempt 'Sweet Kitty' in England until after its first tour in this country. If by chance it should slip up over in London it would hurt our prospects for the play here. While the papers attach very little importance to a play successfully produced in England, they cable over a failure with sensational particulars, and it hurts all throughout the country. I think it would be wise to arrange for the production of 'Sweet Kitty' in London later, making the arrangements during the coming season, but, as I stated, I don't think it would be well to produce it yet.

"Hope that you are meeting with every success. With best wishes to Mrs. Castle and yourself,

"Faithfully,

"DAVID BELASCO."

(*David Belasco to Egerton Castle, in London.*)

"The Belasco Theatre,
"New York, March 3, 1905.

"My dear Mr. Castle:—

"Your letter of February 5 received. I regret very much that 'Sweet Kitty Bellairs' has not done better than it has. But I am constrained to attribute this to the fact that, in order to please you, I put it on during an unpropitious season, when there was little or no interest in plays of the

Georgian period, because the country was surfeited with them—with comic operas of the Eighteenth Century, and revivals of Sheridan. Again, I myself had just finished the production of 'Du Barry,' which, while it is of a more regal nature than 'Bellairs,' is still of the Eighteenth Century, a costume play of manners and customs. All this tended to take from 'Kitty' the charm of novelty, a detraction which could not be overcome by the fact that I spent more than $65,000 on the production and gave it a cast comprising some of the highest salaried artists in America.

"It was my intention to hold the play in reserve for Miss Bates, and produce it this year, with her in the title rôle. She is one of my own stars, and very popular. Had I done so, waiting for the flood of plays of that period to cease, I am convinced the result would have been far different.

"Miss Crosman closes in April, and I shall then recall the company, store the production and send it out when the road conditions in this country are more favorable. I believe it to be a valuable piece of property over here, and that it may yet make enough money to enable me to get back at least my original outlay. My loss up to date on the play is $50,000.

"In regard to the English production, I deem it inadvisable to commit myself at present, because I yet hope to have a theatre of my own in London, and, in consequence, am saving all my material for that time. Moreover, in 'Kitty Bellairs' I know so well the things that made it a great artistic success in this country, and there are so many details about the production to need my personal supervision, that I should really be afraid to let it be put on without me. To make the play 'go' at all, it must have a special cast, without which its fate would be foredoomed, and I do not care to trust the selection of this cast to another. In short, the

English production is a risk I do not wish to take, until I can give it my own personal attention.

"With kindest regards, I am

"Faithfully,

"DAVID BELASCO."

"THE DARLING" IN LONDON.—A HEARTY TRIBUTE.

On December 28, 1903, the English actor and manager Herbert Beerbohm-Tree produced "The Darling of the Gods," with notable success, at His Majesty's Theatre, London,—himself appearing in it as *Zakkuri,* with Miss Marie Löhr as *Yo-San* and George Relph as *Kara.* A characteristic instance of journalistic meanness was then provided by "The London Times," which ascribed the beauty and perfection of Japanese detail in the production to the influence of Mme. Sada Yaco,—a Japanese eccentricity who had appeared on the stage in London and profoundly agitated the esthetic circle of "souls" resident in that city. As Tree's present-ment of the tragedy of Japan was made in faithful adherence to Belasco's prompt book thereof and as Belasco never saw the Japanese actress, either on the stage or off, it would be interesting to learn in what manner her "influence" was exerted on him or his work. It is pleasant to turn from such paltry carping to read the hearty tribute paid by Tree, speaking from the stage of his theatre, in grateful acknowledgment of public approval:

"Ladies and Gentlemen:—I thank you for this splendid, wonderful reception of 'The Darling of the Gods,' but I must tell you that all the credit for what you have seen here goes across the ocean to that great idealist and genius of the Theatre, my comrade David Belasco, whom I so much admire. Never in all my career have I received from anybody [else] such a perfect 'script of a play. Every detail, every bit of costume, every piece of business, every light, is set down for us, and every note of music furnished, making it all so easy to produce this play that we can only claim credit for carrying out instructions! Concerning the genius and imagination that created it all and is responsible for it all,—I must say that, knowing him as I do, I can see that it is all Belasco-Belasco-Belasco, from the rise to the fall of the curtain. Words are inadequate to pay tribute to him; but I shall have the pleasure of sending him a cable to-night, to tell him how tremendously you have all enjoyed and applauded this wonderful play and how grateful we all are to him as well as you!

"Hereafter, it is my hope that Mr. Belasco and I shall do some work in collaboration and that I may induce him to send us more of his productions—perhaps, to bring them over himself and have them acted for you under his own supervision. . . ."

"Tree was always most generous to me," Belasco has said; "and his 'Darling' speech made me very

happy. I like appreciation and encouragement
when I have worked hard and tried to deserve it.
Always after doing my 'Darling' Tree used to
address me as 'Sir David,' and several times in public
speeches he said that if they had me in England
they would knight me—which was very kind and
lovely, but plain 'Mister Dave' is good enough for
me!"

[Just before leaving this country for the last time
Tree read Belasco's striking play about the spiritual
survival of man, "The Return of Peter Grimm,"
and arranged to produce it in London,—an arrangement which was abrogated by his sudden and
untimely death, July 2, 1917.—J. W.]

A STRENUOUS YEAR.

The year 1904 was one of peculiar perplexity and
vexation for Belasco—of incessant strenuous labor
and (as I deem) of most malicious harassment
which might well have broken both his health and
his spirit had he not been sustained by vital enthusiasm and a steadfast, invincible will. In that year
he had not only to bear the heavy expense of producing "Sweet Kitty Bellairs," together with the
loss and anxieties incident to theatrical manage-

ment amid generally disturbed business conditions and the distraction and annoyance of Miss Montagu's monstrous lawsuit, but, also, he had to provide new plays and new productions for Mrs. Carter and for Warfield, to make his plans for the future of Blanche Bates, and to encounter at last the open and unrestricted animosity of the Theatrical Syndicate. "I am," Belasco has truly said about himself (1903), "a patient and peaceful man: I don't want to fight with anybody. I want to attend to *my* business in *my own way*—to do my work unmolested and to interfere with nobody. But neither will I permit anybody to interfere with *me,* or to dictate to me, if I am able to resist." And speaking of Belasco's course in theatrical management, his general representative, B. F. Roeder, publicly declared at about the same time (June, 1903): "Mr. Belasco's policy will remain exactly what it has always been. He will be independent of all factions and [will] place his companies wherever he can get the best terms and time." Such a policy, indisputably right as it is, was not one which the Theatrical Syndicate would brook, and it soon brought that oppressive monopoly into direct and open conflict with Belasco in the conduct of his business. Foreseeing an immense popular interest in the World's Fair (Louisiana Purchase Exposition) at St. Louis, in 1904, Belasco resolved that his superb production of "The Darling of the Gods" should concurrently be presented there. He felt great and wholly natural and frank pride in that production: he knew that he could not much longer hold together the company acting in it, and he desired that as many persons as possible should see his tragedy to the best advantage. When, however, he applied to the Syndicate booking agency, presided over by Mr. A. L. Erlanger, to arrange for an engagement in St. Louis, during "the Fair," he was informed that it could not be done. He thereupon instructed his own booking agent, an experienced manager, William G. Smyth, to arrange for presentment of "The Darling of the Gods" at an independent theatre there, the Imperial, and his order was at once obeyed. It is not worth while to relate in detail the story of the attempt to coerce Belasco into cancelling that engagement: it is enough to state that (as he told me at the time) when it had proved impossible to intimidate him the uncouth Erlanger destroyed the contracts previously executed through his agency, between Belasco and theatre managers in various cities,—and, in profane and insulting language, sent him notice that he could not thereafter present his productions in *any* Syndicate theatre.

WARFIELD IN "THE MUSIC MASTER."—AN
ANIMATED SPEECH.

Once committed to "open war" with the Trust
and having got the St. Louis engagement of Miss
Bates securely arranged, Belasco turned to completion of the plays for Warfield and Mrs. Carter.
He had, at first, intended to write the Warfield
piece unaided, but the demands on his time and
strength had rendered that impossible and he had
employed the late Charles Klein (1867-1915) to
work with him. "I had," he said, "given much
thought to the subject of the play I needed for
Warfield, but with all my other responsibilities and
cares I found that I must get somebody else to do
much of the actual writing. One night while having supper in a restaurant with Roeder, after the
play, I told him that I was going to ask Klein to
undertake it. 'Well,' Roeder said, 'this is a good
time to ask him—here he comes,' and Klein, who
had just come in, walked over to our table and told
me he had been thinking for some time about writing a play for Warfield! I told him what I had in
mind, and before we separated we had agreed to
do the piece together."

The outcome of that agreement was the play of
"The Music Master," which was produced for the

DAVID WARFIELD AS *HERR ANTON VON BARWIG*, IN "THE
MUSIC MASTER"

first time at the Young's Pier Theatre, Atlantic
City, New Jersey, on September 12, 1904. "The
Music Master" is not remarkable for either
originality of design or felicity of construction,
but it is pure in spirit, interesting in story, picturesque in setting, and healthful in influence,
and it was apparent from the first that it would
have a long and abundantly prosperous career.
There has been on our Stage such excessive exposition of vice and degradation, of the possible depravity of human conduct and wickedness of human
motive, that it was an active benefaction to place
such a play before the public, a positive blessing
to receive the privilege of mental contact with its
pure and noble ideal of humanity. It was
announced, without qualification, as having been
written by Charles Klein: that was an injustice. It
is, in fact, a patchwork,—in the form in which Klein
first shaped it being based to some extent on a play
by Felix Morris (1847-1900) called "The Old
Musician," and then made over by Belasco, with
a distinctively perceptible interfusion of dramatic
expedients from that fine old drama "Belphégor; or,
The Mountebank." The central person, *Herr
Anton von Barwig,* the Music Master, is a German
musician, of a familiar type,—peculiar but attractive; impassioned but gentle; droll but piteous;

fervid but patient: an image of moral dignity and
self-sacrifice,—and the posture of situations and
incidents that have been utilized for his presentment
shows him as a loving father, occupied, under conditions of almost sordid adversity, in a quest for his
daughter, whom an unworthy wife and mother has
taken from him, flying, with a paramour, from Ger-
many to the United States, whither he has followed them. That daughter, at last, he finds and,
in circumstances cruel to himself, practically
befriends by keeping the secret of her paternity.
The conspicuous attributes of this person,—attributes blended and interwoven beneath a serio-comic
surface of foreign manner and broken English,—
are, intrinsically (of course with variant investiture), those that have long endeared such characters as *Michonnet, Triplet, Mr. Peggotty, Caleb
Plummer,* and *Doctor Primrose:* attributes, namely,
of love, charity, fidelity, fortitude, patience, humor,
simplicity, spontaneous goodness, and an unconscious
grace equally of conduct, manner, and thought. The
purpose, manifestly, was to place an eccentric, gentle, affectionate, humorous, and somewhat forlorn
elderly man in a predicament of sad circumstance,
and in that way to arouse pity and stimulate the
promptings of charitable impulse. That purpose
was accomplished; and therefore, aside from all con-

sideration of its inspiration and while the play is
neither novel with invention, potent with strong
dramatic effect, nor brilliant with polished dialogue,
it possesses the solid worth of fidelity to simple life,
the charm of diversified character, and the beauty
of deep, tender, human feeling.

It was a wise choice to combine those attributes
into a stage figure, and David Warfield,—finding
himself liberated, mind and heart, into a congenial
character,—gained in embodying it the most substantial success of his professional career,—making
of that figure a vital emblem of heroism that is
never flamboyant and virtue that is never insipid;
an image of paternal affection that typifies innate
dignity of character and the sweet, gentle, lovely
patience of pure self-abnegation. In earlier performances this comedian was almost exclusively
photographic; but time, thought, and practice,—
the forces that constitute experience,—gradually
expanded and ripened his art, and in his performance of this part (when repetition had eliminated
excessive nervous trepidation and made it "a property of easiness" to him) he showed intuitive insight
and was deeply pathetic. That is true success;
because the higher purpose of acting a play is not
proclamation of the talents of an actor, but libera-
tion and enforcement of the utmost of beneficial

influence upon an audience that a play contains. Warfield in "The Music Master" conquered by the two great virtues of simplicity and sincerity. The principal artistic defects in the personation—defects conspicuous in all Warfield's acting and to the elimination of which he seems to be curiously indifferent—were a hard, metallic voice and a poor method of elocution. The best dramatic expedient in the play is that by which the father's dubious, inchoate recognition of the daughter is confirmed. At that point and in the sequent situation ("lifted" from "Belphégor") the actor evinced sympathetic delicacy and tempestuous fervor. The closing scenes of the play are marred by episodes of irrelevant incident and by prolixity, obscurity and artifice, in the long-drawn passage of parental and filial recognition,—which, indeed, requires but a glance.

Belasco has written the following reminiscence of the production of "The Music Master," in which he shows just appreciation of the destructive result of those excessive expedients of stage "realism" which, in some of his earlier productions, impaired precisely the *effect* they were designed to create:

"We always spoke of *von Barwig* as 'the music teacher.' Naturally that became the name of the play; but as the character grew our musician impressed us as a master, and our title was changed to 'The Music Master.'

"I think there were at least fourteen versions of this comedy-drama. Even after the cast was engaged, we went over the manuscript again. The entire Supper Scene in the First Act was written while the company was assembled on the stage; so, too, was the ending of the play. Such radical alterations were made at the last rehearsal that one of the acts was almost entirely rewritten. We had a scene, wherein *von Barwig* dreamed of his past life in Leipzig. While the stage was dark, a double took Warfield's place in the armchair and remained in view of the audience while Warfield himself moved through the following scenes. He was shown as a young man, writing the intermezzo which was to bring him fame and fortune. Then he was seen directing the orchestra, then in his home, where he came fresh from his triumph, to find a note from his wife, telling of her departure, and on the floor a broken toy,—the toy by which after many years he was to identify his daughter. These scenes were mounted on movable platforms, easily set in place without loss of time. They were shown with telling effect at rehearsals, but I felt that the beauty of the actor's art was hampered by machinery. While Warfield was making quick changes, hurrying on and off the stage, the beautiful simplicity of his work was lost. The artist was of less importance than scenic changes and effects. 'This is not a spectacular play,' I thought, 'all these external matters are carrying us too far from this man's performance.' To the surprise of everyone, I ordered the scenes cut out. Instead, I showed Warfield sitting in revery, and by means of his changing expression and a few phrases dropped now and then the story of his past was conveyed to the spectators. His simple acting made it all as clear as though I had really used the various scenes. At the same time attention was centred on the actor, not on canvas. . . . The Last Act represented an attic with a skylight with its cracked panes stuffed with cloths which fluttered violently in the wind until some of them fell out and snow drifted through the openings. I liked the snow-storm very much, as it accentuated the misery of the characters grouped about a little stove. Warfield did not like the storm, but he did not wish to say so; so he took a novel way to be rid of it. 'Brrr!' he said as he walked off the stage, 'I'm cold! The snowstorm is so realistic it has given me a chill!' I ordered the weather changed at once. . . ."

"The Music Master," when first acted in New York,—at the original Belasco Theatre, September 26, 1904,—was cast as follows:

Herr Anton von Barwig		David Warfield.
Signor Tagliafico . . }	Musicians of the	{ . . W. G. Ricciardi.
Mons. Louis Pinac . }	Liberty Café	Louis P. Verande.
Herr August Poons . }		{ . . . Leon Kohlmar.
Henry A. Stanton		Campbell Gollan.
Andrew Cruger		William Boag.
Beverly Cruger		J. Carrington Yates.
Mr. Schwarz		Alfred Hudson.
Mr. Ryan		Tony Bevan.
Al. Costello		Louis Hendricks.
Joles		Harold Mead.
Ditson		H. G. Carlton.
Danny		Master Richard Kessler.
A Collector		Downing Clarke.
Mrs. Andrew Cruger		Isabel Waldron.
Helen Stanton		Minnie Dupree.
Miss Houston		Marie Bates.

Jenny.............................Antoinette Walker.
Charlotte...............................Sybil Klein.
Octavie...................................Jane Cowl.

After the Second Act Belasco was many times called before the curtain and finally, responding to insistent requests, addressed the audience in an exceptionally animated way, saying:

"I hope you will excuse me from making a formal speech; but I am most happy to take this occasion to say that I am glad you like our little play and glad that Mr. David Warfield has succeeded. And I am happy, too, to take this occasion to say publicly how proud I am of him and how very, very grateful I am for his loyalty to me—loyalty that no persecution could shake and no malice undermine! There have been lawsuits, plots, perjuries, and lies; there have been vexations enough to weary the patience of a saint (and I am not a saint, ladies and gentlemen!): but Mr. Warfield has remained through it all unshaken and true to me—and I honor and thank him: and, ladies and gentlemen, as long as I possess your confidence and friendship no theatrical syndicates, with all their money and outside influence, can crush me or dictate to me in what way I shall conduct my business. I rejoice in Mr. Warfield's success, and since this play pleases you, I will only say that our prosperity is just so much more ammunition with which to continue the struggle for Justice and the triumph of Right in American theatrical management!"

The appended letter, written by Belasco during the toil and strain of preparing his "Music Master" and "Adrea" productions, indicates his strenuous labor to make the former a success and his almost diffident estimate of his practically invaluable contributions to it as a playwright:

(*David Belasco to Charles Klein, at Merriewold Park, N. Y.*)

"Shelter Island, Long Island,
"New York, July 10, 1904.

"My dear Charles:—

"Act Second is now in the hands of Miss Edith. As you say you have shipped the Third Act to me I am expecting it any hour. I shall have Act One typed as soon as possible and fire it off to you. I hope you will like the things I have done to it. I am so anxious that your play shall be a sensational hit *that I am giving fifteen hours a day to it.* Whatever I do I think will help the cause,—and after all we are working for a big success. There is too much at stake for us all not to take off our coats and work for life. You have been bully, my dear Charles, from start to finish, and now with good health and with God on our side you shall reap the benefit of your patience and hard work.—I shall drop the acts along to you as they leave Miss Edith, and as I said before, I hope the work I have done on them will please you. "Faithfully, "David Belasco."

CONCERNING WARFIELD, JEFFERSON, THE ELDER
SOTHERN, AND THE "ONE-PART" CUSTOM.—
AN AMAZING RECORD.

In commenting on Warfield's great, indeed phenomenal, success and popularity in "The Music Master," Belasco writes: "I have no doubt that he could become *a one-part actor* and appear as *von Barwig* perennially, just as Jefferson played *Rip Van Winkle* and Sothern *Lord Dundreary*. However, neither he nor I approve of this plan." It is singular, indeed, what a strange, delusive, ineradicable effect the parrot-like repetition of words sometimes creates. Belasco,—like the majority of other persons who mention the subject,—has got it firmly established in his mind that Jefferson and Sothern were what he designates as "one-part actors" (actors who, as he expressly states, follow a professional course of which he does not approve), and he will, I suppose, go to his grave serene in the conviction that such was the case and unconscious of the injustice he does both those great actors. Yet Sothern gave hundreds of performances in "Sam," "David Garrick," "The Crushed Tragedian," "Home," and "An English Gentleman" after his great success in "Lord Dundreary"; while Jefferson's repertory embraced well over 100 parts; for every five performances he gave of *Rip* he gave about three of *Bob Acres,* in "The Rivals," and,—to the delight of audiences throughout our country,—he acted, hundreds of times, as *Dr. Pangloss,* in "The Heir-at-Law"; *Caleb Plummer,* in "The Cricket on the Hearth"; *Mr. Golightly,* in "Lend Me Five Shillings" (which, by the way, was the last part he ever played); *Dr.*

Ollapod, in "The Poor Gentleman"; *Hugh de Brass,* in "A Regular Fix," and *Mr. Woodcock,* in "Woodcock's Little Game." *Every* exceptionally successful actor is *more* popular in some one part than he is in any other, and as it was with Jefferson in *Rip Van Winkle* and Sothern in *Dundreary* so also is it with Warfield in *von Barwig.* Yet Warfield certainly is not a one-part actor,—though for every part he has played in the regular Theatre, aside from that one (exactly four, that is), Jefferson and Sothern each played anywhere from fifteen to twenty-five parts. Warfield, since his initial triumph as *von Barwig,* thirteen years ago [1917], has acted in a revival of "The Auctioneer," and in "A Grand Army Man," "The Return of Peter Grimm," and "Van Der Decken." Yet, time and again, wisely and rightly, Belasco has revived for him "The Music Master," and always the public,—whether in the greatest cities of the country or the smallest "one-night stand" which he has visited,—has hailed him in that piece with joy and flocked in crowds to witness his touching and lovely performance. During the season of 1906-'07, when he fulfilled engagements in that play, of four weeks each, at the Majestic Theatre, Boston, and the Academy of Music, New York, the respective managers of those houses caused to be prepared, attested under oath, and delivered as souvenirs to Belasco statements which show that in eight weeks $171,179.25 was paid for the privilege of seeing Warfield's impersonation of *von Barwig*. That is an amazing record, surpassing any similar and fairly comparable one known to me, and, therefore, I here transcribe the items of receipt:

MAJESTIC THEATRE, BOSTON.

Week ending October 6, 1906 (seven performances),......................	$16,443.50.
Week ending October 13, 1906 (seven performances),......................	16,227.75.
Week ending October 20, 1906 (eight performances),......................	18,676.50.
Week ending October 27, 1906 (eight performances),......................	20,864.00.
	$72,211.75.

ACADEMY OF MUSIC, NEW YORK.

Week ending February 2, 1907,.......	$21,857.25.
" " " 9, "	22,249.75.
" " " 16, "	25,149.25.
" " " 23, "	29,711.25.
	$98,967.50.

During the engagement at the Academy of Music, in 1907, the highest price charged for a seat was $1.50.

[Perhaps nothing more conclusively manifests the unbreakable hold of Warfield on the affections of the American public, in this play, than the facts that in the present season (1917-'18), notwithstanding the stress of war and that the character he portrays is a German, his audiences everywhere have, seemingly, been limited only by the capacity of the theatres in which he has appeared and that, as Mr. Belasco kindly informs me, his average gross receipts have been well over $14,000 a week.—J.W.]

The first engagement of "The Music Master" at the Belasco Theatre lasted until January 7, 1905, when it was withdrawn to make way for Mrs. Carter in "Adrea." On January 9 it was acted at the old Bijou Theatre, and remained there until June 3.

Belasco was subjected to a peculiarly impudent and contemptible persecution when Joseph Brooks (the factotum of Klaw & Erlanger and, as asserted by Belasco, a mere "dummy" for that firm) attempted to maintain a claim of partnership with him in the production and presentment of "The Music Master." The contract signed by Brooks and by Belasco, in 1901, providing for professional exploitation of David Warfield, assigned the contract made in November, 1900, between Belasco and Warfield, to the Belasco-Brooks "partnership"; and

SCENE IN FRONT OF THE BELASCO THEATRE, PITTSBURGH, PA.

Ten o'clock in the morning, December 6, 1906: Opening of the sale of tickets for David Warfield's engagement in "The Music Master"

the Belasco-Warfield contract, which covered the seasons of 1901-'02-'03, provided for a renewal at the end of that term. Brooks, accordingly, after "The Music Master" had been written on Belasco's instigation and in large part by him and after it had been produced solely at his expense and risk, claimed a one-half interest in that prosperous venture and sought an injunction to prevent the play from being presented except under management of "Brooks & Belasco." His claim was flatly disallowed in a decision of the New York Supreme Court, rendered by Justice Leventritt on October 31, 1904, in the course of which the court said:

". . . Undisputed proof by affidavit is offered that the [three] theatrical seasons contemplated [in the Belasco-Warfield contract] ended about the first of May or at all events before the first of June. The *alleged* renewal was made by the plaintiff Brooks several weeks after this latter date." Furthermore, held the court, "Whether the option [of renewal] in fact passed to the firm [of Belasco & Brooks]; whether, if it did, the plaintiff could exercise it, are questions open to grave doubt; but, conceding the right of the plaintiff Brooks, the papers show an exercise of the option after the close of the third theatrical season and insufficient proof of a custom that the right survived the termination of the season. . . . To enjoin a successful actor's lucrative performance of a successful play under (*sic*) such circumstances, when in addition no question of financial responsibility is presented, would be to grant, in advance of trial, on insufficient proof, the very relief which the action itself seeks. Motion denied, with ten dollars costs."

Belasco's feeling about "The Music Master" and his esteem of and loyalty to his friend Warfield are pleasantly shown in a declaration which he made about them several years ago:

"From the time the play opened until the present day I have had many offers for it. George Edwardes promised an enormous guarantee if we would come to England. George Newnes, proprietor of 'The Strand Magazine,' said: 'I am not a theatrical manager, but I want to bring your play and Mr. Warfield to England.' Cyril Maude, Arthur Bourchier, and Sir Herbert Beerbohm-Tree all applied for the acting rights. Another great fortune could be made out of the piece were I to allow it to be played in stock and moving pictures, but I have turned a deaf ear to all inducements. 'The Music Master' is for David Warfield; more than that, The Music Master *is* David Warfield."

A SHEAF OF OLD LETTERS: IN THE MATTER OF
THE THEATRICAL SYNDICATE.

All of the following letters by Belasco were written during the first year of "The Music Master," and they well characterize the purposes of the Theatrical Syndicate and well indicate Belasco's lively opposition to that oppressive monopoly. The second of them is addressed to his cousin, the son of the famous English actor David James, and it refers to a proposal made by the younger actor so named that he should be brought to America, to act in some of his father's parts, under the management of Belasco.

(*David Belasco to Blanche Bates.*)

"Belasco Theatre, New York,
"September 28, 1904.

"My dear 'St. Louis Pet':—

"Thanks for your message. It was sweet of you and your dear mother to think of me. Warfield and his little play hit them *hard,* and we have struck another terrific blow in the *solar plexus* of the Syndicate.

"Mrs. Carter's new play ["Adrea"] is written and I am already at work on yours ["The Girl of the Golden West"]. I am crazy to see you and go over the story before I get at the dialogue. As soon as Mrs. Carter's play is produced I shall join 'The Darling of the Gods' for a few weeks, as we must have a lot of talks together. I am going to do something *bully* for you,—a part that you will love. Won't you be happy when you are again playing in New York at the home theatre!

"Keep well. Love to your mother,—and remember I am

"Always your friend,
"DAVID BELASCO."

(*David Belasco to David James, Jr., in London.*)

"Belasco Theatre,
"New York, October 14, 1904.

"My dear David James:—

"Yours of October the 1st received. Yes, I did answer your former letter. No doubt it followed you about and was finally lost. Things theatrical are in a very bad way over here just now, and I am still in the midst of a big combat with what is known as the Theatrical Syndicate—a combination of men who have got together to disgrace the Stage and commercialize it, root and branch. It is rule or ruin with them, and unless they can force a heavy tribute from a man he is blacklisted forthwith. I am fortunate enough to be on their blacklist, and consequently am obliged, for the present, to move with cautious steps and to make no more productions than I can safely place. But it is to be hoped that a season or two will see the lifting of this dark cloud. When that time comes, I shall be only too happy to introduce you in this country. I know your work and I feel sure that you would make yourself heard over here had you the opportunity. Will you not drop me a line now and then? I am always pleased to hear from you.

> "Faithfully yours,
>
> "DAVID BELASCO."

(*David Belasco to Peter Robertson, San Francisco.*)

> "Belasco Theatre, New York,
>
> "April 25, 1904.

"Dear Peter:—

"[E. D.] Price and Fred [Belasco] have been 'kicking' about the vile cigars in San Francisco, so I am sending you a few weeds that ought to be better than the Barbary Coast perfectos. Sorry I can't deliver them in person, but I cannot get away this year; so when you are smoking them think of your old Four-o'clock-in-the-morning-pie-chum. Heavens, my dear Peter, I often think of those dear old days! They were struggling days for us, to be sure, but sometimes I feel that, at least as far as I am con-

cerned, they were the happiest ones of life. Ambition is
a hard, hard master, and from the moment when I left
'Frisco it has been constant work-work-work with me, morn-
ing-noon-and-night—winter and summer! I don't think I
have had half-a-dozen hours to myself in all that time, and
to make my lot easier, away off here in the East, I am
surrounded by that inartistic, low-lived Theatrical Syndicate, which for some reason or other,—certainly not justly
for anything I have done,—has waged a relentless war
against me. And since I cannot with honor play in Syndicate houses I am sending my stars and productions anywhere that I can find a roof to cover them. So far they
have not crushed me, as they said they would, for the public
and the press throughout the country have stood by me,
and as long as I continue to deserve their sympathies and
friendship I shall be victorious. In this combine against
me, my dear Peter, are Al. Hayman and the Frohmans, to
whom you know I have given the best years of my life,
helping to make fame and fortune for them. Of course,
with Charles Frohman it is jealousy: Daniel Frohman
resents not being able to get my plays for nothing: with
the Syndicate it is because they feared I was getting a little
too strong for them. But you knew me as a boy—in fact,
we were boys together—and no one in the world knows
better than you how I can struggle with privation and
adversity. I shall never surrender to this crowd: *never*—
not even if I am obliged to return to 'Frisco and do
chores about a theatre as you saw me do in the long, long
ago.

"Well, I have written more than I intended to, telling
you my troubles, but I shall make it a rule to send you a
line now and then and let you know all the good and cheerful news of the East. I would give a finger to be able to

drop in on you at this moment for a cup of coffee and a piece of pie in the little old restaurant, if it is still in existence, and to have an old-time heart-to-heart talk. But I hope it won't be very long before I can do this. Hurrah! God bless you!

"Faithfully,

"DAVID BELASCO."

(*Peter Robertson to David Belasco, in New York.*)

"Bohemian Club, San Francisco, Calif.,

"May 9, 1904.

"My dear Dave:—

"I shall smoke the cigars to your continued success. I was glad to hear from you; but I don't sympathize in the least with your suffering from hard work. I did sympathize much more with you in the days when you worked,— often quite as hard and got no salary!—'faking' plays for Maguire, at the Baldwin. You would never be happy, anyway, if you hadn't your head full of schemes, and were not constantly producing. Your work has achieved a great success, and work that has success behind it and success before it is life at its best. There is nothing so hard as work that has failure to pull it backward and the prospect of failure to push it back.

" *I,* too, think of the old days of coffee and cake; they were pleasant, after all; if I had lived much beyond them since they would still be pleasant to recall. However, my life goes on in its even tenor, and I make myself as comfortable as possible, though I do feel something like an old, worn-out hack—so many years I have gone the same old round. Still, I have not quite given up hope of better fortune.

"Go on and make your name and fortune greater than ever, and don't work yourself up over any Syndicates. They need you more than you do them.—My regards to Mrs. Belasco and the family, and Fred and Price.

"Always yours,
"PETER."

Belasco, I surmise, must have smiled a little grimly at this airy admonition "not to work himself up" about the active antagonism of the Syndicate: the cheery advice to the weaker party in a conflict, "Go in and win," is doubtless excellent, but often, unhappily, it is somewhat more difficult to follow than it is to give. Viewed from the secluded tranquillity of the old Bohemian Club—that genial harbor of congenial spirits—a struggle with the Syndicate may have seemed like a fight with a phantom. For Belasco it was, and for many years remained, a hard reality, and had it not been for his wary vigilance and indomitable resolution he would certainly have been defeated, overwhelmed, and ruined.—Poor Robertson never realized his "hope of better fortune": for several years after 1904 he continued to be the dramatic critic of "The San Francisco Chronicle": then, the whole duty of the managing editor (as defined by my old friend, the journalist William Seaver—"first, to wring your brains dry; second, to throw you away") having been performed, he was dismissed from his employment and, after two or three years of anxious, dispirited, lonely waiting, he died—and, save by a few old friends, he is thought of no more.

METHOD OF COLLABORATION.

The tragedy of "Adrea," begun in 1903, was completed before September, 1904, and it was put into rehearsal, at the Belasco Theatre, in October of the latter year. The following letters which passed between Belasco and his friend and associate John Luther Long afford an informing glimpse of their methods of collaboration in authorship, which Belasco has described in these words: "Before the actual writing of 'Adrea' we had the story [worked out] to the smallest detail. He lived in Philadelphia, but spent the latter part of each week with me. After the plot was finished we adopted a new system of collaboration. Mr. Long and I worked on the scenes apart, then met and joined them together. Then he revised the result and then I revised the result, and so on, until the sixth or seventh version found the scene in very good condition."

(John Luther Long, in Philadelphia, to David Belasco, in New York.)

"————, (?) 1903.

"I have now, my dear Goliath, been pretty well over the history of Rome, once more, and I have found only two places where we MIGHT possibly stick in our pin. One is the Augustan Era, and Livia and Julia; the other is the reign of Claudius and Messalina. I don't think you would like either. I am sure *I* don't! Besides, both have been done to death. There were NO woman rulers of Rome, and only one—Messalina—who took much of a hand at politics. I think we shall finally agree upon some island or mountain plateau—the latter commends itself because the other has been so often done. I think we could use either the island of Pandataria in the Adriatic, or the little island of Ilva in the Mediterranean. We could have all the Roman splendor there, without the handicap of being, unhistorically, IN Rome. Here is the scheme which outlines itself in my mind:

"When Rome was finally subdued, in A.D. 476, Romulus was on the throne. He was kicked out and sort of lost—though he is said by some of the histories I have read to have gone to live privately in the Campagna. He does not seem to have left any heirs. But let us give him some. Or *one*. This one seeks out one of these islands and takes with him some Romans to build anew the debased Roman Empire with the blood of the old Patricians alone. It is this kingdom, several hundred years later,—so that four or five of Romulus' descendants may intervene,—where we locate our play. And now, there are no males of the pure Roman blood and the succession falls to the two women.

"I rather dislike the creation of a name, such as Romancia or Ruritania or such like, and I think we could use the real name of the island, if we adopt it. And both are pretty good names. Pandataria. Ilva. Or we could, as you suggested, make some name out of the real names: Pinda —Illus—Illa—and so on. All the histories stop at that wonderful period of ours, 476 A.D., when our Odvokar did the trick. (One of them goes on to say that he stops there because the rest is too indecent for publication!) But I am on the track of some good books treating of that period —though I don't expect to find a woman or a ruler in it all. For, in this period, ALL the sovereigns, without exception, were elected by the soldiers in the field and the corrupt pretorians at home—with, once in a while, the people waking up and saying a word. After I have well looked up this period, I will run over and we will talk—when you can spare the time.

"Don't forget to tell your girl to send me the copies she makes. If anything should happen, by fire or flood, you have all the stuff over there.

"Yours,

"J. L. L."

(*David Belasco to John Luther Long, in Philadelphia.*)

"The Belasco Theatre,

"New York, April 2, 1904.

"My dear Jonathan:—

"You are right about the bench. I had already noted it and called Buckland's and Gros' attention to it, but outside of that correction, when we make the model, both the scenes will be corkers, full of the right sentiment and feeling—the atmosphere perfect. I am running over to see Mrs. Carter to have a talk with her about certain people for the cast

DAVID BELASCO

Inscription:
    "God bless you, dear friend!
      Faithfully,
          David Belasco."
"To William Winter, Esqre."

and also a general chat as to the costumer. She is miles deep planning them already. Before she goes to 'Frisco you and I together will have a talk with her.

"I am on the Fourth Act all the time. It is great—*great* —GREAT. They can't beat us—we are the top notches! Furst is going insane with pleasure over his share of the work. He loves it and is so infatuated that he is good for nothing else at present. In fact, everybody who has anything to do with the play is wild over it. I shall be back on Monday. What day after that can you come over? We will get in some big licks with Buckland, as I want to start him on the properties, etc., as soon as possible. God give us health and strength to knock out the great play!

"Faithfully,
"DAVID."

(*John Luther Long to David Belasco.*)

"Gosh! but that letter is full of good news, Goliath dear! When the scenery and costumes begin to materialize it looks as if the brain-squeezing would really amount to something. I shall have the Fourth ready for you by the middle of next week. Let me know a few days in advance of the time you want it, so that it can be copied. I am leaving a few little things to look up, but they are not important: such as *drums*—whether they had them in the legions; and, if so, what were their forms: and the Roman military salute. But I am practically done with the act. I'd like to see the models for the First. Perhaps I can, soon. I am feeling O.K. Equal to all the work two hands and one head can do. Don't bother about Frohman. We've got him beaten! This Fourth Act, as I get into it, is wonderful! Send on the Epilogue whenever you are ready with it. I am doing nothing but the Fourth and shall not, till I send it on to you.

"Hail, Luna of Adrea!"

"J. L. L."

MRS. CARTER AND THE TRAGEDY OF "ADREA."

The tragedy of "Adrea," by Belasco and Long, is a composition of exceptional imaginative scope and of great dramatic power. Its scene is a royal court of a conjectural kingdom, situated on an imaginary island in, perhaps, the Adriatic Sea. Its time is named as about the fifth century of the Christian era,—a time well chosen for poetic and romantic purposes; for the vast Roman Empire had then become extinguished in Western Europe and was slowly crumbling to pieces in the East, and minor monarchies can credibly be supposed to have flourished in such an era of transition and a martial chieftain out of Noricum to have dallied with the daughters of a Roman Prince. It is a play without historic basis; an authentic creation of the inventive brain; a vigorous and splendid work of art, moving freely in a broad field. It deals with great themes,—great passions, crimes, and sorrows; great and terrible punishments of sin, and the spectacle of great character made sublime by grief.

Much of its movement proceeds in the open air: some of it beneath the vault of night; and its web involves the terrors of tempest and the mystery and dread of spectres from the realm of death. The form and color of it are modern,—a form and color of rosy amplitude and voluptuous luxuriance; but the feeling that pervades it is the ominous feeling of the old Greek tragedies of fate and doom. Its defect is excess—an excess of persons, objects, pictures, emotions, and words; the superflux that proceeds from intensely passionate feeling in the conception of the story and especially in the conception and development of its central character. An affluence of fancy is, however, more grateful than the frigid sense of want. This is a synopsis of it:

The action begins in a spacious scene, in front of the royal palace of the monarchs of the island kingdom. The *Princess Adrea* is the blind daughter of *Menethus, King of the Adrean Isles.* She is older than her sister, the *Princess Julia,* and on the death of her father she would succeed to the throne, if she were not blind: for the law of *Menethus* has ordained that "No sovereign shall wear the crown who is not, both in mind and body, sound." The play opens on the hundredth day after the death of *Menethus.* The *King* is dead, and the hour has come for the crowning of his successor. The *Princess Julia,* long known as "the imperial wanton," with a company of her kind, is holding a festival. *Kaeso,* born a barbarian, but later a pretorian tribune, having come to Adrea, with his troops, intent on usurping the throne of *Menethus,* sees a readier way of conquest, in a marriage with the *Princess Julia,* soon to be *Queen.* He has been made her favorite, and marriage with him is to follow her coronation.

In the course of the revel the blind princess, *Adrea,* passes, led by an Egyptian named *Garda,* on her way to the temple, in which she is to be secluded, so that her presence at court may not trouble her sister *Julia,* whom the people of the kingdom detest. It is premised that in Arcady, where *Adrea* had dwelt with her father, she had known and loved *Kaeso,* then one of the *King's* martial chieftains, and that he had sworn to marry her, but had proved faithless. Now, at the *Princess Julia's* festival, *Kaeso* and *Adrea* meet again, and *Kaeso* kindly greets the blind girl. This enrages the *Princess Julia,* who thereupon commands him to declare to *Adrea* that he does not love her, but loves her sister *Julia.* This cruelty he must commit, as the price of the kingdom. He submits; the imperious *Julia* leads her train away; and he is left alone with *Adrea,* to whom he discloses himself, and who receives him with the deepest tenderness of faithful love. To her his presence can mean only that he has come to keep his oath by marrying her. *Kaeso* forgets *Julia,* his ambitions—everything but the woman who has come into his arms. The watchful *Princess Julia,* apprised by a spy, the *Court Fool,—Mimus, the Echo,*—returns to see the lovers in their ecstasy of reconciliation, and she at once determines on a terrible revenge. *Kaeso,* seeing *Julia,* starts away from *Adrea,* and *Mimus,* who madly loves the blind princess, takes his place. This *Mimus* happens to be in an armor like that of *Kaeso,* which he has put on in a frolic; and when *Adrea* reaches to find *Kaeso* her hands touch *Mimus,* and she eagerly claims him, believing him to to be her plighted lover. "And you shall marry him!" says the *Princess Julia;* grimly adding, as a response to *Kaeso's* look of horror: "It is the price of Adrea!"

A lapse of five hours is supposed. The scene is the same. The time is near dawn. Soldiers are on guard. Challenges pass. Rumors have been heard of ill to the beloved *Princess Adrea. Kaeso's* lieutenant, *Arkissus,* devoted to *Adrea,* has heard these rumors, and he demands an explanation of them from the now drunken and frenzied *Kaeso.* They quarrel, and are about to fight, when a fearful cry is heard and they halt. Then, staggering down the palace steps, moaning in agony, comes the *Princess Adrea,* alone. Her prayer, like that of Ajax, is for light. She beseeches the gods to grant her one moment of sight, so that she may see the man to whom she has been given. The *Fool* enters, to drag her away,—for the *Princess Julia,* now *Queen,* has decreed banishment of *Adrea* and the *Fool,* and they must leave her kingdom before the dawn. There is an ominous roll of thunder. The *Fool* seizes *Adrea.* Suddenly the heavens seem to answer her agonized supplication. A bolt of lightning shatters the statue of her father, to which she has been clinging, and there is an instant of darkness. When the light is restored, a chaos stands revealed, in which *Princess* and *Fool* are prostrated. *Adrea* revives, and, with a wild cry, realizes that she can see. Soon she remembers, and gazing down upon a "painted, hideous, gibbering thing, in red and white," she knows him for the *Fool,* who has been described to her. She lifts his limp body and stares at his vacant eyes: then she drops it and whispers, in horror: "Gods! *You!*"

The action now shifts to a structure called "The Tower of Forgetfulness." To this *Adrea* goes, not thinking to take her throne, but only wishing to die, and thus bury her shame. The Tower of Forgetfulness is an obelisk of great antiquity, built half on the land and half on the sea. Its door is never closed. Here the wretch who is weary of life can drink "the cup of oblivion," and, through "the door of release," sink into the sea, and be at rest. It is *Adrea's* purpose to die. Then suddenly she hears the royal trumpets, the marriage song, and *Kaeso's* song of battle. At the same moment her father's ghost appears and enjoins her to reign, for vengeance. Looking down upon the ocean, she beholds *Kaeso* and *Julia,* who are returning to the palace, after their marriage. They are in her father's royal galley, with his effigy at the prow. "Stop them!" commands *Adrea.* "Bring my father's galley here! Say that *Queen Adrea* rides to her coronation!" *Arkissus* appears with his legions, and executes her will.

The coronation of *Adrea* ensues. *Kaeso* is brought before her, in order that he may sue for pardon—which the heart of the injured *Queen* is ready to grant. But *Kaeso* is haughty, and the *Queen* dismisses her court, that she may judge him alone. She is temperate, lenient, and fond. She pours out all her heart; but it is only to be dazed by *Kaeso's* declaration that his regret is solely for his lost ambition. He tells her that he knew of her spoliation, and allowed it. The *Queen* recalls her court. "Set him upon a horse of state," she says, "drest in a robe of gold. Strew his way with roses! Let heralds go before him and cry 'Conqueror!' 'Imperator!' Let maidens chant songs! And when he has reached my gates, and his men and galleys are in sight,—*whip him!* Whip him to his empty camp, and hold him captive there till the manner of his death is decided."

The scene changes to the *Queen's* Cabinet. *Kaeso* is brought in on the way to execution. It is the supreme moment of *Adrea's* life. The man she loves is on the way to death. In spite of all her wrongs she will look upon his face again, before it is mangled by wild horses' hoofs. Her heart still cries out for him. Even now she would save him, if she could. But frenzied multitudes surround the palace, maddened with knowledge of the outrages that the *Queen* has suffered; and she is powerless to save. *Queen Adrea* must tell *Kaeso* the manner of his death. *Kaeso* had thought to die as a soldier should—upon his sword, but his death is to be that of a beast, trampled beneath the iron hoofs of horses. This fate she proclaims, but, when the first shock of horror is past, *Kaeso* confesses that he deserves his doom, and declares that he will die well: and then he says that he has always loved *Adrea,* but has put his love aside, for the sake of his ambition. Again the *Queen* relents. She will, at least, save him from a death of ignominy. She offers him the sword of *Menethus,* with which to kill himself. But his hands are chained. "You!" he begs. The thought is unendurable. She turns away. But suddenly, turning back, she cries out, "Yes!" and drives the blade through her lover's heart.

The scene changes to Arcady. Eight years have passed. *Queen Adrea* has come to Arcady, and there she would remain at rest. But her people call her back to Adrea. The stanch *Arkissus,*—who has always loved her, whose one thought is of duty, and whose duty is to obey,—brings the prayer of her subjects that she will return and rule over them. But here are green fields, summer skies, and the shepherds and their pastoral music: it is a halcyon place and time; and she would remain, and linger, and die here, and rest beneath the sod that she and her first lover once trod together. A trumpet sounds, and a captive youth is brought into her presence. He is the son of *Kaeso* and *Julia,* and he has sought the throne of *Adrea.* He is vanquished, and his mother, *Julia,* has been slain. But there are tears in *Queen Adrea's* eyes, as she looks upon him, and her arms open to him—for he has the port and lineaments of *Kaeso.* The *Queen* and the captive play a game,—"the Game of Being King." *Adrea* places the youth on her throne, sets her crown on his head, puts her sceptre into his hands, throws her ermine on his shoulders, and bids him "Reign in love." "Open the casement," cries the captive boy, "Let in the sun, if you play fair and set no trap for me!" "At the King's command," she answers; and in those words ordains her fate, for *Adrea* cannot again look upon the sun without loss of her vision. She flings the casement wide open, and, in the sudden blaze of light, goes blind: then, when the agony is past and night has come again, she staggers to the throne and cries, "Long live the King!" For still the law of succession is inexorable,—and so *Prince Vasha* reigns, and *Adrea* is once more only *Adrea of Arcady.*

No student of Roman history needs to be told that among the women of Rome (and at one time all Italy was circumscribed within the capital) there were females illustrious for almost celestial virtues and females portentous for the monstrosity of their hideous crimes. The authors of "Adrea" neither distorted nature nor exaggerated fact in their portraiture of the two princesses, *Adrea* and *Julia,* who are opposed and contrasted in this remarkable drama of love, crime, frenzy, retribution, atonement, and peace. *Adrea* is not nobler or more virtuous than Valentinian's Eudoxia, nor is *Julia* more malignant, treacherous, and cruel than Justinian's Theodora. In this tragedy the purpose, obviously, was to present, amid regal accessories and in all the paraphernalia of semi-barbaric splendor, a woman of lofty mind, potent character, and impetuous passions, and, by making her the victim not alone of blighted affection but of deadly outrage, to involve her in a complex tangle of torment; to make her terrible in the delirium of exasperated feeling; to display her emotional perturbation and fierce and ferocious conduct in a vortex of tempestuous struggle; and, finally, to depict her noble expiatory conquest of herself, and to leave her, in her lonely majesty, a sublime image of triumphant virtue, gentle fortitude, and patient grief. That purpose has been superbly accomplished. To superficial observers, indeed, the presentment of "Adrea" appealed chiefly by reason of its implication of theatrical situation, its startling effects of climax, and its gorgeous scenic investiture. To thoughtful minds it came home as an illuminative and significant exposition of human nature, artfully made through the medium of a wonderful picture of human life in the antique world,—and in that it reached much further than merely to the fulfilment of any immediate theatrical need. Like the more classic dramatists of the Garrick era, its authors drew their inspiration from the great fountain of historic antiquity—adjusting, rearranging, and emphasizing old types and old examples to exhibit actually (and not by any dubious method of old symbolism) what is in our own hearts and of what fibre we are all made. Their play is an honor to them, and it is a rich and permanent addition to the literature of the Stage.

Mrs. Carter impersonated *Adrea,* and finding in it a part into which she could entirely liberate all her emotional power, without losing control of it, she rose to the occasion. She had hitherto acted in comedy, "sensation," or sentimental, drama. The character of *Adrea* is wholly tragic. Through the wide range of conflicting emotions implicated in her experience—the misery of blindness and loss of royal inheritance, the ignominy of desertion by her idolized lover and of betrayal into the lewd embraces of an odious menial, the paroxysm of anguish when, to save her lover from a death of horror and shame decreed by herself, she strikes him dead, and the humility of surrender when, after years of bleak remembrance, she invites again the black eclipse and forlorn disablement of blindness and delivers her kingdom to the rule of her slaughtered lover's son— Mrs. Carter moved firmly, steadily, triumphantly,— commanding every situation and rising to every climax. No denotement in Mrs. Carter's acting of

Du Barry had even remotely indicated such depth of tragical feeling and such power of dramatic expression as she revealed in the scenes of the tempest, in pronouncing *Kaeso's* doom, and, above all, in the terrible, piteous, tragic self-conflict through which the Woman became the incarnation of Fate and the Minister of Death. Mrs. Carter had long been known for her exceptional facility of feminine blandishment, her command of the enticing wiles of coquetry and the soft allurement of sensuous grace,—known, likewise, and rightly admired for the clarity and purity of her English speech, always delightful to hear: but observers studious to see and willing to be convinced had not supposed her to be an actor of tragedy. It took a long time for Belasco to bring her to a really great victory, but she gained it in *Adrea*. The impersonation possessed many attributes of beauty: symmetry, for the eye; melody, for the ear; unity, continuity, sincerity, and sustainment, for the critical sense; poetic atmosphere, for the imagination; but it possessed one supreme attribute of terror,—absolute knowledge of human misery. "Look into your heart, and write," is an old poetic precept. "Look into your heart, and act" ought to be joined with it: but God pity the heart into which the true poet and the true actor must sometimes look!

"Adrea" was first performed in Washington, D. C., on December 26, 1904, and in New York on January 11, 1905,—at the first Belasco Theatre. The following is the original cast of that play:

Kaeso of Noricum	Charles A. Stevenson.
Arkissus of Frisia	Tyrone Power.
Marcus Lecca	R. D. McLean.
Holy Nagar	H. R. Roberts.
Mimus, the Echo	J. H. Benrimo.
Bevilaccas	Claude Gillingwater.
Caius Valgus	Marshall Welch.
Sylvestros	Gilmore Scott.
Dyaixes	Louis Keller.
Bram-Bora	Edward Brigham.
Marlak	H. R. Pomeroy.
Master of the Tower	H. G. Carlton.
Servant of the Tower	Gerald Kelly.
The Shade of Menethus	Charles Hungerford.
Thryssos	Francis Powers.
Idmondus	Gordon West.
A Mock Herald	Arthur Maryatt.
Crassus	Edwin Hardin.
Herald of the Senate	Franklin Mills.
Page of the Senate	Harold Guernsey.
A Bargeman	Luther Barry.
Zastus	Teft Johnson.
Galba	Harry Sheldon.
Sigrad	Charles Wright.
Var-Igon	F. L. Evans.
Slave of the Whips	James H. George.
Slave of the Queen's Door	Joseph Moxler.

BELASCO'S "ADREA" CURTAINS

The Child Vasha (in the epilogue)......... Louis Grimm.
Julia Doma............................. Edith Crane.
Garda.................................... Maria Davis.
Myris............................... Corah Adams-Myll.
Lefta.................................. Lura Osborn.
Lelit.................................... Grace Noble.
A Singing Bird................. Madeleine Livingston.
Adrea............................ Mrs. Leslie Carter.

Coincident with his production of "Adrea" Belasco's fight for freedom in the conduct of his business reached a climax that attracted nation-wide and wondering attention and enlisted the sympathetic assistance of eminent members of the national legislature. Whenever possible, subsequent to his successful presentment of "The Heart of Maryland" in Washington (October, 1895), Belasco has elected to bring out his new plays in that city. There he desired to launch what was in some ways the most ambitious venture of his career,—and there, accordingly, after overcoming every obstacle that could be thrown in his way, he first made known the tragedy of "Adrea." But before narrating the manner in which that production was effected it is desirable here to make somewhat particular exposition of the antagonism he was compelled to encounter and to record the significance of his long and costly conflict with it.

BELASCO AND THE THEATRICAL SYNDICATE.

JUSTICE AND THEATRICAL ACHIEVEMENT.

David Belasco has served the Public and the Theatre, ably and brilliantly, in several fields and for many years, but his achievements as at once theatre manager, stage manager, playwriter, instructor, and "producer," splendid and admirable as incontestably they have been and are, have been equalled by other American managers, of earlier date. In writing Biography it is prudent to remember that "there were heroes before Agamemnon." Much was accomplished on the American Stage long before the advent of either David Belasco or any other theatrical administrator of recent times, and when we review the history of the drama in America for more than a hundred years, and consider the managers by whom it has been fostered, conserved, and directed, we should recall and honor the names,—among others,—of William Dunlap, the elder Warren, William Wood, Francis Courtney Wemyss, James H. Caldwell, Noah Ludlow, Edmund Simpson, Charles Gilfert, the elder Hackett, the elder Wallack, William Evans

Burton, and Thomas Barry,—each of whom, in his day, deserved theatrical eminence and gained it, and all of whom seem now to be forgotten. Lester Wallack, who long preceded Belasco, and who also was theatre manager, stage manager, playwriter, and actor,—and as actor with no superior and scarce an equal in his peculiar realm,—gained laurels which will long endure. John T. Ford, Boucicault, Barrett, McCullough, Edwin Booth, and John S. Clarke,—all were accomplished and highly successful and distinguished in every branch of theatrical management; and, although Belasco has written his name imperishably on the honorable scroll of dramatic renown, he has not eclipsed those eminent predecessors.

BELASCO'S UNIQUE SERVICE TO THE THEATRE.

In one service, however, that Belasco has rendered to the Theatre and the Public he is peculiarly a benefactor, and in doing that service he has encountered an antagonism and prevailed in adverse circumstances with which the elder theatrical managers never had to contend. It would be difficult to overestimate the value of his intrepid opposition to the tyrannical monopoly known as "The Theatrical Syndicate." His conflict with that arrogant, oppressive, pernicious organization, sustained through a period of about twelve years, and finally victorious, required unfaltering courage, tenacious purpose, skilful and prompt action, and tireless persistence. It exacted from him prodigious labor; it entailed upon him great expense and loss, and it compelled an expenditure of time and strength which, if he had been left free to devote it to his artistic labor, would have been productive of lasting benefit to the Drama. But the sacrifice was well made, because the Theatre and the Public profited by it,—as, earlier, and concurrently, they profited by the resolute contest against the Syndicate (a valiant and gallant fight for freedom and justice) waged by Harrison Grey Fiske and Minnie Maddern Fiske. It should be noted that Augustin Daly, Belasco's immediate predecessor in the primacy of theatrical management in America, —who, also, was theatre manager, stage manager, playwriter, and "producer," and who was consummate as an executive,—being assailed by the Syndicate (as he several times declared to me), became one of its active opponents and resisted its aggressions: but Daly, who died before its despotic power had become matured, had long been an established, powerful manager before it was formed, so that it could not do him much harm. Belasco, on the contrary, was constrained to fight his way to independence and influence against its active, relentless opposition and inveterate hostility, from almost the beginning of his career in theatrical management.

WHAT ARE WE DISCUSSING?

In the period of about sixteen years preceding 1912 the newspaper press of America published many thousands of columns, often critical, at times strongly censorious, about the "Trust" or monopoly which commonly is known as "The Theatrical Syndicate." Bitter fights likewise have been waged not only in the press but in the courts relative to that organization. The public has, from time to time, manifested interest in the subject,—as, for example, relative to Mrs. Fiske's appearance in all sorts of unsuitable places, because the Syndicate had "barred" her from the regular and (as they are technically styled) "first-class" theatres, and to Mme. Bernhardt's enforced performances in a circus tent, for the same reason, and, especially, to Belasco's almost preterhuman efforts to present his plays in Washington (from which city strenuous efforts were made by the Syndicate to exclude him). Yet I believe that the public knowledge of the Syndicate,—its origin, aims, character, policy, conduct, and effect,—has never been more than superficial.

THE SYNDICATE-INCUBUS DEFINED.

What *is* "The Theatrical Syndicate," and *why* should it rightfully be denounced and opposed as a pernicious institution?

The Theatrical Syndicate, primarily, was a partnership of six men, all speculative theatrical managers, formed for the purpose of dominating, for the pecuniary profit, advantage, and personal aggrandizement of its members, the theatrical business of America, and of doing this by methods some of which, in their practical operation, are morally iniquitous, and should be, if they are not, legally preventable, in the public interest.

Those six men were: Al. (Albert) Hayman (deceased 1916), Charles Frohman (deceased 1915), Marc Klaw, and Abraham Lincoln Erlanger, all of New York; and Samuel F. Nirdlinger (known as Nixon) and J. Frederick Zimmermann, both of Philadelphia, Pennsylvania. The contract under which those persons formed their copartnership and carried on their syndicate business was made in August, 1896, and it was renewed, in substance, in April, 1900.

SPECIOUS PRETENSIONS TO JUSTIFY THE INCUBUS.

The founders of the Theatrical Syndicate have, with much fulsome commendation of themselves and their purposes, directly or by implication, sought to justify the position they have assumed by specious assurances substantially to this effect:

That the theatrical business of America was disorganized, unstable, and, in general, so conducted as to entail loss on many or most persons engaged in it, by reason of *competition,* poor judgment, and lack of discrimination in its transactions; that the prevalent administration of it was not favorable to the development of actors and the promotion of the art of the Theatre; that their combination was made to cure, and that it did cure, the defects of theatrical business, stabilize it and render it reputable and responsible,—placing it, in this respect, on a level with other business; and that, incidentally, it would, and did, tend to prosper the means whereby the Theatre must live—namely, Acting and the exhibition of Acting. A. L. Erlanger, executive of the Booking Department of this organization (that is, of the firm of Klaw & Erlanger, the particular business of which was, and is, to "book," *i. e.,* to arrange, the tours of theatrical companies), has thus stated a part of his views relative to the character and doings of the Syndicate:

"The American [theatrical] manager of to-day is *unique, contrasting* him with the *managers of long ago,* and that still exist in England, France, and elsewhere, in that *he* is *qualified* and *experienced* in staging *all kinds* of theatrical entertainments. . . . As for the question of Commercialism *versus* Art in Stage matters, I cannot see where the fact that financial solvency, *making the business of the theatrical world comparable* in its *integrity* with that found in other occupations, lessens the artistic value of the question [*sic*]. No actor will act the worse because he knows his salary will be paid promptly; and the fact that the business of the theatres is conducted on *firm lines* is calculated to encourage, rather than dismay, the actor, the dramatist, and everybody else whose interest in the Stage is primarily artistic."

In support of those views and in advocacy of the Syndicate of which he was an active member the late Charles Frohman wrote ("The New York Herald," March 13, 1910): "Several men united to systematize the conduct of the Theatre, *put the actor's profession on a self-respecting footing,* guard the playwright against piracy, protect the managers of theatrical companies against unfair competition [*i. e.,* competition not profitable to the members of the Syndicate.—W. W.], at the same time obliging them *to keep faith* with managers of theatres."

A third voucher for the exalted integrity and far-reaching beneficence of the methods exemplified in the operations of the Syndicate was furnished by Charles Burnham, at that time manager of Wallack's Theatre, not himself a member of the benign brotherhood, but obviously congenial with it, and President of "The Theatrical Managers' Association," a society which the Syndicate practically dominated:

"The commercialism of the drama," so said that manager, "*has justified itself.* . . . The Theatre of to-day is no Chicago University or Carnegie Library. If you look after the *financial end* of the Drama, *which is the main thing*, the public may be trusted to maintain a high standard."

TENDENCY TO COMBINATION IN MODERN BUSINESS.

An honest, just, equitable organization of business is always right, and no one but a fool or a knave would ever question the legality or propriety of it. The drift of the present age, in commercial affairs, is, and for a considerable time has been, toward combination, organization—in a word, *efficiency*. Business men of the United States, little by little, have awakened to the imperative necessity of conservation of energy and resources, systematic labor, economy; the sensible use of every force that tends to the advancement of civilization, the increase of public prosperity, and the diffusion of intelligence. One of those forces is the Theatre, and it is one of prodigious influence. No intelligent observer acquainted with its history would maintain that its condition, particularly as a business institution, has ever been perfect or is perfect now. It is certain, however, that its commercial condition has, within the last half-century, very considerably improved, because not only have the ban of the Church and the stigma of Society been, to a large extent, removed from it, but great wealth has been bestowed on its enhancement, and expert executive talent has sometimes been enlisted in the management of its affairs.

CAUSES OF THEATRICAL PROGRESS.

It was not a commercial manager of the Syndicate type who first urged the efficient management of the Theatre; it was an idealistic critic and a great poet. Many years ago that ripe scholar and accomplished man-of-letters Matthew Arnold exclaimed, in one of his Essays, "The Theatre is irresistible—*organize* the Theatre!" Arnold, as a youth, had been entranced by the acting of Mlle. Rachel, and as a man had naturally been charmed by the acting and greatly influenced by the propulsive reformatory and constructive theatrical administration of that great actor and theatrical manager Henry Irving. It is from such sources of thought and of intellectual energy as Arnold and Irving, in England, and as Wallack, Booth, and Daly, in America,* that the impulse properly to organize the Theatre has proceeded; not from the mere money-grubbing schemes of monopolistic cliques or speculators in public amusement. Members of such cliques,—of which the Theatrical Syndicate is one,—are, at times, frank enough to admit that (as they are fond of expressing it) they are not engaged in theatrical business "for their health," and undoubtedly they are within their rights when they seek, *by fair means,* to make their business profitable. So much is understood and conceded: who would deny it? Monopolies, however, frequently pose as public benefactors, and such, as already shown, is the pose assumed by the Theatrical Syndicate. Many persons have, in one way or another, been deceived by it, or brought to approve it. In 1898, beginning to be conscious, in my critical and editorial work on "The New York

* And, preëminently, William Winter, who was not only the friend but in many instances the guide, adviser, and assistant of all those managers, as well as of many others: no other single person has ever, directly and indirectly, exerted a greater or more unselfish influence for the good of the Theatre than that of Winter.—J. W.

Tribune," of an oppugnant influence emanant, apparently, from that source, I determined to have a clear understanding with the late Donald G. Nicholson, then the editor of that paper, and I formally asked him whether "The Tribune" favored or opposed the Syndicate. In reply I received from him the assurance that "of course 'The Tribune' *opposed* it," and also I received a printed list of newspapers which, Mr. Nicholson informed me, had explicitly declared their opposition to the Syndicate as being an unjust organization, hurtful to the Theatre and adverse to the public interest. That list contained the names of most of the leading journals of our country. But—"There are no birds in last year's nest." Most of the opposers of the Syndicate seem, like the *Witches* in "Macbeth," to have "made themselves air, into which they vanished." Active opposition to that incubus in the press is, at present, conspicuous chiefly by its absence.

The pretensions of the Syndicate are one thing: its proceedings are quite another. Equitable conduct has not been the spring of its prosperity. Not by fair means has it become rich and powerful. Aside from having somewhat facilitated the making possible of economically practical routes over the country for travelling companies and the transaction of business between resident theatrical managers and representatives of travelling companies, it has done, literally, nothing for the good of the Theatre; but it has done everything for the good of itself. It is not to be supposed, for example, that because the making of economical routes is *feasible* through the booking agency of the Syndicate, once such routes have been booked they are inviolate. "Dates" are cancelled and "routes" are changed, when such change is requisite to the advantage of the Syndicate, with total disregard of any other consideration. "Where," exclaimed Gladstone, "can you lay a finger on the map of Europe and say, 'Here Austria did good'?" Where can you lay a finger on the map of progress in the Theatre in America and truthfully say, "Here the Syndicate did good"?

THE RIGHT PRINCIPLE.

That the Theatre, to exist, must be self-sustaining; that its administration "must show a profit," is a proposition so elementary in its truth and so universally conceded that it would be folly to restate it, if there were not so much stupidity in the generally attempted exposition of Commercialism in Art. But as a matter of right and duty (and this is what, apparently, the Syndicate and congenial managers *cannot comprehend*), theatrical managers are under distinct obligation to consider the public good *before* they consider their individual prosperity. In other words, when a man assumes to make use of one of the fine arts as a means of "doing business," he assumes to wield an indirect educational power; he undertakes,—whether he knows it or not, whether he means to do so or not,—to affect the public taste, the public thought, and the public morals. Therein, accordingly, he assumes a responsibility much broader and much more important than that which is incurred in an ordinary "business" pursuit; and, as it happens, he assumes it under less restriction, by law, as to the possible effect of his conduct than is imposed on the speculator in almost any other "business."

THE OBLIGATION OF INTELLECT.

Obligation of honesty and honor rests with equal force on all workers in all branches of industry: but it is one thing to sell boots or pickles, and another thing to disseminate thoughts and emotions. The more a man ascends in the scale of labor the more exacting becomes his duty to Society. A writer of novels, for example,—a Scott, a Dickens, a Thackeray, a Cooper, or a Collins,—might, perhaps, find the largest amount of personal emolument in writing stories calculated to vitiate taste, injure public thought and public morals, and thus debase the community, but, if he wrote such books, he would be a criminal, and it would be no defence for him to say that he made money by his crime, or to allege that because he made money the public approved of his actions. Intellectual men have *no right* to make money by misusing their powers. The same sense of rectitude,—but broader, higher, finer,—that bids an honest tradesman sell nothing that will injure the buyer enjoins upon the worker in the arts that he should consider not merely the payment he is to receive for his work, but the effect of that work upon the lives and destinies of the human beings to whom it is addressed and whom it is likely to influence. Theatrical managers stand in that position toward the public. Thoughts and feelings are the wares in which they deal, and, much as they are bound to consider financial profit (because they have heavy burdens of expense to carry), they are also solemnly bound, first and most of all, to consider the taste, the morals, and the intellectual advancement of the community. The manager who aims at monetary gain as the first and dominant object of his ambition and endeavor, to the exclusion of all higher purpose, is a disgrace to his profession and an enemy to social welfare. To him, as to the *Weird Sisters,* "fair is foul and foul is fair."

There are many vocations in which little is to be considered above the till. No person is *compelled* to assume the management of a theatre or the direction,—invariably of potent force,—of an educational, influential art. If he deliberately chooses such occupation and does assume it, he assumes it with all its inherent responsibilities,—and the greatest of these is moral and intellectual duty. No mistake more foolish or more culpable could be made than to regard this standard of conduct and responsibility as visionary, impracticable, or what this deplorably slang-ridden community flippantly mentions as "highbrow stuff." No strenuosity of asseveration from theatrical janitors, "Great Moguls," "Napoleons of the Theatre," bullies or gamblers, flatulent with the wind of self-complacency and conceit, that conduct of the Theatre justifies itself by mere financial gain can vindicate a theatrical administration which benefits a few individuals at the expense of the public good and by the oppression of honest competitors; and that, practically, is the administration of the Theatre which is provided by the Theatrical Syndicate.

The covenant made by the six members of the Syndicate contains much of that verbiage which customarily encumbers legal documents. Some facts, however, as to the results of its operation are apparent. Under the contract, covering "different cities of the United States and Canada," independent theatrical companies, seeking to compete for public favor and support, "were not permitted to play against" "other companies of the same or different class," owned, operated, controlled, or directed, by the Syndicate. According to that covenant, "No attraction [*i. e.,* no company presenting a theatrical entertainment or performance] shall be booked in *any* of the said theatres or places of amusement [*i. e.,* theatres or places of amusement owned or controlled by the Syndicate] which will [*sic*] insist on playing *in opposition* theatres or places of amusement in any of the cities" named in the Syndicate agreement, unless by written permission of a Syndicate member, controlling a theatre or theatres in such or such specific places where an independent manager desired to present his company in an independent theatre. By this arrangement the Syndicate, in effect, could say, and has said, to managers of theatres outside its ownership or direct control: If you wish to "play" *any* of our "attractions," at any time, you must play *all* the attractions we book in your theatre when we book them and on the terms which we specify,—otherwise you *cannot have any* of the attractions which we book. To persons, whether star actors or managers directing theatrical companies on tours through the country, desirous to secure "bookings" in certain cities in which first-class theatres are controlled by the Syndicate that organization could say, and has said, in effect: If you wish to play in *any* theatre owned or controlled by us, you must play in every theatre, whenever and wherever we choose to direct you to play, on whatever terms we choose to make for you. If that is not, in effect, blackmail and extortion, compelling the transaction of business under duress, what is it? The theatres owned, leased, controlled by members of the Syndicate *are* their theatres, and they assert the right to conduct those theatres to suit themselves. Owners of property certainly *are* entitled to use it for their advantage; but would any well-informed and fair-minded person maintain that the members of the Theatrical Syndicate, using their property in the way I have described, use it according to the dictates of justice? When that kindred beneficence the Standard Oil Company desires to drive a small, independent dealer out of business how does it go about the task? It sets up a contiguous, superbly managed competing oil shop and undersells the independent dealer, till he, lacking money to maintain a hopeless struggle for his liveli-

"THE DOLLAR SIGN IS THE SIGN OF SUCCESS"

$

"I KEEP A DEPARTMENT STORE" CHARLES FROHMAN

¢   ¢

THE MEMBERS OF THE THEATRICAL SYNDICATE

Al. Hayman   Charles Frohman

Marc Klaw

Abraham L. Erlanger

Samuel F. Nixon (Nirdlinger)   J. Fred. Zimmermann, Sr.

" It is often true, as old *King Duncan* declares, that 'There's no art to find the mind's construction in the face.' Nevertheless, study of the faces of the men who compose that sacred institution of beneficence, The Theatrical Syndicate, is worth making. Such study renders it easier to understand the condition of the Theatre in America to-day."—W. W.

hood, is forced to sell his business and desist from competition. Then the benevolent national octopus gradually advances the price of oil until at last the public in the neighborhood has paid the cost of driving the small competitor out of business, the field is occupied solely by the Standard Company, and it sells oil to the people for "all the traffic will bear." That method may be as *lawful* in selling "theatricals" as in selling oil, but—is it *right?*

If Belasco desired to present one of his "attractions," in thirty cities under the Syndicate domination (acceding to the terms imposed upon him), but could, in one other city, present that "attraction" for ten weeks, at an independent theatre, receiving eighty per cent. of the gross receipts, while in the same city the Syndicate would "book" his "attraction" at one of its theatres and graciously exact fifty per cent. of the gross receipts, then Belasco would be necessitated to submit to that predatory dictation, or else lose his "bookings" in the thirty other cities, —in *all* other cities,—in which the Syndicate controlled the "first-class" theatres.

"THOSE SHALL TAKE WHO HAVE THE POWER."

Perhaps that may seem an extreme case. Yet that is exactly what happened to him. In 1902

Belasco produced "The Darling of the Gods," Miss Blanche Bates appearing in it as a star, in association with an exceptionally fine and expensive company. That was a very costly production: after two years of presentation of it Belasco had gained a net profit of only $5,000,—while, had he chosen to do so, he could have gained that profit in a fortnight with many an inferior vehicle. He was, naturally, proud of his achievement. He desired that the play should be represented within reach of the multitude assembled to view the World's Exposition, which was opened at St. Louis, in 1904, and he arranged to present "The Darling of the Gods" at the Imperial Theatre, in that city. As soon as this fact became known he was notified by Mr. Erlanger, on behalf of the Syndicate, that he would not be permitted to do so,—the reason being that the Syndicate would not tolerate the presentment there of Belasco's play in any but a Syndicate house, though the Syndicate could not, or would not, provide him a theatre there for as long a term as he could secure the Imperial. Belasco's reply was that he would certainly produce "The Darling of the Gods" in St. Louis, whereupon Mr. Erlanger, in the presence of Belasco's representative, destroyed and threw into a waste basket a number of contracts, signed and executed, providing for the presentation of that and other

Belasco "attractions" in theatres under Syndicate control in various cities of the Union and Canada. This peremptory repudiative action, accompanied by much violent expletive, no doubt was one of Mr. Erlanger's genial ways of illustrating the conduct of business on those "firm lines" he had prescribed as so essential to theatrical regeneration, and of illuminating the Syndicate's righteous purpose, as stated by the late Mr. Charles Frohman, to compel the managers of theatrical companies "to keep faith with managers of theatres." It clearly was. a conclusive example of the Syndicate's beneficent methods.

"Thus bad begins and worse remains behind": if the general policy which I have specified is iniquitous, how shall certain other proceedings, conducted by the executive of the Syndicate, in the development of the business of the Theatre, be characterized? Let the reader assume that he wishes to bring out a new star or a new play, in New York, and does so: his venture is successful: he plays for a considerable term in the capital: he wishes to "book" his "attraction" on the road. The charges made for such booking service are, I understand, reasonable,—somewhere from about $250 to $300 for a season's tour. But does the reader suppose he can get his play booked and his tour arranged as simply as by paying an agent's commission? Let him try: perhaps he will succeed: "circumstances alter cases": his play may have proved so popular in New York that theatre managers throughout the country clamor to have it exhibited in their theatres, in which case the Syndicate might become placable; but such good fortune is dubious. It is far more probable that, in order to obtain a desirable route through the first-class theatres of the country, he will find it obligatory to make "a free gift" of an interest of from one-third to one-half of his successful venture (in which he has done all the original work and borne all the expense and risk) to the benevolent and protective firm of Messrs. Klaw & Erlanger,—as, for example, it appears from his sworn testimony (see *ante,* pp. 18-19) that Belasco was forced to do when presenting David Warfield in "The Auctioneer."

DIVERGENT VIEWS OF THE SYNDICATE: GROUNDS FOR REASONABLE BELIEF.

It is not feasible to include in this Memoir a complete History of the Theatrical Syndicate, examining every detail of its organization, conduct, influence, and effect,—though such a history

is a necessary part of the annals of our Stage. In
the absence of such exhaustive record the partially
informed reader may be confused, perhaps misled,
by dissentaneous views of the Syndicate—about
which, be it observed, I write as an uncompromising
opponent. On the one side that Syndicate is found
portrayed by its advocates as an institution of light,
leading, and beneficence. On the other side, it is
found represented as an arrogant, ruthless, grasping
monopoly,—exerting an actively injurious influence
on the Drama and the Art of Acting,—and as being
composed of ignorant, avaricious, vulgar men, unfit
to dominate any art—and in particular the *quasi*-
educational art of the Theatre,—and regardless not
only of the public welfare as affected by the Stage
but, at least in some instances, regardless even of the
public safety. The disparity of sentiment is dia-
metrical. But though a whole history of the Syndicate is not here practical, is it not possible briefly
to present essential information bearing on the subject in such a way that the reader may disregard the
discordant and disputatious views of advocates and
opponents and form an independent opinion based
merely on facts of record? I think that it is. First,
then, as to disregard of the public safety by some
members of the Theatrical Syndicate:

Soon after the burning of the Iroquois Theatre,

in Chicago, December 30, 1903, during a performance there of "Mr. Bluebeard,"—a disaster in which 602 persons horribly perished,—the New York weekly journal "Life" published a cartoon portraying the exit of a theatre, with the door padlocked and with smoke streaming through it, while women and children were shown struggling to force it open and escape. A symbolic figure of Death was shown standing beside that portal, and beneath the picture was a caption reading: "Messrs. Klaw & Erlanger Present Mr. Bluebeard." The implication of that cartoon was, unquestionably, an accusation of wholesale manslaughter. Messrs. Klaw & Erlanger, claiming that the publication of it was a libel upon them, instituted a suit against "Life" for $100,000 damages. That suit was tried in the United States Circuit Court, New York, January 3 to 6, 1905, before Justice William J. Wallace and a jury. The publication complained of was, in fact, beyond question a libel. Under the law publication of libellous matter is justified if it be *true* and if it be made without malice, in the way of legitimate comment or criticism. The issue in this case, therefore, was perfectly clear. The jury decided in favor of "Life" after deliberating less than five minutes—thus, in effect, certifying to the truth and legitimacy of comment which amounted

to an accusation against Klaw & Erlanger of wholesale manslaughter through negligence.

Second, as to the characters and reputations of
the men composing the Syndicate and the question
of their fitness to dominate the Theatre:

"The New York Dramatic Mirror," on October
30 and November 13, 1897, published articles, written by its editor, then Harrison Grey Fiske, which
stigmatized the members of the Theatrical Syndicate as a *"band of adventurers,* who imagined that
they could manipulate the amusement business *for
their sole gain"*; as men actuated by "clannish greed
and selfishness"; as "mercenaries" who threatened
"the welfare of the Stage"; as persons who, in
their business, were guilty of maintaining a *"system
of double-dealing,* of *false pretences,* and of *misrepresentation"*; as "illiterate managers"; as an "insolent
and mischievous clique of theatrical middlemen"; as
"insolent jobbers," "theatrical throttlers," "crooked
entrepreneurs" and "an un-American and intolerable
combination of greedy, narrow-minded tricksters."

The several members of the Syndicate, resentful
of these explicit strictures, instituted suit against
Fiske, asserting that in making and circulating the
statements about them just quoted he had uttered
a "false, defamatory, scandalous, and malicious libel"
which had "injured the complainants in their good

name, fame, and reputation," and otherwise damaged
them, all in the sum total of $100,000. The com-
plaint in this action was filed on November 19, 1897.

Fiske answered, in effect, that his charges against
the Syndicate were "made in behalf of the public and
[of] those engaged in the theatrical line or profession in the United States" and were set forth as *"a
fair and true statement* of the object and purpose
of the Syndicate"; that his articles complained of
were true and not malicious, denying that they constitute a "false, defamatory, scandalous, and malicious
libel"; asserted that "Al. Hayman was not a person
of good name, fame, and reputation," but "that he
[Hayman] with his co-complainants did by a system of double-dealing and false pretences and mis-
representations to the public and those engaged in
the theatrical business unite and band together by
wrongful and improper expedients" to mislead and
defraud the public; "that the said J. Fred Zimmermann is not a person of good name, fame, and
reputation"; that A. L. "Erlanger is not a person
of good name, fame, and reputation, but that, on the
contrary, the said A. L. Erlanger has been arrested
and convicted of crime in the State of Pennsylvania," and that "the name, fame, and reputation" of
the plaintiffs had been "truly set forth in the said
articles mentioned in the plaintiffs' complaint."

Of course, to *make* such damaging accusations is not to *prove* them,—whether they be made in a newspaper or in a legal instrument: the noblest and best men and women the world has ever seen, or ever will see, all are liable to traduction and attack. But the members of the Syndicate, after taking cognizance of these accusations, after declaring under oath that they had been damaged by the making of them in the amount of $100,000, and after the braggart spokesman for the group had asserted in print that "we mean to make Mr. Fiske prove his allegations or publicly acknowledge his mistake," dallied and delayed in the case for two and one-half years (during all of which time Mr. Fiske, as he personally and repeatedly assured me, was not only willing but eager to go to trial on the facts),—and then, April 18, 1900, *discontinued their action*. Commenting on this proceeding, Fiske said, in "The Mirror":

"No pretence of legal unreadiness and no motion for delay of this case have ever proceeded from the defence. . . . 'The Mirror' has been not only ready but eager at all times since the joining of issue in this case to thoroughly thresh the matter out in open court. . . . The case never has been pushed in court, and *it is evident that the plaintiffs never had any intention to try it.*"

Judicious readers will, I believe, agree that the course of the members of the Syndicate amounts, practically, to a confession of the truth of Fiske's charges; and surely, in the circumstances, they can neither wonder nor complain because those charges have been generally believed.—As to the power exerted by A. L. Erlanger over Belasco and the quality of the Theatrical Syndicate as a monopoly, I consider the arraignment made by Samuel Unter-myer, before the Appellate Division of the Supreme Court, to be perhaps the best and most entirely just that I have ever read:

". . . Of course Belasco went to Erlanger's house and was a suppliant to the tender mercy of Erlanger to permit him to hire theatres in which to produce his play. He went there because the Syndicate's unholy and criminal alliance which controlled the principal theatres throughout the country had made it impossible for any man with a play, a company, scenery, costumes, and all the requirements for a complete production to *book* his play (which means to find a roof under which to produce it) except by the grace of Klaw & Erlanger, who controlled the Syndicate and the theatres. And they could ask just such proportion of the profits by way of rent and impose such other conditions as they chose. Of course Belasco went to Erlanger's house, and when he confronted 'the great man' he not only agreed to pay the rent, generally *fifty per cent. or more of the gross receipts* of every performance, for the theatres, but he was also forced to agree to give secretly to Klaw & Erlanger under cover of Brooks' name fifty per cent. of all the profits of that production. No wonder Erlanger did not want that little arrangement known to his Syndicate

THE CROWNING ROOM,—BELASCO'S PRODUCTION OF "ADREA"

partners! Why should not Belasco go to Erlanger and smilingly consent to be fleeced? His venture was ruined unless Erlanger would furnish 'bookings' on any terms Erlanger chose to extort. Should the King go to the Beggar? Or was it meet that Belasco the Beggar for a chance to pay for the use of theatres in which to produce his own play with his own company, should go humbly to Erlanger, the King of the Syndicate that controlled the theatres?

"No such despotism has ever been known or dreamed of in this country and none so fatal to the development of art as the evidence discloses this Theatrical Syndicate. Every monopoly that has been dragged into the court pales into insignificance and seems almost harmless beside it. Every owner of a theatre contracted with throughout the country was required to agree not to permit his theatre to be used for any performance not under the direction [of] or assented to by the Syndicate even during the times it was not in use or being paid for by the Syndicate! . . ."

CONVERTING CONVENTION HALL:—"ADREA" IN WASHINGTON.

Using the despotory power alluded to by Mr. Untermyer, the Syndicate closed all the theatres of Washington against Belasco when he attempted to arrange for the presentment of his tragedy. "My *penchant* for giving the first performances of my plays before the Washington public, because I got the real start of my independent career there," Belasco remarked to me, "may be, as some unfriendly critics have declared it, a 'sentimental folly,' but it pleases me to do so, and it seems to me to be a matter for *me* to decide. The less likely it became that I could get into Washington with 'Adrea' the more determined I became to do so." The result of his determination was that Belasco suddenly and privately hired Convention Hall, a vast, barn-like place in Washington, inconvenient of access, situated over a market, with seating capacity for more than 5,000 persons. It contained no stage and was in every way unfit for theatrical use: in brief, what Belasco did was, first, to hire a roofed space, and then build a theatre beneath it,—incidentally complying with all the mysteriously sudden and preternaturally exacting requirements of various administrative departments of the District of Columbia. "In all my experience," he remarked to me, "I never knew such vigilance to be exercised about a theatrical performance, and I should never have been able to meet the almost incessant and sometimes most unreasonable demands upon me if it had not been for the kindly advice, guidance, and assistance of Senator Gallinger and of Speaker Cannon, who had been interested in my fight by a *protégé* of his, Mr. Sidney Bieber; but, one way or another, every demand was met." About one-third of the hall was partitioned from the rest of it by a temporary wall and a proscenium arch. Behind this a commodious stage was erected,—all the labor of building being performed by a company of mechanics brought by Belasco from his New York theatre. The iron girders supporting the roof and also the exposed parts of the ceiling were draped and covered with fireproof cloth and gauze, dark green in color. Several carloads of rich hangings and furniture which Belasco had originally purchased for use in "Du Barry" and "The Darling of the Gods" were taken to Washington and used to decorate the interior of this improvised theatre. Seats were arranged, the aisles were carpeted, "boxes" were built, a gallery was erected at the rear; a chill and barren loft was converted into a spacious, warm, and handsome playhouse, and on Christmas Eve all seemed to be in readiness for the opening—and then the Fire Department condemned the electric-lighting system. "For a little while," said Belasco, in relating the story of this enterprise, "I thought they had me beaten, and after I had spent thousands of dollars. But I put my case before the Edison Electric Company—and between Saturday and the following Monday evening the Edison people tore out the condemned system of wiring, put in a new one, laid a special main for the supply of current, got it all inspected and passed, and we opened as advertised

on Monday night! *I* wanted to get out on the footlights and crow! As to safety—everything had been
done and we had, for an audience of 1,400, the
spaces, exits, and stairways previously considered safe
for crowds of from 5,000 to 6,000."

Belasco's conversion of Convention Hall into a
theatre, for the production of "Adrea," and the
difficulties encountered by him in doing so caused
much comment in the newspapers of the capital, and
shortly before the first performance he published
the following letter in "The Washington Post":

"The editorial in this morning's 'Post,' under the title,
'Theatre Regulations in Washington,' conveys several erro-
neous impressions, and I ask this intrusion on your space to
state certain facts with which the Washington public has
not hitherto been made familiar. When I conceived the idea
of using Convention Hall for Mrs. Leslie Carter, my very
first step was to come to Washington personally, to learn
directly from the heads of the building, fire, and electrical
engineering departments what changes or safeguards would
be required by each to enable me to use Convention Hall
with their entire approval and in conformity with the law.
During a series of subsequent conferences plans were made
and submitted, embodying not only all the requirements of
each department, but several additional improvements—
such as wider aisles, more exits, broader exit space, etc.
These plans were fully approved by the necessary officials
of the District.

"Having thus secured the proper indorsement, and having placed myself right with the municipal departments, I

proceeded at great expense to make these extensive alterations, seeking, above all, in the interest of the public, to
fulfil not only the letter but also the spirit of the law. I
already have done more than I was asked to do, and no
obstacle was raised until after the work was completed.
The structural changes have been made in strict and ready
compliance with the requirements of the District officials,
and under their supervision. *My one thought, first, last,
and all the time, was to comply with the law and protect
the public.* I fully believe that I have done so."

The representation of "Adrea" was received with
extraordinary enthusiasm by a large and brilliant
audience, not a single member of which left before
the close of the performance, long after midnight.
During the Fourth Act a violent rainfall, beating on
the iron roof of the hall, rendered much of the dialogue inaudible, and soon, the roof leaking in many
places, water poured down through the cloth and
gauze hangings, deluging the audience with green
rain. "I saw Admiral Dewey, in one of the boxes,"
said Belasco, "holding an umbrella over a lady
whose beautiful white gown was ruined with green
blotches; and in another Secretary Morton and
Admiral Schley with the green water splashing
down on them. But, even though they had to sit
under umbrellas or be soaked, *my audience stayed to
the very end! Is it* any wonder I love the Washington public?"

In the local newspapers, on Christmas Day, Belasco published the following notice "To the Washington Public":

"Mr. Belasco begs to state that his occupancy of Convention Hall for Mrs. Leslie Carter's initial performances of her new play is because of the opposition of the Theatrical Trust, through whose dictation no theatre in Washington is permitted to book his attractions. Unwilling, however, to surrender his custom of making his productions first in this city, he has rebuilt the interior of Convention Hall, in strict observance of the legal requirements of the District departments, and with every regard for the comfort and safety of his patrons. He begs also to thank the people of Washington for the friendship and most liberal support which already assure the success of his independent enterprise."

When called upon the stage during the opening performance of "Adrea" Belasco made a brief speech of thanks, the first sentence of which brought an outburst of applause that lasted for more than two minutes:

"Well, ladies and gentlemen, they did not prevent my opening in Washington. And as long as this is a free country and I am able to fight for independence in theatrical management, I will open my companies in Washington, or in any other city that I elect to visit. It is very late: I won't detain you but a moment, just to thank you in words that can't convey my thanks for your approval,

your sympathy and support. Mrs. Carter, Mr. Long, all
my company, my staff—my loyal, splendid staff, carpenters and mechanics who have worked here, ladies and
gentlemen, for as much as forty-eight hours at a stretch
to make this opening possible—they all are grateful to
you, and I thank you, and thank them, again and again.
It would be strange indeed if we were not willing to fight
for the chance to play before you when you are all so kind
to us and when the man who fought the Battle of Manila
Bay and the man who fought the Battle of Santiago are
willing to sit in a sort of green shower-bath to watch us!"

Belasco gave seven performances of "Adrea" during his week in Washington, the gross receipts from
which were more than $15,000. And when that
engagement was over and the accounts had all been
made up and paid he had suffered a loss of a little
more than $25,000.—On the first night in New York
he made a significant speech in which he said:

". . . Nobody could ask—nobody could wish—for any
more splendid loyalty, support, and encouragement than I
have received from you, from the people of New York, from
the people of every place in Amrica where I have presented my companies, and I am grateful, very, very deeply
and lastingly grateful, ladies and gentlemen. But conditions in the American Theatre are bad, ladies and gentlemen,—very bad indeed—and they ought to be remedied.
The institution we all love should not be left at the mercy of
high-handed, brow-beating, un-American hucksters. We are
not afraid of anyone, ladies and gentlemen: we—all of us;

my associates, my business staff, my splendid, loyal mechanical staffs, my actors—have had a long, a hard and bitter
struggle and have suffered very serious annoyances and
loss. I have just paid more than $25,000 for the privilege
of presenting this tragedy for one week in the City of
Washington. We do not ask or expect that life should be
made easy for us; we can fight, just as you can, for our
rights. But I say, ladies and gentlemen, that it is a crying outrage and a burning shame that men and women who
simply want to go about their own business in their own
way should be forced, in this day and country, to undergo
what we (all of us here behind the curtain and in the offices
of my theatre) have to undergo from week to week. And,
ladies and gentlemen, it is you, the public all over this great
country, who are most injured by it all—because we cannot
give you what you are entitled to get from us when you
pay your money to see our plays and what we want to
give you,—that is, the very best there is in us: we cannot
give you that, ladies and gentlemen, when we have to give so
much of our time and strength and energy and enterprise
and courage to fighting a criminal monopoly when we ought
to be giving it and want to be giving it to writing and producing plays and acting in them, for your entertainment
and pleasure."

EXIT MRS. CARTER.

"Adrea" was the last new play in which Mrs.
Leslie Carter appeared under the direction of
Belasco. Her first season in that tragedy closed at
the Belasco Theatre, May 4, 1905; the second (in
the course of which she acted *Du Barry* and *Zaza*

MRS. LESLIE CARTER AS *ADREA*, IN THE TRAGEDY OF
THAT NAME

as well as *Adrea*) began there, September 20, that
year, and lasted until June 23, 1906, when it was
ended at Williamsport, Pennsylvania. Differences
of opinion and divergence of interests had been
growing for some time between the manager and the
actress who owed so much,—everything, in fact,—
to his sagacity and guidance. On July 13, 1906, at
Portsmouth, New Hampshire, Mrs. Carter was
married to William Louis Payne, and withdrew
from the direction of Belasco,—Mr. Payne assuming the care of her affairs. In *Adrea* she touched
the highest point of all her greatness and, thereafter,
may fairly be said to have hastened to her setting.
At the time of her withdrawal from Belasco's management he was at work on a new play for her,
dealing with the experience of an Hungarian immi-
grant. It was to be called "Repka Stroon":
although it has been finished it has not yet been
acted. Mrs. Carter has done nothing of lasting
importance since her personation of *Adrea*. Her
acting, at its best, was far stronger in the emotions
than it was in the intellect; but, in *Adrea,* she met
and endured the test of tremendous situations involving conflict of various passions, and in that respect
she proved her possession of tragic power. In fact,
the defects of her performance of that part were
wholly in the superficial texture of the method, and

it came home to the heart with an exceeding effect of pathos because of the sad knowledge with which it was freighted,—the knowledge of affliction and of grief.

SIGNIFICANT MESSAGES.

The following telegrams, sent by Belasco and his general manager, Roeder, are significantly indicative of the consideration shown by the former toward the players in his employ, as well as of the character of his mind, and for that reason they are printed here: the actor referred to, Mr. Benrimo, who played the *Fool* in "Adrea," might properly enough have been transferred to Mrs. Carter's company, without discussion:

(*Telegram, David Belasco to Blanche Bates, in St. Louis.*)
"New York, October, 1904.

"You know I would not do anything to imperil your cast or to jeopardize our western tour. Always thought it unadvisable to double *Prince* and *Kato* in San Francisco and always intended sending another man to play *Prince*.

"If it were not absolutely necessary for me to have Benrimo in my new play, I would not ask for him. There happens to be no man disengaged at present to suit this peculiar part, which means so much to the success of the play. You may not quite understand why it should be so, but so it really is. At the present moment I am engaged in the greatest fight of my life and everything depends on this new production. Its success will leave me free to give all my attention to your new play for next season and will ensure the working out of all my plans. It is only with our triumphs that I can hope to beat the Syndicate. My dear girl, by this time I am sure you have reconsidered your telegram and will help me out. Please—please, do! There is nothing within my power that I will not grant if you ask it, so I beg of you again, please help me out.

"DAVID BELASCO."

(Telegram, Benjamin F. Roeder to Blanche Bates in St. Louis.)

"New York, October, 1904.

"In making original cast 'Darling' Mr. Belasco requested other of his stars, who gladly consented. Regret, as one of your best friends, that you don't follow dictates your own heart and accord what is, after all, only a courtesy. Mr. Belasco has been kind and generous to you always. Money has never stood in way when he could do anything to make you happy. In consequence Chicago fire we are still much money behind on original investment 'Darling' and Mr. Belasco has more than fulfilled his contract with you. We paid out thousands to secure your new play—have been obliged to forfeit all and Mr. Belasco has been forced to write one himself to give you 'Blanche Bates part.' I have not shown him your telegram and don't want to. This is the time he needs good soldiers. Be one like the rest of us. You will lose nothing in the end. Anyway, Benrimo is not 'Frisco favorite. Under no circumstances could we allow two such important parts to be played by one man in 'Frisco. Mr. Belasco is rehearsing the new men. They leave Wednesday and will strengthen the cast.

"B. F. ROEDER."

(*Telegram, David Belasco to Blanche Bates, in St. Louis.*)

"New York, November, 1904.

"Thanks! Thanks! You're a dear brick and some day I will do as much to relieve you of anxiety. Buy the prettiest and finest rider's dress, with hat and cloak to match, and send the bill to me. I am sending you two good actors, one for the *Prince,* the other for the *Fisherman.* I am rehearsing them myself. After all, it would have been dangerous for us to permit any one actor to double the parts in 'Frisco. You must think so too, so instead of weakening the cast I am strengthening it.

"But never mind that, you have helped me out of a dilemma and you're a bully girl. As soon as the play is on I shall join the company and spend some days with you to talk over your new piece and the cast. It will be well to begin to get the eight people under contract. If all goes well,—and it will,—you'll be in New York *all next year!* Love to your mother and yourself.

"DAVID BELASCO."

VARIOUS LETTERS AND INCIDENTS OF 1905.

In June, 1905, Belasco, accompanied by Mr. Roeder, sailed for England, his purpose being to purchase, if possible, or else to arrange to build, a theatre for his own use in London,—as Daly had done many years before. This ambitious project, however, proved impracticable of execution and, though he has never finally abandoned it, he found himself forced by circumstances to set it aside and he soon returned to America. While he was in

England the subject of his fight against the dominion of the Syndicate was discussed in various newspapers: in one of them I find the following letter:

(*David Belasco to "The London Referee."*)

"Hotel Russell, Russell Square,
"London, W. C., June 17, 1905.

"To the Editor of 'The Referee':

"Sir:

"A sympathetic article in an evening paper, speaking of the methods of the American Theatre Trust, and their efforts to crush me, also stated: 'Let there be no misunderstanding. Mr. [Charles] Frohman may be entirely exempted from inclusion in this indictment. His operations in London are in direct competition with those of the Trust.'

"In order to prevent any 'misunderstanding' I would like to ask: '*Why* should Mr. Frohman be exempted from this indictment?' In my suit brought against Messrs. Klaw & Erlanger in New York, in April last, among other things for the purpose of exposing the methods of the Theatrical Trust, there was produced in court the original Syndicate agreement, made in August, 1896, and renewed in August, 1901. This agreement was signed by Charles Frohman, Klaw & Erlanger, Al. Hayman and Nixon & Zimmermann, and according to the evidence is still in operation. Further comment is, I think, unnecessary.

"I am,
"Faithfully yours,
"DAVID BELASCO."

Soon after his return to New York Belasco received a message from the great singer Mme. Ernestine Schumann-Heink, who had been much impressed by his presentment of Warfield in "The Music Master," who desired to adventure on the dramatic stage, and who proposed that Belasco should undertake her management and write a play for her use. This he gladly agreed to do, and the play, which was to have been a sort of sister piece to "The Music Master" and was to have been called "The Opera Singer," was planned and in part written; but the demands on Belasco's energies and time were more than any one person could meet and he was regretfully forced to relinquish that project. "It hurt me to let go," he said: "I had a good story. Mme. Schumann-Heink had great natural talent for acting, and I believe that if I could have carried it through, working in a tremendous scene for her, as a singer on the opera stage, we should have set the country wild. But—there is a limit, and I was pretty near to mine, so *that* little scheme went up in smoke!"

The following letters all are characteristic of Belasco in varying moods:

(*David Belasco to Blanche Bates.*)

"Belasco Theatre, New York,
"April 3, 1905.

"My dear Blanche Bates:—

"I have received a note from Mr. William Courtleigh of

the Actors' Society in which he asks if it is possible for you to appear with Mr. Wm. Gillette at their benefit. I have promptly said 'No.' In the first place, you are not going to support Mr. Gillette. You would do all the hard work— yelling, shouting and running about like a maniac,—while he sat calmly smoking his cigar, with a calcium light upon him. Besides, this would be no novelty, as Gillette did the same thing at the Holland Benefit and I saw the poor little ——————— girl disgrace herself. There is nothing at all in these 'benefits,' and I hope you are pleased that I got you out of this one.

"With all good wishes,

"Faithfully yours,

"DAVID BELASCO."

(David Belasco to John Luther Long, in Philadelphia.)

"Belasco Theatre, New York,

"April 26, 1905.

"My dear John:—

"I have just received the beautiful Tennysonian verses. I shall *dramatize* them, of course, and you were bully to send them to me.

"But really, Jonathan, haven't we given that gang of grafters a shake-up? It cost me a lot of money,—but (thank Heaven!) I had it to spend, and could unmask them. If I have done a wee bit of good in helping to clear away the rubbish, I am more than rewarded.

"Good luck to you, and my best affection!

"Faithfully,

"DAVID BELASCO."

(*David Belasco to Mrs. F. M. Bates.*)

"Belasco Theatre, New York,
"July 13, 1905.

"My dear, dear Mrs. Bates:—

"I am so sorry I did not see you the other morning when you called at the theatre, but I have been nearly crazy with neuralgia for the past week.

"I am a little bit behind on Blanche's play, and am hurrying off to Shelter Island to take off my coat and go to work on it. Tell our Blanche it is a *bully play*, and that the character of '*the girl*' is sky-high—fits her from her head to her feet! I expect to have it in shape shortly now, and in her hands to study. I am getting together a *bully* cast for it. I really think the new play *is my very best*, and I know she will be happy. Give her my love.

"Faithfully,
"DAVID BELASCO."

(*David Belasco to Blanche Bates, in San Francisco.*)

"Belasco Theatre, New York,
"July 20, 1905.

"My dear Blanche B.:—

"Your letter received.

"I got a little behind on the play; you know I had to run off to London to do big things for the future, and when I got back I went under with my old attacks of neuralgia. You know how I suffer with them, and really, this time the pain was excruciating. I'm glad to say that I am all right again and I am working night and day, hoping that it is the best play I ever wrote. Your part fits you from your dear little feet up to your pretty head. It's a *bully part*, and I know you will like it. If you don't,—well, you need never kiss me again! I call the play 'The Girl of the Golden

HENRY IRVING IN THE LAST YEAR OF HIS LIFE—1904-'05

West.' The characters call you *The Girl.* The models of
the play are fine—the last scene of all, 'In the Wilderness,'
is a gem. There are some beautiful speeches in the play—
very 'Batesesque'; the lines just *crackle* and all the situations
are human.

"Yes, send along the photo, and I will have a poster made
of you.

"*Entre nous,* we open in Pittsburgh, before coming into
New York, playing there for two weeks at the new Belasco
Theatre, as the stockholders have named it. It will be a
great night.

"Just keep well, enjoy your summer, and the moment I
have finished the play,—which will be in about three weeks,
—I will rush it into your hands.

"With love, hugs, kisses and things,

"Faithfully,

"DAVID BELASCO."

(*David Belasco to Frederick F. Schrader, in
Washington, D. C.*)

"Belasco Theatre, New York,
"July 22, 1905.

"My dear Mr. Schrader:—

"Many thanks for your letter and for your kindly
interest. I am so glad that the press out West has taken
up the question of the Theatrical Trust so splendidly. It
helps us in the big fight. There is a hard year before us,
and if we win I think we shall have succeeded in breaking
the tyrannous ring. The London press was bully. I was
interviewed extensively and succeeded in getting many leading papers interested. They have taken up the Trust question seriously over there. I hope you read 'The Referee.'
They began a series of Trust articles in the number before

the last. The article was written in a very forcible style.

"Regarding the theatre in Washington, what you write is very interesting and I shall be most happy to hear more about it.

"Mr. [Fuller] Mellish called to see me, and there is an understanding that at the first opportunity I shall gather him in. Then,—he may remain with me for life, if he wants to.

"With kindest regards to yourself and your wife, I am,

"Faithfully,

"DAVID BELASCO."

TRIBUTE TO IRVING.

While Belasco was in Washington, with his new play "The Girl of the Golden West," there befell one of the saddest bereavements and one of the greatest losses the Stage has ever known,—the sudden, pathetic death of that great actor and manager and even greater man Henry Irving, which occurred at Bradford, England, October 13, 1905, immediately after the close of his performance in "Becket." Belasco, always one of his disciples and most ardent admirers, when informed of his death, paid him this tribute:

"There are no more such masters! The English-speaking, the modern, Stage has lost its greatest inspiration! The name of Henry Irving stood for all that was artistic in the highest sense. He was the loyalest servant of the public; the friend, the champion of the Stage. He belonged to us almost as much as to England. And what is saddest of all, he leaves no one behind him to take his place. He was a great, a marvellous, actor, a dramatic genius; he was the greatest stage director of modern times; he was the prince of managers; and, what was best of all, he was the best and kindest of men and the truest of friends. God rest his great soul! He has died as he would have wished, but we shall not look upon his like again."

BLANCHE BATES AND "THE GIRL OF THE GOLDEN WEST."

Belasco's stirring play of "The Girl of the Golden West" was first produced at the new Belasco Theatre, Pittsburgh, Pennsylvania, on October 3, 1905. It is a fabric of situations contrived for the advantageous display of that old, familiar, everlasting, always effective theatrical personage, the Rough Diamond. The Girl was beautiful, intrepid, passionate, vivacious; the soul of innocence; the incarnation of virtue; the blooming rose of vigorous health; and she could swear fluently, play cards, and shoot to kill. She kept a drinking shop, she was adored by all "the boys"; and the fame of her probity and her many fascinations filled the countryside of California, in the halycon days of '49. That fortunate State, according to the testimony of novelists and bards, was densely populated at that time by girls of this enchanting order; but this particular *Girl* seems to have transcended all rivals. She was beloved by a picturesque and expeditious outlaw, *Dick Johnson,* known as *Ramirez,* who had gained brilliant renown by means of highway robbery, and likewise she was beloved by the local *Sheriff, Jack Rance,* a grim, obnoxious officer, self-dedicated to the wicked business of causing that outlaw's arrest and death. Both those lovers were ardent, and, between those two fires, her situation was difficult; but she always rose to the occasion, and when her outlaw was entrapped by his pursuer the ingenuity of her love and the dexterity of her stratagem delivered him from bondage, and, upon his promise of reformation and integrity, launched him upon a new and better career. The most conspicuous display of her passionate devotion and adroit skill occurred on a night when he was captured in her dwelling. The circumstances were essentially dramatic,— because the *Girl* and her favored swain were storm-bound in a mountain cabin, whither the *Sheriff* had tracked his prey; and the robber had been shot and wounded, so that there seemed to be no method of escape for him, till the *Girl* proposed a game of poker with his foe, staking herself against the liberty of her sweetheart, and won it by successful emulation of the *Heathen Chinee,*—substituting "an ace full" for an empty hand, at the decisive moment.

BLANCHE BATES AS *THE GIRL,* IN "THE GIRL OF THE
GOLDEN WEST"

There came a time, however, when even Love could do no more; but at that crisis Fate interposed, in the shape of Public Opinion,—that is to say, the friendship of "the boys,"—and the *Girl* and her lover were united.

The condition of California in 1849 was, to say the least of it, turbulent. Some parts of that State are in a turbulent condition now. Groups of "the boys" can still be discovered. They are not paragons, though, and they never were. The existence of good impulses in uncouth persons. does not make them less uncouth. Fine qualities can, and do, exist in beings who are unfamiliar with soap and the toothbrush; but it would seem that the study of human nature can be pursued, more agreeably than elsewhere, among saponaceous branches of the race. It is more pleasant to read about "the boys" than it is to see them. But, broadly speaking, in Belasco's drama the *Girl* is the play, and with Miss Bates as the *Girl* there was little more to be desired. Shorn of all extraneous fringes—variously impious, improper, vulgar, and offensive interjections of profanity and violent expletive—the play is the image of a lovely, impetuous woman's devotion to her lover,—a devotion that is shown in a series of actions by her to save him from danger and ruin and to make him happy. Feminine heroism is the theme, and the *Girl* selected to exemplify it is meant to be "a child of nature," simple, direct, and true—and Belasco was entirely accurate when he wrote that the part fitted the actress for whom he made it from her head to her feet. Given the specified ideal to interpret, Miss Bates placed her reliance on Acting, and there were moments in her performance,—as, for example, in the First Act, as the *Girl* speaks of the protective instinct in the heart of woman,—when the soul that showed itself in her face was beatific. She gave, throughout, a personation of extraordinary variety and strength. In the situations devised for the heroine,—situations, which, while not radically new, are ingeniously contrived and are fraught with the dominant spell of suspense,—the actress had to express the growth of love; the blissful sense of being loved; the bitter pangs of jealousy; the passionate resentment of a heart that thinks itself betrayed and wronged by the object of its love; the conflict of anger with affection; the apprehension of deadly peril, and the nobility of self-conquest. The exaction of the part is tremendous, equally upon physical resource and nervous vitality, but, at every point, it was met and satisfied. The play exemplifies its author's remarkable faculty of continuation in the making of characteristic dialogue, together with ample felicity of invention, and it is overlaid with profusion of details. The midnight tryst of the *Girl* and the *Road Agent* is not altogether a credible device, but, once assumed and arranged, that situation,—comprehending the outlaw's detection, as such, by the *Girl,* the awakening of furious jealousy, her turning him out into the storm, her subsequent harboring of him, and the game of cards with the outlaw's life and liberty staked against the *Girl's* whole future,—is handled with consummate skill and moulded to splendid results, and there the acting of Miss Bates rose to a magnificent climax of emotion, fully expressed and yet artistically controlled and directed,—a triumph of intellectual purpose.

This was the original cast of "The Girl of the Golden West":

The Girl...........................Blanche Bates.
Wowkle, an Indian squaw..............Harriet Sterling.
Dick Johnson........................Robert Hilliard.
Jack Rance..........................Frank Keenan.
Sonora Slim.........................John W. Cope.
Trinidad Joe........................James Kirkwood.
Nick................................Thomas J. McGrane.
The Sidney Duck.....................Horace James.
Jim Larkens.........................Fred. Maxwell.
"Happy" Haliday.....................Richard Hoyer.
"Handsome" Charlie..................Clifford Hipple.

Deputy Sheriff.....................T. Hayes Hunter.
Billy Jackrabbit, an Indian.............J. H. Benrimo.
Ashby............................J. Al. Sawtelle.
José Castro.........................Roberto Deshon.
Rider of the Pony Express.............Lowell Sherman.
Jake Wallace, a travelling camp minstrel....Ed. A. Tester.
Bucking Billy........................A. M. Beattie.
The Lookout.........................Fred. Sidney.
A Faro Dealer.......................William Wild.
The Ridge Boy........................Ira M. Flick.
Joe................................H. L. Wilson.
Concertina Player.....................Ignazio Biondi.
Citizens of the Camp and Boys of the Ridge.

A THRILLING STORY—AND A TRUE ONE.

One of the most tense and effective passages in contemporary drama is that contrived by Belasco, in this play, when the *Sheriff* detects the concealment of the *Road Agent, Johnson,* in the *Girl's* home. Through the swirling snow he has caught a glimpse of a man's figure near to the cabin of the *Girl,* has shot at it, and has, in fact, hit and grievously wounded *Johnson,* who has then been given refuge in the cabin and concealed by the *Girl* in a low loft. *Rance,* having come to the cabin and been assured that nobody is concealed there, is about to leave. He goes toward the door, he is about to open it and step out, but turns to speak to the *Girl,* holding a white handkerchief with which he has wiped the snow from his face; as he does so, a drop of blood falls from the helpless wounded man above him upon the handkerchief, then another,— and *Rance,* watching the little crimson stain grow, instantly comprehends. Belasco, referring to this device, which, obviously, is as simple and as possible as it is effective but which was somewhat censured by captious fault-finders, writes this interesting account of its origin:

"It was from my father that I first got the idea which afterwards so well served me in 'The Girl of the Golden West,'—the incident of the Sheriff and the blood dripping on his handkerchief. The experience occurred during the Cariboo mine period. My father and his friend, Shannon, with several others, had a hut together. There had been a heavy snow, so for awhile they had to give up all idea of prospecting. Food was growing very scarce, until finally the twenty-four huts that constituted the expedition could boast of but three or four loaves of bread, one bottle of whisky, a scant supply of bear meat, and some straggling fish. The miners were apt to be careless, and the food supply became so low that it was necessary to form a committee to guard the precious stores. A Sheriff and a commission of deputies made a law that anyone taking more than was handed to him should be shot without trial. Thus things went on for a few weeks. A poor fellow from Philadelphia who was in camp had had the blues for months before this, and had made every effort to start for home. In the midst of the famine he was taken with the hunger fever, and when the boys told him that he was very low he cried out that he did not want to die. So one night he sneaked over to the box, and stole a bit of bread and beef and some gold dust. Then he fled from camp. The next day he was missed, and the loss in the chest discovered. The Sheriff immediately went after him. Instinctively the poor fellow must have felt that he was being followed, for he doubled on his own tracks, and came back to the hut. My father was playing poker at the time, and presently heard a shot outside. The missing man staggered into the room and fell at the feet of the players. 'Humphrey,' he gasped, 'for the sake of my wife, don't let them do me up. Save me!' My father told him to get out or be plugged, and he pulled his gun from his belt. But at the same time my father did not say anything when the fellow crawled upstairs into the loft. Hot upon this came the Sheriff, asking all sorts of questions, but never a guiding answer did he receive from the players. Then he joined the game, just as he did in 'The Girl of the Golden West,' my father living an eternity while the man was above them. They let the Sheriff win so as to make him feel good, and the game finally broke up. As he held his hand out to my father for a good-night shake a drop of blood fell upon his arm. A blanched face looked down through the rafters, a hand clutched nervously at a shirt, now deep-stained in red. The Sheriff gazed at the telltale spot on his arm, and smiled cynically as one can afford to do who is master of such a situation.

" 'Did you fellows know he was up there?' he asked, taking his gun from his pocket.

"There was nothing to be said; the facts were against it. The victim was caught. There was no staying the hand of the law; one could see this very well as the Sheriff gripped his gun and drew himself up to his full height. Standing there, his gaunt shadow thrown against the wall, his white face etched deep with marks of hardship and of toil, he poked the muzzle of his gun between the rafters and fired. He had done his job, and so he left without another word.

"Now, the morning after 'The Girl of the Golden West' opened, one or two critics declared that I did not know the times; they said that my gambler, so distinctively played by Frank Keenan, was a caricature, that he was taken from prints rather than from life. Why, I know the period of 'Forty-nine as I know my alphabet, and there are things in my 'The Girl of the Golden West' truer than many of the incidents in Bret Harte!"

A MASTERPIECE OF STAGECRAFT: THE STORM IN "THE GIRL OF THE GOLDEN WEST."

Considered technically, Belasco's production of "The Girl of the Golden West" was a genuine masterpiece of stagecraft, and it is specially memorable for the perfect example it exhibited of the right use of "realism" in the Theatre,—the use, in this instance, of an artfully created and perfect semblance of Nature in one of her wildest, most terrible moods as a background,—always felt, yet never obtruded,—for dramatic action the effect of which it steadily augmented and enforced. Nothing of the kind which I have ever seen in the Theatre has fully equalled in verisimilitude the blizzard on Cloudy Mountain as depicted by Belasco in the

Second Act of this fine melodrama—such a bitter and cruel storm of wind-driven snow and ice as he had often suffered under in the strolling days of his nomadic youth. When the scene, the interior of the *Girl's* log-cabin, was disclosed the spectators perceived, dimly, through windows at the back, a far vista of rugged, snow-clad mountains which gradually faded from vision as the fall of snow increased and the casements became obscured by sleet. Then, throughout the progress of the action, intensifying the sense of desolation, dread, and terror, the audience heard the wild moaning and shrill whistle of the gale, and at moments, as the tempest rose to a climax of fury, could see the fine-powdered snow driven in tiny sprays and eddies through every crevice of the walls and the very fabric of the cabin quiver and rock beneath the impact of terrific blasts of wind,—long-shrieking down the mountain sides before they struck,—while in every fitful pause was audible the sharp click-click-click of freezing snow driving on wall and window.

The means by which this effect of storm was produced could easily be specified and described; in themselves they are as simple as those employed by Belasco to make the almost equally impressive tempest in "Under Two Flags": but it is a capital mistake to take the public behind the scenes of the Theatre and thus uncover the very heart of the players' mystery and destroy illusion. In this instance it is enough to say, as revealing Belasco's liberality, thoroughness, and care in placing his plays before the public, that operation of the necessary mechanical contrivances required a force of thirty-two trained artisans,—a sort of mechanical orchestra, directed by a centrally placed conductor who was visible from the special station of every worker. And it will, perhaps, be usefully suggestive to misguided exponents of literal "spontaneity" in Acting to mention that the perfectly harmonious *effect* of this remarkable imitation of a storm necessitated that at every performance exactly the same thing should be done on the stage at, to the second, exactly the prearranged instant.

A pleasing device utilized by Belasco in the investiture of this melodrama was a variant of the long familiar panorama which, moving from bottom to top of the stage, instead of across it from one side to the other, showed, first, a beautiful and romantic view of Cloudy Mountain and of the *Girl's* cabin, perched, like an eyrie, high upon a canyon's side; next, a winding mountain path leading down to a settlement and ending outside her saloon, the Polka: then, in a fleeting instant of darkness, the scene was changed to the interior of that saloon, where the action of the play begins. In this production, also, Belasco banished the usual orchestra and substituted for it a band of homely instruments,—the concertina, the banjo, and "the bones" of the old-time minstrels,—which discoursed such old, once familiar but now long-forgotten, airs as "Coal Oil Tommy," "Campdown Races," "Rosalie, the Prairie Flower," "Pop Goes the Weasel," and "Old Dog Tray."

THE PARTING OF BLANCHE BATES AND BELASCO.— "THE FIGHTING HOPE" AND "NOBODY'S WIDOW."

"The Girl of the Golden West" proved to be as successful as its author had expected: also, greatly to the disadvantage of the public, it proved to be the last important production in which, down to the present day (1917), Blanche Bates has appeared,— although she continued to act under the management of Belasco for about seven years. Three of those years were devoted to "The Girl," which was presented throughout the country. Then, September 7, 1908, at the Belasco Theatre, Washington, Miss Bates was brought out in a new play by Mr. William J. Hurlbut, entitled "The Fighting Hope," which was acted in New York, September 22, at the Stuyvesant Theatre. It held the stage there until January 16, 1909; was transferred to the Belasco Theatre, January 18, and remained visible there until April 10. This was the cast:

Burton Temple	Charles Richman.
Marshfield Craven	John W. Cope.
Robert Granger	Howell Hansel.
Anna	Blanche Bates.
Mrs. Mason	Loretta Wells.

"The Fighting Hope" served as a professional vehicle for Miss Bates during two seasons. On October 24, 1910, at the Euclid Avenue Opera House, Cleveland, Ohio, Belasco presented her in "Nobody's Widow," by Mr. Avery Hopwood: that play was first acted in New York, November 14, that year, at the Hudson Theatre, with the following cast:

Roxana Clayton	Blanche Bates.
Betty Jackson	Adelaide Prince.
Countess Manuela Valencia	Edith Campbell.
Fanny Owens	Dorothy Shoemaker.
Duke of Moreland	Bruce McRae.
Ned Stephens	Rex McDougall.
Baron Reuter	Henry Schumann-Heink.
Peter	Westhrop Saunders.

Both those plays, though they enjoyed profitable careers, were, in fact, stop-gaps: they had never been produced but that "the strong necessity of the times enforced": "Blanche wanted to appear in 'drawing-room' drama," Belasco has said to me; "I was hard pressed and I took what I could get." Both those plays owed their profitable careers entirely to Belasco,—to his unremitting and unacknowledged diligence in the labor of revising them and making them feasible for stage use and to the perfection of detail with which he invested their production and caused them to be acted. A whimsical remark which he once made to me, in conversation about another play, applies with force to both these ventures: "I have," he said, "first and last, paid many authors handsome royalties for the privilege of working like a slave on their plays, without credit and generally without thanks, and making them into popular successes. Each time I have solemnly sworn I'll never do it again—yet, somehow, I do! But I live in hope that some day somebody will bring me a *finished play* that only needs production."

"The Fighting Hope," even as rectified and notwithstanding its measure of popular success, was but a flimsy fabric,—crude in construction and improbable in plot, though at times theatrically effective. In it is displayed an experience of a loyal wife, *Anna Granger,* who clings to "the fighting hope" of vindicating her husband and rescuing him from the consequences of crime. That husband, a peculiarly contemptible scoundrel, has been detected in a forgery; has been tried, convicted, and imprisoned. His wife, believing him to be innocent and the victim of *Burton Temple*, president of a fiduciary institution, obtains employment in the service of that person and becomes his confidential secretary. In that capacity, after discovering and shamefully destroying a letter which establishes the guilt of her husband, she discovers, also, that she is beloved by *Temple* and that a reciprocal sentiment is developing in her own bosom. And then, having confessed her identity, her wrong conduct, and her regard, she is relieved from a distressing dilemma by the convenient taking off of her husband,—who, having escaped from the State Prison at Sing Sing, is overtaken, shot, and killed by officers of the law who pursue him. In the hands of any other manager than Belasco, instead of enduring for two years, this piece—if it had ever been produced at all— would have been relegated to the regions of tall timber and high grass within a fortnight.

"Nobody's Widow" is an ephemeral farce, the central idea of which is denial of an established relationship in circumstances which might cause absurd perplexities and ridiculous consequences,—

such, in general character, as ensue when *Charles Courtly,* in "London Assurance," on being introduced to his father, *Sir Harcourt,* blandly greets him as a new acquaintance. The chief female character, *Roxana,* acted by Miss Bates, has, in Europe, met and married a *"Mr. Clayton,"* who, actually, is an English nobleman, the *Duke of Moreland;* but having, on their wedding-day, found him in the embrace of a former mistress, *Roxana* has repudiated and left him,—privately instituting proceedings for divorce, and presently apprising her friends in America that her husband, of whom they have heard, but only by his assumed name of *Clayton,* is dead, and that she, accordingly, is a widow. Later she visits some of those friends at Palm Beach, Florida, and there she is, by chance, confronted by her husband, then a visitor to the same hostess, but bearing his right name. *Roxana's* husband endeavors to reinstate himself in her affections, but, persistently and with alternate pleasantry and sarcasm, he is treated by her as an accidental acquaintance. *Roxana* assures him that, as *"Mr. Clayton,"* he is "dead"; that she has never seen him before; that to her he is, as the *Duke of Moreland,* nobody; that she is nobody's widow. That attitude she maintains until apprised of her divorce, when she becomes conscious of a sudden access of tenderness for him;

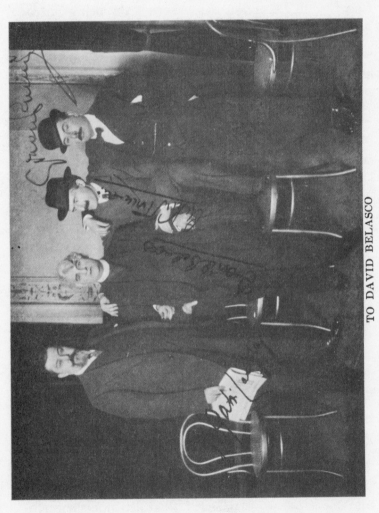

TO DAVID BELASCO

A souvenir of the production of the opera, "The Girl of the Golden West," by Giacomo
Puccini

G. Gatti-Casazza   David Belasco   A. Toscanini   Giacomo Puccini

and, eventually,—though not until after various trips and stumbles on the track of reconciliation,—she first allows herself to be again married to him, and then allows herself to be convinced of his honest intentions and the sincerity of his love. A farce is well enough in its way: but to record industry of such a manager as Belasco and such an actress as Blanche Bates in such stuff as "Nobody's Widow" is only to record wasted opportunity and disappointed expectation. In conversation with me Belasco has once or twice intimated some thought of proposing the resumption of Miss Bates' management: it might be greatly to the public gain if that actress should return to his direction; but, while I earnestly hope it may come about, I do not believe it ever will:

"The Bird of Time has but a little way
    To flutter—and the Bird is on the Wing."

A GREAT NIGHT.—BELASCO AT THE METROPOLITAN.
    —A GENEROUS ACKNOWLEDGMENT.

During the season of 1906-'07 Belasco's friend the Italian musical composer Puccini, who desired to write an opera on a characteristically American subject, made a visit to our country for the purpose of selecting one. While in New York, in January, 1907, he attended performances by Miss

Frances Starr in "The Rose of the Rancho" and by Miss Bates in "The Girl,"—at the Academy of Music. After considerable cogitation his choice fell upon the latter, and while travelling to his home in Italy he wrote the following letter to Belasco:

(*Giacomo Puccini to David Belasco.*)

Hôtel de Londres, Paris [France],
March 7, 1907.

"Dear Mr. Belasco:—

"I was exceedingly sorry to have left New York without seeing you once more. I have been thinking so much of your play, 'The Girl of the Golden West,' and I cannot help thinking that with certain modifications it might easily be adapted for the operatic stage. Would you be good enough to send me a copy of the play, to Torre del Lago, Pisa, Italia? I could then have it translated, study it more carefully, and write to you my further impressions.

"I cannot express to you all the admiration I feel for your great talent, and how much impressed I was at the drama I saw at your theatre.

"With kindest regards, and hoping to hear from you soon,

"Yours sincerely,

"GIACOMO PUCCINI."

Puccini's wish was immediately complied with, and upon the basis of Belasco's melodrama he wrote his opera of "La Fanciulla del West,"—which was sung, in Italian, "for the first time on any stage," December 10, 1910, at the Metropolitan Opera House, New York: the libretto was "arranged" by

IN REMEMBRANCE

PUCCINI'S OPERA "THE GIRL OF THE GOLDEN WEST"

Giacomo Puccini   Arturo Toscanini

Belasco

G. Gatti-Casazza   Otto H. Kahn

Emmy Destinn

Pasquale Amato   Enrico Caruso

Signori G. Zangarini and C. Civinni: it is, substantially, a translation, until the last act, when a scene is introduced showing the imminent lynching of *Johnson* by "the boys" in a convenient grove of redwood trees and his rescue by the *Girl*. This scene, as I understand, was originally planned by Belasco for use in his play but was by him discarded. "La Fanciulla del West" was sung for the first time by an extraordinary cast, which should be recorded. This is it:

Minnie	Emmy Destinn.
Dick Johnson, (*Ramirez,* the road-agent)	Enrico Caruso.
Jack Rance	Pasquale Amato.
Nick, Bartender at the "Polka"	Albert Reiss.
Ashby, Wells-Fargo Agent	Adamo Didur.

Sonora		Dinh Gilly.
Trin		Angelo Bada.
Sid		Giulio Rossi.
Bello	Miners	Vincenzo Reschiglian.
Harry		Pietro Audisio.
Joe		Glenn Hall.
Happy		Antonio Pini-Corsi.
Larkens		Bernard Bégué.

Billy, an Indian	Georges Bourgeois.
Wowkle, his Squaw	Marie Mattfeld.
Jake Wallace, a Minstrel	Andrea de Segurola.
José Castro	Edoardo Missiano.
The Pony Express Rider	Lamberto Belleri.

Men of the Camp and Boys of the Ridge.

CONDUCTOR......................ARTURO TOSCANINI.

Belasco felt profound interest in the production of his friend's opera and directed many of the rehearsals, intent, as he has declared, "to make the artists act as well as sing." That, doubtless, was a laudable ambition,—but, practically, it is, in the very nature of things, impossible of fulfilment, whether by Belasco or another. Opera singers may be, indeed, frequently are, dramatic in temperament: they are not and can not simultaneously be excellent as actors and as singers. Sometimes a comparatively poor singer becomes, in opera, a tolerably good actor,—but that is the limit of achievement in this direction. True *impersonation,* as made known on the dramatic stage,—in, for example, Forrest's *Othello,* Davenport's *Macbeth,* Jefferson's *Rip Van Winkle,* Barrett's *Cassius,* Irving's *Mephistopheles,*—never has been and never can be displayed on the operatic stage.

Talking with me about the first performance of this opera, Belasco said: "It was a great night for me, and I took unbounded pleasure in it and felt much honored when I found myself taking curtain calls with the author, Toscanini, Gatti-Casazza, Caruso, Miss Destinn, and the rest. Puccini, as always, was simple and frankly demonstrative in his delight. The singers were all wild with enthusiasm —I was never so much be-kissed in my life!—but I think I was, perhaps, most interested in that wonderful man Arturo Toscanini. He seemed to me one of those self-contained fellows—calm on the surface but burning white-hot inside. To me it was thrilling to watch him conduct, and he did so at that first performance without a score, as though the work were a classic long familiar to him and held in memory."

Belasco's labor on the production of "La Fanciulla" was wholly one of love, as he declined to accept any payment for all his arduous work at rehearsals. In the programme of the first performance appeared a notice saying: "The Metropolitan Opera Company desires to make public acknowledgment of its indebtedness, and to express its cordial thanks, to Mr. David Belasco for his most valuable and kind assistance in the stage production of 'The Girl of the Golden West.'" And among his most cherished possessions is a sumptuous album containing signed portraits of all the principal singers who participated in the opera, as well as of Puccini, Toscanini, and Gatti-Casazza, together with an exquisitely illuminated copy of the programme on vellum and an appreciative inscription, also illuminated on vellum. This gracious token was taken to Belasco's studio and delivered to him by a committee, representing the opera company, composed of Messrs.

Otto Kahn, Henry Rogers Winthrop, Robert Goe-
let, and John Brown.

BELASCO AND THE MESSRS. SHUBERT.

'An incident of Belasco's career in management
which can conveniently be recorded here is his
alliance with the Messrs. Shubert. That alliance
was arranged in 1904-'05, when Belasco was in
active conflict with the Theatrical Syndicate, by the
late S. S. Shubert, of whom and of their business
association he writes: "I found him an earnest
young man, with the power to make friends and
possessed of an irrepressible enthusiasm." Shubert,
with two brothers, began theatre management (or,
rather, correctly speaking, theatre control) in Syracuse, New York, where they leased the Bastable
Theatre. They subsequently obtained control of
the Herald Square Theatre in New York, and then,
directly or indirectly, of many other theatres in various cities of the country, especially in the smaller
places which are known as "the one-night stands."
"You have attractions and a reputation," urged
Shubert, addressing Belasco, "but no theatres out of
New York: we have theatres but lack attractions
and reputation. Join us, and all our out-of-town
houses shall be at your disposal." The arrangement

PRESENTED TO

MR. DAVID BELASCO

BY THE BOARD OF DIRECTORS OF THE
METROPOLITAN OPERA COMPANY
AS A TOKEN OF ITS DEEP APPRECIATION OF HIS
GREAT ASSISTANCE AND SPLENDID WORK IN CONNECTION
WITH THE PREPARATION AND PRODUCTION OF——

"THE GIRL OF THE GOLDEN WEST"

AT THE METROPOLITAN OPERA HOUSE — NEW YORK
DECEMBER TENTH — NINETEEN HUNDRED AND TEN

THE OPERA OF "THE GIRL OF THE GOLDEN WEST"—

A Souvenir, to Belasco

thus proposed was made and it had mutual advantages, but it was more valuable to the Shubert Brothers than to Belasco. Possessed of contracts to "book" the latter's "attractions" the Shuberts were strengthened in their relations with theatre managers not dominated by the Trust who desired to have those attractions presented in their houses,—and thus they were, in turn, strengthened in dealings with managers of other "attractions." The Belasco-Shubert alliance lasted for about four years. The time came when Mr. Lee Shubert (who had become the head of the Shubert Company) condescendingly intimated in public that he did not believe that anything could be accomplished by the methods of opposition to theatrical despotism which were long employed by Belasco and by the shrewd, indefatigable, vindictive H. G. Fiske and his intrepid, brilliant, accomplished wife; nevertheless, if it had not been for their opposition, the subjugation of the American Theatre to injurious monopoly would, in all human probability, have been so complete that Mr. Lee Shubert and his associates would never have found an opening through which to break.

S. S. Shubert died, May 12, 1905, in consequence of injuries sustained in a train wreck on the Pennsylvania Railroad, near Lochiel, Pennsylvania, on the 11th. Belasco considers his death "a hard blow" and is "sure he would have occupied a great place in the history of the American Theatre. He had keen business instincts, a lovable nature, and was the soul of honor." He would have required to possess a more extensive equipment to entitle him to the eminence Belasco believes he would have attained. I had no personal acquaintance with Mr. Shubert: he never *did* anything of notable importance as a theatrical manager, properly so called. His brother, Mr. Lee Shubert, through the shifts and chances of fortune, at one time almost held the destiny of our Theatre in his hand,—but he is merely a commercial exploiter of the Stage and consequently made nothing of his opportunity.

Belasco was to have accompanied S. S. Shubert on the journey which proved his last and, had he done so, might have perished with him. "I have had three such 'close calls,'" he has said to me: "Once, when I was a lad, I gave up an excursion trip on the Sacramento River to please my mother,— and the excursion boat was blown up soon after she left the dock. The second was when, at the last minute, I cancelled a trip to Cincinnati, with Charles Frohman. He took a secretary with him, the train was wrecked, and the secretary, sitting beside him where I would have been, was killed. The third was the trip with 'Sam' Shubert. We were to have gone to Pittsburgh together, on business connected with the Duquesne Theatre there, which, with the Shuberts, I took over and which was renamed the Belasco. If I had gone I am sure that I should have been killed in the wreck." It is probable that he would have been: the train on which Shubert travelled to his death "side-swiped" a freight train, loaded with dynamite: many lives were lost.

THE ADVENT OF FRANCES STARR.—BELASCO'S "THE ROSE OF THE RANCHO."

Frances Starr was born at Albany, New York, June 6, 1880, and made her first appearance on the stage as *Lucy Dorrison,* in Robertson's "Home," with a stock company, in that city, under the management of the late Frederic Bond. During the next six years she gained experience in various stock companies,—at the Murray Hill Theatre, New York; in San Francisco, in Boston, and at Proctor's 125th Street Theatre, New York,—and, February 12, 1906, she appeared, in association with Charles Richman, as *Nell Colfax,* in "Gallops,"—a weak echo of Boucicault's horse-racing plays of "The Flying Scud" and "The Jilt." Belasco first saw her when she was acting at the Murray Hill, and his attention was again called to her by his brother Frederick, who, in 1905, wrote to him from San

Francisco, praising her in high terms. Writing about Miss Starr, Belasco has given this account of her employment by him—certainly the most fortunate event of her life:

"When I first saw her play I watched her performance with the closest attention. Her entrance was greeted by a spontaneous outburst of applause. She was just a young girl then, a sweet-faced girl, delicately formed, with a beautiful forehead and fine, intelligent eyes. I was most favorably impressed by her performance, but at the time I had no part for her. . . . Her opportunity came during the second season of 'The Music Master.' Miss Minnie Dupree was to leave the company before the close of the season and I needed some one to take her place. I remembered Miss Starr and, with my friend and stage manager, William Dean, I went to the Garrick to see her in 'Gallops.' . . ." In that play "the hero staked his all on a horse race, and the future happiness of the young lovers hung in the balance as the race took place. The heroine and a coaching party were near the track, and Miss Starr stood on the steps of the coach, facing the audience. As the race was being described Miss Starr's facial expression was so remarkable that she held the audience for several minutes. The various expressions of hope, despair, and joy came and went according to the movements of the horse. The tumult of applause was a tribute not to the play nor to the scene, but to the perfection of Miss Starr's art. And as an exhibition of pantomime I have seen nothing to surpass it. . . . I decided that I must have her under my management, and I gave instructions to Mr. Dean to send for her to ask her to sign a contract as soon as possible.

Just before the final curtain fell the young actress looked at me, and as our eyes met I fancied I read in them the question: 'Have I pleased you?' On the way back to my theatre I was haunted by the pathetic appeal so silently thrown across the footlights, and I determined to do what I could to save one little girl the sleepless night I felt sure was in store for her. 'Dean,' I said, 'don't wait until morning. Telephone Miss Starr to-night and say I wish to see her to-morrow.' Mr. Dean advised me to wait. He thought it would be poor judgment on my part to show any eagerness; that Miss Starr would be sure to take advantage of it and raise her salary, but I insisted and he telephoned to her. As I expected, she was in her room, anxious, nervous, and wondering if my visit to the theatre would mean an engagement for her. Later, she told me of her relief and happiness when the telephone call came. It did not save her from a sleepless night after all, but her wakefulness was the result of joyous anticipation rather than anxiety. The appointment was made for 10.30 in the morning. When I arrived at 9, Mr. Dean came to me, smiling broadly. 'Miss Starr is in my office,' he said; 'she has been waiting since 8 o'clock.' I found her even more attractive than I had imagined. Her hair was soft and light, her eyes deep blue, varying into gray, and the changing expressions of her earnest face were delightful. She was pale and tearful. 'It has always been my wish to work for you,' she said. I learned that her manager at the Garrick Theatre intended to 'star' her in a play, but she expressed a willingness to come with me if only in a 'bit' five lines long. I offered her the leading part of *Helen* in 'The Music Master,' and she was delighted. I told her to go to Mr. Dean and make business arrangements. 'I don't care what salary I get,' she exclaimed. 'The only agreement I want is that you

don't change your mind.' I insisted, however, that a contract be signed, and when Mr. Dean made it out she
wanted to put her name to it at once, but I advised her
to take it home and read it over. She took it away with
her, but afterwards confessed that she stopped in a telegraph
office on the way to her hotel and signed it! . . ."

The first play in which Belasco presented Miss
Starr as a leading performer, heading an important
theatrical company—less than six months after he
had seen her in "Gallops"—was "The Rose of the
Rancho." This piece is based on an earlier one,
by Richard Walton Tully, called "Juanita," which
had been produced in Los Angeles with the excellent actor John H. Gilmour in the principal male
part. Mr. Tully's play was verbose, diffuse, and
coarse in texture. Belasco, after once rejecting it,
being in urgent need of a vehicle for Miss Starr,
read it again and agreed to "accept it, provided I
might have the privilege of rewriting it." This
"privilege" Belasco has exercised in many instances
—to his loss and the immense advantage of various
inconsequential and ingrateful amateurs of dramatic
authorship. His stipulation was acceded to by Mr.
Tully, and Belasco, working as usual under the
stress of haste and the distraction of many projects, revised, curtailed, amended, and reconstructed
"Juanita," which, in its final form as "The Rose

FRANCES STARR

nscription:
*"To him who made me what I am and inspired what I hope to be,—
with ever living love and gratitude."*

of the Rancho," gained abundant success. It was
first acted, under that name, at the Majestic Theatre, Boston, November 12, 1906, and was brought
out in New York, at the Belasco Theatre, November
27: it held the stage there until June 29, 1907.

There is, in this play, a glance at a disgraceful
episode in American history,—the technically legal,
but outrageously unjust and brutally tyrannical,
seizure of the estates of Spaniards in California,
after the Mexican War; but the purpose was not
so much to relumine a remote and half-forgotten
rascality as to display the incidents of a romantic
love story associated with the nefarious proceedings
of that distressful and turbulent time and place.
That purpose Belasco accomplished in pictorial settings of uncommon beauty. The scenery of Southern California is inexpressibly charming, because it
combines tranquil loveliness with awful grandeur
and is everywhere invested with poetic mystery.
The stupendous and austere mountains, the boundless, lonely plains, the balmy orange groves, the
graceful palm trees, the fragrant magnolias, the
abundance of wild flowers, the glorious blue skies
and the pure, sweet air,—these and many other
beauties unite to make that region a paradise. It is
in Southern California that the *Rose of the Rancho*
blooms, and Belasco, who knows and loves that coun-

try well, made his stage a garden of luxury and a dream of splendor to convey that charm—presenting a series of pictures which have never been excelled and seldom equalled. The investiture of this play, indeed, blending old Spanish architecture with a semi-tropical wealth of natural beauty, was literally magnificent and considerably excelled the worth of the play itself. This is a synopsis* of that fabric,—from which it will be seen that the theme is, to some extent, the same as that treated in Helen Hunt Jackson's prolix and tedious novel of "Ramona":

The scene is laid amid the sleepy, picturesque Spanish missions of Southern California. The plot deals with the great tragedy that underlies California history—the taking of the Spanish inhabitants' homes by land-jumping Americans. *The Rose of the Rancho* is *Juanita,* the youngest daughter of the *Castro* family. Through pride and indolence the *Castros* have neglected to make their property secure to them by filing an entry with the American land agent, and things have come to a serious pass with them. One of the most notorious land-jumpers in the state, *Kinkaid,* of Beaver, Neb., has come to San Juan, with his outfit, to take the

---

*Whence derived I do not know: obviously, it was not written by Mr. Winter,—but it is accurate.—J. W.

whole valley. At the same time another American
has appeared on the scene,—*Mr. Kearney,* of Washington,—a government agent sent to investigate the
land disputes.

Previous to the rising of the curtain upon the
beautiful mission garden the latter has met and
fallen in love with the fascinating *Juanita.* Because
of enmity toward all gringoes she refuses to treat
him civilly, but she meets him by accident every
day, unknown to her mother, who arranges (according to the custom) that *Juanita* shall marry a young
Spanish spark, from Monterey—*Don Luis de la
Torre.* The girl's father was an American, and
there begins a struggle between her loyalty to her
mother, her Spanish relatives and friends, on the one
side, and the young American who comes with the
offer of his love and aid, on the other. *Juanita,*
given her first kiss, lets the blood of her father direct
her actions. She gives the data necessary for a
registration to *Kearney,* who has no authority to
interfere with *Kinkaid,* but who sends his friend,
Lieutenant Larkin, to Monterey to make the entry
for the *Castros. Kearney* remains behind to delay
Kinkaid as long as he can. *Larkin* agrees to bring
back the state militia for *Kearney's* protection.
Meanwhile, the mother has learned that her
daughter has tossed a geranium to a gringo (signify-

ing, "I love you"), and *Juanita* is locked in her room.

The Second Act takes place in the patio-court of the old *Castro* ranch house. In spite of the danger that threatens, the mother is giving the engagement party she has planned. *Juanita's* friends are present. There are Spanish dances and the throwing of cascarones, and *Don Luis* appears to claim his bride. *Juanita* is defiant, and when they are about to betroth her she declares herself to be a gringo and the promised wife of a gringo. For this her mother disowns her, and is about to turn her out of the house, when *Kinkaid* and his men attack it and break in, and *Juanita* is thunderstruck to find the man she has trusted among them. The crowd of riffraff insult the women, who are protected by *Kearney*. He, however, must pretend that he is upon *Kinkaid's* side. *Juanita* appeals to him, and is rebuffed. *Kinkaid* agrees to wait until dawn before taking possession—thereby giving *Kearney* the time desired. The latter gets away from the land-jumper and finds *Juanita* to explain. She lashes him with her tongue for his betrayal of her people, and when he tries to make her listen she strikes him. Nothing daunted, he forces her to listen to his explanation. She tells him that she thinks he is a liar, but—she will wait till morning to see if the militia comes.

The Third Act takes place upon the roof of the
ranch house. Dawn is coming, and no help has
arrived. *Kearney* makes *Kinkaid* a prisoner as a
hostage to protect the women. Unfortunately, *Don
Luis,* jealous of the American lover of *Juanita,* in
an effort to compel him to fight a duel, lets *Kinkaid* go. The latter joins his men and an attack is
imminent. The old Franciscan, *Father Antonio,*
assembles "his children" in prayer for delivery,
the sunrise hymn of the Californians. This delivery
comes in the shape of the long-awaited militia from
Monterey. The rancho is saved, but the mother will
not see her daughter go to an American. She forces
her daughter to choose, and this she does—in favor
of the gringo.

———

That is a simple, almost trite, story; but Belasco
contrived to tell it in *action* more than in words,
and his telling of it proceeds from one sensation to
another with cumulative effect. Divested of all outward flourishes, it is seen to be the portrayal of a
conflict between virtue, animated by love, and vil-
lany, impelled by cupidity and brutal license. The
vulgarian would seize the estate of the old Spanish
family. The hero, who loves its young mistress,
would save it for her; and in order to accomplish

that object he is compelled to pretend fraternity with her oppressor,—for which reason she temporarily mistrusts him; but his purpose is accomplished, his fidelity is proved, and his love is rewarded. In all this, happily, there is no examination of the remote causes of the universal passion; no philosophic essay on masculine strength as opposed to feminine weakness; no treatise on elective affinities. The play, in short, is an old-fashioned melodrama in a new-fashioned dress; one of those plays that the spectator observes with an interested desire to ascertain how it will turn out. No new type of character is presented, nor is a special attempt made to variegate the old types. *Kearney,* of Washington, is the handsome, gallant, expeditious young cavalier who has loved and rescued the endangered maiden in a hundred plays of the past. *Kinkaid,* of Beaver, is the same old blackguard and bully who seems victorious for a moment, but is always finally discomfited, in the chronic story of the Far West. *Don Luis* is the debonair but disappointed suitor, from whom the *Bride of Netherby* always rides away. *Father Antonio* is the good and gentle priest who cheers the drooping spirit and bestows ecclesiastical benediction. The only persons who savor of exceptional quality are *Señora Kenton* and her daughter *Juanita, the Rose,*—the one a stern and formidable

woman, vital with Spanish hatred of the invading
American; the other, a passionate, capricious, wilful
girl, who can be sweet and tender, but who is customarily piquant, independent, and resolute in her
own course: characters strongly reminiscent of the
matron and the heroine in "Ramona." But, all the
same, the old tale of strength protecting weakness,
stratagem defeating duplicity, and love triumphant
over hate, pleased, as it always has pleased, and as
it always will continue to please—"till all the seas
run dry." Although, intrinsically, not exceptional
as a work of dramatic art, "The Rose of the
Rancho" has positive and abundant felicity of theatrical merit, imparted by the skilful hand of
Belasco, and the production of it was worthy of
his brightest fame. This was the original cast
of it:

Kearney, of Washington.............Charles Richman.
Don Luis de la Torre..............A. Hamilton Revelle.
Padre Antonio............................Frank Losee.
Lieutenant Larkin......................William Elliott.
Kinkaid....................................John W. Cope.
Rigsby.......................................Wayne Arey.
Sunol...............................J. Harry Benrimo.
Tomaso...........................Frank Westerton.
Ortega.....................................Norbert Cills.
Goya..................................Candido Yllera.
Pico..Fermin Ruiz.

Fra Mateo...........................Frank de Felice.
A Gardener......................Richard S. Conover.
Salvador..............................Gilmore Scott.
Pascual.............................Salvatore Zito.
Benito...........................Vincent de Pascale.
Estudilla................................Julio Grau.
Yorba...........................Francesco Recchio.
Cadet..............................Regino Lopez.
El Tecolero........................Virgilio Arriaza.
Bruno...............................C. A. Burnett.
Manuel........................Leonardo Piza Lopez.
Señora Doña Petrona Castro...........Marta Melean.
Señora Kenton....................Grace Gayler Clark.
Juanita, called *La Rosa del Rancho*........Frances Starr.
Trinidad.................................Jane Cowl.
Beatriz............................Catherine Tower.
Carlota........................Atalanta Nicolaides.
Guadalupe............................Maria Davis.
Señora Alcantara.......................Regina Weil.
Agrada............................Louise Coleman.

Kinkaid's Ranchmen, Caballeros, Vaqueros, Musicos,
Servants, Etc.
Señoritas, Dueñas, the Child of the Dance, Etc.

Miss Starr, in her performance of *Juanita,* manifested impetuosity of temperament combined with charm of personality, and by her arch behavior as a coquette, together with the vigor and sparkle of her demeanor as a wounded, doubting, resentful, and angry young woman, gained and merited general admiration.—A significant thought as to expedition

FRANCES STARR AS *JAUNITA*, IN "THE ROSE OF THE RANCHO"

and indolence in the fibre of contrasted races is
conveyed in two casual remarks in this play: "Civilization," says the "land-jumper," *Kinkaid,* with bla-
tant vulgarity of manner, when announcing his
purpose of legalized robbery, "must progress"; and
when it is found that certain muskets which have
been collected for use in defending the *Castro* ranch
are useless because of lack of powder, the Spanish
cavalier is heard to murmur: "I meant to have got
that powder *to-morrow.*"   Charles Richman, as the
intrepid *Kearney,* and John W. Cope, as the sinister *Kinkaid,* gave performances of sterling merit,
because true to life and symmetrical and fluent in
expression,—the one presenting, in a notably earnest spirit, a sonsy, healthful, interesting, thoroughly good fellow: the other assuming, in a pain-
fully natural way, the obnoxious characteristics,—
including a repulsive personal appearance,—commonly, and correctly, ascribed to the Western breed
of ruffian.

Belasco has, in drama, made use of the element of
natural accessories,—meaning peculiarities of climate, cloud, sunshine, rain, storm, calm, the sound
of the sea, the ripple of leaves in the wind, the swirl
of dust, the gentle falling of flower petals, the incessant variations of light according to place and time,
whether morning or evening, noonday or midnight,

and so following,—with an unerring skill akin to
that of Wilkie Collins in the writing of fiction. In
"The Rose of the Rancho" he took almost unparalleled pains to render his effects perfect. Writing
of this work, he has recorded:

"To get the strong sunlight of my beloved California
and the wonderful shades and tones of sunset, night, and
dawn as they come out there I had my electrician, Louis
Hartman, carry our experiments to the point of making
our own colors for our lamps, as we could find none on the
market that would give me the desired result. At the
present time we mix all our own colors for the lights used
in my productions, but in those days this had not been
done. I took *twenty-five electricians* with me to Boston,
for the opening of 'The Rose': usually, two or three are
enough with any company. . . ."

A NEW PROJECT:—THE SECOND BELASCO THEATRE.

Although Belasco held the Belasco Theatre under
a lease with an option of renewal, he was at all times
during the early years of his theatre management
conscious of a certain weakness in his position: an
unforeseen disaster—a fire, for instance,—might
leave him with many theatrical enterprises and no
metropolitan theatre to present them in. "Besides,"
he writes to me: "not only was I always confronted
by the fact that the lease of my Forty-second Street

house might not be renewed, but also it was natural
that I should desire to have a theatre *all my own,* in
the making of which I could carry out, fully, my
ideas of stage construction, lighting, and seating."
The result of this desire and of his wary vigilance
to maintain managerial freedom is the second
Belasco Theatre (which originally was named David
Belasco's Stuyvesant Theatre), which was built
by Meyer R. Bimberg (18—-1908), on designs
made by Belasco and under his personal superin-
tendence. The cornerstone of that theatre was laid
on December 5, 1906. David Warfield came from
Philadelphia, where he was acting, to participate;
Miss Bates came from Boston; Miss Starr was at
the time filling her first engagement in New York
in "The Rose of the Rancho." Belasco, those players, his business associates, and a numerous company
of friends gathered round the site of the new theatre.
Miss Starr deposited in a niche beneath the bed of
the cornerstone a copper casket containing various
records and programmes of Belasco's productions,
photographs of himself and of the chief players then
appearing under his direction, and a miscellaneous
assortment of souvenirs, cards, and "good luck
pieces" contributed by various friends. Miss Bates
then spread the mortar upon which the stone was to
be laid and uttered this touching sentiment as she

did so: "Here's hoping that Mr. Belasco will stick to all of us, and we and all his friends will stick to Mr. Belasco, as this mortar will eternally stick to this stone."

The cornerstone was then swung into place, settled, and declared to be "well and truly laid," whereupon Belasco's daughters, Reina and Augusta, each broke a bottle of champagne against it, saying, in unison, "David Belasco's Stuyvesant Theatre." The dramatist Bronson Howard (who had risen from a sick-bed to attend this ceremony) then spoke, saying:

"My dear Public and Friends: This is one of the greatest pleasures of my whole life—to be here to-day to dedicate the theatre that David Belasco is building. He has always given of his best in the past and you know what he is doing now. This theatre and the plays that it will house will live in the Future even as Wallack's, Daly's, and Palmer's, of the Past, live now in the Present. Here, where we stand to-day, will stand the future Temple of Dramatic Art in America. David Belasco has played a great part in the advancement of the drama in this country and he will play a greater one. He has never disappointed us and he never will. His heart and soul will be in every brick of this theatre and in every production he makes on its stage.

"Belasco and I have been friends and co-workers for many years. We first met when the gods were favoring me most,—when, long, long ago, he came, a young man out of the West, with black hair and eager face, to begin his career here. I was fortunate enough to put into his hands, in his first position as stage manager, at the Madison Square Theatre, the manuscript of my play 'Young Mrs. Winthrop.' I want to tell you an anecdote connected with that. I expected, when I gave it to him, that I should be obliged to do a lot of work on it; but after he had had it a few days he came to me and told me of many beautiful things in my play that I did not know were there! I decided, then, to keep away and did not see the play until the dress rehearsal. I found I had done well to leave it all to him. [Turning toward Mr. Belasco and stretching out his hand to him.] Come here, David! I am proud to clasp your hand, to utter a word of thanks for all you have done for us, for the workers in the Theatre; to congratulate you and say 'God bless you and give you success!'"

Writing of this occasion and of his new theatre, Belasco says:

"With all my associates gathered round me I felt like the *Vicar of Wakefield* when he got out of gaol and once more assembled his family round his hearth!

"How quickly a theatre grows old-fashioned! Every summer I make improvements in this house and have already spent enough money to build another theatre. At the present time of writing I have just installed a new lighting system, the result of years of experimenting by Louis Hartman, my valued old friend and electrician, who is to be found in the theatre from morning until night, and whose only pleasure is in his work. I think we have revolutionized stage lights, and I have no doubt that our innovations will find their way to foreign countries. . . . As my whole life is passed in my theatre, I have a studio there of several rooms devoted to my work and collections. In the latter I take great pride. . . .

"I have picked up much interesting furniture for my work-room, but, despite the joy I take in these things, I write with greatest comfort on a little sewing-table covered with green baize,—a relic of my attic days. . . . I really know of no other manager whose delight in his playhouse is greater than mine. . . . Here I spend my life and here I shall, I hope, end my days."

The second Belasco Theatre (originally called David Belasco's Stuyvesant Theatre, by which name it was known until the fall of 1910) stands on the north side of West Forty-fourth Street, between Broadway and Sixth Avenue, on lots Nos. 111 to 121, inclusive. The site has a front of 105 feet and a depth of 100 feet. The building is of red brick and white stone, simple and graceful, in the style of architecture denominated as Colonial. It was, originally, three stories high, with a rectangular, tower-like eminence at the southwest corner. The entrance from the street is into a small lobby, at the right of which are large swinging doors opening into a clear space which extends, behind the orches-tra seats, parallel with Forty-fourth Street, from side to side of the auditorium. In this playhouse,

BELASCO IN HIS WORKSHOP

as in the first Belasco Theatre, there is a handsome
screen of carved wood and crystal glass at the rear
of the orchestra, which protects the audience from
drafts of air. The orchestra and balcony chairs are
of heavy wood, upholstered in rich, dark brown
leather, the back of each chair being embossed with
the emblematic bee. The decoration of the interior
is opulent and dark in tone,—deep browns, blues, and
greens with dull amber and orange being the pre-
vailing colors. There is a large painting above the
proscenium opening and on either side are several
mural paintings, of various sizes, with here and there
a rich tapestry hanging. The groups and figures
in these paintings are symbolical,—Music, Grief,
Tranquillity, Allurement, Blind Love, Poetry, and
the like being depicted. The ceiling is raftered into
twenty-two panels, which are set with rich-colored
stained glass and illumined from above. Each panel
contains two shields, with heraldic mantling,—among
the coats-of-arms displayed being those of Shakespeare, Goethe, Schiller, Racine, Molière, Goldsmith, Sheridan, and Tennyson. The seating
capacity of the theatre is now (1917) about 1,000
persons,—430 on the orchestra floor, 320 in the balcony, and 240 in the gallery. There are no supporting pillars in the auditorium, the balcony and
gallery being constructed on cantilevers, so that an

unobstructed view of the stage is afforded from every part of it.

The stage was carefully designed with the purpose of facilitating in every possible way the setting and shifting of scenery. It is eighty feet wide and twenty-seven feet from the curtain-line to the back-wall. The proscenium opening is thirty-two feet wide and thirty feet high. The "gridiron" is seventy-six feet above the stage; the fly galleries, of which there are two, one on each side of the stage and thirty feet above it, have forty-five feet of clear space between them. In recent years an adjustable apron, five feet wide, has been constructed in front of the curtain-line, covering the musicians' pit. The stage can be opened at any desired spot, and the centre of it is an elevator-trap, ten feet from front to back and twenty feet long. Upon this trap the paraphernalia of an entire scene can be lowered to, or raised from, the level of a cellar floor, thirty feet below the stage.

The original cost of this theatre, including the land upon which it stands, was more than $750,000, and various alterations and improvements made in it down to the present time (1917) have increased the total investment to nearly $1,000,000. In the summer of 1909 a one-story and mezzanine addition was built upon the roof of the Stuyvesant, in which

Belasco has made his studio,—a strange, romantic place in which he has assembled priceless objects of art and antiquarianism. That studio (an adequate description of which would necessitate weeks of examination and would, alone, fill a large volume, and which, here, can be given only passing notice) is entered by a narrow, low, heavy-latticed door from the business offices of the Belasco Company. The first room is a small, low-roofed one, in itself somewhat suggestive of an old cathedral crypt. Along the walls are ranged shelved cases containing a wondrous collection of specimens of precious glass, the most recently made piece of which is more than eighty years old. A sort of alcove opens from this room, at the right side, which is stored with scores of relics associated with that arch-villain the great Napoleon,—a collection which includes a lock of his hair, cut from his head after death, and in which Belasco takes special pride and joy. Beyond the entrance room is a larger one; beyond that are low, dim passages; a library with stairs to a gallery; a dining-room; an odd little bedroom, exquisitely furnished in Japanese style,—with a miniature Japanese garden built outside its window,—and luxurious facilities for bathing. These passages, rooms, and stairs,—ceilinged with multi-colored banners, carpeted with soft, rich rugs, and almost everywhere

lined with shelf on shelf of books,—are somewhat
maze-like to a stranger, and in them is gathered a
vast, confusing medley of collectors' treasures: here,
a sinister, black-steel armor; there, a stand of French
halberds; beneath that old table, an unmatchable set
of rapiers; upon this one, nearly twoscore different
styles of dagger; yonder, a huge carved wooden
chest, blackened with age and stuffed with antique
velours; against it, a great two-handed sword,—
"such a blade as old Charles Martel might have
wielded, when he drove the Saracen from France";
across that opening, an antique wooden window-
lattice, with heavy shutters, taken from an English
house built more than 700 years ago; beside it, a
chair once used by England's King Henry the
Eighth; against this wall, a stone mantel brought
from Italy, with a hearth made of tiles stolen by
slaves from the Alhambra. In the walls are many
odd nooks and hidden cupboards, which open by
the release of secret springs,—in which, when illumined by small, concealed lamps, are revealed collections of jewelled rosaries; or of crucifixes wrought
in ivory, ebony, and iron; or of specimens of the
potter's art; or of trinkets once worn or owned
by members of the gentle Borgia Family. The
stranger, wandering through this reclusive domain,
—into which few strangers ever are permitted to

penetrate,—opening low Gothic doors, will blunder into angular hutches or long, low tunnels filled with shelves and cases of rare pamphlets and old books; will pause with awe before a superb window of purple stained glass; or gaze with wonder on a massive globe suspended in a well over which a translucent canopy is so arranged that it takes and intensifies all the changing colors of the covering heavens; or will come with startled delight upon a grot in which a small fountain of crystal water flings its spray over a little pool half-filled with violets, sweetpeas, and full-blown roses.

Belasco, unlike many other collectors, has an intimate personal knowledge of every article in his collection; can recall at once where, when, and how each was acquired; and, notwithstanding the number and seeming confusion of the different pieces, knows exactly where each one is placed and instantly perceives and vituperatively denounces any disarrangement of them such as occasionally is caused by members of that pestiferous sisterhood which plies the duster and the brush without sense of the sacredness of an antiquarian's sweet disorder,—a sisterhood which has stirred up consternation and wrath since long before *Mr. Oldbuck's* time. His writing is done there among his treasured collections, now in one corner, now in another, upon a small, battered, baize-covered cutting-table, such as ladies use for sewing, which he carries about from place to place as the fancy suits him. And there, also, his principal recreation is found when, wearied by labor or oppressed by care, he turns to contemplation and enjoyment of the heaped-up beauty which he has gathered about him.

IN THE MATTER OF STAGE LIGHTING.

A much needed addition to the technical literature of the Theatre is a comprehensive, authoritative, and just account of the origin and development of modern stage mechanism and of the art of stage lighting. The pioneer achievements of Edwin Booth, at Booth's Theatre (opened, February, 1869), and of James Steele Mackaye and Augustin Daly are, as a rule, blandly ignored in writing on those subjects, and the movement for "Stage Reform" which began in Austria in 1879-'80 is taken as the starting-point. If ever such an account is written, laborious experiments and fine achievements by David Belasco, especially in the latter field, will, of necessity, occupy a conspicuous place in it. His active practical interest in the problems of stage lighting began as early as 1876 and it has not abated. The first attempt in America to use electric light for stage illumination,—at least, the first attempt of which I have found a record,—was made at the California Theatre, San Francisco, February 21 to 28, 1879. Belasco was there at that time and carefully observed the experiment, which was not notably successful.* From 1879 to 1902 he closely studied all methods of lighting and experimented much: since 1902, when he opened his first theatre and obtained satisfactory facilities for the work, his experimentation in that field has been incessant. The lighting system at the Stuyvesant Theatre was designed by Belasco in collaboration with his chief electrician, Mr. Louis Hartman, and was installed under their supervision. When that theatre was opened, the lamps of the footlights on the stage, and also those in each of the overhead "border light strips," were arranged in seven sections, each section connected upon separate resistance, in order that any desired part of the stage or any figure or group of figures might be illumined or shadowed as desired. There were five sets of the border lights, with 270 lamps in each; there were eighty-eight con-

---

* The first recorded instance of a theatre lighted throughout by electricity is that of the Savoy, in London, 1882,—but I think it probable that practical stage lighting by electricity had been achieved in this country at an earlier date. Electric light was used to illumine a cyclorama in Paris, France, as early as 1857,—but that, of course, was light from a primitive arc lamp.

nection pockets in the fly galleries and upon the stage through which large or small "bunch lights" could be connected as required; the switchboard (one of the largest, if not the largest, then in use in an American theatre) was equipped with seventy-five dimmers, in order that the lights should be under perfect control. Since the opening, in 1907, the lighting system has repeatedly been altered and improved. The most radical change is one made about two years ago [1917], whereby footlights are entirely dispensed with. The objection to footlights is, of course, an upward thrown shadow: this, however, can be satisfactorily dealt with, and, in my judgment, it is seldom if ever advantageous wholly to discard them. Belasco, however, thinks otherwise: his productions are the only ones made without footlights, which I have seen, in which the absence of those lights is adequately compensated. In his present theatre there is a contrivance, placed in the front of the first balcony, which, while the curtain is down, appears to be an ornamental glass panel about six feet long. When the curtain is raised, however, shutters in the front of that panel are opened by an electrical device operated at the switchboard on the stage, and a singular bright light, which is transmitted without casting perceptible rays, is diffused upon the stage, bringing the

SWITCHBOARD OF THE SECOND BELASCO THEATRE, NEW
YORK

actors into clear vision.—It is not practicable to pursue this subject further in this place; but readers will, perhaps, realize the importance Belasco attaches to the art of lighting as an adjunct to acting and the care he lavishes upon it when they are informed that the experimental workshop in his theatre is operated all the year round and that in many instances the expense of his *light rehearsals alone* has exceeded the total of all other costs of production. Perhaps the most perfect example of stage lighting ever exhibited was provided in Belasco's presentment of "The Return of Peter Grimm,"—and that was the result of nine and a half months of persistent experimentation. Dilating on this subject, Belasco has said with justified wrath:

"I think that we may fairly and without vanity claim to have revolutionized stage lighting. I confess that I have at times felt some annoyance when I have been informed by young writers in the press,—who were not born until long after I had made great improvement in lighting,—that in dispensing with footlights I have 'imitated' Mr. Granville Barker, Mr. Max Reinhardt, and various other so-called 'innovators.' Such statements are nonsensical. My first regular production without 'foots' was made in 1879,* when I staged Morse's 'Passion Play' in San Francisco. And I did without them in several other productions, at the Madison Square Theatre, in 'The Darling of the Gods,' and in 'Adrea.'

* At which time Mr. H. Granville Barker was two years old!—J. W.

When I produced 'Marie-Odile' there was a lot of newspaper talk on this subject, but the talkers were such poor observers that they didn't know I had been using the *same system of lighting* I used in 'Marie-Odile' for more than three months before, in 'The Phantam Rival'!   A little of Mr. Barker's work as a producer has been seen in this country and he has had success in England.   He seems to be a very talented man and I always admire ability and so I admire him and am glad to see him succeed.   But without unkindness I must say that I have no need to 'borrow' from Mr. Barker; and as he must know that I never have done so I wonder a little that he has not rebuked these writers who would push him up by pulling me down.   Many of the appliances we use in my theatre are invented and made in my own shop; many others are made outside, to specifications we provide.   My new system is, I believe, a great step toward the perfection of stage illumination.   By means of it footlights, in my opinion, are made unnecessary for any play, and they are no longer a part of the illumination of my stage.   All the light comes from above, as in nature; but in order to accomplish this I built an entirely new proscenium arch.   A great iron hood, following the lines of the stage, hangs behind the proscenium. The hood contains lights of varying power, and by means of reflectors, invented and manufactured in my own shop, the illumination is diffused without casting shadows.   The glare of the footlights is a thing of the past so far as I am concerned.   My stage was also reconstructed so as to extend out into the auditorium over the orchestra pit.   These changes bring the audience into more intimate touch with the scene on the stage."

Belasco opened his Stuyvesant Theatre, October 16, 1907, with a play entitled "A Grand Army Man," written by himself in collaboration with Miss Pauline Phelps and Miss Marion Short,—that is, rewritten and made practical by Belasco, working on the basis of an amateur essay in dramatic authorship provided by those ladies. That play was first acted on any stage at the Hyperion Theatre, New Haven, Connecticut, September 23, the same year. It presents neither surprising ingenuity of construction nor uncommon felicity of style, but it tells a plain story in a plain way. The chord that is struck in it is that of romantic, almost paternal, altogether manly and beautiful affection. As a work of dramatic art it appertains to the class of comedies represented by such plays as "Grandfather Whitehead," "The Porter's Knot," and "The Chimney Corner,"— plays in which the theme involves unselfish love and the sentiments and emotions that cling to the idea of Home. In that respect it reverts to a style of drama once, fortunately, dominant—at a time when the American Stage was illumined and adorned by such actors as Henry Placide, John Gilbert, John Nickinson, Charles W. Couldock, William Warren,

and Mark Smith. The authors of it provided Warfield with a vehicle of dramatic expression that
exactly conformed to the bent of his mind. The plot
is simple, but by reason of being natural and being
fraught with true, as opposed to false, emotion, its
simplicity nowhere declines into insipid commonplace. The chief character, *Wes' Bigelow,* is a
veteran of the Grand Army of the Republic. He
has never married. In youth he has loved a girl, but
has not won her, and she has become the wife of one
of his comrades. Years have passed, and the American Civil War has occurred. That comrade has
been slain in battle. The widow has died: but she
has left a child, that comrade's boy, and *Bigelow*
has adopted and reared him. The substance of the
play is his experience with the fortunes of that
ward.

It happens sometimes that a man whom a girl has
rejected, and who remains unmarried because of his
absorbing love for her, will fix his affection on her
child,—she having married a more favored suitor
and produced a family,—and will love that child
as if it were his own. That happens to *Bigelow.*
The son of his loved and lost idol is the light of his
eyes and the joy of his heart. There is no labor
that he will not do and no sacrifice that he will not
make for the lad, of whom he ardently prophesies

success and honor. The boy, *Robert,* has been intrusted with money, the property of the Grand Army veterans, and, instead of placing it in the bank, as directed to do, he has used it in speculation, and lost it. When the knowledge of that fault comes to the veteran he is, at first, stunned by it; then enraged; and then broken by the conflict between the sense of shame and the struggle of affection. He tries to thrash the boy with a horse-whip, but in that manifestation of wrath he fails: his cherished pet cannot have done wrong; has only erred through accident; can surely be redeemed; must, of course, make amends,—and all will be well. The case comes to trial, before a judge who, privately, is hostile to *Bigelow,* and measures are taken to insure conviction. The veteran offers to replace the money that has been taken by his ward,—supposing that the complaint will then be dismissed. That money he has obtained by sale of his personal effects, and also by means of a mortgage imposed on his farm. The old soldier makes an impassioned, pathetic appeal to the court, but the hostile magistrate cannot be appeased. *Robert* is convicted and is sent to prison for one year. A little time passes, and *Robert's* sweetheart, the daughter of that malicious judge, leaves her father's abode and seeks **refuge** with *Bigelow* and the kind old woman who keeps house for him. *Robert* is pardoned, at the intercession of the veteran's military comrades, and he comes back, to his guardian and his love, on New Year's Day.

Nothing could be more simple than that unpretentious idyl of Home. It is in situations of simplicity, however, that an actor is subjected to the most severe tests of his inherent power, his fibre of character, his knowledge of the human heart, his store of experience, his resources of feeling, and his artistic faculty of expression. Warfield endured that test, allowing the torrent of feeling to precipitate itself without apparent restraint, and, at the same time, controlling and guiding it. Such artistic growth he had evinced in his impersonation of the *Music Master,* and he evinced it even more effectively in his assumption of the *Grand Army Man,*— going to Nature for his impulse and obeying a right instinct of Art in his direction of it. In the portrayal of the noble, sweet-tempered, yet fiery old soldier he aimed especially at self-effacement, at abnegation of every motive or trait of selfishness. On finding that his boy loves the daughter of his enemy, and is by her beloved, the veteran is, almost at once, disposed to placate that enemy and favor those young lovers. There is, to be sure, a little reluctance, a little struggle in his mind; but that is soon over. The actor denoted that struggle and that surrender in a lovely spirit. In the tempestuous scene of *Bigelow's* horrified consternation, the agonized conflict between anger and love, when the misconduct of the boy is exposed and confessed, and the old man, after trying to beat him as a felon, clasps him to his heart as only the victim of an unfortunate, venial error, the anguish and the passionate affection of a strong, even splendid, nature were expressed with cogent force. The appeal spoken in the courtroom,—an outburst of honest, simple, rugged eloquence, all the more fervid and poignant because unskilled and fettered,—had the authentic note of heartfelt emotion. In circumstances those situations, which are the pivotal points of the play, recall certain supreme effects in "Olivia" and "The Heart of Mid-Lothian," but Warfield's histrionic treatment of those situations was fresh and his achievement in them displayed him as an actor to whom the realm of pathos is widely open and who can move with a sure step in the labyrinth of the domestic emotions,—one of the most perplexing fields with which dramatic art is concerned. All observers know how easy it is, in treatment of themes of the fireside, the family, the home, to lapse into tameness. An actor must possess an ardent and beautiful spirit, and must be greatly in earnest,

who can sustain such themes and invest them with
the glow of passionate vitality. Some of the best
of the managers and actors of an earlier, and as I
believe in many ways a more fortunate, generation
might well have been proud of placing before the
public such a play and such an impersonation as
Belasco and Warfield provided in "A Grand Army
Man,"—a play and an impersonation instinct with
fidelity to common life and yet far removed from
commonplace. Warfield, as a player, possesses in a
marked degree the charm ascribed to John Ban-
nistere (one of the greatest serio-comic actors in
theatrical annals), that he wins you immediately
by seeming to care nothing about you. His identi-
fication with the character of *Bigelow* was absolute and he never, for even a moment, lapsed out of
it. It had been long since such complete absorption,
such living inside of a fancied identity, had been seen
on the stage. The blending of humor and pathos was
exceedingly fine, and it touched the heart even while
it brought a smile to the lips.—"A Grand Army
Man," together with "The Music Master," was acted
at the Stuyvesant Theatre until May 2, 1908, when
Warfield's season closed. On the opening night
Belasco, called upon the stage by a brilliant
and enthusiastic audience, made a brief speech,
saying:

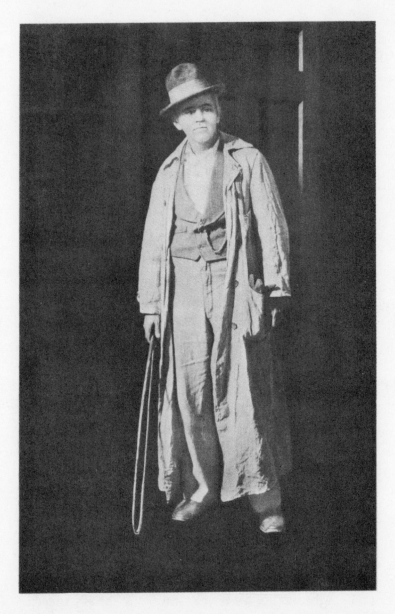

DAVID WARFIELD AS *WES' BIGELOW*, IN "A GRAND ARMY MAN"

"I am very grateful, ladies and gentlemen, that you have given me this opportunity to speak a few words of welcome to you—of welcome warm as heart can make it, to each and every one of you, the friends who have been kind enough to honor me by coming to this little house-warming to-night in our new, and, I hope, our permanent, home. It is a privilege to come before you; to see you here; to see and recognize, as I do, so many of the faces of those who have given me their support ever since I came here from that dear, far-off city of the West where I was born. It gives me such great happiness, ladies and gentlemen, to see you here; to know, as I do know by your generous applause, that you like the play we have produced for you and that you still love, as I am sure you do, that splendid actor and loyal and dear friend of yours and mine, Mr. David Warfield, who is playing here so beautifully to-night. Ladies and gentlemen, I hardly am able to express myself to you. In one of the great plays in which I myself used to act, many, many years ago—and which, before I die, I hope to have the privilege of placing before you, here, in New York—there is a speech that has kept coming back into my mind all this evening, as I have listened to your applause and tried to think what I could say to you:

"'You have bereft me of all words,
Only my blood speaks to you in my veins.'

"But I think that you must know what I wish to express, that you must understand without any words what it means to me to have you here to-night, and to know that all the lies and all the perjuries that have been printed and spoken against us cannot shake your approval and support. We need it! Remember, we are only a handful, fighting against a mighty Trust: but, ladies and gentlemen, this

little theatre flies the flag of independence, and as long as
we have your approval and support and sympathy nobody
can dictate to us and nobody can 'put us out of business.'
And I am sure that we shall have you with us just as long
as we deserve it, and we shall strive to deserve it and to
serve you and the beautiful Art we all love just as long as
we live. I thank you, again and again, for all of us,—
for Miss Phelps and Miss Short, and for Mr. Warfield and
for my company and all my associates as well as for
myself,—and again and again I bid you heartily welcome to
this little new theatre."

This is the original cast of "A Grand Army
Man":

Wes' Bigelow......		....David Warfield.
Judge Andrews....		......Howard Hall.
Captain Bestor....		.......Reuben Fax.
Jim Bishop.......		.George Woodward.
Cory Kilbert......	Of the G. A. R.	....James Lackaye.
Let' Pettingill.....		....Stephen Maley.
Comrade Potter....		......Tony Bevan.
Comrade Tucker...		....Thomas Gilbert.
Comrade Tate.....		...Henry F. Stone.

Robert, Wes' Bigelow's adopted son.......William Elliot.
Rogers Wellman......................Taylor Holmes.
Hickman...............................John V. Daly.
The Drummer-Boy of the Rappahannock....John Morris.*
Hallie...............................Antoinette Perry.
Letitia................................Marie Bates.

* In the original cast: this character was cut out of the play before
the New York opening.

Mrs. Bestor..............................Amy Stone.
Alida Bestor.........................Veda McEvers.
Mrs. Pettingill.............................Jane Cowl.
Mrs. Kilbert........................Louise Coleman.

A DEFEATED PLAN: "THE PASSING OF THE
THIRD FLOOR BACK."

Belasco had planned to open his new theatre with a play by the eccentric Jerome Klapka Jerome, entitled "The Passing of the Third Floor Back." In his "Story" he gives the following account of his plan and purposes and of the way,—surely most unjust,—in which they were defeated. The actual reason for Mr. Jerome's "misunderstanding" undoubtedly was that he preferred to have Forbes-Robertson, instead of Warfield, act the principal part in his "idle fancy," as he designated his monotonous but amazingly popular fabric of insipid colloquy:

"I was about to make a new version of 'The Lone Pine,' which I wrote for Denman Thompson many years ago, when Mr. Jerome K. Jerome came to see me. He and I had travelled from London on the same ship, and I found him a most interesting companion. He was the author of the charming little Christmas story, 'The Passing of the Third Floor Back,' and suggested turning it into a play for Warfield. I was delighted. The contract was signed and a payment made in advance. 'I shall sail for home at once,' said Mr. Jerome, 'to go into the country, for I shall need the trees and flowers and birds about me as I work. I am going to write it with David Warfield in mind. He shall be the *Stranger* and I shall dip my pen into my heart as well as into the ink.' Mr. Jerome suggested that the action of the entire play take place in one scene. 'But I wish the actors could face the audience as though a wall of the room were between them and the auditorium,' he said. 'You want the fireplace in front of the footlights,' I suggested. A sketch of the scene was made then and there.

"Our contract stated that the play was to be completed in time for the opening of the present Belasco Theatre, which was being built. 'I'll have your play finished,' said Mr. Jerome; 'I'll bring it over myself.' With my mind at rest, I turned to other matters. It was not long before Mr. Jerome wrote for an extension of time. I readily agreed to this and shortly after Mr. Jerome wrote again to ask for another postponement. The play depended largely upon the mood in which it was written and moods are not to be summoned at will; so once more I agreed to a delay. Mr. Jerome sent me a model of the scene and costume sketches by Percy Anderson. They bore Mr. Jerome's 'O. K.,' and I cheerfully paid a fee of $500 for them. I still have the sketches in my possession. The time for the opening of the new theatre was drawing near and I engaged the company. Mr. Warfield was eager to have the script, that he might begin to study the part. Then came bad news from England. Mr. Jerome could not finish the play in time. I saw that I could not depend upon it for the opening of my new theatre and must find something else. I once heard Mr. Warfield recite James Whitcomb Riley's 'The Old Man and Jim,' and I knew that a character like the *Old Man's* would be delightful in his hands. I had in my possession a manuscript, written by Pauline Phelps and Marion Short. It contained the very idea for the character I wanted, so I made arrangements with the ladies and rewrote parts of the play. By the time my work was done and I had engaged a company I received a cable from Mr. Jerome: 'The manuscript is finished. Am bringing it to you.' I had been obliged to disband the company selected for 'The Passing of the Third Floor Back,' and preparations for 'A Grand Army Man' were completed. I doubted if the other play could possibly be made ready for production in so short a period. When Mr. Jerome arrived, he read his piece to Mr. Warfield, Mr. Roeder and me, and we found the idea more and more to our liking. I felt, however, that the play should be held over until the following season. Before I could reach a decision Mr. Jerome left unexpectedly for London. It was my moral, to say nothing of legal, right to postpone the production, as it was no fault of mine that the script had not been delivered sooner. I told Miss Marbury, Mr. Jerome's representative in this country, to cable to him to that effect. He showed some surprise in his reply. But in a long communication I explained my dilemma. In response to this he sent a very satisfactory answer, and I was about to write another letter to him, enclosing an additional advance on the contract— so anxious was I to have the piece—when Miss Marbury abruptly inquired what steps I intended to take in the matter. She insisted upon another large payment, which displeased me, since I had so willingly complied with every request Mr. Jerome had made, and I hastily scribbled an impatient note. To my astonishment, I received a telegram from her saying: 'The play is sold to Forbes-Robertson.' Three years after, when Mr. Jerome asked me to read a new piece, we spoke of 'The Passing of the Third Floor Back.'

I explained the matter, and he said it was all the result of a mistake. I was of course very sorry the mistake had occurred. This mistake was most fortunate for Sir Johnson Forbes-Robertson, who might have missed the greatest success of his career. The piece could not add to his fame, but it certainly added to his fortune."

"THE WARRENS OF VIRGINIA."

Belasco opened the season of 1907-'08, at the Belasco Theatre, August 31, with a revival of "The Rose of the Rancho," which he continued to present there until November 9. On November 11 Miss Bates appeared at that theatre, where she acted for three weeks, in "The Girl of the Golden West." On December 3 he there brought out, for the first time in New York, a play called "The Warrens of Virginia," written by William C. De Mille, son of his old friend and early collaborator, Henry C. De Mille, and retouched by himself. It had been acted at the Lyric Theatre, Philadelphia, on November 18. In that play the interest is concentrated on the character of a general in the service of the Southern Confederacy, toward the close of the American Civil War, and on the conduct of his daughter, in a well-contrived emergency, involving the conflict,— perennial as a dramatic expedient,—between love and duty. The story is interesting, and it illustrates, in a manner that is both pictorial and pathetic, the contrasts of circumstances and the vicissitudes of domestic experience that, necessarily, were incident to the harrowing condition of fraternal strife then prevalent in this country. The play, however, is not in any sense either political or sectional. It has no didactic drift. It does not discuss the war. It does not advocate either union or disunion. It tells a story, and, necessarily therefore, it portrays characters. The predominant element in it is picture, but it contains much incident, of a kind more notable for utility than novelty, and some of its situations are fraught with the dramatic element of suspense. Its special charm is a sweet and gentle domestic atmosphere.

The action is supposed to pass during the twenty-four hours immediately preceding the surrender of the Confederate army, at Appomattox, April 9, 1865, and to close five years later. Act First occurs in a woodland glade, near to the abode of the *Warrens* of Virginia. Acts Second and Third proceed in a room in that dwelling. Act Fourth, and last, is placed in a rose garden adjacent to the *Warren* home. *General Warren,* a Confederate commander, is ill, broken by care and privation, and he has been ordered from the field, for rest. *General Griffin,* a Union commander, has acceded to the request of

General Lee that *Warren* should be passed through the Union lines to his home. *Warren's* daughter, *Agatha,* trying to reach the Confederate forces, with such little relief as the *Warren* family could supply, has been stopped by *Lieutenant Burton,* a Union officer,—known to her before the outbreak of the war,—who loves her, and who is by her beloved, although she has repulsed him. *Lieutenant Burton,* in turning *Agatha* back to her home, begs the privilege of visiting her, if he can obtain leave of absence, but his request is denied. *General Warren,* however, on the way to his dwelling, meets with *Burton* and consents to the proposed visit. A supply train is expected by the Confederates, and its arrival is vital to them, while the stoppage of it is equally essential to the forces of the Union. Stratagem is planned. A bogus despatch is prepared, ordering the interception of the train at a certain point, and it is desired that this despatch be captured by the Confederate commander, so that he will be deceived by it and will send the train another way. The Union commander utilizes *Lieutenant Burton's* wish to visit his sweetheart, and compels him to carry the despatch,—having previously ascertained that a movement of the Confederates is intended which will insure *Burton's* capture at *General Warren's* home. Various reasons constrain *Burton* to carry the despatch,—

although his expectation is that he will be shot as a spy. When the scene shifts to the *Warren* home *Agatha* and *Burton* meet and they plight their faith as lovers. *Burton* is captured by the Confederates, but *Agatha* has obtained the despatch and has concealed it in her shoe. Her purpose is to shield her lover; but *General Warren,* surmising that she knows where the document is concealed, appeals to her in such a way that she breaks down and surrenders it. The *General* is deceived. The supply train is despatched in a wrong direction and is captured by the Union forces. The conduct of *Burton* thereupon is stigmatized as grossly dishonorable; *Agatha* renounces him; and, making no defence, he is likely to be shot. The surrender of the Confederate army terminates the war, and thus *Burton's* life is saved. After the lapse of five years he once more repairs to the *Warren* home and renews his suit for the hand of *Agatha.* At first his prayer is denied,—notwithstanding the girl still loves him. The talk of the lovers is heard by *General Warren,* who appears all the while to have been asleep, and presently the father recalls the departing lover, and, for his daughter's sake, consents to a reconciliation and a marriage: and thus a pretty picture of happy love and peace is made to close an ordeal of trouble and grief. It seems a pity that some device could not have been found to make the young soldier carry the despatch without being aware of the treachery that was intended. He is forced to act in a dishonorable manner, and he forfeits all sympathy in the action of the play.

There is no limit to the pathos of conflicting emotions that can be pictured, incident to war, and especially to a civil war. Some of that pathos is indicated at moments in this drama. The little children, concocting a letter to their soldier brother; the agonized lover, who while waiting for the moment in which the trick to which he has lent himself will be accomplished, is fondly treated by the girl whom he loves, and toward whom he feels that he has been deceitful; the worn, ill, suffering Confederate general, gleeful in his supposed triumph, waiting for the safe arrival of the supplies that will relieve his wretched troops, and sitting with his wife by his side and their two young children at their knees; the blind, almost insane fury of that deceived, resentful old man when he learns of the capture of those supplies—those incidents and others like to them are exceedingly effective. There is excess of dialogue and there is too much attention to unimportant detail delaying the action. The incident of the father's kneeling to his daughter is copied from Wills's splendid play of "Charles I"

CHARLOTTE WALKER AS *AGATHA WARREN*, IN "THE
WARRENS OF VIRGINIA"

—in which the betrayed *King,* in a similar situation, begs *Lord Murray* to bring his forces to the rescue of the royal arms. The opening incident—the meeting of the Union and the Confederate soldier—is reminiscent of the opening of Boucicault's "Belle Lamar." The acting was, in several instances, superb. Frank Keenan was, in appearance, true to the indicated ideal of *General Warren* and his performance was instinct with the truth of Nature, shown with the delicate exaggeration of proficient art. Power, dignity, authority, and blended humor and pathos were its attributes, and it was especially admirable for its repose. The finest moment in it was that of the outbreak when *Warren* is apprised of the loss of the supply train and cannot believe that his son has obeyed orders. Miss Emma Dunn, who acted *Mrs. Warren,* gave a touching and interesting, because carefully considered, well-planned, and smoothly and fully executed, impersonation of an affectionate wife and mother,—the result of close study informed by exact observation and the intelligence and feeling native to the nature of the actress. Miss Charlotte Walker as *Agatha Warren* was extremely handsome and winning, and, in the lighter moments of the play, acted with charming effect. The stage dresses and pictures were, in every detail, historically correct and characteristic of the period to which the

play relates; in fact, the production was a memorable example of taste and excellence in the pro-
vision of harmonious and helpful stage environment.—"The Warrens of Virginia" was acted at
the Belasco Theatre until May 2, 1908; on May 4
it was transferred to the Stuyvesant Theatre, where
it was presented until the 16th, when that house
was closed for the season.   This was the cast:

General Warren	....	Frank Keenan.
Ruth Warren	....	Emma Dunn.
Agatha	....	Charlotte Walker.
Arthur	....	Cecil de Mille.
Bob	....	Richard Story.
Betty	....	Mary Pickford.
Miss Molly Hatton	....	Blanche Yerka.
Gen. Griffin...... ⎫	Of Gen.	⎧ ....William McVay.
Gen. Harding.... ⎬	Grant's Staff	....DeWitt Jennings.
Gen. Carr....... ⎭		⎩ .....E. Allen Martin.
Lieutenant Burton	....	C. D. Waldron.
Blake	....	Raymond L. Bond.
Corporal DePeyster	....	Stanhope Wheatcroft.
Zack Biggs	....	Frederick Watson.
Billy Peavy	....	Willard Robertson.
Tom Dabney	....	Ralph Kellerd.
Sapho	....	Mrs. Chas. G. Craig.

Of the Mary Pickford who appeared in this cast
as Betty Warren—and who gave an agreeable performance—Belasco affords this reminiscence, which

it is specially pleasant to quote here because instances of appreciation and gratitude among actors of the present day are not frequent:

"In 'The Warrens of Virginia' two children, a boy and a girl, had very important parts. I could not find a little girl to suit me, when one day my stage manager asked me if I would see a child named Mary Pickford. Little Mary was then a vision of girlish beauty—with long golden-brown curls. She said she had been hanging about my stage door for a week, wanted the part and was in fact at that very moment ready for it. I gave it to her at once, and the next day she came to rehearsal letter-perfect. In the course of time she became the 'Queen of the Movies.' After a few years I sent for her to ask her to play in 'A Good Little Devil.' She was then earning $500 a week, but she told me I might name my own price, as she knew I could not afford to pay that sum. She said she was willing to lose financially that she might gain artistically. I regret that she is giving her time to the moving-pictures houses, for she is a genius in her line."

"THE EASIEST WAY."

Mr. Eugene Walter's play called "The Easiest Way" is one of the most obnoxious specimens of theatrical trash that have been obtruded on the modern Stage. It depicts a segment of experience in the life of a shallow, weak, and vain prostitute, who makes a feeble attempt to reform but who fails to

do so. The significant impartment of that play—
in so far as it possesses any significant impartment
—is an intimation that "the easiest way" in which
a woman can obtain and hold a position on the stage
and live in luxury off it is by the sale of her chastity;
but that "the easiest way" will, at last, prove to be
the hardest, ending in misery and a broken heart.
The ethical platitude is supposed to constitute a
"moral lesson," and this disgusting play was pro-
claimed as instructive and admonitory in its purpose. The assumption of a right and duty to "teach
good moral lessons" in the Theatre by causing the
public mind to dwell with tolerant familiarity on
wholly commonplace and sordid proceedings and
experiences of blackguards, rakes, pimps, and har-
lots, as such, is as stupid as it is impudent, but it
has been made by some of the most eminent men and
women of the Stage.   Lester Wallack produced
Boucicault's tainted drama of "Forbidden Fruit,"
and trailed the banner of the noble Wallack tradi-
tion in the gutter by doing so; Richard Mansfield,
to the end of his life, retained in his repertory the
feculent play of "A Parisian Romance" (produced
by A. M. Palmer); Mme. Modjeska introduced in
our Theatre Mr. Sudermann's radically pernicious
"Heimat" ("Magda"); William and Madge Kendal
exploited the "Tanqueray" scandal; that great man-

ager and actor John Hare (one of the loveliest artists that ever graced the Stage) sullied his fair fame by presenting, and attempting to defend, "The Gay Lord Quex"; Belasco brought out "The Easiest Way"—and so it goes. Dispute as to the propriety of presenting such plays is unending. It is not, however, essential to continue that dispute (of which I have long been sick almost to death) in this place: my views on the whole subject of the drama of demi-repdom have been explicitly stated in the chapter of this work relating to the play of "Zaza." When "The Easiest Way" was first made known in New York I wrote and published these words of comment:

It is melancholy and deplorable that he should have lent his great reputation to the support of the vicious play which now disgraces his Stuyvesant Theatre. . . . No lover of Dramatic Art, no admirer of David Belasco, can feel anything but regret that he should give the authority of his great managerial reputation,—the greatest since Augustin Daly's death,—and the benefit of his genius and his rich professional resources to the exposition of a drama that cannot do good. . . . We do not want to see in the Theatre the vileness that should be shunned; we want to see the beauty that should be emulated and loved!

These words expressed my conviction then—and they express my conviction now. And I am encouraged to believe that my old friend (whose productions of "Zaza" and "The Easiest Way" I opposed by every means in my power) has come to my way of thinking on this subject because in a recently published newspaper article I find him declaring: "Art is not confined to the gutter and the dregs of life. Rather, real art has more to do with the beautiful. Perverted and degenerate ideas are the easiest to treat of in literature, the drama, and the stage."

"The Easiest Way" was produced with vigilant attention to detail. Nothing was forgotten: the rooms shown were reproductions of fact,—from the rickety wardrobe, with doors that will not close and disordered sheets of music and other truck piled on top of it, in the boarding-house chamber, to the picturesque, discreetly arranged disorder of the opulent apartments, the signs of a drunken orgy, and the artfully disclosed and disordered bed. All that stage management could do to create and deepen the impression of reality was done, and the result was a deformity magnificently framed to look like nature,—another example of a thing done perfectly that ought not to have been done at all and one from which I gladly turn away. This was the cast of "The Easiest Way":

John Madison......................Edward H. Robins.
Willard Brockton....................Joseph Kilgour.
Jim Weston..........................William Sampson.
Laura Murdock......................Frances Starr.
Elfie St. Clair.....................Laura Nelson Hall.
Annie.............................Emma Dunn.

"WESTWARD, HO!"—THE SYNDICATE SURRENDERS.—
INCIDENTS OF 1909.

Belasco, accompanied by several friends, left New York on February 7, 1909, for San Francisco, where he arrived on the 12th and where he remained for nearly a month. He had been apprized that the health of his father was failing and that, in the course of nature, his death was likely to occur soon. His expedition was prompted by filial affection and it was undertaken with a heavy heart. His visit, however, greatly cheered and benefited his aged parent, and the sojourn in his native city was made a time of festival and happiness. On February 24 a dinner was given at the Bismarck Café by surviving pupils of the Lincoln Grammar School, of the classes from 1865 to 1871, at which Belasco was the principal guest; and on the 27th a supper was given in his honor at the Bohemian Club. He has written for me this account of his visit:

". . . The only really sad time was when at last I had to say 'Good-bye' and come away: that was a sorrow. But

I would not have missed the visit back home for all the world! The happiness of seeing my old father and the pleasure my coming gave him are priceless memories to me, and I like to think my visit helped him to hold on: he lived nearly two years longer. I would have gone back the next year, but I was warned against the agitation our parting would bring to both of us. . . . I was so hospitably received on every hand that I entirely forgot my enterprises in New York and I felt like a boy again, without a worry. Although it was less than three years after the earthquake-fire, prosperity was in evidence everywhere; the spirit of the people was simply wonderful, and it sent me home encouraged and inspired to attempt greater things. I am proud that I was born in San Francisco, and I cannot say too much for the hospitality and overwhelmingly friendly reception accorded me. . . . The night at the Lincoln School Dinner was wonderful. There were about seventy of the 'boys' there, and dear old Professor Bernhard Marks, who had been the principal and who was nearly eighty, presided and called the roll, just as he used to do when we were all lads. Sometimes a silence followed a name; many times there came the answer 'Dead,' and now and then somebody responded 'Present.' I cried! Then the principal put us through our paces again, at the old lessons, and dealt out cuts on the hand with very little of the old-time vigor. After that there were speeches, and so many lovely things were said about me that I was too embarrassed to reply properly: I remember that I began by saying it was the happiest night of my life—and then stood there with tears running down my cheeks! But I managed to say a few words that pleased them, and then there were many calls for me to recite 'The Madman' and at last I got up to do it. I started in with restraint, to

DAVID BELASCO AND HIS FATHER, HUMPHREY ABRAHAM BELASCO, IN SAN FRANCISCO, FEBRUARY, 1909—THEIR LAST MEETING

give it properly, as I would now, but the 'old boys' wouldn't have it. They began to catcall and cry 'Nix! Nix!' 'The old way! the *old* way!' and they made me get up on one of the tables and begin all over again and give it in the good old way, raving and shrieking and tearing my hair, as I used to do when a boy, when the audiences used to say I'd break a blood-vessel if I kept on! So I went through with it, though it was pretty hard work, and they were so delighted they made me give 'The Vagabonds' for an *encore*, but I 'stuck' dead, halfway through that, and couldn't go on to save my soul, so they let me off. . . .

"I didn't know the names of all those who came, but by and by I would recognize a glance of an eye or the turn of a head and recall that I knew that fellow when he was a boy. They were so much altered—one of the greatest scamps of the school was a staid, respected banker, and another was a portly physician of the highest standing, and so on. It was all very interesting to me—and at times very pathetic and touching. . . .

"My night at the Bohemian rather overwhelmed me—when I looked about and saw many of the leading men of San Francisco and remembered the days when I couldn't even get into that club! They gave a play in my honor, by Dr. Shiels, and there were many charming speeches and I made my acknowledgments as well as I could, and then they gave me a cartoon, painted by Neuhaus. It shows me kneeling at the shrine of The Owl [the symbol of the Bohemian Club], presenting my offering, 'The Rose of the Rancho,' to their patron bird of Bohemia."

I have endeavored to obtain reports of the speeches at these festivals but have been unable to do so. At the Lincoln Grammar School Dinner the speakers

were Professor Marks, Charles A. Miller, Joseph
Greenberg, James I. Taylor, Charles F. Gall, and
J. J. McBride, all of San Francisco, and Arthur
L. Levinsky, of Stockton. Among the speakers at
the Bohemian Club supper were Dr. J. Wilson
Shiels, Joseph D. Redding, Charles J. Fields, Willis
Polk, Waldemar Young, and Mackenzie Gordon.—
Belasco left San Francisco for New York on March
2 and arrived there on the 7th.

In the spring of 1909, soon after he returned
from his visit to San Francisco, the Theatrical Syndicate practically surrendered in its fight to exclude
Belasco from the theatres which it dominated. The
reason for this surrender was, of course, purely selfish. The Belasco theatrical productions were not
only the best that were being made in America but,
also, they were among the most profitable. He had
long been firmly established in public favor: he was
managing two splendid theatres in New York: he
controlled, directly or indirectly, others in other
cities: each season he had grown more influential: it
was a manifest impossibility to crush him: many
janitorial managers of theatres in different parts of
the country were bitterly dissatisfied because his
popular and remunerative productions were not
"booked" in their theatres: the obvious course of
commercial expediency was to terminate a losing

conflict and utilize and prosper by the leading theatrical manager in America: to the Syndicate, as
to *Petruchio* in *Grumio's* description of him, "nothing comes amiss so money comes withal," and the
greatest wonder is not that it forgave Belasco the
heinous crime of working for his own advantage but
that, at heavy financial loss, it so long debarred him
from the "first-class territory." The upshot of the
various considerations indicated was an understanding between the parties in opposition (namely, the
booking agency of the Messrs. Klaw & Erlanger,
representing the Syndicate, on the one side, and Mr.
and Mrs. Harrison Grey Fiske and Belasco, on the
other), whereby,—as set forth in a statement issued
by Fiske,—it was arranged that "Klaw & Erlanger
and Fiske and Belasco will hereafter, *whenever
mutually agreeable,* play attractions in each other's
theatres." Since that understanding was reached,
April 29, 1909, they have, as far as I know,
done so.

I am far from regarding *any* association between
Belasco and the Theatrical Syndicate as being either
for his best interest or for that of the American
Stage. Belasco, however, thinks differently, and in
a recent conversation with me he summed up his
feeling about the Syndicate in these words: "In the
conferences initiated by our lawyer Mr. Gerber

[David Gerber was attorney for Belasco as well as for Klaw & Erlanger] it was found that we could enter upon business relations for the betterment of the American Stage without any sacrifice of principle or integrity, and I think our arrangement has been beneficial for the Stage. I am older than I used to be; I have no ill-feeling; our relations are very friendly, and *I* am satisfied to 'let the dead past bury its dead.'" That is very well—but, as it happens, all that was truly urged by Fiske and Belasco (among others) in opposition to the Theatrical Syndicate *before* the business understanding above recorded remained equally true *after* it; newspaper files and many legal instruments are accessible and anybody can consult them who wishes to do so; the public record cannot be evaded. I am thoroughly familiar with the annals of the Syndicate and I do not agree with Belasco in his present friendly and favorable attitude. On the contrary, I am satisfied that the influence of the Syndicate upon matters of dramatic art must, in the nature of things, remain vulgar and degrading, and in matters of business oppressive and sordid, to the end of the chapter. Public opinion, however, and that of the newspaper press has long been indifferent on this subject, and I am now convinced that it is only by the passing away of the men who compose the Syndicate (in whom, happily, "nature's copy's not eterne") and the accession to theatrical management of men of higher character and ideals and finer intellect that the American Theatre will be measurably redeemed from its impaired estate.

Belasco's course, meanwhile, in dealing with the Syndicate has been incorrectly described as "a surrender" on his part and he has been much misrepresented therein. From the first of difference and dispute he maintained his right to *independence* in the conduct of his managerial business. In various conversations with me, many years before the arrangement with his opponents was reached, he declared, in substance, half-a-score of times or more: "I have no wish to try to interfere with these people [meaning the Syndicate] in *their* business. What *I* am fighting for is *my* right to book *my* productions with whatever managers want to book them, for *my* best advantage."

A newspaper intimation that Belasco, while booking through the Syndicate agency, would "fear to offend the Trust" brought from him (1909) the following specific disclaimer of subserviency:

"Please deny for me, emphatically, the statement that I 'hesitate to give offence to the Theatrical Trust.' My position regarding the Theatrical Trust is too well known, I hope, for anyone to believe that!"

Mr. Lee Shubert, who controlled theatres competing with Syndicate houses in which Belasco productions were presented for a long time after the Syndicate agreed to book for him, made the following comment on the understanding:

"So far as myself and my associates are concerned we cannot disapprove of a development which shows advancement of the policy of the 'open door,' for which we have fought. It is gratifying to us to note that the tendency toward a general letting down of the bars, which were up so long and so unjustly against independent producers, is so emphatically in evidence in the change of attitude both on the part of Erlanger and Belasco and Fiske. We have produced and procured our own attractions, and will continue to do so with such measure of success as may be ours. *I have contended always that the time would come when the bars must be let down and successful producers welcomed wherever they were willing to play their attractions.* . . . We are independents, and Messrs. Belasco and Fiske are independents. Whatever steps they may take in an independent way we cannot with consistency disapprove. It is really of little moment to the public, which cares little about whose attractions it may pay to see and in what theatre it may see them so long as the attractions are worth the money."

One immediate result of the Fiske-Belasco arrangement with the Syndicate was the settlement out of court of the lawsuits over "The Auctioneer," implicating Klaw & Erlanger, Belasco, and Joseph

Brooks, and the withdrawal of the appeal by Belasco, in that matter, which had been filed April 13, 1906.

A painful incident of this year (1909) was a bitter attack on Belasco made by his former friend and professional associate Mrs. Leslie Carter. That singular woman, having appeared in John Luther Long's absurd play of "Kassa" and made a failure, was pleased to ascribe that regrettable result not to a bad play and a tiresome performance but to the malign influence of Belasco! A long and silly "statement" was issued in her behalf to the effect that there was a plan on foot to interfere with "her career" in that play, and it was intimated that Belasco was the instigator of this alleged nefarious scheme. Later Mrs. Carter gave out another screed, which was circulated throughout the press of the country, reflecting in the most gross and unwarranted way upon the man who had made her theatrical career possible, and in which she declared: "If I were going to die and could save my life by playing again for David Belasco, I would not do it!" As nothing could ever have induced him to resume the management of Mrs. Carter this declaration was a trifle superfluous. Belasco's only comment on this matter was explicit: "It is," he said, "absolutely false that I have sought, or desired, in any way, to injure Mrs. Carter. It is monstrous that such a thing should be said against me, and monstrous that anybody should dare to ask me if it is true."

During the summer of 1909 Belasco proposed to his old friend Lotta that she return to the stage under his management (she had retired from it about 1890) and make a farewell tour of the country. "I urged her all I could," Belasco writes, "because I knew I could make her reappearance and tour a sensational success and that the public would be delighted to see the little Lotta of other days. At first I wouldn't take 'No' for an answer, and for a while Miss Lotta was inclined to accept my proposal. But, finally, she declined, saying: 'I've seen so many people make the same mistake, when they've grown old and outlived their public, of coming back to appear in the parts that were written for them in their youth. "Other days, other ways." It is better to let my old friends remember me as they saw me many years ago. I shall never act again.'" That was a wise decision. No doubt there would have been much friendly interest in a formal farewell by Lotta; but the elfin charm of her youth was gone and the venture would have inspired sadness: "Yesterday's smile and yesterday's frown can never come over again!"

THE SEASON OF 1909-'10: "IS MATRIMONY A FAILURE?" —"THE LILY"—AND "JUST A WIFE."

Belasco produced three new plays in the season of 1909-'10,—"Is Matrimony a Failure?", "The Lily," and "Just a Wife." "Is Matrimony a Failure?" is a clever farce, adapted by Leo Ditrichstein from a German original, "Die Thür ins Freie," by Oscar Blumenthal and Gustav Kadelberg. It relates to the ancient, evergreen subject of conjugal friction,—which, in this instance, seems intolerable but proves indispensable,—and it implicates ten married couples and one pair of prospective connubialists. The scene is a pleasant country town in New York. A coterie of husbands has grown restive under what is deemed to be an excessive exercise, by their wives, of matrimonial authority. A lawyer named *Paul Barton* visits the town to settle the estate of an old Justice of the Peace, recently deceased, ascertains that the wedding ceremonies of the various couples implicated were performed by that official's clerk, in the absence of his employer, and declares them to be illegal. The husbands decline to validate their marriages unless their wives agree to permit them greater freedom than they have enjoyed, and, leaving their homes, establish themselves at a neighboring inn,—where they soon find that, however irksome may have seemed the dominion of their wives, it is immensely preferable to the total lack of their society. More particular rehearsal of the complications, cross-purposes, and conflicts woven about this posture of circumstance would be superfluous: they were not less comic 'and amusing because the legal quirk upon which the original play was based is inapplicable under the law of the State of New York. The farce was exquisitely set and admirably played,— especially by that excellent light-comedian and lovable man, the late Frank Worthing,—and it enjoyed acceptance bounteous and remunerative. "Is Matrimony a Failure?" was first acted at Atlantic City, New Jersey, August 29, 1909, and, in New York, at the Belasco Theatre, on the 23d of that month,— with the following cast:

THE HUSBANDS.

Skelton Perry	Frank Worthing.
Hugh Wheeler	W. J. Ferguson.
Frank Bolt	James Bradbury.
Albert Rand	Edward Langford.
Jasper Stark	John F. Webber.
David Meek	F. Newton Lindo.
Dr. Hoyt	Robert Rogers.
George Wilson	Marshall Stuart.
Lem Borden	Gilmore Scott.
Herman Ringler	Frank Manning.

NANCE O'NEILL AS *ODETTE DE MAIGNY* AND JULIA
DEAN (THE YOUNGER) AS *CHRISTIANE DE
MAIGNY*, IN "THE LILY"

"Jane Cowl," said Belasco, "had been with me for several years, understudying many parts in different plays, acting 'bits,' and working hard. I felt that she had earned her chance, and I gave it to her in 'Matrimony.' Her performance was splendid and she has been successful ever since."

"The Lily" is a play in four acts, adapted by Belasco from a French original, "Le Lys," by MM. Pierre Wolff and Gaston Leroux. It was produced for the first time, December 6, 1909, at the Belasco Theatre, Washington, and was first acted in New York, at the Stuyvesant, December 23. The story of this play is one of domestic tyranny, possible in

France but impossible in America, and one which, accordingly, inspired only tepid interest in the American public,—although the treatment and presentation of it were in a high degree theatrically effective. This is the substance of that story: The *Comte de Maigny,* a profligate Frenchman who is also a father and a widower, tyrannizes over his children. The eldest of those children, *Odette,* is "the lily,"—a woman of thirty-five who, in girlhood, has been parted by her father from the man she wished to marry and who has become a mere domestic convenience, dwelling in lonely celibacy as her father's housekeeper and lavishing her affection upon her sister, who is ten years younger. That sister, *Christiane,* is destined by their father for the same barren existence, but she meets a strolling artist, who wins her love and with whom, because he cannot wed her,—being already married to an uncongenial woman who will not divorce him,—she enters into an illicit relation. *De Maigny* has contrived to arrange a loveless marriage between his son and the young daughter of a man of great wealth,—being intent thus to obtain money for libidinous self-indulgence. The relation of *Christiane* and her artist becoming known to that person, he breaks off the marriage of his daughter with *Christiane's* brother, not explicitly stating his reason but with ambiguous givings out which intimate it. The chief scenes of the play then follow. The infuriated licentiate badgers his unfortunate daughter, who, at first, lies to protect herself, until, at last, he elicits from her a rebellious, exultant declaration of the truth. Then, in the fury of his disappointed cupidity, he is about to beat her, when the long-suppressed, meek-seeming but actually passionate *Odette,* opening her valves under an immense and rising pressure of emotional steam, intervenes, denouncing the conventions of society in general and the iniquities of *de Maigny* in particular, certifying to the propriety of her sister's conduct in the wretched circumstances existing, and declaring her purpose to protect that sister in her natural desire for "love and happiness." *Christiane* then departs with her lover and the expectation of deferred matrimony, and her disgruntled parent, practically ejected from his home, goes off to Paris, whining that a waiter will probably close his eyes in death,—a pious kindness which the spectator hopes may be performed at an early date.

The play, of course, was devised for the sake of the sudden, blistering outburst by the elderly spinster—which in representation is undeniably effective—and, in the French original, for the sake of emitting some specious special pleading in extenuation and justification of illicit conduct. As to the doctrine which *Odette* declares in this play and which *Christiane* and her unhappily married swain exemplify,—the doctrine, namely, that when two persons who love each other are held asunder by cruel chance of social circumstance they are warranted in setting aside convention in order to come together,—its utter fallacy is too obvious for detection. Practical application of it, however, has often provided variously dramatic results: pathetic exposition of some of its possible consequences, to helpless, innocent persons, is made in Collins' great novel of "No Name." Belasco, in presenting his modified version of "Le Lys," sought to evade the ethical issue, but he added one more to his long list of plays perfectly environed and admirably acted. Miss Nance O'Neil, who appeared in it as *Odette,* has been designated as a "tragic actress" (which she is not) and has been extravagantly extolled. She possesses rough natural ability, animal strength, vocal capacity, some sensibility and considerable power of forceful simulation. Most of her performances have been monotonous: in this one, in which, practically, she had only one scene and in which, furthermore, she had the advice and assistance of a consummate stage manager, she was interesting and impressive,—uttering the verbal explo-

BELASCO, ABOUT 1911

sion of voluble vehemence addressed to *de Maigny*
with fine abandon, passionate intensity, and powerful
effect.—The cast of "The Lily" is appended:

Comte de Maigny	Charles Cartwright.
Vicomte Maximilien de Maigny	Alfred Hickman.
Huzar	Bruce McRae.
Georges Arnaud	Wm. J. Kelly.
Bernard	Leo Ditrichstein.
Emile Plock	Dodson Mitchell.
Joseph	Marshall Stuart.
Jean	Douglas Patterson.
Michel	Robert Robson.
Odette ⎱ *De Maigny's* daughters	⎰ Nance O'Neil.
Christiane. ⎰	⎱ Julia Dean.
Lucie Plock	Florence Nash.
Suzanne	Ethel Grey Terry.
Alice	Aileen Flaven.

"Just a Wife" was written by Mr. E. Walter
and was first acted at the Colonial Theatre, Cleveland, Ohio, January 17, 1910, and at the Belasco
Theatre, New York, on the 31st of that month. As
a playwright that writer has exhibited a persistent,
morbid preoccupation with the subject of illicit
sexual relations which suggests the possible utility
of vigorous open-air exercise, the cold sitz-bath and
potassium bromide. In this play a libertine named
John Emerson, who has consorted with a widow
named *Lathrop* until their relation has become a

public scandal, by way of "keeping up appearances" marries an impecunious vestal from South Carolina, named *Mary Ashby*. As he immediately installs *Mrs. Emerson* in a luxurious rural habitation somewhere on Long Island and practically deserts her, this expedient would hardly seem to be of much social service. However, after neglecting his wife for about six years, *Emerson* grows weary of his mistress, quarrels with her and runs away from her to visit his wife. The mistress, much incensed, follows him, and a sort of three-cornered debate,—protracted, sophistical, and indelicate,—on the sexual relation is held at *Mrs. Emerson's* country residence, in the course of which that lady manifests a sweet temper and admirable self-control. After it is over, *Mrs. Lathrop* (to whom it has been intimated that in men the ruling passion is sex impulse and that she is growing somewhat elderly) goes away in a peaceful and much chastened mood. *Mrs. Emerson* then snubs her neglectful spouse and signifies that he may not hope to possess her as his wife until he has recognized the supremacy of Love, which it is implied he will soon do. It is all very edifying, of course,—especially as the author of it, apparently, knows as much about love, as distinguished from carnal concupiscence, as a tomcat on the tiles does. This was the cast:

John Emerson........................Edmund Breese.
Bobby Ashby......................Ernest Glendinning.
Maxcy Steuer........................"Bobby" North.
Wellesley...........................Frederick Burton.
Mary Ashby Emerson...............Charlotte Walker.
Eleanor Lathrop....................Amelia Gardner.

A CHANGE OF NAMES.—THE FARCE OF "THE CONCERT."

Belasco's management of the theatre in West Forty-second Street which was the first to bear his name extended over a period of twelve years. In the spring of 1910 he began to feel dubious as to whether he would,—perhaps as to whether he could, —renew his lease at the end of its term, two years later. He therefore determined to restore to that house its former name of the Republic, and thereafter to designate the Stuyvesant as the Belasco Theatre. That change, accordingly, was made, in July, 1910; and on August 22 the Republic Theatre was reopened under that name with a performance of a play made by Mr. Winchell Smith, on the basis of a clever and amusing story by Mr. George Randolph Chester, called "Bobby Burnitt": that play was produced by Cohan & Harris. On October 10 the second Belasco Theatre was opened with a performance of "The Concert," adapted by Leo Ditrichstein from a German original by Herman

Bahr: it had been acted, for the first time, at the Nixon Theatre, Pittsburgh, September 19.

The theme of "The Concert" is an old one,— Woman's infatuation relative to the Musical Performer. The intention is to satirize that foolish state of the female mind, and also to expose and ridicule a despicable combination of febrile sensuousness, splenetic temper, and insensate egotism, often, and unjustly, designated "the artistic temperament." That intention is accomplished in a manner certainly ludicrous, though heavy-handed and cynical: it is characteristic that the Stage of the Present, reflecting some aspects of life in the Present, while from time to time it exhibits much that is clever, brilliant, hard, satirical, exhibits little—whether of writing or of acting—that is amiable, playful, engaging, pleasant, and therefore potent to make the spirit gentle and happy. The chief postulate of "The Concert" and the manipulation of it are strongly reminiscent of "Delicate Ground" and "Divorçons." The musician, *Gabor Arany,* having lied to his wife as to a purposed excursion from his home, which he says is undertaken for the purpose of "giving a concert,"—goes to a secluded retreat in the mountains of New York with one of his pupils, the wife of another man, intending an amorous intrigue with her. The other man, in

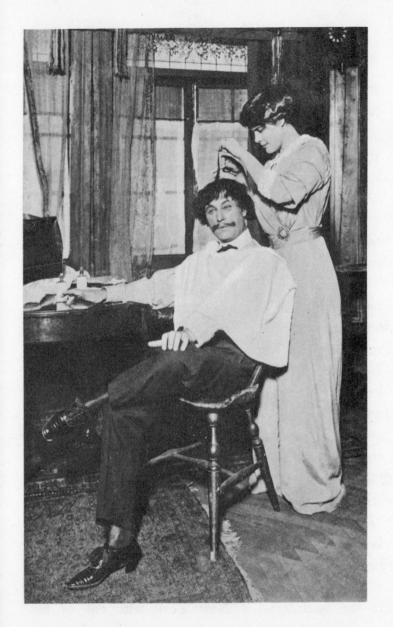

LEO DITRICHSTEIN AS *GABOR ARANY* AND JANET
BEECHER AS *HELEN, MRS. ARANY*, IN
"THE CONCERT"

company with the wife of the musician, pursues those fugitives, and, when the two couples are confronted, the insulted husband, after the manner of *Citizen Sangfroid*, blandly proposes that the complication of domestic affairs shall be solved and adjusted by an exchange of wives, sequent on the attainment of divorce. The silly woman who admires the musician is rescued by exposure of his selfishness and her folly, the musician is baffled and rebuked, and domestic peace is supposed to be restored.

Mr. Ditrichstein called his adaptation of Mr. Bahr's play "a comedy." The terms applied to plays, by way of classification, are somewhat indefinite at the best, but as to *Comedy*,—the general understanding is that it should be a dramatic composition which, in delineating character and manners, while piquant by virtue of delicate exaggeration and amusing by virtue of clever equivoke, moves within the limits of reason and probability. "The Concert" begins with farce and proceeds with violent absurdity. The persons implicated would not, in real life, act in a manner even approximate to that which is prescribed for them. The note that is struck, considered at its best, is that of burlesque. The play, in as far as it is a play,—the clash of character and the exposition of conduct,—begins in the Second Act. Sixteen persons are implicated in the action of the piece, but only seven of them are seen after the first curtain has fallen. The tone of the Second and Third acts, except at moments, is radically and extravagantly farcical. But toward the end an opportunity occurs, and it is duly improved,—perhaps in jest, perhaps in earnest,—of saying the magnanimous words that are usually attributed to philosophical lovers: "If you love a woman, and that woman happens to be your wife, you wish her to be *happy,* and if you discover that she thinks she can be happier with another man than she is with you your wish is that she should join him, if she can be sure of her feelings"; and so forth. At the close of this piece the wife of the genius affectionately assures him that she has all along understood his conduct, but is willing to pardon him if he will be faithful in future, and, by way of emphasizing her docile, charitable, and eminently tolerant spirit, she produces bottles of hair-dye and proceeds to rejuvenate his fading locks.—The scenic setting, the stage management, and the acting by which this farce were commended to public approbation were so appropriate, so resourceful and deft, so careful, zealous, spirited, and effective, that it gained immense popularity. This was the original cast of "The Concert":

Gabor Arany......................Leo Ditrichstein.
Dr. Dallas...........................William Morris.
McGinnis...........................John W. Cope.
Helen Arany........................Janet Beecher.
Flora Dallas..............................Jane Grey.
Eva Wharton.....................Alice Leal Pollock.
Mrs. McGinnis.......................Belle Theodore.
Miss Merk........................Catherine Proctor.
Fanny Martin.......................Edith Cartwright.
Claire Flower...................Margaret Bloodgood.
Natalie Moncrieff.....................Adelaide Barrett.
Edith Gordon......................Cora Witherspoon.
Georgine Roland.......................Elsie Glynn.
Laura Sage...........................Edna Griffin.
Mrs. Lennon-Roch..................Kathryn Tyndall.
Mrs. Chatfield........................Mary Johnson.

LOSS AND GRIEF.—"NO MAN BEARS SORROW BETTER."

"Thanks for your kind sympathy, dear William Winter," Belasco wrote to me, in July, 1911. "I have thought of you so often in my grief. I should be glad to come over to your island to see you, but I am not able. . . . I am trying to be resigned; and, though the pain is great, I must be. Nothing can ever be the same again, and it is all very, very hard. Yet I must go on, and I shall. There is nothing but our work. . . ." He had, within less than two months of each other, lost his father and his dearly loved daughter Augusta,—Mrs. William Elliott. His father was stricken on April 6th, and he died on the 11th, at his home, No. 1704 Sutter Street, San Francisco. Belasco, however, was at that time in almost distracted attendance on his daughter, at Asheville, North Carolina, and could not leave her when he received news of his father's illness; nor was he able to attend his funeral. Humphrey Abraham Belasco was buried beside his wife in Hills of Eternity Cemetery, San Mateo, California, April 12th.

The death of Belasco's daughter,—"my little guardian," as he has called her in talk with me,— was a bereavement more than usually bitter. She was a creature of extraordinary goodness and beauty, of exquisite sensibility, gentle and lovely in nature, childlike in disposition, the pitiful friend of all sorrowing and suffering persons, the special comrade and comfort of her father, and her death came within less than five months after her marriage—to the actor William Elliott. When Belasco was informed of his child's attachment to Elliott (whom she had met when he was a member of the company supporting Miss Starr in "The Rose of the Rancho") he, at first, opposed their marriage,—"Not," as he has told me, "that I had any personal objection to 'Billy,'—who is a dear fellow

"*Oft in the still night*
    Ere Slumber's chain has bound me
Fond Memory brings the light
    Of Other Days around me."

and whom I always liked,—but because I had hoped she would choose a husband out of the theatrical profession, one who could live all his life with her,—which the inevitable travelling of theatrical life makes practically impossible. But when I saw that my little girl was pining for him, that a great love had come to her and that she could never be happy without him, I brushed all my own hopes and wishes away and urged their immediate marriage. I thought to keep her always near her mother and me, so as a wedding gift I had an apartment fitted up for them in the Marie Antoinette, where we live, and we were all going to be together and happy: but it was not to be."

William Elliott and Augusta Belasco were wedded, at the home of her parents, January 27, 1911: as they were about to start on their honeymoon, the bride, while bidding good-bye to her father, was stricken with sudden illness and collapsed. At first it was believed that her illness was merely a transient disorder, which would soon yield to treatment. For a few weeks her condition fluctuated, but seemed, on the whole, to improve: then, at the end of March, she began rapidly to decline, and Belasco was informed that she was afflicted with an acute form of tuberculosis, which must soon cause her death. That was an issue which

her father could not and would not accept without
a bitter struggle. "I had seen so many desperate
cases of consumption saved, for years," he said,
"that I *could not believe* my little girl, who had
always seemed so strong and well, who was so young
and lovely, on the threshold of her new life, with
everything to live for, must die. I gathered her
up, overnight, and fled with her to Asheville."
There Belasco leased Witchwood, a fine residence,—
the home of the late Colonel Charles W. Woolsey,—
and installed his daughter in it. Her fatal malady
could not, however, be stayed, though every expedient was tried that love could prompt or wealth
employ, and she grew rapidly worse. On May 1,
in a forlorn hope that the climate of Colorado
might prove beneficial, Belasco chartered a special
train and removed her to Broadmoor, a beautiful
place in the environs of Colorado Springs,—where,
on the afternoon of June 5, after great suffering
borne with patience and fortitude, she died. Her
body was taken to New York; funeral services were
held there, at the Temple Ahawath Chesed, on June
9, and late on that day she was laid in her grave in
Ahawath Chesed Cemetery, at Linden Hills, Long
Island.

"My little Augusta," writes Belasco in a note made
for me, "was the gentlest creature I have ever known and

the kindest. No one but myself will ever know how many poor girls and young men have had places *made* for them in my companies because she came and asked it, with her dear little arms about my neck. And she had good judgment, too; I never have regretted employing any of the people she interceded for. She was just a child to the very end. She had caught some of my foolish little superstitions, and when she died she was surrounded with pretty little painted butterflies that she had pinned about her to help her to get well—'and I know they will,' she told the doctor, 'because my father believes in them and says so!' Each of my girls was my 'favorite' child, but the younger was my special companion, who always took care of me. Though she might have been up till all hours the night before, she never missed getting up to see that I had my breakfast properly, and I never got home too late for her to come pattering to my room to see me safely tucked into bed. I think that, in her heart, the poor child must have had some premonition that she was going to die soon, because she was so fascinated by my play of 'Peter Grimm.' I had no thought, when I was writing it, that she was to be taken away from me; but I had long wanted to write something that might show death in a beautiful way; something that would touch on immortality as a vivid reality, just a flash beyond this life, and so help to inspire hope. I used to talk to my little girl about it, and she was the first to read my play when it was finished. I gave it to her one evening and waited for her verdict far into the night, and her approval meant much to me. She attended all the rehearsals, and one night she told me that after seeing 'Peter Grimm' no one should be afraid to die. It was the last play she ever saw,—and it is my comfort to believe that its message entered her soul."

Belasco's elder daughter, Reina Victoria, was married to the theatrical manager Morris Gest, of New York, at Sherry's, in that city, on June 1, 1909.

A DRAMA OF SPIRITUALISM.

(Fragmentary Notes, Not Revised.)

The extreme dissatisfaction of the *Ghost,* who, on returning from the spirit world to this mundane sphere, ascertains that his, or her, earthly sweetheart or husband has formed a nuptial alliance with somebody else has been noticed by various poetical writers in deeply affecting verse, dramatic, descriptive, and pathetic, . . .

Belasco's play "The Return of Peter Grimm" deals with the mysterious and certainly important subject of Spiritualism,—a subject which deserves all the thoughtful, studious inquiry which has, in recent years, been bestowed on it by many persons of exceptional intellectual capacity and power. It is, nevertheless, a subject which is generally treated with pitying contempt or scornful antagonism, especially by those persons,—the vast majority of humanity,—who are most comprehensively ignorant of its history and its apparent phenomena. It was, accordingly, a bold choice which selected that subject for exposition in a drama of prosaic, contem-

AUGUSTA BELASCO, MRS. WILLIAM ELLIOTT

poraneous setting, and it is a significant testimony at once to Belasco's managerial perspicacity and to his skill as a writer and a stage manager that his play of "Grimm" achieved unusual success. . . .

In the days of my youth, when I was a student at the Dane Law School of Harvard College, it was my good fortune to gain the friendship of the erudite lawyer Theophilus Parsons, who was a preceptor there, and to listen to much interesting and instructive discourse by him on many subjects —among them, the Swedenborgian faith, to which he was an absolute and happy adherent. "Death," he remarked, in expounding to me the tenets of that faith, "is no more than walking from one room into another." The same thought (which has, of course, been cherished by many persons) seems to have been predominant in the mind of Belasco when he was writing "The Return of Peter Grimm." . . .

BELASCO'S "THE RETURN OF PETER GRIMM."

In drama, whether prose or verse, the device has frequently been used of bringing back to our material world the spirits of persons who have passed out of mortal life, and causing them to pervade the scenes with which they were associated in the body. That device is employed in Belasco's "The Return of Peter Grimm," in which David Warfield made his first and, thus far, his only approach to the realm of Imagination [since this passage was written Warfield has appeared, 1915-'16, as *Van Der Decken*, in a drama by Belasco on the subject of "The Flying Dutchman."—J. W.]. *Peter Grimm*, a prosperous, self-willed, kind, good old man, who in the government of his family and the arrangement of his worldly affairs has made serious errors,—the most deplorable of them being the separation of his ward, a docile, affectionate girl named *Kathrien*, from a youth who loves her and whom she loves, and her betrothal to his nephew, *Frederik Grimm*, a hypocrite and a scoundrel,—is suddenly stricken dead, of heart disease, and, after a little time his spirit returns to the place which was his earthly home, intent on retrieving those errors, discomfiting the rascal by whom he has been deceived, and making his foster-child happy. Warfield, personating *Peter Grimm*, first presented him as a mortal, afterward as a spirit. The character,—honest, sturdy, opinionated, worldly-wise, somewhat rough and imperious, yet intrinsically genial,—was correctly assumed and expressed, but the actor's denotement of spiritual being was neither

REINA BELASCO, MRS. MORRIS GEST

imaginative nor sympathetic, and it did not create even the slightest illusion.

The purpose of the dramatist seems to have been to intimate a notion, comfortable to the general mind, that spiritual existence of beings once mundane is merely a continuation of their everyday condition in this world. In the absence of knowledge on the subject that assumption is as tenable as any other. Persons who are commonplace in what we call Time may reasonably be held to remain commonplace in what we call Eternity. No one knows. The Book of Destiny has not been opened. But the rationality of assumption which makes of "that undiscovered country" only a prolongation of this earthly scene at once dissipates, especially for dramatic purpose and effect, all atmosphere of *spirituality,* all glamour of the ideal, which happily might be superinduced by imaginative treatment of a mysterious subject. However prosaic the quality of a disembodied spirit may remain, it seems reasonable to assume that there must be some essential difference between the material body and the spiritual body, and the person undertaking to represent a spirit could succeed, if at all, in denoting that difference not by stage tricks but only by mental power and affluence of emotion, by weird strangeness of individuality, by exquisite sensibility, by magnetism, and by the artistic skill to liberate those forces and so elicit and control the sympathy of his auditors. Warfield's personation of *Grimm* gave not the faintest intimation of spirituality, and there was not one gleam of imagination in his presentment of the spirit.

Few actors have ever succeeded in conveying to an audience any really convincing, absorbing sense of *spiritual presence.* The dramatist of "Peter Grimm" probably did not intend that any such sense should be conveyed. Warfield, apparently, did not attempt to convey it, and if, as appears true, it was the actor's purpose to present *Grimm* as essentially the same person after death as before, then his personation, undoubtedly, was the rounded result of a definite plan, and was, as such, entirely successful.

The part of *Peter Grimm* has been described as one of great difficulty. It is, on the contrary, very easy. Its requirement is sincerity. *Grimm,* as a spirit, clothed as in mortal life, must move among persons who were his friends, unseen by them, unheard when he speaks, eagerly desirous to influence their conduct, but practically helpless to do so, except at moments when accession of extreme sensibility on the part of one or another of them provides occasion, until, at last, force of circumstances and the impelling guidance of the dead man achieve his purpose. Acted in the spirit precisely as in the flesh, as a good old man, the part makes no draft upon the resources of mind or feeling or upon the faculty of expression that any good actor might not easily satisfy. The situations wherein *Grimm,* ostensibly, is ignored by the other persons on the stage in fact revolve around him and are dependent on his presence; he engages the sympathy of the audience practically to the exclusion of all the other characters, and the almost universal interest —whether assenting or dissenting—in anything relating directly to the theme of spiritual survival after death, together with the novelty of a ghost displayed in the environment of every-day, centres observation on *Grimm* and his personator.

Warfield's performance, notwithstanding the prosaic atmosphere of it, was interesting, and his excursion into the realm of the occult was, at least, calculated to stimulate thought on a serious subject. In this, as in many other matters, the degree of approval gained by the play and its performance will ever be variably accordant to taste. To some persons, no doubt, the ideal of a newly dead child being borne away on his spirit-uncle's shoulders, singing about "Uncle Rat has gone to town to buy his niece a wedding gown," and musically inquiring,

"What shall the wedding breakfast be? Hard-boiled eggs and a cup of tea?" will be delightful. Others, equally without doubt, will fail to find it impressive.

"The Return of Peter Grimm" was acted for the first time, January 2, 1911, at the Hollis Street Theatre, Boston; and for the first time in New York, October 18, the same year, at the present Belasco Theatre. This was the original cast of that play:

Peter Grimm	David Warfield.
Frederik Grimm	John Sainpolis.
James Hartman	Thomas Meighan.
Andrew MacPherson	Joseph Brennan.
Rev. Henry Batholommey	William Boag.
Colonel Tom Lawton	John F. Webber.
Willem	Percy Helton.
Kathrien	Janet Dunbar.
Mrs. Batholommey	Marie Bates.
Marta	Marie Reichardt.
The Clown	Tony Bevan.

CONCERNING THE EUNUCHS OF CRITICASTERISM.

The gentle Goldsmith, commenting on a meanness in human nature which causes little minds to envy and disparage the achievements of large ones, remarked that "There are a set of men called

DAVID WARFIELD AS *PETER GRIMM*, IN "THE RETURN
OF PETER GRIMM"

answerers of books, who take upon themselves to
watch the republic of letters and distribute reputation by the sheet: they somewhat resemble the
eunuchs in a seraglio, who are incapable of giving
pleasure themselves and hinder those that would."
Such emasculated perverters of the function of
criticism,—scribblers bloated with envy engendered
by conscious intellectual impotence,—flourish more
or less in all periods; they are peculiarly prosperous
in this one, and their envious malice is employed with
at least as much industry in the "answering" and
defaming of dramatists and actors as in the "answering" of books. Before Belasco had produced "Peter
Grimm" in New York and almost in the hour of
his personal bereavement, a representative specimen of that wretched brotherhood, itching to detract
from the achievement of an author whom he could
not hope ever to approach, published the false statement that Belasco was only *part* author of that
play. Among the papers loaned to me by Belasco is
a copy of the following letter, which I print here
because the misrepresentation alluded to has been
several times iterated and the refutation of it should
be placed on record:

(*Belasco to a Quidnunc.*)
"Belasco Theatre, New York,
"July 22, 1911.

"In your article in the current '———— ————' there is a misstatement which I should be much obliged to you if you would rectify, as it places both Mr. Cecil De Mille and myself in a false light.

"Your article states that Mr. Cecil De Mille is my '*collaborator*' in Mr. Warfield's new play, 'The Return of Peter Grimm.' I am not aware whether you saw the play when it was presented in Boston, Chicago and Pittsburg last season. If you did so, however, you must remember that on the play bill I gave full credit to Mr. De Mille *for an idea*—WHICH I PURCHASED FROM HIM AND PAID VERY HANDSOMELY FOR. As for the play—in its construction, its dialogue, its plot and its characterizations—the play is *mine* and MINE ONLY.

"Mr. De Mille, I know well, will be the first person to verify this statement of mine, and in view of the fact that my play has not yet been presented in New York—and may possibly prove a failure there—I think it is only fair that *I* should be held exclusively responsible for *my own work.* . . ."

"THE WOMAN"—AND MR. ABRAHAM GOLDKNOPF.

Belasco devoted most of the summer of 1911 to work on William C. De Mille's play entitled "The Woman," which he produced for the first time in New York, September 19, that year, at the Republic Theatre: a trial production of that play had been effected, April 17 preceding, at the New National

Theatre, Washington, D. C. It is a highly effective melodrama, of the "contemporaneous interest" type, and it implicates twelve persons, nine of whom are germane to its action. It is neat in construction; it skilfully utilizes the invaluable element of suspense, and interest in its progress is cumulative to the dramatic climax. This, in brief, is its story:

A corrupt politician, the *Honorable "Jim" Blake,* a member of the national legislature, is scheming to get a specious bill enacted into law, whereby over-capitalization of railroad corporations and wholesale swindling of the public can be perpetrated in the guise of legality. Another member of the legislature, the *Honorable Matthew Standish,* perceptive of the latent iniquity of that measure and of the predatory intent of *Blake,* has so vigorously opposed the enactment of it and so bitterly assailed its sponsors that *Blake* and his associates fear to force its passage. They determine, therefore, to divert attention of the people from the opposition of *Standish* to their corrupt measure and purposed malfeasance by blasting his personal reputation with social scandal. In their effort to do this they ascertain that several years previous the *Honorable Matthew,* inflexible before Plutus, has succumbed before Venus—has, in short, registered at an hotel with a woman not his wife. The name of that woman is not known to their informant, and it is the despicable task of *Blake* and his adherents to ascertain her identity in order to ruin his public career by convicting him of private misconduct. That task they attempt to perform by endeavoring to extort from a young woman, *Wanda Kelly,* the operator in charge of a telephone exchange desk, a telephone number in New York which *Standish,* in Washington, has called for, immediately after being apprised of the dastardly purpose of *Blake* and his associates. The identity of the concealed and errant she as *Blake's* daughter, the wife of one of his chief supporters, the *Honorable Mark Robertson,* is deftly discovered to the audience by the device of a second telephone message to her, by her husband, immediately after the close of the warning of impending disclosure by *Standish.* The sympathetic *Miss Kelly* resolutely persists in her protective secrecy as to *The Woman* at the other end of the wire, and the climax is then attained when *Standish* refuses to be driven from his public duty by the threatened assault on his private character and when *Mrs. Robertson,* having in an agony of dread listened to the unsuccessful coaxing and badgering of *Miss Kelly,* with sudden and desperate courage terminates the anxious situation by avowal of her delinquency, thus providing her corrupt parent and spouse with considerably more information than they desire to publish as to the amatory weaknesses of the obdurate *Standish*. This was the cast with which that play was first presented in New York:

The Hon. Jim Blake......................John W. Cope.
Tom Blake..........................Harold Vosburgh.
The Hon. Mark Robertson.................Edwin Holt.
Grace, Mrs. Robertson....................Jane Peyton.
The Hon. Matthew Standish............Cuyler Hastings.
Ralph Van Dyke.......................Carleton Macy.
The Hon. Silas Gregg..............Stephen Fitzpatrick.
The Hon. Tim Neligan.................William Holden.
A Guest..............................Langdon West.
A Page...........................George Van Blake.
A Waiter................................José Rossi.
Wanda Kelly............................Mary Nash.

The exceptional success of Belasco's production of "The Woman" prompted a genius thitherto unknown to fame, a certain inspired and amiable barber of New York, Mr. Abraham Goldknopf, to assert that it was stolen from a sublime drama indited by himself in the intervals of tonsorial exercise and entitled "Tainted Philanthropy." Belasco, in defending himself against this preposterous claim, resorted to a unique and costly though conclusive expedient. But before describing the trial of Mr. Goldknopf's allegations, it is convenient here to

examine with some particularity the general subject of

BELASCO AND PLAGIARISM.

"FOLLY LOVES THE MARTYRDOM OF FAME."

No person rises to eminence without exciting
antagonism and incurring detraction. Malice is
quick to perceive any possibility, however trivial,
of tarnishing a distinguished character, and hatred
is ingenious in devising specious means of disparagement. The slightest appearance of weakness in any
talented person favorably conspicuous in the public
eye is eagerly seized as a ground of condemnation.
Every close student of biography must have
observed, relative to almost every eminent person
commemorated, that there is always some one particular form of reproach which, by diligent, persistent iteration, is made to adhere to that person's
name, so that at last the one is seldom mentioned
without association with the other. Eminent actors
of the Past have been particularly singled out for
defamation in this way. Barton Booth, for example,
scholar and poet as well as actor, is stigmatized, on
no competent authority, as a gross voluptuary; Garrick, because he was prudent, especially while he
was poor, is styled an avaricious niggard; Kemble,

an opium sot; Edwin Booth, a drunkard, which is
a specially contemptible slander. Henry Irving was
one of the greatest of actors, but, because he happened to be a person of many peculiarities, perfectly
natural to him, we are forever hearing that he had
"affected mannerisms"—which is distinctly untrue.
Every department of biography furnishes examples
of this form of aspersion. In the case of Belasco
the customary disparagement takes the shape of an
iterated charge of *Plagiarism*. In this work an
examination of that charge is essential.

"It is an old trick of Detraction," says Moore, in his
"Life of Sheridan," "and one of which it never tires, to
father the works of eminent writers upon others; or, at
least, while it kindly leaves an author the credit for his
worst performances, to find some one in the background to
ease him of the fame of his best. . . . Indeed, if mankind
were to be influenced by those *Qui tam* critics . . . Aristotle
must refund to one Ocellus Lucanus, Virgil must make a
cessio bonorum in favor of Pisander, the Metamorphoses of
Ovid must be credited to the account of Parthenius of
Nicæa, and Sheridan . . . must surrender the glory of having written 'The School for Scandal' to a certain anonymous
young lady who died of a consumption in Thames Street.
. . . Sheridan had, in addition to the resources of his own
wit, a quick apprehension of what suited his purpose in the
wit of others, and a power of enriching whatever he adopted
from them with such new graces as gave him a sort of claim
of paternity over it and made it all his own. *'C'est mon*

bien,' said Molière, when accused of borrowing, 'et je le reprens partout ou je le trouve.' "

THE "TRICK" AS APPLIED.

"Plagiarism," says The Dictionary, is "the act of appropriating *the ideas* or the language of another and passing them for one's [*sic!*] own; literary theft." It would not be very difficult, testing Belasco's plays by that definition, and excluding all other considerations, to invest the charge of plagiarism against him, in some instances, with validity. The last part of "Hearts of Oak" is borrowed from Leslie's "The Mariner's Compass"; "La Belle Russe" is based on situations taken from "Forget Me Not" and "The New Magdalen"; the thrilling situation in the Third Act of "The Girl I Left Behind Me" is based on a similar situation in Boucicault's "Jessie Brown; or, the Relief of Lucknow"; the agonizing situation in the Third Act of "The Darling of the Gods," in which a military despot extorts information from a woman by forcing her to gaze on her lover subjected to torture, is derived (and bettered) from Sardou's "La Tosca." Other instances of similarity could be specified. It would, however, be a manifest injustice to stigmatize Belasco, *and only Belasco,* as a plagiarist on the

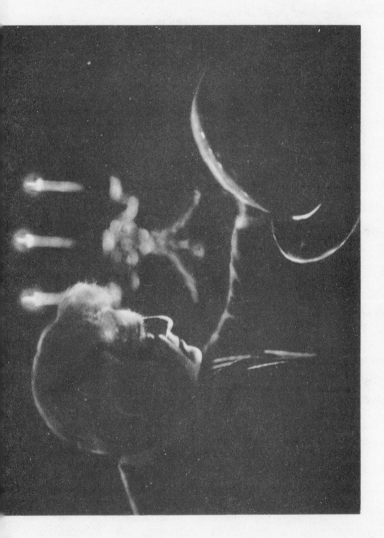

"THE STUDENT"—DAVID BELASCO

ground of his indebtedness to plays earlier than his. He has done only what all other dramatists have done since the beginning of the craft; that is, he has based *some* of his plays on dramatic expedients and situations that have long been considered to be common property.

AN 'ANCIENT USAGE.

Several of Shakespeare's plays were based by him on plays of earlier date, by other authors. Dryden borrowed freely from Spanish plays and sometimes from Corneille and Molière,—a fact which caused Scott to remark (Preface to "The Assignation") that "originality consists in the mode of treating a subject more than in the subject itself." English dramatists, from Wycherly onward, have freely borrowed from Molière. Fielding, there is reason to believe, derived an occasional hint from the great Frenchman, as also from Thomas Murphy. Goldsmith was a little indebted to Wycherly. Hoadley borrowed from Farquhar; Steele from Bickerstaff; Colman from Murphy; Sheridan from both Wycherly and Congreve, and perhaps from his mother's play of "The Discovery" and her novel of "Sydney Biddulph"; Boucicault from many French sources and some English ones. I would not be understood as approving or defending that practice in dramatic authorship: on the contrary, in the whole course of my long service as a dramatic critic and historian I have condemned it. These words, written by me many years ago, relative to Boucicault, indicate my view of *the practice:*

Dramatic authorship, indeed, seems to have been regarded by him,—and by many other playwriters,—as a species by itself, exempt from obligation to moral law. The bard who should "convey" Milton's "Lycidas" or Wordsworth's great "Ode," and, after making a few changes in the text and introducing a few new lines, publish it as a composition "original" with himself, would be deemed and designated a literary thief. The dramatist, taking his plots from any convenient source and rehashing incidents and speeches selected from old plays, can publish the fabric thus constructed as an "original drama," and, so far from being discredited, can obtain reputation and profit by that proceeding. ["Old Friends," by W. W.: 1909.]

If the large majority of dramatic authors,— Sophocles, Shakespeare, Racine, Molière, Sheridan, and the rest, down to the present day,—be convicted of plagiarism on the ground that they have rehashed old material, that charge will stand against Belasco. But the dramatist who, with manifest truth, pleads, as Belasco can plead (and as I understand that he does plead), "a well-known, universal, recognized custom" cannot, justly, be singled out and stigmatized for plagiarism,—any more than a respectable Turk, resident in Constantinople, with four wives, can be singled out and stigmatized for bigamy. I no more approve the custom of what I call "play-wrighting" than I approve or advocate polygamy,— but I speak for justice. Moreover, it is essential to be remembered that the number of basic situations, in fiction as in fact, is limited, and consideration of *the method* of combining and treating them must vitally affect the question of "originality." To make an avowed adaptation of the work of another, or, with credit, to base a passage on suggestion derived from an incident in the work of another is not plagiarism.

The fair investigator of the charge of plagiarism against Belasco will find that it is twofold: it accuses him of appropriation from the works of other writers precedent to him, and of appropriation from other writers contemporary with him to whose writings he has had, or, as alleged, may have had, access.

CHARLES READE ON PLAGIARISM.

In considering the first part of the accusation I would recommend all inquirers to read the masterly exposition of the subject of Plagiarism made by Charles Reade (himself one of the successful writers frequently, in his day, accused of the offence), which is printed, in his collected Works, as an appendix to his capital story of "The Wandering Heir,"—a story first made public in dramatic form. That exposition is too long to be quoted here in full, but the appended extract from it, which deals with what Reade calls "the mere intellectual detraction" involved in the charge that he had stolen "The Wandering Heir" from Dean Swift's "The Journal of a Modern Lady," is illuminative:

"It ['the mere intellectual detraction'] is founded on two things—1. The sham-sample swindle, which I have defined. 2. On a pardonable blunder.

"The blunder is one into which many criticasters of my day have fallen; but a critic knows there is a vital distinction between taking ideas from a *homogeneous* source and from a *heterogeneous* source, and that only the first mentioned of these two acts is plagiarism; the latter is more like jewel-setting. Call it what you will, it is not plagiarism.

"I will take the fraud and the blunder in order and illustrate them by a few examples, out of thousands.

"By the identical process Pseudonymuncle has used to entrap your readers into believing 'The Wandering Heir' a mere plagiarism from Swift, one could juggle those who read quotations, not books, into believing:—

"1. That the Old Testament is *full* of indelicacy.

"2. That the miracles of Jesus Christ are none of them the miracles of a God, or even of a benevolent man—giving water intoxicating qualities, when the guests had drunk enough, goodness knows; cursing a fig-tree; driving pigs to a watery grave. This is how Voltaire works the sham-sample swindle, and gulls Frenchmen that let him read the Bible for them.

"3. That Virgil never wrote a line he did not take from Lucretius or somebody else.

"4. That Milton the poet is *all* Homer, Euripides, and an Italian play called 'Adam in Paradise.'

"5. That Molière is *all* Plautus and Cyrano de Bergerac, 'en prend *tout* son bien ou il le trouve.'

"6. That the same Molière *never* writes grammatical French.

"7. That Shakespeare is *all* Plautus, Horace, Holinshed, Belleforest, and others.

"8. That Corneille had not an idea he did not steal from Spain.

"9. That Scott has not an original incident in all his works.

"10. That five Italian operas are *all* English and Irish music.

"11. That the overture to 'Guillaume Tell' is *all* composed by Swiss shepherds.

"12. That 'Robinson Crusoe' is a mere theft from Woodes, Rogers, and Dampier.

"Not one of these is a greater lie, and few of them are as great lies, as to call 'The Wandering Heir' a plagiarism from Swift.

"Now for the blunder. That will be best corrected by putting examples of jewel-setting and examples of plagiarism cheek by jowl.

"Corneille's 'Horace,' a tragedy founded on a *heterogeneous* work,—viz., an historical narrative by Livy,—is not a plagiarism. His 'Cid,' taken from a Spanish play, is plagiarism. Shakespeare's 'Comedy of Errors' and Molière's 'Avare' are plagiarisms, both from Plautus.

Shakespeare's 'Macbeth,' taken from a *heterogeneous* work, a chronicle, is no plagiarism, though he uses a much larger slice of Holinshed's dialogue than I have taken from Swift, and follows his original more closely. The same applies to his 'Coriolanus.' This tragedy is not a plagiarism; for Plutarch's Life of Coriolanus is a *heterogeneous* work, and the art with which the great master uses and versifies *Volumnia's* speech, as he got it from North's translation of Plutarch, is jewel-setting, not plagiarism. By the same rule, 'Robinson Crusoe,' though Defoe sticks close to Woodes, Rogers, and Dampier in many particulars of incident and reflection, is not a plagiarism, being romance founded on books of fact. The distinction holds good as to single incidents or short and telling speeches. Scott's works are literally crammed with diamonds of incident and rubies of dialogue culled from *heterogeneous* works, histories, chronicles, ballads, and oral traditions. But this is not plagiarism; it is jewel-setting. Byron's famous line—

'The graves of those who cannot die,'

is a plagiarism from another poet, Crabbe; but *Wolsey's* famous distich in Shakespeare's 'Henry the Eighth' is not a plagiarism from Wolsey; it is an historical jewel set in a *heterogeneous* work, and set as none but a great inventor ever yet set a fact-jewel. . . ."

"FOR THE DEFENDANT."

Examination of Belasco's plays will reveal that they are, for the greater part, founded on what Reade designates *"heterogeneous works,"*—that is,

while he has in some instances borrowed or utilized
material long generally regarded as common property, he has gone, far more, to history and record,—
and that his/ plays contain more original writing than ninety per cent. of the plays which
are customarily acted on the English-speaking
Stage.

Turning from the question of what Belasco may
or may not have derived from elder dramatists, we
come to a field in which it is easy to move with
definite, assured steps. The first accusation against
him of plagiarism from a contemporary, as far as
I have been able to ascertain, was made by Albert
M. Palmer, on information and belief, in regard
to the play of "The Millionaire's Daughter," first
produced at the Baldwin Theatre, San Francisco,
May 19, 1879. Palmer had been given to understand that Belasco, in this play, had infringed
Bronson Howard's play of "The Banker's Daughter," first produced at the Union Square Theatre,
November 30, 1878, and which Maguire had endeavored to secure for Baldwin's. He sent his attorney,
W. Barnes, to see Belasco's play of "The Millionaire's Daughter," accompanied by assistants, who
took down as much as possible of the dialogue.
After the performance Belasco said to Maguire:
"It is not necessary for Mr. Barnes to try to

take down my dialogue: he has *seen* the play: tell him he can have a copy of the manuscript, if he wishes." Barnes advised Palmer that there was *no plagiarism* by Belasco, and there the matter ended.

The second accusation was that of Howard P. Taylor, alleging that Belasco took material portions of "May Blossom" from "Caprice": Taylor would not bring that charge into court, though Belasco invited him to do so; and Harrison Grey Fiske, the editor of "The Dramatic Mirror," the publication in which the false accusation had been repeatedly made, publicly declared it to be unwarranted.

Beyond these, I have been furnished by my friend Judge A. G. Dittenhoefer (acting with Belasco's permission) with a list showing that six distinct, formal charges of plagiarism have been made against Belasco and redress sought by legal action for injury thus alleged to have been done by him. The plays as to which these charges have been made are (1) "The Wife"; (2) "Du Barry"; (3) "Sweet Kitty Bellairs"; (4) "The Woman"; (5) "The Case of Becky"; (6) "The Boomerang."

In the first of these cases suit was instituted, in 1888, by Fannie Aymar Matthews, against David Belasco and Henry C. De Mille, praying for an

DAVID BELASCO

injunction to restrain the further presentation of their play of "The Wife," on the ground that it was a plagiarism of her play entitled "Washington Life." The action was tried before the Hon. Miles Beach, Justice of the Supreme Court of New York. Judge Beach decided in favor of Belasco and De Mille, finding that there was no infringement, *no plagiarism.*

The second case was an action brought by the French writer M. Richepin, January 25, 1902, in which he demanded an accounting for the receipts from representation of Belasco's play of "Du Barry," on the ground that it was, in fact, a play written by the Plaintiff. M. Richepin would not bring this case to trial, and it was finally discontinued, in January, 1908.

In the third case Grace B. Hughes (otherwise known as Mary Montagu) began an action, in the Circuit Court of the United States for the Southern District of New York, February 3, 1904, against Belasco, Maurice Campbell, and Henrietta Crosman. The action was brought to restrain further representation of Belasco's play of "Sweet Kitty Bellairs," on the ground that it was, in fact, an infringement of the Plaintiff's play of "Sweet Jasmine." Motion for an injunction was argued before Judge Lacombe, on March 18, 1904, and on March

26 it was denied, Judge Lacombe holding that there was *no plagiarism*. The case was never brought to trial, and it was stricken from the calendar, on March 3, 1913.

The fourth case (which is dealt with in detail, page 336, *et seq.*) was the action brought against Belasco and William C. De Mille by Abraham Goldknopf, in February, 1912, in the United States District Court for the Southern District of New York, praying for an injunction to restrain the further representation of their play of "The Woman" on the ground that it was, in fact, an infringement of Goldknopf's play of "Tainted Philanthropy." Judge Holt, before whom the case was tried, held that there was no infringement by Belasco and De Mille, *no plagiarism,* and on March 3, 1913, final judgment was entered dismissing the Plaintiff's complaint, upon the merits.

In June, 1912, the fifth action against Belasco was brought by Amelia Bachman and George L. McKay, seeking to restrain him from further presentation of "The Case of Becky," on the ground that it was, in fact, a plagiarism of their play entitled "Etelle." Trial of this action was begun May 13, 1913, before Judge Julius M. Mayer, of the United States District Court, and was concluded the next day. On July 9, 1913, Judge Mayer rendered his decision, holding that there was *no plagiarism* by Belasco, and dismissed the Plaintiffs' complaint, upon the merits.

The sixth case was an action begun on January 14, 1916, by Lila Longson, to restrain Belasco, Winchell Smith, and Victor Mapes from further presentation of their play of "The Boomerang," upon the ground that it was an infringement of her play of "The Choice." The case was tried in the District Court of the United States for the Southern District of New York, on September 19-21, and, at the close of the trial, Judge W. B. Sheppard held that there was no infringement and dismissed the complaint. Final judgment, dismissing the complaint upon the merits, was entered September 25, 1916.

In all these cases only one judgment in favor of Belasco was appealed,—that by Judge Mayer, in the action by Amelia Bachman and George L. McKay, *in re* "The Case of Becky." Their appeal was taken to the United States Circuit Court of Appeals for the Second Circuit and was argued April 6, 1914. On May 12, following, the Circuit Court of Appeals handed down its decision in favor of Belasco, affirming Judge Mayer's decision dismissing the complaint. The opinion of the Court was written by Judge E. Henry

Lacombe, and can be found in 224 Fed. Rep., page 817.

The significance of this summary of *facts* is obvious. Belasco has been, and is, freely accused of literary theft,—but on each and every occasion when accusation has been made and investigated in Court he has defeated his defamers and been completely vindicated.

CONCERNING BENEFITS—REMEMBERED AND FORGOT.

While Belasco, in common with the generality of dramatic authors, has certainly profited by the example and sometimes by the labor of others (a fact which he does not seek to conceal or deny, but which, on the contrary, he has freely and fairly recognized and admitted), there is a *per contra* aspect of his relation to other play-writers which none of his detractors,—and, for that matter, as far as I am aware, none of his admirers and advocates except myself,—ever mentions,—namely, the immense and direct advantage and profit derived by other play-writers *from him.* Nor is that indebtedness confined to makers of plays: as theatre manager, stage manager, mechanician, success for others if not always for himself has walked

with him, and for scores of persons connected with
the Theatre (many of them void of appreciation)
his has been the touch of a Midas, turning dross to
gold and, incidentally, establishing them in reputation. Among the makers of plays who, first and
last, have greatly profited by his sagacity, skill, and
labor are James A. Herne, Peter Robertson, Bronson Howard (who always handsomely acknowledged the obligation), William Young, H. H.
Boyesen, Henry C. De Mille, A. C. Gunter, Clay
M. Greene, P. M. Potter, Franklyn Fyles, Charles
Simon, Pierre Berton, Charles Klein, Lee Arthur,
John Luther Long, Richard Walton Tully, Miss
Pauline Phelps, Miss Marion Short, William C. De
Mille, William J. Hurlbut, Eugene Walter, Avery
Hopwood, Edward J. Locke, Miss Alice Bradley,
George Scarborough, and Winchell Smith.* In all
the mass of letters addressed to Belasco and
examined by me in preparing this Memoir I have
found fitting acknowledgment of benefits conferred
by only two of those persons, aside from Howard,—

---

* Several other names could appropriately be added to that list—
notably, those of Willard Mack (whose play of "Tiger Rose" owes its
extraordinary success entirely to the revision and stage management of
Belasco and the remarkably interesting and sympathetic acting of Miss
Lenore Ulric), George Middleton, and Guy Bolton. Messrs. Middleton
and Bolton figure as authors of "Polly with a Past,"—which, though it is
an extremely slender farce, was one of the few substantial successes of
the current (1917-'18) theatrical season: it was entirely reshaped and
made practicable by Belasco.—J. W.

Franklyn Fyles and Mr. Scarborough. The latter wrote:

(*George Scarborough to David Belasco.*)
"150 Madison Avenue, Tompkinsville,
"Staten Island, February 28, 1916.

"My dear Governor:—

"Just a brief line before the drop falls on poor little 'Wetona' ["The Heart of Wetona"] to-morrow night:

"It has been a great honor to sit at your feet the past few months—to go to school to you. An infinite pleasure, also, to have seen you work and known you.

"If the play gets over, the great measure of the success will be yours. If it fails, the fault will be with the material which came to you.

"Whatever the issue is, I want now to thank you for your many personal courtesies, for your enthusiasm and your friendship. Hereafter, when some would-be author 'hits the ceiling' at some change you suggest in his 'script, please have him get me on the telephone and I will cheerfully tell him how many kinds of a d—— fool he is not to know a master touch and not to appreciate the Master's interest.

"May you be preserved to the Theatre for a long, long time.

"Affectionately,
"GEORGE SCARBOROUGH."

The scope and variety of his labor as an author are impressively signified in the following partial list of his writings:

THE DRAMATIC WORKS OF DAVID BELASCO.

(Note.—The dates given in the following table refer to the years in which the plays specified *were written,*—and, therefore, in some instances, they differ from the dates given in Chronology, and elsewhere, which refer to *presentation* of the plays.)

JUVENILE EFFORTS.

"Adam and Eve in the Garden of Eden."

"Aladdin and the Wonderful Lamp."

Angel in Hell," "An

Barmaid's Revenge; or, The Fatal Corkscrew," "The (burlesque).

Bohemian Girl," "The (with music).

Bronze Statue," "The.

Butcher's Revenge; or, The Seven Buckets of Blood," "The (burlesque).

Death of Benedict Arnold," "The.

Dying Boy's Last Christmas," "The.

"East Lynne" (burlesque).

Hanging of Nathan Hale," "The.

"Jim Black; or, The Regulator's Revenge" (*his first play*).

Roll of the Drum," "The (before 1869).

Signing of the Declaration of Independence," "The.

"Spiritland."

Trovatore," "Il (with music from the opera of that name).

WRITTEN BEFORE 1882-'83 (BELASCO'S NEW YORK CAREER BEGAN IN SEPTEMBER, 1882).

Ace of Spades," "The (1877—or earlier).

"American Born" (based on "British Born": 1882).

Assommoir," "L' ("Drink": based on Zola's novel: 1879).

Belle Russe," "La (1880-'81).

"Bleak House" (from the novel—about July, 1875).

"Capitola" (a version of "The Hidden Hand": 187[6?]).

"Cherry and Fair Star" (revision of the old spectacle so named: 187—).

"Chums" (1879—see "Hearts of Oak").

Christmas Night; or, The Convict's Return," "The (1877).

Creole," "The (based on Adolphe Belot's story, "L'Article 47": 1879-'80).

Cricket on the Hearth," "The (from Dickens' "Christmas Story": 1877-'78).

Curse of Cain," "The (with Peter Robertson: 1882).

"David Copperfield" (from the novel—before 1878).

Doll Master," "The (1874-'75?).

"Dombey & Son" (from the novel—before 1878).

"Dora" (alteration of Charles Reade's play: 1875).

"Faust" (1877).

Fast Family," "A (adaptation of Sardou's "La Famille Benoiton!": 1879).

Haunted House," "The (1877).

"Hearts of Oak" (based on "The Mariner's Compass," originally called "Chums": with James A. Herne: 1879).

Hidden Hand," "The (from Mrs. Southworth's book—at least three different versions: before 1878).

Lone Pine," "The (187[5?]).

Millionaire's Daughter," "The (1879).

Moonlight Marriage," "The ("The Marriage by Moonlight": based on Watts Phillips' "Camilla's Husband": 1879).

New Magdalen," "The (from Collins' novel—1874).

"Nicholas Nickleby" (from the novel—before 1879).

DAVID BELASCO

"Not Guilty" (alteration of Watts Phillips' play of that name: 1878).

Octoroon," "The ("retouched and altered" version of Boucicault's play: 1878).

"Oliver Twist" (version of, from earlier play and the novel—before 1878).

"Olivia" (dramatization of "The Vicar of Wakefield": 1878).

"Our Mysterious Boarding House" (1877).

"Paul Arniff" (based in part on "The Black Doctor": 1880).

Persecuted Traveller," "The (1877).

Prodigal's Return," "The (1877).

Scottish Chiefs," "The (from the novel—before 1878).

Storm of Thoughts," "A (1877).

Stranglers of Paris," "The (based on Adolphe Belot's story of that name: 1881: re-written, 1883).

"Struck Blind" (from a story: 1875).

"Sylvia's Lovers" (1874-'75?).

"Thaddeus of Warsaw" (from the novel—before 1878).

"True to the Core" (alteration of T. P. Cooke's "prize drama": 1880).

"Uncle Tom's Cabin" (at least two dramatizations of the novel—before 1878).

"Wine, Women and Cards" (1877).

"Within an Inch of His Life" (based on Gaboriau's story: 1879).

WRITTEN SUBSEQUENT TO 1882-'83.

Auctioneer," "The (rewritten from a play made at his direction by Charles Klein and Lee Arthur: 1901: again, 1913).

"Caught in a Corner" (revision of a play by Clay M. Greene—and others: 1887).

Charity Ball," "The (with Henry C. De Mille: 1889).

Darling of the Gods," "The (with John Luther Long: 1901-'02).

"Du Barry" (1900-'01).

Girl I Left Behind Me," "The (with Franklin Fyles: 1892).

Girl of the Golden West," "The (1904).

Governor's Lady," "The (with Alice Bradley—1911-'12).

Grand Army Man," "A (with Misses Pauline Phelps and Marion Short: 1906-'07).

Heart of Maryland," "The (1890-'95).

Highest Bidder," "The (based on "Trade"—which never was acted—by Morton and Reese: 1887).

Kaffir Diamond," "The (revision of play by E. J. Schwartz: 1888).

Lily," "The (adaptation from "Le Lys" by Pierre Wolff and Gaston Leroux: 1908-'09).

"Lord Chumley" (with Henry C. De Mille: 1888).

"Madame Butterfly" (based on a story of the same name by John Luther Long: 1900).

Marquis," "The (version of Sardou's "Ferréol": 1886).

"May Blossom" (based in part on his own play of "Sylvia's Lovers": 1882-'83).

"Men and Women" (with Henry C. De Mille: 1890).

"Miss Helyett" (rewritten from the French of Maxime Boucheron: 1891).

Music Master," "The (altered and revised from play by Charles Klein: 1903-'04).

"Naughty Anthony" (1899-1900).

"Pawn Ticket 210" (with Clay M. Greene—based on an idea in Baring-Gould's novel of "Court Royal": 1887).

Prince and the Pauper," "The (revision of a play by Mrs. Abby Sage Richardson, based on Mark Twain's novel: 1889-'90).

Return of Peter Grimm," "The (1908-'10).

Rose of the Rancho," "The (based on "Juanita," by Richard Walton Tully: 1905-'06).

Secret," "The (adaptation from French of Henri Bernstein: 1913).

"She" (revision of William A. Gillette's dramatization of Haggard's novel—1887).

"Sweet Kitty Bellairs" (based on the novel of "The Bath Comedy," by Agnes and Egerton Castle: 1902-'03).

Ugly Duckling," "The (revision of a play by P. M. Potter: 1890).

"Under the Polar Star" (with Clay M. Greene: 18—: revised, 1896).

"Under Two Flags" (revision of play by P. M. Potter, based on Ouida's novel: 1901).

"Van Der Decken" (1913-'15).

"Valerie" (alteration of Sardou's "Fernande": 1885-'86).

Wall Street Bandit," "A (revision of a play by A. C. Gunter: 1886).

Wanderer," "The (revision of Maurice V. Samuels' adaptation of Wilhelm Schmidtbonn's "Der Verlorene Sohn": 1916-'17).

"Wife," "The (with Henry C. De Mille: 1887).

"Younger Son," "The (adapted from a German play named "Schlimme Saat": 1893).

"Zaza" (based on a French play of that name by Pierre Berton and Charles Simon: 1898).

PLAYS AS YET UNACTED.

"Bubbles."
"Jennie."
"Jimsie, the Newsboy."
Opera Singer," "The.
"Repka Stroon."

BELASCO AS A DRAMATIST:—A FRAGMENT.

Careful study of the plays of Belasco has convinced me that, much as he has accomplished, he has not yet fully developed his powers or fully expressed himself as a dramatist. There is ample evidence in his writings that he abundantly possesses the natural faculty of dramatic expression. That faculty is born—not made. The dramatic mind comprehends a story not in narrative but in action, sees the characters which are involved, each as a distinctive individual, perceives their relations to one another, notes their movements and hears them speak. To the dramatic mind the spectacle of human life is, essentially, one of *movement*. But that spectacle is vast, tumultuous, bewildering, not to be comprehended at once, perhaps not ever to be comprehended fully, and certainly not to be comprehended without the reinforcement of large experience and a profound, peaceful meditation.

The reader of Shakespeare feels that the fully developed intellect of that great dramatist calmly brooded on the world: but there is no Shakespeare now, and there has been no such thing as tranquillity in the world for many long years.

Belasco, when he began to write, was a poor boy, imperfectly educated, in a disorderly environment, subject to all sorts of distractions and impediments, and throughout the whole of his career he has struggled onward under the sharp spur of necessity, without leisure or peace.   In scarcely one of his many dramas is it possible to discern an *unforced* dramatic impulse, spontaneously creative of an exposition of diversified characters, acting and reacting upon circumstances, in dramatic situations, and constituting an authentic picture of human nature and life.   In many of those dramas the *existence* of that impulse is perceptible, but almost invariably the growth of it is checked and the sway of it is impeded by the necessity of haste, or of conformity to the demand of some arbitrary occasion or of deference to the requirement of some individual actor, or to weariness and dejection. Fine bits of characterization appear; flashes of fancy frequently irradiate dialogue; imagination imparts a splendid glow to striking situations,—as in "The Darling of the Gods" and "The Girl I Left Behind

Me,"—and pathos is often elicited by simple means; but sometimes probability is wrested from its rightful place, and extravagance of embellishment mingles with verbosity to cause prolixity and embarrass movement. In a word, a sense of *effort*, a strenuous urgency for the attainment of violent *effect*, is largely perceptible in Belasco's plays,—as, indeed, it is in nearly the entire bulk of modern American Drama. How could it be otherwise?

> "Like children bathing on the shore,
> Buried a wave beneath,
> Another wave succeeds before
> We have had time to breathe."

Belasco, a good son, affectionate and faithful, ever solicitous to contribute to the support of his parents and their family, began labor in childhood, and he has never ceased to labor. At an early age he married, assuming the duties and incurring the responsibilities of a husband and a father in harsh surroundings. In about twenty-five years, working as factotum, secretary, teacher, agent, mechanical inventor, actor, stage manager, theatre manager, and playwriter, and battling against a powerful, unscrupulous, malignantly hostile commercial antagonism, he raised himself from poverty-ridden obscurity to independence, general public esteem, and international celebrity as a theatrical leader. Throughout the ensuing fifteen years he increased his eminence, becoming at last the representative theatrical manager of our day [meaning, here, about 1902 to the present, 1917] in America. He has adapted or rewritten more than 200-odd plays, has collaborated with other writers in making twenty-odd new ones, and is himself the sole author of about thirty more, most of which have been acted but several of which have not. The wonder is not that his writings exhibit some defects, but that, at their best, they contain so much truthful portrayal of character, pictorial reflection of life, fine dramatic situation, and compelling power to thrill the imagination and touch the heart. The time, it seems to me, has not yet come for attempting a comprehensive and final estimate of his faculty and achievement as a dramatist. Whether as an author or a character, he presents a singular, elusive, and perplexing study. The constitution of his mind, I have often thought, shows a striking resemblance to that of the romantic and copiously inventive old English novelist William Harrison Ainsworth. The same prodigal vitality, the same intensity of interest, the same audacious recklessness of probability, the same facility of graphic characterization, the same exuberance of detail, and above all the same wild romanticism peculiar to Ainsworth's novels are perceptible in Belasco's plays. The imagination that conceived "Adrea" might well have conceived "The Lancashire Witches" or the first book of "Jack Sheppard." But Belasco is not merely an imitator. He has pursued a course natural to himself, and he has created much in Drama that is both original and beautiful. If he had written nothing but "The Girl of the Golden West" and "The Return of Peter Grimm" his name would live as that of one of the best dramatists who have arisen in America.

[Written May 18, 1917. Given to me by my father with instruction to mark it, when setting it for him:

ADD, AND REVISE.

The last phase of his illness began on May 24, and he never saw this passage after he wrote it as it stands.—J.W.]

THE GOLDKNOPF TRIAL.—A UNIQUE DEMONSTRATION.

The trial of the Goldknopf action against Belasco, based on the pretence that "The Woman" was plagiarized from "Tainted Philanthropy; or, The Spirit of the Time," was begun, July 31, 1912, with a hearing before Commissioner Gilchrist, at

DAVID BELASCO

the Federal building, New York, and it proceeded, the Hon. George C. Holt, Justice, presiding, in the United States Circuit Court, on August 5. It was established by sworn testimony that Gold-knopf's "play" was submitted by him to the Belasco Play Bureau in May, 1910, and that under date of July 10 Mr. Henry Stillman, the play reader of that bureau, wrote to Goldknopf a letter in which he said:

"Mr. Belasco has gone away for the summer. I sent your play to him, two or three days after reading it myself. He returned it to me to-day. While he was interested in reading it, it is not quite adapted to his present requirements. Will you please call for the manuscript?"

Mr. William C. De Mille testified that after the production of "The Warrens of Virginia," in January, 1908, he had suggested to Belasco that if they could "throw up a good heart story against the general background of political 'graft' it would make a good play"; that Belasco had been favorably impressed by the suggestion, and that a contract had been entered into between them, in that year, for the writing of such a play,—several drafts of which, bearing different titles ("The Princess of the Wire," "The Machine," "1035, Plaza," etc.), were made before the final one was put into rehearsal. It also was established that Mr. De Mille had read his play to friends,—among them Professor John Erskine, of Columbia University,—in 1908.

Belasco corroborated Mr. De Mille; specified that he had instructed Mr. Stillman "to be kind to aspiring dramatists," which fact he surmised "might account for the courteous tone of his note to" Goldknopf; testified that he had never seen the manuscript of "Tainted Philanthrophy" prior to July 31, 1912, and had *not even heard of it* until the suit was started. Then, becoming exasperated, he exclaimed: "I am heartily sick of being sued by nurserymaids, waiters, and barbers every time I bring out a new piece, and I should like very much to give a performance of both these plays before your Honor, in the fall." To this startling proposal Judge Holt assented, remarking that he could doubtless have the merits of the case better placed before him by witnessing both the plays in representation than by merely reading them,—adding: "But it will be be very expensive for you to have the case decided in this way, will it not?" To this inquiry Belasco replied: "Yes, sir; it will cost me about $5,000, but I want to show these unknown authors, once and for all, that they cannot come into the courts and attack every successful production I make without submitting their plays to a comparison that will dispose of their claims very quickly." On Belasco engaging himself to provide as good a cast for "Tainted Philanthropy" as that with which he was presenting "The Woman," his proposal was accepted by counsel for Goldknopf.

The comparative performances were given, November 26, at the Belasco Theatre, in the presence of Judge Holt and invited audiences—Belasco desiring that as many journalists and members of his own profession as possible might see for themselves the shameful injustice to which he was subjected by the charge of plagiarism. "The Woman," which was then filling an engagement at the Grand Opera House, New York, was acted first, beginning at eleven o'clock in the morning. After an interval of an hour "Tainted Philanthropy" was presented, "exactly as written,"—manuscript copies of both plays having been submitted to the court in order to make impossible any dispute on grounds of alleged changes during representation. The Goldknopf fabrication proved to be the veriest farrago of impalliable trash,—and, as it was performed with absolute sincerity by conscientious and capable actors, it became ludicrous in the extreme. On November 29, Judge Holt rendered his decision, finding, necessarily, that there is *no plagiarism* from

"Tainted Philanthropy" in "The Woman." The chief parts in the former were cast thus:

Mrs. Elizabeth Dalton	Teresa Maxwell-Conover.
Grace Dalton	Helen Freeman.
Theodore Thompson	Milton Sills.
Jack Bud	Joseph Kilgour.
John Watts	Albert Bruning.
Harold Dalton	Eugene O'Brien.
A Bellevue Doctor	Harry C. Browne.
Attendants	{ James Grove. Mark Powers.
Servant	Judith Snaith.

The following letter on the subject of the Gold-knopf accusations gave Belasco much satisfaction:

(*The Society of American Dramatists and Composers to David Belasco.*)

"New York, November 27, 1912.

"Dear Mr. Belasco:—

"At a special meeting of the Board of Directors of The Society of American Dramatists, held immediately after witnessing the performances of 'The Woman' and 'Tainted Philanthropy,' a resolution was passed congratulating and thanking you for your splendid work in behalf of the dramatists of America in having called the attention of the public and the press to the efforts of irresponsible writers and lawyers against authors and producers of successful plays. We are of the opinion that these 'strike' suits, having no basis or ground for legal action, are a great hardship to the professional dramatist, and [that] the attention of the Bar Association should be called to this particular suit as an aggravated instance of sharp practice and unwarranted attack on the dramatist's name and pocket.

"Yours most sincerely,

"CHARLES KLEIN,

"Secretary."

In his decision Judge Holt said:

"This suit is to restrain the [alleged] infringement of a copyright. . . . Both pieces have been presented by experienced and skilful actors, with excellent scenery and stage appointments. I have carefully read the manuscripts of each play and have seen the representations of them. . . . In my opinion the proof *wholly fails* to establish the charge. There is *nothing* to prove, *or to suggest,* such a comparison of the two plays—that 'The Woman' was copied from 'Tainted Philanthropy,' or that any part of the one was taken from any part of the other. There is *nothing* to indicate that either the words, the ideas, or the plot of the defendant's play were suggested by complainant's play. The two plays, in my opinion, are wholly dissimilar, and I see *no ground whatever* for the charge that one infringed the copyright of the other in any particular. There should be a decree for the defendants, dismissing the bill on the merits, with costs."

Final judgment to that effect was entered March 3, 1913. Belasco's unique demonstration of the shameful injustice of the Goldknopf charge, however, cost him $5,700. Writing on the subject of this suit and of the performances offered in evidence in it, he has said:

"A lawsuit charging plagiarism is an expensive affair, even though the accused manager may win. Because of this, a compromise is frequently effected. There are many unscrupulous people who make a business of submitting impossible manuscripts in order to bring suits when a successful play is produced. Others keep long lists of registered titles, with the same idea in mind. Thousands of dollars have been paid by American authors and producers to end these blackmail suits, because they are more cheaply settled out of court. I have never yielded to this swindle,— and I never will. . . . My actors played 'Tainted Philanthropy' beautifully, and I gave it a dignified setting. It was a case of 'Look here, upon this picture, and on this!' The audience laughed at 'Tainted Philanthropy' until the theatre echoed. . . . I think it was the first instance in the history of American jurisprudence when a judge adjourned court to go to the theatre for the day, as a matter of legal duty. . . .

"As a result of this wretched, contemptible suit, and others like it, I discontinued my Play Bureau, which I had established several years previously to encourage young American dramatic authors. I have produced more plays by such authors than any two other managers, and I wanted to help them further. My Bureau cost me from $15,000 to $20,000 a year to maintain and never paid me a cent, though sometimes as many as 100 plays were received through it in a single day. When I realized that instead of helping young authors it was merely helping blackmailers to attack me as a plagiarist, I closed it up."

A DRAMA OF PSYCHOLOGY.—"THE CASE OF BECKY."

Belasco produced "The Case of Becky" for the first time, October 30, 1911, at the New National Theatre, Washington, D. C., but it was not until October 1, 1912, that, at the Belasco Theatre, the piece was first made known in the metropolis. It is a psychological "study," in dramatic form, based on a play by Edward Locke, entitled "After Many Years." Locke (who entered Belasco's employment to study stage management and who for a time acted a small part in "The Music Master") read his play to Belasco,—who, perceiving in it possibilities of novel and striking dramatic effect, at once accepted it, with the understanding that it should be rewritten under his supervision. That stipulation was agreed to and partially fulfilled,—the rewriting being (as in a great many other similar instances) done largely by Belasco. The members of the company which eventually acted in the drama could conclusively testify to this fact, since much of that labor was performed in their presence, at rehearsals.

The name finally bestowed upon this piece is "The Case of Becky." It is in three acts, requires only two scenic settings, implicates seven persons, and is an ingenious and interesting play on a painful but important subject,—namely, disease or disorder affecting human personality. The chief characters in it are *Dr. Emerson,* an eminent physician who employs hypnotism in psychiatry; *Professor Balzamo,* an itinerant and unscrupulous hypnotist of extraordinary power, and a girl named *Dorothy.* This girl is the victim of a dreadful metempsychosis and is often mysteriously changed from her normal, lovable personality,—in which she is sweet-tempered, affectionate, gentle, and refined,—into a common, mischievous, vindictive hoyden who is designated as *Becky. Dr. Emerson* is laboring to reëstablish her permanently in her normal consciousness by means of hypnotism,—an object which, ultimately, he attains. It is incidentally revealed that many years earlier *Balzamo,* exercising his hypnotic faculty, has compelled *Emerson's* wife to leave her husband and travel with him, as a subject for use in brutal and degrading exhibitions of hypnotism. While in that helpless bondage the daughter, *Dorothy,* has been born (her psychic disorder being attributable to the prenatal effect of abuse of her mother)' and the miserable woman has died. Chance has installed *Dorothy* as a patient in the home of her father, who, while ministering to her in affliction, does not know her

FRANCES STARR AS *BECKY*, IN "THE CASE OF BECKY"

as his child. *Balzamo,* learning the whereabouts of the girl and desirous of recovering custody of her, in order to utilize her as a subject, visits *Emerson* and seeks to reëstablish his control over *Dorothy,* begun when she was a little child. The *Doctor* is led to suspect the originative facts in "the case of *Becky"* which are unknown to him; a conflict of wits and powers ensues between him and *Balzamo;* the latter is, by a trick, subdued and thrown into hypnosis,—in which state he is compelled to confess the truth and is then deprived of his hypnotic power.

Belasco, writing about this singular play—in which he presented Miss Frances Starr for more than two years—has recorded:

"I had begun work on the manuscript of my play for Miss Starr called 'Jennie' when I received a letter from Mr. Locke about 'After Many Years.' . . . It was rewritten and renamed 'The Case of Becky,' and in the writing of it we were guided by Dr. Morton Prince's 'The Dissociation of a Personality.' I felt that in a hypnotic study of this kind I must not resort to the broad theatricalism of 'Trilby' or 'Dr. Jekyll and Mr. Hyde.' I was dealing with a dual personality, and I gave Miss Starr the arduous task of slipping from innocence into viciousness, in the presence of an audience, without resorting to any outward trickery. Those hypnotic scenes were written while the company was rehearsing on the stage."

It is interesting to note that the method prescribed for Miss Starr by Belasco, in acting *Dorothy* and *Becky,* is the same which Henry Irving declared should be employed in acting *Jekyll* and *Hyde:* Irving bought the English dramatic rights to Stevenson's story about that dual character, intending to put his theory about impersonating it into practice, but he never did so.—This was the cast of "The Case of Becky":

Dr. Emerson	Albert Bruning.
Dr. Peters	Harry C. Browne.
John Arnold	Eugene O'Brien.
Professor Balzamo	Charles Dalton.
Thomas	John P. Brawn.
Miss Pettingill	Mary Lawton.
Dorothy ("*Becky*")	Frances Starr.

"I was as much surprised as I was delighted," said Belasco, "by the popular success of 'The Case of Becky,'—which was entirely unexpected." His delight was considerably moderated by the prompt appearance of a couple of discontented playwrighting amateurs, alleging plagiarism. Their names were Amelia Bachman and George L. McKay; they asserted that "The Case of Becky" was taken from a drama which they had written, called "Etelle"; their suit was brought in June,

1912; it was tried, May 13 and 14, 1913, before Judge Julius M. Mayer, in the United States Circuit Court, and it was decided against them, "upon the merits," on July 9. That decision was appealed, the appeal was argued before the United States Circuit Court of Appeals, April 6, 1914, and decision in favor of Belasco was affirmed. In rendering the original decision Judge Mayer said:

". . . The writing of the play by Mr. Locke was the natural outcome of his interest in themes dealing with hypnotic influence and multiple personality, and when he was attracted by 'How One Girl Lived Four Lives,' by John Corbin, and [by] Dr. Prince's book, he was at work on 'The Climax,' a play in which hypnotism or mental suggestion is the predominant feature.

"I am also satisfied, beyond any doubt, that Mr. Belasco never saw, read or heard of 'Etelle' prior to his acceptance of Locke's play and Miss Bachman testified that her play had its foundation in the idea suggested by John Corbin's article. That being so, and the facts found by me being as stated, it follows that complainants have no case. 'The Case of Becky' is, in substantial respects, different from 'Etelle.' . . . It is to be expected that two playwrights, working independently from a common source, may develop similarities in their plots, but 'The Case of Becky' displays the skill of the experienced playwright in a number of important particulars and details not found in 'Etelle.' "

"A GOOD LITTLE DEVIL."

"Children of an idle brain,
Begot of nothing but vain fantasy."

"A Good Little Devil" is a fairy fantasy, written in French by Mme. Edmond Rostand (using the pen name of Rosamonde Gerard) and her son Maurice Rostand. It was adapted to the American Stage by Austin Strong, and Belasco produced it, for the first time in this country, December 10, 1912, at the Broad Street Theatre, Philadelphia: January 8, 1913, it was acted in New York, at the Republic Theatre. An immense amount of space, first and last, has been filled in the American newspaper press with sentimental rhapsody about such fabrications as "Peter Pan," "The Blue Bird," and "A Good Little Devil." They are well enough in their way, but they possess nothing of authentic importance, whether literary, poetic, or dramatic, and the success gained by them is due solely to the interest of children and of those who enjoy the amusements of their children: "The sports of childhood satisfy the child."

In "A Good Little Devil" experiences are depicted of a Scotch orphan, a lad named *Charles MacLance,* who is abused by his aunt, a witch, *Mrs. MacMiche;* comforted and befriended by fairies;

loved by a little blind girl named *Juliet,* from whom he is separated; saved from evil beings (*Old Nick, Sr.,* and *Old Nick, Jr.*); and raised to high social rank, where he forgets the comrades of his boyhood and is about to wed unworthily, when he returns to the home of his aunt. There he is visited by the spirit of his youth; his better nature and his memory of olden times and friends are awakened, and he returns to the arms of his early love—whose sight has been restored by the fairies—declaring his intention to live the life of the affections.

The stage accoutrement in which Belasco presented this fabric of whimsical extravagance was so beautiful, so full of the poetic feeling and allurement conspicuously absent from the piece itself, that it gained and for some time held, and deserved to hold, popular favor: it was played at the Republic Theatre until May 3, 1913,—152 consecutive performances being given.

"A Good Little Devil" was presented with the following cast:

A Poet..............................Ernest Lawford.
Betsy................................Iva Merlin.
Mrs. MacMiche......................William Norris.
Charles MacLance, a Good Little Devil......Ernest Truex.
Old Nick, Sr.......................Edward Connelly.
Old Nick, Jr.......................Etienne Girardot.

Juliet.................................Mary Pickford.
Marian...............................Laura Grant.
Queen Mab...........................Wilda Bennett.
Viviane..............................Edna Griffin.
Morganie.............................Lillian Gish.
Titania..............................Claire Burke.
Dewbright...........................Reggie Wallace.
Thought-From-Afar..............Georgia Mae Fursman.
Jock.................................Louis Esposit.
Wally...............................Gerard Gardner.
Mac.................................Adrian Morgan.
Tam................................Jerome Fernandez.
Sandy...............................Edward Dolly.
Allan...............................Norman Taurog.
Neil................................Harold Meyer.
Jamie..............................Carlton Riggs.
Davie..............................David Ross.
Robert.............................Roland Wallace.
John...............................Charles Castner.
Angus..............................Lauren Pullman.
Huggermunk........................Pat Walshe.
Muggerhunk........................Sam Goldstein.
The Solicitor from London..............Dennis Cleugh.
The Doctor from Inverary............Joseph A. Wilkes.
The Lawyer from Oban.................Robert Vivian.
Rab, the dog........................Arthur Hill.

"THE SECRET."

"A secret and villanous contriver."

"When I produced 'The Secret,'" writes Belasco, in a biographical note made for me, "I was told by most of the writers for the [news]papers, and by many friends, that the principal character in it, *Gabrielle,* is untrue to life—is *impossible!* Well, all I have to say is:—It is *not* impossible. She is very exceptional, no doubt, and morbid; but she is *true* to life and I know it, because I have seen and known and had to deal with exactly such women as *Gabrielle.* They are unpleasant, of course,—but they are real, a part of the Comedy of Human Life that I have aimed to show in the Theatre, and that is the reason I produced 'The Secret,' notwithstanding much advice against it. I did not expect financial success."

When Belasco first heard of "The Secret,"— which, written in French by Henri Bernstein, was originally produced, in March, 1913, at the Théâtre Bouffes-Parisiens, in Paris, with Mme. Simone (Mme. Simone Le Bargy) in the principal part,— Charles Frohman had just relinquished the right of producing it in America. He was so much impressed by the published accounts of the plot and of the performance that he went to Paris (sailing, June 18, 1913, on the Campania, *via* Fishguard) to see it, and there, after witnessing several representations of the drama, he personally arranged with its author for an 'American produc-tion. "Bernstein," he writes, "wanted me to have

Mme. Simone act *Gabrielle* in America; but, although she is a fine actress and gave a good performance, she did not, in my opinion, make the part credible. I could see nobody for it but little Miss Starr—and Bernstein waived his wishes and left everything to me. I knew from the first that it was impossible to make money with the piece in America; but I was determined to do it, and I did; and I am content, though it cost me $57,000 in order to show the American public a perfect piece of modern playwriting and (as I think) acting."

The qualities in Bernstein's "The Secret" which won Belasco's profound admiration are its technical constructive deftness and its cumulative theatrical effectiveness. While repellent in subject, it is, for stage purposes, extraordinarily well made. The principal character in it is *Gabrielle Jannelot,* a wife, young, accomplished, beautiful, admired, and loved,—apparently a paragon of feminine excellence; in fact, a personification of malignant jealousy and malicious envy. This charming female, blessed with everything that should make her contented, cannot endure the sight of the happiness of others and, while cloaking her wickedness with an assumption of generosity, gentleness, and goodness which for years completely deceives her husband and her

BELASCO, ABOUT 1914

friends, she industriously spreads misery all about
her. She has contrived to establish bitter estrangement between her devoted husband and a dearly
loved and loving sister; and, ascertaining that
another sister-in-law, *Henriette Durand*,—who is
her closest friend and who has confided in her,—is
beloved by a high-principled, jealous young man,
Denis Le Guern, she schemes to wreck their prospective happiness. The fair *Henriette* (whose
amorous receptivity appears to be comprehensive)
has secretly been the mistress of a profligate man
of fashion, named *Charlie Ponta-Tulli*, to whom
she would have been wedded had not *Gabrielle*
surreptitiously suppressed missives passing between
them and thus caused their intrigue to be ended.
Aware of *Guern's* jealous disposition and strong
preference for early vegetables, *Gabrielle* counsels
Henriette, when he shall formally propose marriage
to her, to make a full confession to him of her
relation to *Ponta-Tulli*,—being confident that *Guern*
will then withdraw his proposal. This advice *Henriette* promises to act upon; but, through fear, she
fails to do so, and presently she and *Guern* are
wedded and for a while dwell in bliss. *Gabrielle*,
unable to endure the spectacle of their felicity, plans
to destroy it by contriving to have all the persons
implicated in the action assembled as guests in

a country residence, thus bringing the new-wedded couple into close contact with the ardent though alienated *Ponta-Tulli*. There the former lover protests to the distressed *Henriette* his unchangeable passion, and there they are surprised together by the suspicious *Guern* in the moment when *Tulli* is demanding her reasons for having broken with him. A violent wrangle ensues, during which *Gabrielle*, under pretence of attempting reconciliation, neatly manages to make known the former illicit relation of *Tulli* and *Henriette* to the latter's husband. In the passages of bitter recrimination which follow *Tulli* at last establishes the fact that he had not wilfully abandoned the charming *Henriette*, and then (with remarkable dramatic dexterity) the spiteful treachery of *Gabrielle* is little by little elicited and "the secret" of that vicious and contemptible little mischief-maker is finally revealed when she is forced to confess to her wretched husband all her years of wicked intrigue and perverse malice. There, dramatically, the play ends,—where so much of human experience ends, in heartbroken misery and despair. A superfluous "tag" is, however, provided in which *Jannelot* first induces *Guern* to forgive *Henriette* and then himself casts the mantle of indulgence over the sins of *Gabrielle*— the fervid *Ponta-Tulli* being left to recede into the dim perspective of Paris, there to comfort himself as best he may.

The performance of this painful play was, in the main, excellent, Miss Marguerite Leslie acting the errant *Henriette* with deep and sympathetic feeling, and Miss Starr, as *Gabrielle,* giving perhaps the most completely finished and artistic performance of her career,—because definite and intelligible in ideal, sustained, fluent, precise in expression, and entirely plausible in effect. Mr. Frank Reicher appeared as the excitable and jealous *Guern* and provided a significant exhibition of the radically artificial, insincere, and finical method so common to the Continental European Stage and so much admired and commended in America for the reason, apparently, that it is European.—"The Secret" was exquisitely set upon the stage, in scenery designed by Ernest Gros, and was presented by Belasco with the following cast:

Constant Jannelot..........................Basil Gill.
Charlie Ponta-Tulli..................Robert Warwick.
Denis Le Guern.........................Frank Reicher.
Joseph..................................John P. Brawn.
Gabrielle Jannelot....................Frances Starr.
Henriette Durand..................Marguerite Leslie.
Clotilde DeSavageat..........Harriet Otis Dellenbaugh.
Marie.............................Beatrice Reinhardt.

"MARIE-ODILE."

[Of all the productions which he has made, excepting only that of "Madame Butterfly," Belasco feels most pride in that of Edward Knoblauch's play entitled "Marie-Odile,"—a work esteemed by him to be one of great artistic excellence and beauty. It was brought out in Washington, January 18, and at the Belasco Theatre, New York, January 26, 1915. Through a series of mischances it happened that neither my father nor I saw that production. Therefore, as critical consideration of it should not be omitted from this Memoir, I here copy, from "The New York Evening Post," the review of the representation written by my father's old friend and co-worker John Ranken Towse, now the most experienced and authoritative writer on the drama connected with the New York press.—J. W.]

"The 'Marie-Odile' of Edward Knoblauch, which was presented for the first time in the Belasco Theatre last evening, is in many respects a remarkable play, which would have been still more noteworthy if it did not slip now and then below the highest level of its ideal. For the most part, it is sweet, idyllic romance, with an undercurrent of satirical symbolism and a tincture of somewhat perilous philosophy, and it is told with delicacy and imagination, except for occasional touches of rougher realism, which are unnecessary and inartistic, and have a harsh and jarring effect in a rarefied and sentimental atmosphere. The object of them —one of contrast—is obvious and legitimate, but it might have been attained by less violent methods.

"On the surface, at first, the tale is one for the nursery, but beneath is deep and earnest purpose, the enforcement of the distinction between the essential goodness of loving and unselfish innocence, delighting in service, and the hard and cruel Pharisaism of a narrow, egoistic bigotry. Presently the parable illustrates the savagery which perfect innocence may experience at the hands of arrogant and sophisticated virtue. But a brief outline will most clearly show the motive of Mr. Knoblauch's story. The scene is laid in a convent in France, during the Franco-German conflict of 1870. *Marie-Odile*, the embodiment of childish innocence, is virtually the servant of the sisterhood. As an infant she had been found on the door-step. Now she is serving her novitiate and doing the domestic work, until ready for the final vows. She is a bright, affectionate, devout, and indefatigable little creature, who has never been outside the convent walls, has never seen a man—except an old priest and a decrepit, half-witted gardener—and is absolutely ignorant of the world and the ways of life. She has been taught that babies are the rewards which kindly angels bring from heaven to deserving mothers. By the *Mother Superior*, a martinet and zealot, she is persistently bullied. Even her tenderness for her pet pigeon is accounted a mortal sin, and, by way of spiritual discipline, she is ordered to tell the gardener to kill it for the *Mother Superior's* table. At this she revolts. Sooner than obey she hides herself, and is not to be found when the terrible news arrives that the French have been hopelessly beaten, and that the *Uhlans* are at the convent door. The priests and the nuns flee and *Marie-Odile* and the old gardener are left behind alone. Soon the first German, a handsome young corporal, arrives, and *Marie-Odile*, who has never seen a male figure of such splendor before, concludes that he is Saint Michael—the convent's patron saint—and kneels to him in rapturous worship. Other soldiers come in, led by a rough sergeant, and are disposed to take liberties, but are promptly disarmed by her fearlessness, her simplicity, and her transparent innocence. They even affect to respect the laws of the *Mother Superior*, which she quotes as paramount. She feeds them, presides at their table, and holds them in subjection—all but one or two—by magic of the ignorance that knows no wrong. The corporal champions her against the advances of his more brutal fellows, and to him she appeals with the confidence of a child. When the troops depart the sergeant, learning that the corporal has never had a love affair of any kind, purposely leaves him behind, bidding him take advantage of his manifest opportunity.

The *Corporal*, who is not vicious, is so moved by *Marie-Odile's* unsuspecting confidence that he resolves not to molest her, but she begs him so earnestly to remain, and so willingly lets him kiss her, that he yields to temptation, and the curtain falls upon the second act as she reposes happily in his arms. The scene is natural and charming, and the sentiment that of pure, youthful romance. In the third and last act, after the lapse of a year, the convent has another tenant. *Marie-Odile* and the old gardener are no longer alone. There is an infant, which *Marie-Odile* accounts for as a miraculous gift from Heaven. She is conscious of no ill, has followed unhesitatingly the promptings of nature, and rejoices in her new possession with boundless exultation. But now the war is over and the nuns are returning. *Sister Louise*, the personification of true Christian charity, is the first to enter, and sorely afflicted is she as she listens to *Marie-Odile's* grateful pæans, and thinks of what the *Mother Superior* will say. That austere judge is inflexible from the first. Straightway she orders the amazed but unrepentant young mother from the sacred precincts, in spite of the protests of *Sister Louise,* who declares that the true responsibility lay with the sisterhood which had failed to instruct or guard innocence.

"Simple as the play is in external form, it deals with more than one difficult and complex problem. Concerning the particular instance of the heroine—who becomes in Mr. Knoblauch's sketch a fresh and delightful ideal of ignorant and untainted innocence—there need be no question. Like *Haidée,* she flew to her love like a young bird. She was guiltless, and her story—with the exceptions hinted at— is told very prettily, with an unaffected naturalism which is rare, and with many charming little poetic interludes. Her love episode is handled with notable tact and fancy, and is an eloquent plea for the sanctity of nature's own laws. But obviously it is less ingenuous than *Marie-Odile* in its wilful disregard of certain awkward and wholly incontrovertible facts. The Pharisaism of the *Mother Superior* is, of course, utterly indefensible upon any count, but may be set down partly to the credit of poetic license. Unfortunately, the innocence of love is not, in the present state of this imperfect world, sufficient to exempt it from the material penalties of unrestricted freedom. And the instruction of ignorance is not altogether so simple a matter as some of our younger social philosophers seem to suppose.

"But in 'Marie-Odile' Mr. Knoblauch has produced a work of superior calibre, and has acquitted himself of a difficult task with ingenuity and tact. His first act is too much overladen with (dramatically) trifling details, but the piece acquires strength and impetus as it proceeds. *Marie-Odile* is one of the most credible examples of complete unsophistication that has been put upon the stage for a long time, and she is admirably impersonated by Miss Frances Starr. The part does not, it is true, present many difficulties, but most actresses would have betrayed in it a self-consciousness of the superfine quality of the innocence which they were portraying, and this Miss Starr did not do. She did really suggest the purity of a completely isolated maidenhood. Her completely natural maternal exultation in the possession of a baby was really excellent acting. Harriet Otis Dellenbaugh showed warm womanly feeling as the kindly *Sister Louise*, Jerome Patrick did very well as the *Corporal*, and Frank Reicher furnished a clever character bit as the senile old gardener. The setting in the convent was perfect—a notable specimen of Mr. Belasco's handiwork."

This was the cast of "Marie-Odile":

Mother Saint Dominic, Mother Superior of the
    Convent.........................Marie Wainwright.
Sister Clotilde............................Ada C. Nevil.
Sister Louise.................Harriet Otis Dellenbaugh.
Sister Monica.........................Alice Martin.
Sister Anatole.........................Sally Williams.
Sister Angela..........................Mildred Dean.
Sister Cecilia......................Amy Fitzpatrick.
Sister Joseph...........................Mary Green.
Sister Elizabeth......................Nona Murray.
Sister Catherine.......................Alice Carroll.
Marie-Odile, a novice...................Frances Starr.

FRANCES STARR AS *MARIE ODILE*

Father Fisher		....Edward Donnelly.
Peter		....Frank Reicher.
Sergeant Otto Beck..	Uhlans in a Prussian Regiment.	......Henry Vogel.
Corp. Philip Meissner.		....Jerome Patrick.
Steinhauser		......Paul Stanley.
Hartmann		....Alphonse Ethier.
Horn		.Edward Waldmann.
Mittendorf		Charles W. Kaufman.
Schramm		.....Robert Robson.
Sisters		..Margaret Cadman.
		........Edith King.
		....Dorothy Turner.
		...Edythe Maynard.
		.Madeleine Marshall.
		...Gertrude Wagner.
Soldiers		Hugo Schmedes.
		August Nelson.
		...Albert Mack.

RECONCILIATION WITH CHARLES FROHMAN—AND JOINT
PRESENTMENT OF "A CELEBRATED CASE."

The antagonism of Belasco and the Theatrical
Syndicate, which he fought for so many years, naturally led to friction between him and Charles
Frohman,—a person of extraordinary self-conceit,
who loved to have applied to himself the ridiculous
designation of "the Napoleon of the Theatre"; who
aspired to be thought the greatest of theatrical managers, and who, necessarily, felt himself rebuked
under the superior talents of the man with whom,
in early years, he had been so closely associated and

who had done so much to make his career possible. In 1903 he had a personal quarrel with Belasco (about what I do not know), and for twelve years thereafter they were more or less actively at enmity and treated each other as strangers. Frohman, however, appears to have possessed engaging qualities, which endeared him to many of those who knew him well. Belasco, for example, has assured me that through all the time of their estrangement he "cherished a great affection for 'Charlie,'" and that he is "grateful beyond words that our misunderstanding was cleared up and our friendship renewed before he sailed away to his death." Frohman left New York on board the steamship Lusitania, May 1, 1915, and he lost his life, May 7, when, to the eternal infamy of the German nation, that vessel was sunk off Old Head of Kinsale, Ireland. "I was alone in my studio, one evening early in 1915," Belasco has told me, "and by chance I noticed a newspaper paragraph about Charles Frohman being ill, at the Hotel Knickerbocker. It set me thinking about our first meeting so long ago in San Francisco, and of all that followed; of our first venture in Chicago and of all the years when we worked together and had rooms side by side, when 'Charlie' used to consult me about everything and I used to read my 'May Blossom' to him. As I sat there thinking it all over I realized that the shadows were beginning to slant toward the east—and suddenly I decided that if 'Charlie' should die without our being reconciled it should not be my fault. I started to write a little note to him but got no further than 'Dear Charlie' when my telephone-bell rang. The caller was Roeder—and the first thing he said was: 'I've just had a telephone message from Charles Frohman. He wants to see you'! We met that night, in his rooms, and forgot that we ever had a disagreement."

Soon after that reconciliation Belasco held a little festival in honor of Frohman, in his theatre-studio, and there, at first in jest, it was proposed that they should make a joint revival of some notably successful play of earlier days. This proposal led to a serious discussion and eventually to an agreement whereby the two managers covenanted to make a joint production every season during a term of years. At Frohman's request Belasco agreed to choose the first play to be presented by them, and his election fell upon "A Celebrated Case."

That play (first produced in America at the Union Square Theatre, New York, January 23, 1878) is a melodrama in six acts, translated, in rough English, from the French of Adolphe D'Ennery (1811-1899) and Eugène Cormon (18—-

18—). It presents the image of a murder which was done in France, on the eve of the Battle of Fontenoy (May 11, 1745), and for which an innocent man was made to suffer years of cruel punishment, till, at last, in a mysterious and circuitous way, it was brought home to its perpetrator. The circumstances of the crime are peculiarly hideous and the circumstances of the belated retribution are peculiarly complex. The innocent man, *Jean Renaud,* is condemned, for the murder of his wife, on the testimony of their child. *Lazare,* the guilty man (as in many other fictions on this antiquated pattern), assumes the identity of another person connected with the crime, the *Count de Mornay,* and, after various escapes from exposure and much suspense, he is baffled in his maintenance of the assumed identity and is brought to justice. The parting of the condemned father with his innocent, prattling child, who has unconsciously convicted him of murder, and their meeting in after years, he a wretched galley-slave and she a young woman, afford a poignantly affecting contrast. Adroit use, likewise, is made of a certain singular jewel as the instrument for discovery of the actual criminal. Although there are no remarkable characters in the piece and nothing extraordinary in its dialogue, it possesses substantial dramatic merit in its occasional scenes of acute agony, relieved by the violent action of natures taxed beyond endurance. Its sentiment, moreover,—that of filial affection,—is pure; and in its complication of the lives and the emotional troubles of two young girls it deals skilfully and tenderly with difficult and lovely themes. Its choice by Belasco (who had several times directed performances of it in the days of his youth and in whom predilection for tense situation and sharp effect is dominant) was a natural one. Affiliated with Frohman, he presented it in a slightly revised form— some of its dialogue being a little "modernized"— but substantially unaltered and in picturesque and rich dress. It was well acted and kindly received. The first performance of this Belasco-Frohman revival occurred at the Hollis Street Theatre, Boston, March 28, 1915, and, April 7, they brought it out at the Empire Theatre, New York. This was the cast:

Count d'Aubeterre................Frederic de Belleville.
Lazare ⎫
Count de Mornay ⎭ ....Robert Warwick.
Chanoinesse........................Elita Proctor Otis.
Viscount Raoul de Mornay..............Eugene O'Brien.
Jean Renaud...........................Otis Skinner.
Dennis O'Rourke.....................N. C. Goodwin.
Corporal............................Walter F. Scott.
Seneschal............................George Allison.

Captain.............................John Warnick.
Duchess d'Aubeterre...............Minna Gale Haynes.
Little Adrienne.........................Mimi Yvonne.
Martha........................Beverly Sitgreaves.
Julia...................................Ruth Farnum.
Madeleine Renaud.........................Helen Ware.
Adrienne Renaud......................Ann Murdock.
Annette..............................Esther Cornell.
Valentine de Mornay...................Florence Reed.
Julie....................................Marie Sasse.

LENORE ULRIC—AND "THE HEART OF WETONA."

Many players of talent and present eminence
have been fostered and developed under Belasco's
management—that being, indeed, one of his most
important services to our Stage. He is an inveterate theatre-goer,—attending performances everywhere and, sooner or later, seeing practically everything and everybody visible on the American Stage.
This customary vigilant observance of all activity
within his profession he facetiously describes as "my
fishing trips," and, conversing with me on the subject, he has remarked: "It is often a long time
between 'bites,' but one of the delights of the sport
is that you never know, as the curtain goes up, how
soon you may 'hook a big one.' Among the biggest
I have ever landed is, I believe, little Miss Ulric: I
think she will grow bigger every season she is before
the public."

Miss Lenore Ulric, to whom Belasco thus referred, was born at New Ulm, Minnesota, July 21, 189—. In childhood she knew the meaning of hardship, and she has studied and learned in the often harsh school of experience. Whether or not she will fulfil Belasco's high expectation time alone can tell, but one thing about her is certain: she belongs to a class of which there is urgent need on our Stage,—she is "a born actress." She resorted to the dramatic calling not through mere vanity, the impulse of personal exhibition, or the acquisitive hope of profit, —motives which actuate a majority of the young women who go upon the Stage,—but because her natural vocation is acting. As far as known, no precedent member of her family was ever associated with the Theatre, and for some time her choice of that calling met with severe paternal disapproval. Her novitiate was served in various stock companies in Milwaukee, Grand Rapids, Chicago, and Syracuse. In August, 1913, Miss Ulric appeared as *Luana,* in "The Bird of Paradise," under the management of Mr. Oliver Morosco: she acted that part for two seasons. In 1914, while playing at the Standard Theatre, New York, she wrote to Belasco asking him to witness her performance of that part and expressing the hope that after having done so he might find a place for her in some one of his companies. "I have

long made it a rule," writes Belasco, "to comply
with such requests from young players whenever it
is possible for me to do so. I well remember how
long *I* pleaded with dear John McCullough for a
hearing before I got it and I know the discourage-
ment of 'hope deferred.' Besides—nobody can make
a fairer proposition than 'watch my work and, if you
think it is good, engage me.' But I was extremely
busy when I received Miss Ulric's request and
couldn't give the time,—so I sent my secretary,
Mr. Curry. His report was so favorable that I felt
I must see her at work—so, since I could not go
to her, I had Mr. Roeder bring her to me by making her a tentative offer of an engagement to act in
George Scarborough's play of 'The Girl.' She
accepted, of course (she has told me, since, that she
had set her heart on getting with me and would
have accepted almost any offer to do so), and I
had my stage manager call a rehearsal. I was not
supposed to attend,—but I slipped into the gallery
unknown to anybody (a little trick I have) and
watched her carefully. After twenty minutes I
knew I was watching a very talented and unusual
young woman—one who with opportunity and
proper training might do great things. Before the
rehearsal was over I had told Roeder to close the
arrangement with her to play the leading part in

'The Girl,' which, afterward, became 'The Heart of Wetona.' "

In its original form the scene of that play was "A Middle Western Town" (Missouri), its five characters were Caucasian, and its story was one of erring love, deceit, shame, and rescue set in a commonplace rural environment,—a main purpose of its author being, presumably, to exhibit a group of conventional persons impelled by violent passion yet restrained by religious feeling. In that form it received a trial presentment, June 28, 1915, at Atlantic City, New Jersey, with this cast:

In the Prologue.

David Greer....................William H. Thompson.
Elizabeth Greer.........................Lenore Ulric.

In the Play.

Jonathan Wells, D.D....................Arthur Lewis.
Anthony Wells.......................Lowell Sherman.
The Rev. Frederick Forbes..............John Miltern.
Elizabeth Greer........................Lenore Ulric.
David Greer....................William H. Thompson.

"Although its material was undeniably good, I had felt strong doubts about the piece, from the first, but I gave it a 'try-out,' anyway," said Belasco. "Then I saw that it would not do as it stood and took it off, and, at my suggestion and under my supervision, with such assistance as I could give, Mr. Scarborough rewrote 'The Girl' and eventually we had a real success with it."

The rewritten play was first acted, January 20, 1916, at Stamford, Connecticut, under the title of "Oklahoma"; soon after it was called "The Heart of Wetona," and under that name it was brought forth, February 29, at the Lyceum Theatre, New York, where it held the stage until May 20.

In its definitive form the scene of "The Heart of Wetona" is an Indian Reservation, in the torrid State of Oklahoma; several of its persons are aborigines of the Comanche tribe, and,—though its action and incidents are sometimes arbitrarily directed,—it is a remarkably good melodrama of a long-familiar kind. Belasco's purpose in directing the revision was to provide an effective play for the exploitation of the young actress whose talents had so favorably impressed him, and that purpose was well accomplished,—the interest centring continuously in the principal female part, a girl named *Wetona,* the child of a Comanche chieftain and a white mother, deceased. This girl, who has been seduced under a lying promise of marriage by *Anthony Wells,* a visitor to the Indian Reservation, is chosen as a sort of vestal virgin in ceremonial rites of the Comanches, and thereupon, in the

Tribal House, before her father and his assembled warriors, though concealing her lover's identity, she confesses her transgression. The girl is then subjected to a harrowing inquisition by the Indians, who desire to find and slay her lover. At last, unable to endure longer, she agrees to reveal his name on condition that she first be permitted to warn him of his danger. She seeks him in the home of his friend *John Hardin,* the Indian Agent on the Reservation (who secretly loves the girl and desires to make her his wife), and is followed by her father, *Chief Quannah,* who, finding her in conference with *Hardin,* furiously accuses him of being the wronger of his daughter and demands that he instantly marry her—as an alternative to being instantly slain with her. To save the girl, himself, and her to him unknown lover, *Hardin* agrees to do so, privately assuring *Wetona* that the marriage shall be one in name but not in fact, and, a clergyman being conveniently accessible, the wedding is at once performed. Afterward *Wetona,* collapsing, calls upon the name of her *Anthony*— thus discovering to her husband her resolutely guarded secret. Later, *Wells,* ensconced in the home of *Hardin* and supposing himself unsuspected and secure, seeks to resume his relation with *Wetona,* but is repulsed by her until a divorce (to

which *Hardin* will connive) shall have been obtained
and he shall have fulfilled his promise of marriage.
Then the perfidy of *Wells* is revealed to *Wetona*
and she revolts from him; *Quannah* discovers the
truth; *Hardin,* though righteously wrathful against
Wells, tries to save him from the vengeance of the
Indians (providing him with weapons and a steed)
but fails,—that rascal being shot and killed as he
attempts to ride away in the night,—and the
injured, forlorn Indian girl humbly and thankfully
confesses to *Hardin* her contrition, her gratitude
for his protective generosity, the affection with
which he has inspired her, and her glad willingness
to remain with him as his wife.

The ethics of all this will hardly bear scrutiny—
but the dramatic effect of it in representation was
undeniable; and, perhaps, where virtue is, presumably, intended it is to consider too curiously to
consider further. Miss Ulric presented with vigor,
skill, simplicity, sustained continuity of identity,
and remarkable force a true, pathetic, and alluring
ideal of unsophisticated girlhood, confiding feminine
ardor and passionate distress, and she gained an
auspicious success.—The cast of "The Heart of
Wetona," as acted at the Lyceum under the management of Belasco and a corporation called
"Charles Frohman, Inc.," is appended:

LENORE ULRIC AS *WETONA*, IN "THE HEART OF
WETONA"

Quannah, Chief of the Comanches......William Courtleigh.
Wetona...............................Lenore Ulric.
John Hardin..........................John Miltern.
David Wells.........................Edward L. Snader.
Anthony Wells........................Lowell Sherman.
Mary Greer.........................Isabel O'Madigan.
Comanche Jack........................Curtis Cooksey.
Nauma...............................Ethel Benton.
Nipo................................H. G. Carleton.
Pasequa.............................Langdon West.
Eagle...............................Chief Deer.

VARIOUS PRODUCTIONS — MISCELLANEOUS RECORD:
"WHAT'S WRONG."—"THE VANISHING BRIDE."
—"THE LOVE THOUGHT."—"ALIAS."

During the last five years [that is, the five years preceding April, 1917] Belasco has made productions of various plays which do not require extended consideration, though they must be specified and briefly described in this Memoir in order to complete the record of his labors. Those plays are "The Governor's Lady," "Years of Discretion," "The Temperamental Journey," "What's Wrong," "The Man Inside," "The Vanishing Bride," "The Phantom Rival," "The Boomerang," "The Love Thought," "Seven Chances," "Alias," "The Little Lady in Blue," and "The Very Minute."

Of these, "What's Wrong," by Frederick Ballard; "The Love Thought," by Henry Irving Dodge;

"The Vanishing Bride," adapted by Sydney Rosenfeld from a German original called "Tantalus," by Leo Kastner and Ralph Tesmar; and "Alias" (based on a story by John A. Moroso and originally called "The Treadmill"), by Willard Mack, are plays to which Belasco gave trial productions, and all of which, except "The Vanishing Bride," he purposes to present in New York hereafter, when they have been smoothed and polished and are deemed by him to be ready for metropolitan presentment. "What's Wrong" was brought out at the National Theatre, Washington, D. C., May 4, 1914; "The Vanishing Bride" at Long Branch, New Jersey, July 27, the same year; "The Love Thought," at the Parsons Theatre, Hartford, Connecticut, April 26, 1915; and "Alias," first under its original title, at the Apollo Theatre, Atlantic City, May 8, 1916, then, February 5, 1917, at the Belasco Theatre, Washington. "The Vanishing Bride" would have been produced in New York soon after its trial had not Belasco found Mr. Rosenfeld (who is an industrious and moderately clever writer but flatulent with self-conceit) excessively fractious and troublesome to deal with. "I had spent $18,000 on that play," Belasco has told me, "and I know it could be made a success, because it has excellent material in it. But life is

too short for disputes with Mr. Sydney Rosenfeld.
I am always glad to do my best for the men and
women, writers or actors, who work with me, but
I am not willing to wrangle and fight with them
for the privilege of doing so! Therefore, I preferred to pocket my loss and let the piece go—with
my blessing and the hope that its adapter will find
a more satisfactory producer."

The casts of the trial productions enumerated
are here appended:

CAST OF "WHAT'S WRONG."

George H. Smith	Frederick Burton.
Perry Dodge	Richie Ling.
Eddie	William Dixon.
Woodrow	Percy Helton.
Heavy ⎫	Henry Weaver.
Bill ⎬ Farm hands	J. W. Kennedy.
Red ⎭	Russell Simpson.
Jennie Brown	Janet Beecher.
Mrs. Perry Dodge	Maidel Turner.
Mrs. Lee-Hugh, S.P.A.I.H.	Louise Sylvester.
Phoebe Snow	Dorothy Walters.
Flossie	Susanne Willa.
Agnes	Grace Vernon.
Tillie	Jane Shore.

CAST OF "THE VANISHING BRIDE."

Zachary Hollis	Thomas A. Wise.
Dick Hollis	Howard Estabrook.
Baron Von Berndorff	Gustav Von Seyffertitz.

Eric Von Berndorff....................Frank Gillmore.
Phelim O'Hara........................Denman Maley.
An Upholsterer.......................Conrad Cantzen.
A Postman............................Lee Metford.
Letty Von Berndorff..................Janet Beecher.
Eva, the bride.......................Ottola Nesmith.
Eileen O'Hara........................Angela Keir.
Mrs. Miller..........................Margaret Seddon.
Anna.................................Edith Houston.

CAST OF "THE LOVE THOUGHT."

Stephen Bennett......................Ramsey Wallace.
Howard Johnson.......................Lowell Sherman.
Squire Miley.........................George Gaston.
Jake Means...........................Hardee Kirkland.
Dupley Reed..........................Henry Forsman.
George Culligan......................Daniel Moyles.
Lew Bates............................George Berry.
Billy................................Edwin Dupont, Jr.
Anne Gardner.........................Janet Beecher.
Mary Miley...........................Isabel O'Madigan.
Frances Avery........................Katherine Proctor.
Nellie Avery.........................Antoinette Walker.
Mrs. Means...........................Harriet Ross.
Mrs. Bates...........................Lois Frances Clark.
Mrs. Culligan........................Elizabeth Hunt.

CAST OF "THE TREADMILL"—"ALIAS."

Herman Strauss, "Old Dutch"..........Willard Mack.
Warden John Healey...................Edwin Mordant.
"Biff" Schulte.......................Jay Wilson.
Dan Davis............................E. J. Mack.
Toby.................................Jack Jevne.
Mrs. John Weldon.....................Margaret Moreland.

Mrs. Franklyn Joyce..................Carmilla Crume.
Amanda Joyce...................Constance Molineaux.
Titheradge Joyce......................Francis Joyner.
Jacob Fralinger....................Arthur Donaldson.
John Weldon...........................William Boyd.
Oscar Spiegel..........................Gus Weinberg.
Mrs. Mary Gilligan................Annie Mack Berlein.
Dick................................Tammany Young.
Harry.................................Cornish Beck.
Greta..................................Ruth Collins.
Bertha.................................Jean Temple.
Andrews.............................Tex Charwate.

"THE GOVERNOR'S LADY."

Belasco produced "The Governor's Lady" for the
first time, May 1, 1912, at the Broad Street Theatre, Philadelphia, and, September 9, that year, at
the Republic, he brought it out in New York. It
is a drama of domestic dissension and tribulation
sequent on the surrender to selfishness and vanity of a
wilful man who is indicated as being, notwithstanding his faults and errors, innately kind and good.
The name of him is *Daniel S. Slade.* He has been
a miner and poor. Having acquired riches he has
become ambitious and aspires to social and political
eminence; would, in fact, be Governor of the State
of Colorado, wherein he dwells. *Mrs. Slade,* his
wife, is an exemplary but homely and home-keeping
person and she cannot adapt herself to the ways of

the rich and fashionable society in which *Slade* desires to be a leader. She is, at first, disposed to consider their newborn incompatibility and her husband's dissatisfaction as fanciful. But when *Slade* intimates that he regards her as a hindrance to his advancement and signifies that there had better be a formal separation, or a divorce, between them she is deeply wounded. She agrees, however, to separate from him, while indignantly repelling his suggestion that he obtain a divorce. Later she ascertains that he has chosen as her successor a young, beautiful, and unscrupulous woman who he believes will be useful in furthering his ambitions and who is willing to abandon the youth she loves in order to make a better match. *Mrs. Slade* then rounds on her discontented spouse and, being thrice armed in the justice of her quarrel, notwithstanding his wealth and influence, brings upon him and his prospective consort public odium, confronts and defeats him in court, and, bringing a counter suit, is granted a divorce from him. She leaves Denver and goes to New York,—where, two years later, *Slade,* who has meantime become Governor of Colorado, finds her in one of Child's restaurants. The *Governor* makes known to her that he is perceptive of the impropriety of his course; that in spite of his conduct he has always loved the wife who has divorced him, and proposes that they remarry. This *Mrs. Slade* declines to do, not, however, concealing the fact that she still cherishes affection for *Slade,* and the play ends with his picking her up and carrying her off in his arms, in quest of a parson, in order to establish her as the *Governor's Lady.*

Belasco described this fabric as "a play in three acts and an epilogue in Child's," and it was announced as having been written by Miss Alice Bradley. During its first performance in New York Mr. Emmett Corrigan (who impersonated the character of *Slade*) came before the curtain and, in a brief speech on behalf of Miss Bradley, made known that she disclaimed credit for anything more than "the central idea" of the play. Neither that "central idea" (the idea, presumably, of showing the patient acquiescence of *Mrs. Slade* suddenly turned into resolute and triumphant opposition by discovery of the full extent of her husband's baseness) nor anything else in the piece is dramatically precious or extraordinary. Many other "collaborators" with Belasco might, however, fairly emulate Miss Bradley's frankness. The construction of "The Governor's Lady" is sometimes arbitrary and the characters in it are in some respects extravagantly drawn—causing more the effect of rough sketches than that of finished portraits. The dialogue possesses the merit of suitability to the situations and, in general, of seeming to arise spontaneously from them. The notable excellence of the production was its exact fidelity to the surface details of everyday life and the really remarkable smoothness, harmony, and sincerity with which it was acted—imparting to much that was crude and improbable an aspect of veracity.—The play was cast as follows:

Daniel S. Slade......................Emmett Corrigan.
Senator Strickland..................William H. Tooker.
Robert Hayes...........................Milton Sills.
Wesley Merritt........................S. K. Walker.
Brigham Hunt............................Bert Hyde.
Ex-Governor Hibbard..................John A. Dewey.
Colonel George Smith................Will H. Nicholson.
John Hart...............................Albert Lane.
Charles Ingram......................Harry B. Wilson.
William...................................Jack Smith.
Martin...................................Frank Hand.
Jake..................................John N. Wheeler.
A Passerby............................James Singer.
A Bookworm...........................Stuart Walker.
Jake's Friend........................Edward Horton.
A Cashier..........................George H. Shelton.
A Man Behind the Pastry Counter.......Robert J. Lance.
Waiter No. 7.......................John H. McKenna.
Waiter No. 2........................Harrison Fowler.
Mary Slade..............................Emma Dunn.
Katherine Strickland..................Gladys Hanson.
Mrs. Wesley Merritt............Teresa Maxwell-Conover.
Susan....................................Jane Briggs.

A Girl of the Streets....................Eloise Murray.
A Scrubwoman.........................Judith Snaith.

"YEARS OF DISCRETION."

Satirical and amusing use has been made in various works of fiction of the old, or elderly, parent who behaves in an inappropriately youthful manner. Charles Mathews built the capital old farce (I wonder if anybody else ever recalls it now?) of "My Awful Dad!" around that idea: Collins utilized it when he sketched *Madame Pratolungo's* "Evergreen Papa." It is one of the expedients of comicality in "Years of Discretion," a farcical comedy by Frederick Hatton and Fanny Locke Hatton which Belasco presented, November 4, 1912, at the Empire Theatre, Syracuse, New York, and at the Belasco Theatre, New York, on December 12, following. In that entertaining play a buxom widow of fifty, *Mrs. Farrell Howard* by name, growing intolerably weary of a humdrum life, leaves the little rural town where she resides and repairs to New York,—where, with the aid of hair dye, tight lacing and a fashionable dressmaker, she puts on the semblance of a gay young woman and recklessly participates in frivolous dissipations, fascinating many ardent males and scandalizing her somewhat sedate and priggish son. At the last she consents to marry one of her numerous admirers, to whom she is honestly attached. After a little struggle with vanity and the fear of losing his regard she confesses to him that, with her, things are not what they seem; that she is not really a roguish young woman eager for social festivity, but rather an elderly one who has grown tired of it, who is inclined to be stout and is extremely uncomfortable by reason of restrictive stays and tight shoes. She is surprised and delighted when he, in turn, confesses to rheumatism, years equal to hers, and a strong preference for easy old slippers instead of dancing pumps. They then agree to abandon a projected honeymoon trip around the world, to which both of them have looked forward with dread, and to take their ease sensibly, in the home surroundings which they prefer.—This was the cast of "Years of Discretion":

Christopher Dallas	Lyn Harding.
Michael Doyle	Bruce McRae.
John Strong	Herbert Kelcey.
Amos Thomas	Robert McWade, Jr.
Farrell Howard, Jr.	Grant Mitchell.
Metz	E. M. Holland.
Mrs. Farrell Howard	Effie Shannon.
Mrs. Margaret Brinton	Alice Putnam.
Anna Merkel	Mabel Bunyea.
Lilly Newton	Ethel Pettit.
Bessie Newton	Myrtle Morrison.

"THE TEMPERAMENTAL JOURNEY."

Leo Ditrichstein adapted "The Temperamental Journey" from a French original called "Pour Vivre Heureux," by André Rivoire and Yves Mirande, and Belasco produced it, for the first time, at the Lyceum Theatre, Rochester, New York, August 28, 1913, and, September 4, following, for the first time in New York, at the Belasco Theatre. It is an unusually clever, sometimes humorous, sometimes bitterly satirical, farce blent with elements of comedy and constructed around the struggles and tribulations of a sincere, capable, "temperamental," and unappreciated painter named *Jacques Dupont,*—a part that was admirably acted (with discretion, humor, feeling, and even a touch of passion) by Mr. Ditrichstein. Notwithstanding the merit of his art *Dupont* is unable to sell his paintings. In a moment of despair, having been meanly upbraided for his ill-fortune by his wife,—a shallow, selfish hypocrite,—*Dupont* resolves to destroy himself. He writes a farewell letter to his wife, which he leaves with his clothes on the shore and, forgetful of the fact that he is a capital swimmer, flings himself into the waters of Long Island Sound to drown. The immersion so much refreshes him that he changes his mind about dying, swims lustily, and, being hauled on board of a sailing craft, makes a voyage to Halifax. Upon returning home a fortnight or so later he finds his hypocritical wife and friends, indulging to the full in "the luxury of woe," about to hold funeral services over a dead body which they receive as his; and, also, he finds that his paintings, previously the objects of contumely, are selling for high prices,—public interest having been inspired by the pathetic circumstances of his supposed suicide. After observing from an unsuspected coign of vantage in their home his hypocritical "widow's" ready acceptance of the embraces of one of his "friends," and after witnessing with ironic contempt the funeral over what are supposed to be his remains, *Dupont* betakes himself to Paris, where he paints many landscapes. After an interval of three years he returns to America, representing himself to be a collector of pictures, named *Lenoir,* who has gathered together a large number of paintings by the defunct *Dupont*—whose works now sell for enormous sums. He finds his "widow" married to his former "friend" and the mother of a child by him, and also he finds that person to be industriously engaged in forging paintings by *Dupont*. During an auction sale of his works *Dupont,* stung by manifestations of injustice, sordid meanness, and duplicity, declares his identity and rebukes those who have wronged and contemned him. Then, for the sake of the child, he agrees to arrange for a divorce from his unworthy wife,—signifying his purpose, in due course, to unite himself in matrimony to a loving young girl who has befriended him in his earlier afflictions and remained faithful to his memory while supposing him to be dead.

The opportunity for gibes and railings provided by the successive postures of circumstance thus indicated are obvious and many. Yet, at best, the comicality evoked by them is bitter and painful.— "The Temperamental Journey," which was much admired and exceptionally successful, was cast as follows:

Jacques Dupont		Leo Ditrichstein.
Prof. Babcock Roland		Henry Bergman.
Vernon Neil		Frank Connor.
Billy Shepherd		Richie Ling.
Dorval		Edouard Durand.
Howard Locke		Julian Little.
Carrington McLiss		Lee Millar.
Tamburri		M. Daniel Schatts.
Roy		Edwin R. Wolfe.
Max		Earle W. Grant.
Edna	*Prof. Roland's* Pupils.	Carree Clarke.
Eleanor		Anna McNaughton.
Marjorie		Dorothy Ellis.
Lina		Annette Tyler.
Messenger		William Dixon.

Delphine.............................Isabel Irving.
Maria..............................Josephine Victor.
Fanny Lamont.....................Cora Witherspoon.
Teresa.............................Gertrud Morisini.
Maid...............................Alice Jones.

A REVIVAL OF "THE AUCTIONEER."

An incident of the theatrical season of 1913-'14 which requires passing record here is the revival by Belasco of "The Auctioneer,"—a play which, in all essentials, was original with him and which for this revival he again revised, making it somewhat more closely-knit and effective than it was when first he brought forward David Warfield in it. "The Auctioneer" was acted at the Knickerbocker Theatre, New York, September 30, 1913, with the following cast:

Simon Levi..........................David Warfield.
Mrs. Levi.....................Mrs. Jennie Moscowitz.
Mrs. Eagan........................Marie Bates.
Callahan..........................Louis Hendricks.
Isaac Leavitt.....................Harry Lewellyn.
Mrs. Leavitt......................Helena Philips.
Meyer Cohen......................Harry Rogers.
Mrs. Cohen.......................Marie Reichardt.
Mo Fininski........................Frank Nelson.
Richard Eagan......................George LeGuere.
Minnie............................Charlotte Leslay.

Dawkins.............................Horace James.
Customer............................John A. Rice.
Helga..............................Janet Dunbar.
Miss Manning........................Frances Street.
Misses Crompton .... { Margaret Johnson.
{ ....Maud Roland.
Miss Finch..........................Ethel Marie Sasse.
Mrs. Smith, a shopper..............Geraldine de Rohan.
Policeman...........................George Berliner.
Chestnut Vendor.....................Tony Bevan.
Visitors................... { ....Watson White.
{ ....Douglas Farne.
{ ....Irving Laudeutscher.
{ Frank L. Van Vlissingen.
Man from Hester Street..............Michael Levine.
Newsboys .... { Meyer Howard.
{ ....Jess Kelly.

A MANIAC'S PLAY—"THE MAN INSIDE."

A singular yet characteristic incident of Belasco's career was his production of a play called "The Man Inside," written by a madman who had been the central figure in one of the most notorious murder cases in modern criminal annals,—Roland Burnham Molineux. That poor wretch is the son of a much respected citizen, General Edward Leslie Molineux, who gained rank and honorable distinction in the Union Army during the Civil War. He was arrested, February 7, 1899, charged with the murder of Mrs. Katherine J. Adams, who died, December

28, 1898, of poisoning by cyanide of mercury, which she unwittingly swallowed mixed with a medicine received through the mails and which it was alleged that Molineux had prepared and sent. His trial began, November 14, 1899, before Recorder (now Supreme Court Justice) John B. Goff and continued for fifty-five days, ending, January 7, 1900, with his conviction of murder in the first degree. On February 16 Recorder Goff sentenced Molineux to death and he was then taken to the Sing Sing Prison, where, for many months, he was incarcerated in the "Death House." His case was carried to the Court of Appeals and, October 15, 1901, he was granted a new trial which began, before Justice Lambert, in Part — of the Supreme Court, October 17, 1902, and ended, November 11, with his acquital,—an issue which, at the time, was regarded by some persons as a miscarriage of justice. The second jury which heard all the testimony, however, found him not guilty and he therefore stands vindicated. Mrs. Adams, meanwhile, certainly was murdered and the guilt of that crime has never been legally placed.

Throughout the ordeal of his trials, his condemnation, and his imprisonment under sentence of death Roland Molineux was sustained by the unwavering support of his devoted parents—his sturdy old father resolutely maintaining the son's innocence and laboring without remission to establish it. The younger man's health, however, was hopelessly undermined by the dreadful strain to which he was subjected and after his release he became ill and morose. In 1912 his parents obtained an introduction to Belasco and appealed to him for help. "His mother said to me," writes the manager, " 'My boy's life has been ruined. His health is gone—he has never been the same since he was released from prison. He has written a play which he believes will do great good and he has set his heart on getting it acted. If he is disappointed in this, on top of all the rest that he has suffered, we fear that he will die. If his play should be a success it might open a new life to him. Will you read it and help us, if you can?' They told me other things—dreadful and afflicting things some of them, that I need not repeat. I had been tremendously impressed by General Molineux's great fight for his son; I felt a great sympathy and pity for them— and I consented to read the young man's play and to do it, if I found it practicable.

"When the manuscript came to me I found the piece long and crude, but I saw possibilities in it and I told the parents I would produce it. Their gratitude was very touching. Soon afterward, I met young Molineux, gave him several interviews, and went to work to knock his play into shape. At the beginning everything seemed all right and he accepted my first cuts and suggestions in a proper spirit and worked hard. But toward the end, along about August or September [1913], when I put the piece into rehearsal and began to make extensive changes, he turned sullen and very ugly. Sometimes, instead of working, he would sit and roll his eyes or glare at me; and, what was very dreadful, he gave off a horrible, sickening odor like that of a wild beast. I shall never forget the last night I ever had him with me. He was furious because of the changes I was making and I am sure he was going to attack me. Suddenly I stopped arguing with him and, picking up a heavy walking stick, I said: 'See here, Molineux, stop looking at me like that; I'm not afraid of you. If you had brought me a finished play instead of a lot of words I wouldn't have had to change your manuscript. Now, it's hot and I'm tired, so we'll call the whole thing off for to-night and you can go home and think it over.' He pulled himself together then and tried to apologize and say how much he appreciated all I was doing, but I wouldn't have it and just showed him out of my studio as quickly as I could—and I took care *he* should walk in front, all the way! There wasn't another soul in the place, except the night watchman, away down at the stagedoor. I never let him come near me again."

When "The Man Inside" had been made ready for production Molineux was permitted to attend the dress rehearsal in New York, during the first act of which he was self-contained and quiet. But after the curtain had been lowered he became so violently excited and created so much disturbance that Belasco was constrained to order him to be taken out of the theatre. "It was hard to do, but it had to be done," he writes; "I didn't know whether to go on or drop the whole thing, and I really expected the man would break out and kill somebody." Molineux's unfortunate family and friends were, however, happily able to intervene and restrain him and no act of violence was committed. On November 7, 1914, he was placed in the King's Park State Hospital, Long Island, and there he is still confined,—hopelessly insane. His brave, devoted old father, worn out and heart broken, died, June 10, 1915: his mother, a few months earlier. [Roland B. Molineux died, in the King's Park State Hospital for the Insane, on November 2, 1917, of paresis. There is no doubt that he was a dangerous madman when first Belasco met him.—J. W.]

The Man Inside of Molineux's play is, sym-
bolically, Conscience; and the fundamental idea
which it expounds is that Society errs in its treatment of criminals, because crime cannot be prevented by punishment but only by an effective appeal
to the self-respecting moral nature and "better
self" of the criminal,—who must first be taught to
"think right" before he can be made to *do* right.
Sublime discovery! No intimation is made as to
what method Society ought to employ in cases—
unhappily numerous—of criminals who do not possess any "better selves" and who cannot by any
means, not even the threat of death, be restrained
from crimes which profit them or gratify their ruling passions. There was, without doubt, an honest
altruistic purpose in the distempered, tortured mind
of Molineux,—though, since he did not possess the
power to elucidate it, there is no need to dwell upon
the subject in this place. Belasco, having through
kindness undertaken to produce an ill-digested,
"talky" and undramatic play, revised it as well as
possible in the circumstances, making of it a moderately effective melodrama, dealing with crime and
injustice. In that melodrama a philanthropic young
man, who is also an Assistant District Attorney of
the City of New York, resorts to the haunts of
criminals in order to ascertain, if possible, why they

persist in crime in spite of efforts to reclaim them. He there becomes deeply interested in a girl named *Annie,* the daughter of a desperate forger known as *Red Mike,* and also he becomes so incensed at the viciousness and cruelty of some methods employed by the Police Department and officials from the District Attorney's Office to insure convictions of accused criminals that he assists *Annie* in the theft of a forged check, upon possession of which the fate of her father depends,—thus himself becoming party to a crime, and, later, participating in a general bath of "whitewash." The First Act of "The Man Inside" passes in an opium den of the New York "Chinatown"; the Second, in the office of the District Attorney—with the Tombs Prison visible through the window; the Third, in a squalid tenement house. Belasco placed the play on the stage in a setting of extraordinary verisimilitude and caused it to be acted in a well-nigh perfect manner. It was first produced at the Euclid Avenue Opera House, Cleveland, Ohio, October 27, 1913, and, November 11, was brought forward in New York at the Criterion Theatre. Public interest in it, however, was languid and it did not long survive. This was the original cast:

Mr. Trainer .... A. Byron Beasley.
James Poor .... Charles Dalton.

Richard Gordon	Milton Sills.
"Red" Mike	A. E. Anson.
"Big" Frank	Edward H. Robins.
"Pop" Olds	John Cope.
Josh Hayes	John Miltern.
Larry	Joseph Byron Totten.
"Whispering" Riley	Lawrence Wood.
Cafferty	Erroll Dunbar.
Clusky	Jerome Kennedy.
Wang Lee	J. J. Chaille.
Chong Fong	H. H. McCollum.
"The Major"	Herbert Jones.
Murphy	Karl Ritter.
Raleigh	Charles B. Givan.
"Frisco" George	Joseph Barker.
"Monk" Verdi	J. A. Esposito.
Annie	Helen Freeman.
Maggie	Clare Weldon.
Lizzie	Gertrude Davis.

BELASCO IN CHINATOWN.

While Belasco was preparing "The Man Inside" for the stage he made several expeditions into the "Chinatown" of New York, accompanied by members of his staff and his theatrical company, in order that some of the ways and denizens of that place— the very prose of the earth—might be pictured with literal exactitude. On those occasions he and his companions, including Mr. Gros, the scenic artist, were convoyed and protected by an eccentric being once well known in the purlieus of vice and crime, whose disreputable acquaintance he had made by chance and to whom he had commended himself by kindness. Describing the last of those insalubrious visits Belasco wrote the following characteristic letter to the young woman who afterward played the principal female part in his adaptation of the Molineux play:

(*Belasco to Miss Helen Freeman.*)

"My dear Miss Helen:—

"We went on the postponed, and probably the last, trip into the 'underworld' last night. It might have been useful to have had you see it once more; but, on the whole, I think you have seen enough for the purpose and am glad you weren't along. Familiar as I am with the sights of such places (and far worse, such as I used to visit in old San Francisco) I found some of it last night rather shocking. But as I promised to give you an account of this trip I will write a little description of our adventures— which, perhaps, you may find suggestive.

"At half-past nine my boys [meaning some members of the technical staff of the Belasco Theatre and two actors] and I met at the stagedoor and left for Chinatown, where, by appointment, we met a very ardent admirer of yours— Mr. 'Chuck' Conners, no less! Perhaps one of the reasons why I like the man is because, in his unpicturesque, rough, human fashion, he felt and expressed your sweetness—the quality which will help you so much in this play, and in all parts. I shall tell you more particularly what he said about you presently, and if you will translate his primitive speech into the finer shaded meanings of a cultivated man, I am sure it will touch your heart as it did mine. But I must get to my story. . . .

"First we sat in the Chatham Club, and had a few 'rounds,'—which I had a hard time to avoid drinking. I don't know what the others did with theirs—I was too busy with my own troubles to watch! While human beings put such stuff inside themselves I can't wonder at anything they do. While there, the girls came and did some 'ragtime' for us. 'Chuck,' I must tell you, was dressed for the occasion,—'to kill,'—with a white 'kerchief about his neck and *one* shoe polished! The other was a characteristic contrast. We listened to the same old stories and 'our hero' sang the same old songs. Also, as aforetime, to punctuate his remarks he found it necessary to *punch* me in the ribs, and so to-day I find myself more or less black and blue. The old pianola was set to the wildest airs, and they had a new one, for our especial benefit, called 'In the Harem,'—which is so good that I am going to introduce it in our play. Do you remember the big, tall girl, with the flat nose and her poor teeth out? She was still sitting in her corner, more forlorn than ever, and with her sad 'lamps' looking into my very heart. I gave her another five dollars and told her that if I came again I should expect to see her wearing a new pair of shoes,—for her poor toes were peeping out of frayed stockings, through the impossible boots, and it was all very sad.

"Well, from there we went to the same old opium bungalows and the same old 'Chink' 'hit the pipe' for us,—afterward, however, taking us into a female 'joint,' where we saw several regular denizens of the place. It is all part of the show; but I am glad Conners did not take us to it when you and the other ladies were along. . . . One of

the women there had been a belle of Philadelphia: another,
a runaway wife. Gradually, they have slipped down the
ladder of shame and remorse, until their poor, wavering
little hands could hold the rungs no longer, and so they
fell into that 'Slough of Despond,' with the 'pipe' for their
favorite companion. I was glad to get away from it, for
it made my heart ache. With infinite understanding there
would be infinite tolerance; and if we knew the springs of
action, the circumstances and environment, of these poor,
stray souls, perhaps we shouldn't judge them very harshly.

"But to return to my story: 'Chuck' was in his element. Never did I know that such unmentionable slang,
such mere depravity of phrase, could come from human
lips, although my experience has been a varied one! The
night you ladies were with us the 'choicest gems' of his
vernacular were bottled up: last night the cork was drawn
—with a vengeance! And yet, after all (though I'm glad
you did not hear him), it was only words. At heart, the
man is kind and generous, and he lives up to his code
closer than many another who has had every advantage.

"Of course, he asked all about you. He said you were
'Der real t'ing,' 'der right stuff,' 'der whole cheese,' etc.
'Next day,' said he, 'all der fleet wanted t' know who der
swell little skoit was. "And," I sez, "why dat's der Princess Nicotine!" I sez.'

"He was anxious to know your opinion of him, and
so I said that he had made 'a great hit' with you. This
pleased him mightily. I then said that he 'was tearing
every skirt's heart wide open!' 'Stop dat—stop dat!' he
said; 'Go 'way back! She was kidding of yer!'

"We wound up by dining at the Chinese Delmonico's
on tea and rice and chop suey. Of course, I ordered some,

but not daring to eat it I slipped my plate to 'Chuck,' whose chop-sticks soon made short work of the concoction. He ordered *more*, afterward, and I wish you could have seen his expression when he had at length reached a stage of repletion and exclaimed 'Hully gee! dis is goin' some! I wouldn't change me feed-bag dis minute wif Rockefeller!' . . .

"We parted with 'Chuck' about three in the morning. He escorted us to the same old car, which was piloted by the same old chauffeur. As we were leaving he blew me a kiss! 'Hully gee!' he said, 'I likes youse; an' don' yer ferget to tell de little skoit dat she's der *real t'ing!*' We were about to start when he gave a yell that frightened us and said he had forgotten something. He pulled the enclosed book from his pocket and, using the chauffeur's back as a desk, wrote the inscription on the fly-leaf! . . .

"The last act will soon be in final shape. Study hard, but don't over-do,—and everything will be all right. Goodnight and good luck.

"Faithfully,

"DAVID BELASCO."

AN ADMONITION TO STAGE ASPIRANTS.

(*Belasco to a Recalcitrant Novice.*)

Another letter which Belasco wrote at about the same period as that above quoted is characteristic and informative as to his views concerning the Stage and stage aspirants and can conveniently be placed here:

"The Belasco Theatre.

My dear Mrs. H.————:—

"It is not an easy task to write what I have to say, but it is time that it should be written and understood. If I am to do for your cousin, Miss V————, what I want to do and have hoped to do; if I am to open the way for her to a career, she must be guided by me; *my* influence, not yours nor that of anybody else, must predominate. The Stage is a harsh master. Real success on it does not 'happen': it is *made*—made of striving and sacrifice and self-denial and *hard work*.

"What you do is, of course, no concern of mine and I have no wish to meddle in anybody else's business, having far more of my own than I can properly look after. But I have every reason to think that, if it were not for your influence, I might not have so many causes to be dissatisfied with Miss V————. At present, my wishes are not heeded by her. And so that we may all reach an understanding, I want to say to you that I resent Miss V————'s recent conduct; that, in view of the fact that I have taken the trouble to interest myself in her future as an actress, I resent it *very much*, and will not any longer tolerate it.

"If I am in some ways a strict master I am always a fair and considerate one. But,—and please realize this,—in everything connected with my theatre, from the water-boys in the smoking room to the 'star' on the stage; from the carpets to be laid on the floors to the plays that are produced, *I am the Master, and my word is the absolute and final law.*

"Miss V———— is a very young girl, who has seen very little of the world. She is not only exceptionally talented but pretty, attractive, and charming. Consequently she is admired by the idlers who have time to kill in dangling after young women of the Stage—and nothing better to do. Miss V—— is much sought after by matrons who are ever on the look-out for pretty girls to attract men to their dances and their 'week-end' visits. Such women care nothing at all about a girl's career or whether they ruin it or not—and they will ruin it, every time, if the girl is weak or foolish enough to be persuaded. Miss V—— likes this kind of attention, which is natural, but it won't do—not if she is to remain with *me*. No big man or woman has time for frivolities; it is either one thing or the other: we work and work and rise and rise; or else we try to flutter through life on butterfly wings—and then we fall by the wayside.

"Miss V—— has, I am informed, been neglecting her duties at the theatre. True, at present she has only the minor position of an understudy; but she should at least be conscientious enough to attend to its duties. She knows very well that she should keep Mr. L—— informed of her whereabouts. She has no right, no excuse, to go anywhere, or to be in any place, where he cannot reach her at a moment's notice, by telephone. An understudy is just a reserve soldier, subject to instant call. If Mr. Dean had been well, of course he would have attended to this matter of Miss V——'s neglect. But as it is, Mr. L—— has too many details to look after. Her conduct is not fair to him, to say nothing of me, nor does it show any proper respect for the theatre, for Miss V—— so to ignore her obligations. Last evening, through an indisposition, Miss ——, whom she understudies, was nearly obliged to remain away. If she had done so, the house would have been dismissed, and Mr. L——— would have been discharged, through her negligence. Have you any conception what it would mean to me to disappoint an audience, *in my theatre?*

"If Miss V——— is to remain under my guidance she must obey *my* wishes: not yours, or her own, or anybody else's, but *mine*—at all times and in everything. If she does not see fit to follow my advice, I shall reluctantly leave her to her own resources. Inasmuch as I have made myself responsible for her artistic success, her mental and physical condition are matters of much moment to me and I will not have them jeopardized as [they are] by her present mode of life. Automobile rides, midnight suppers and dances until daylight are all very well—but they are not conducive to health. They are a sapping of the vitality which, if she wishes to succeed, should be reserved for higher things. . . .

"Do you realize that, for months past, I have given two nights a week to Miss V———,—time and work that no money could buy and no influence induce me to waste? *I* realize it! I once refused a fortune, a theatre in London and an endowment for life, in return for which I was to give a popular actress what I have given Miss V——— for nothing, simply because she has great talent and I have believed in her. And I refused to direct that actress because I knew she would never sacrifice her society life and pleasures for her work. Understand, please; *I* have a reputation to maintain, a standard to live up to. Sickness, weariness, accident, trouble, death—the Public does not want and will not take excuses. That is not what they [it] comes into my theatre for. It comes to see the best plays I can put on, acted by the best artists I can engage and train. Miss V——— can be one of these, if she will pay the price; if, like the women who have made a success of their lives she can be strong enough to give up everything else, 'for the love of the working.' Miss ——— did, and little Miss ———; otherwise, they would not be where they are to-day. . . .

If it is your intention for Miss V——— to make her *début* in society, with matrimony in view for her, then I suggest that you and she be frank enough to let me know, so that I may make my plans accordingly. Matrimony is a career with which *nothing else* can compete. . . .

"I have been very lenient and have written at length and explained myself, because Miss V——— is very young, and because I hold you more to blame than I do her. But if I am to continue the moulding of her artistic career it must be with the distinct understanding that my wishes and my influence shall dominate, in everything.

"If Miss V——— wishes to continue under my direction,—absolute obedience, application, study, effort, and constant hard work are the conditions. On the other hand, when you have read this letter to her, she is at liberty to consider herself released from all engagements to me if she so desires.

"Yours faithfully,

"DAVID BELASCO."

"THE PHANTOM RIVAL."

"The Phantom Rival," adapted by Leo Ditrichstein from an Austrian original by Ferenc Molnar, postulates that a woman idealizes the man whom she first loves and never forgets him; and, by presenting her extravagant notions about him in a dream and then showing,—in an individual case,—that he turns out to be a commonplace person, implies that the ideals founded in youth and cherished by females in after life are mistakes and absurd. It may be so. It probably is true that all ideals of human perfection are unsound and even ridiculous. It certainly is true that the longer we live and the more we see of human nature the more disappointed we are, in ourselves as well as in others, till we come at last to believe, as Lockhart wrote:

"That nothing's new and nothing's true
And nothing signifies!"

The "visible dream" is an old device of the theatre and a good one. It was exceedingly well managed in this play—the only blemish, indeed, being a certain effect of monotony which, being inherent in the dramatic fabric, was ineradicable in the stage exhibition of it. The principal persons in this drama, which centres around "the dream," are an American woman, *Mrs. Marshall,* and an Austrian, named *Sascha Taticheff.* In youth they dwelt in the same Brooklyn boarding house. Propinquity had a usual consequence. The girl, romantic, admired the youth and became fond of him. The youth was flattered and reciprocated. Then, suddenly, he went away, called back to his native land, taking a sentimental farewell and writing a letter filled with ardent vaporings. Years have passed. The girl has met and loved and married a successful American lawyer; they dwell together; they would be happy, in a staid, conventional way, were it not for the preposterous, boorish jealousy of the husband. He suspects his wife of having had an earlier lover and he tortures himself and her because of this suspicion, this paltry jealousy of "the phantom rival" of a youthful attachment. And then, by chance, in a public restaurant, *Taticheff* and *Mrs. Marshall,* who is with her husband, meet again. Scarce able to recall each other, they exchange formal bows. Having returned to their home *Marshall* badgers his wife about the stranger in the restaurant until, exasperated, she admits that she once knew *Taticheff* and was fond of him; and, finally, she surrenders to her husband, who reads it, the farewell letter of her youthful sweetheart. The sentimental folly of that screed so amuses *Marshall* that he declares himself cured of his jealousy, speaks of the writer with contempt, and, laughing heartily, goes out to a business conference. The wife, incensed by this cavalier attitude toward the object of her girlhood affection, rereads his perfervid protestations: then, falling asleep, she has a dream

in which her *Sascha* returns to her, at a fashionable
ball, in, successively, the different characters suggested by his letter:—first, as an all-conquering military hero; then as a world-dominating statesman;
next as a peerless singer, the idol of two hemispheres;
finally,—after she has been turned out of doors by
an indignant hostess because of the scandal of her
conduct with her multiform lover,—in the guise of
a wretched, one-armed street-beggar, upon whom her
husband makes a furious assault, whereupon, shrieking, she awakes. Then, her husband returning with
the actual *Sascha* (who proves to be subordinately
concerned with the business which *Marshall* has in
hand), she is left alone with him. The interview
that then occurs between them is much the cleverest
passage in the play. The woman, rather forlornly,
tries to discover in the man before her some trace of
the romantic glamour with which she had fancifully
invested him, but finds only a plebeian dullard,
stupidly embarrassed, inveterately selfish and petty,
and much interested in her husband's brandy. At
last, when she is relieved of his tiresome presence,
she drops his long-cherished letters into the fire and
joins her husband in his contemptuous amusement at
her sentimental memories and the sorry figure of
his "phantom rival."—Belasco's preservation of an
unreal, dream-like atmosphere throughout the dream

scenes of this play was perfect. And, of the kind, nothing so good as the acting of Miss Laura Hope Crews and Mr. Ditrichstein in the last scene of it has been visible on our Stage for many years. "The Phantom Rival" was first produced, September 28, 1914, at Ford's Opera House, Baltimore: on October 6, it was presented at the Belasco Theatre, New York. This was the original cast:

Sascha Taticheff	Leo Ditrichstein.
Frank Marshall	Malcolm Williams.
Dover	Frank Westerton.
Earle	Lee Millar.
Farnald	John Bedouin.
Oscar	John McNamee.
Waiters	{ Louis Pioselli. / Frank E. Morris.
Louise, Mrs. Marshall	Laura Hope Crews.
Mrs. Van Ness	Lila Barclay.
Nurse	Anna McNaughton.
Maid	Ethel Marie Sasse.

"THE BOOMERANG."

It was an opinion of the philosophic Bacon that women "will sooner follow you by slighting than by too much wooing." That is an opinion shared by many and one which observation perceives to be grounded on fact: *some* women *will*. It is the basic idea underlying the play by Messrs. Winchell Smith

and Victor Mapes, called "The Boomerang," which
Belasco produced at his New York theatre, August
10, 1915,—and which, slender as it is, has proved one
of the most richly remunerative of all his ventures.
In that play a youth, *Budd Woodbridge* by name,
loves a girl, *Grace Tyler,* so unreservedly that she
finds him wearisome and is inclined to repel his
devotion and bestow her affections upon another
youth. Young *Woodbridge* so peaks and pines
under his mistress' disdain and the pangs of juvenile
jealousy that his mother fears that he is passing into
a decline and insists on his consulting a physician.
That physician, *Dr. Gerald Sumner,* finds the young
man depressed, irritable, and in extreme nervous distress. He questions him shrewdly and soon ascertains the nature of the distemper for which he is
desired to prescribe. He rather cynically undertakes to cure the youth and his directions are obeyed.
His patient is sent home and put to bed; a daily
hypodermic injection is ordered of a mysterious,
vivifying serum (in fact, water), and a young
woman nurse, beautiful and peculiarly kind and
sympathetic, is employed to administer the injection
and to amuse and cheer the unhappy sufferer, who
is obediently responsive to her angelic ministration. The capricious *Miss Tyler,* seeing her adorer
apparently succumbing to the fascinations of the

lovely nurse and finding herself rather slighted off, discovers that she cannot live without him and *Woodbridge's* amatory anguish is soon in a fair way to be assuaged. The relevancy of the title of this farce, "The Boomerang," is revealed in a dictionary comment on that implement of Antipodal warfare which declares that: "in inexperienced hands the boomerang recoils upon the thrower, sometimes with very serious results." This is illustrated by the fate of *Dr. Sumner,* who, having been scornful on the subject of love and jealousy, becomes violently enamoured of the charming nurse and for a time suffers much because of her affectionate tendance upon his patient,—until, at last, he learns that her regard is really fixed upon himself.

This play was designated as a "comedy,"—and, if Dr. Johnson's definition of a comedy as something to make people laugh be accepted, that definition is plausible. The piece is, in fact, a farce and, in my judgment, rather a slight one; but it was so exquisitely stage-managed and so admirably acted that it passed for being something far more substantial and worthy than, intrinsically, it is. With the view that it is slight and merely ephemeral Belasco emphatically disagrees. "I maintain," he has declared to me, "that 'The Boomerang' has a vital theme, cf universal appeal, no matter how much you may ridicule it:

I mean Calf Love. Everybody has had it—and, while it lasts, it's terrible. No matter how much we may laugh at the boys and girls suffering from juvenile love and jealousy, we sympathize with them, too. That's why everybody in the country wants to see our little play—why men and women have stood in line all night (as they have done in many places) to buy tickets for the performance. I believed in the little piece from the very first. I wish I knew where to get another as good!"

One of many scores of letters received by Belasco, commendatory of this play and its exemplary presentment, came from perhaps the most generous of contemporary patrons of the Theatre and it may appropriately be quoted here:

(*Otto H. Kahn to David Belasco.*)

"52 William Street, New York,
"November 8, 1915.

"Dear Mr. Belasco:—

"I need not tell you that I have frequently and greatly admired your art and skill, but there are gradations of achievement even in an acknowledged master and, having just seen your latest production, 'The Boomerang,' I cannot refrain from sending you a few lines of particularly warm appreciation and congratulation. Nothing is more difficult in art than to produce great effects with simple means, to do a simple thing superlatively well. Nothing is more rare in art than restraint. Nothing is a greater test of the art of the producer than to maintain throughout an entire evening the atmosphere, the illusion and the effect of comedy, unaided as he is by either the stirring incidents of drama or the broad appeal of farce. Your wisdom in picking out one of the very best and most genuine comedies that I have seen in many a day, your judgment in providing an admirable cast, and your skill and art in producing, have combined to bring about the most happy result, and I owe you thanks for that rare treat, a wholly delightful evening at the theatre, unmarred by any jarring note.

"Believe me,

"Very faithfully yours,

"OTTO H. KAHN."

"The Boomerang" was originally produced at The Playhouse, Wilmington, Delaware, April 5, 1915. This was the cast:

Dr. Gerald Sumner......................Arthur Byron.
Budd Woodbridge...................Wallace Eddinger.
Preston de Witt.......................Gilbert Douglas.
Heinrich...........................Richard Malchien.
Hartley.............................John N. Wheeler.
Mr. Stone..............................John Clements.
Virginia Xelva.......................Martha Hedman.
Grace Tyler...........................Ruth Shepley.
Marion Sumner.......................Josephine Parks.
Gertrude Ludlow....................Dorothy Megrew.
Mrs. Creighton Woodbridge.............Ida Waterman.

"SEVEN CHANCES."

"Odds life, sir! if you have the estate, you must take it with the live stock on it, as it stands!"

exclaims *Sir Anthony Absolute,* in "The Rivals,"
to his son, when mentioning that his proffer of "a
noble independence" is "saddled with a wife." Such
arbitrary bestowal of wealth contingent on matrimony—frequent in actual experience—is one of the
best established and most respected expedients of
comical stage dilemmas, and it recurs, at intervals,
in one form or another, with much the inevitability
of death and taxes. It is the basis of another entertaining farce, called "Seven Chances," which Belasco
produced at the George M. Cohan Theatre, New
York, August 8, 1916, and which also enjoyed a
long and prosperous career. That farce was built
on a "suggestion" derived from a short story by Mr.
Gouverneur Morris, entitled "The Cradle Snatcher,"
and, originally, it was called "Shannon's Millions."
It was several times rebuilt, under Belasco's supervision,—Mr. Roi Cooper Megrue being the last of
his coadjutory playwrights. It was produced,
April 17, 1916, at the Apollo Theatre, Atlantic City,
New Jersey, under the name of "The Lucky Fellow." Its comical incidents revolve around *Jimmy
Shannon,* an amiable young bachelor with a vigorous
antipathy to matrimony, whose sardonic grandsire,
dying, leaves to him by will a fortune of twelve
million dollars, conditional upon his being married
by the time that he is thirty years old. *Shannon*

is informed of that contingent bequest on the eve of his attainment of the specified age. He is at a Country Club where, also, there are seven young women. "The affair cries haste and speed must answer it." The impecunious *Shannon* will propose marriage to each one of those females, if necessary: thus he has "seven chances" of obtaining the impendent fortune,—which, at last, he gets, along with a bride so young and beauteous as to reconcile him to the imposed change in his state. The opportunities for fun in all this are obvious; critically to dilate upon them would be much like breaking a butterfly on the wheel. They were utilized to the full under Belasco's direction by a good company,—the parts being cast as follows:

Jimmie Shannon......................Frank Craven.
Billy Meekin.............................John Butler.
Earl Goddard.........................Hayward Ginn.
Ralph Denby.........................Charles Brokate.
Joe Spence............................Frank Morgan.
Henry Garrison.......................Harry Leighton.
George................................Freeman Wood.
Anne Windsor........................Carroll McComas.
Mrs. Garrison........................Marion Abbott.
Lilly Trevor..........................Anne Meredith.
Peggy Wood..........................Emily Callaway.
Irene Trevor...........................Beverly West.
Georgiana Garrison....................Gladys Knorr.

Florence Jones......................Florence Deshon.
Betty Brown.........................Alice Carroll.

"THE LITTLE LADY IN BLUE": THE LAST PLAY EVER SEEN BY WILLIAM WINTER.

[The last play ever seen by my father was "The Little Lady in Blue," which Belasco produced on October 16, 1916, in Washington, and, on December 22, at the Belasco Theatre, in New York. It is a very agreeable piece, with a somewhat trite but expertly handled story. The period of it is 1820. The scene of it is England. The principal character in it is named *Anne Churchill.* She is an impoverished little governess who sets out to be an adventuress. She wins the affection of a wild young naval officer named *Anthony Addenbrooke,* incidentally rescuing him from the clutches of a much be-painted Circe of the Portsmouth waterfront. Next she helps him to meet the conditions under which he will inherit £60,000, intending to marry him for the sake of that money. Then she discovers that she really loves him, she is ashamed of her conduct, and she cannot go through with the part of a mercenary adventuress. She confesses to *Addenbrooke* the real origin of her interest in his affairs and releases him from his engagement to marry her. Being recognized as an earthly paragon she is not permitted to

414 THE LIFE OF DAVID BELASCO

retire into indigence but is wedded to her lover, who has gained a lieutenant's commission through her assistance and is about to sail away to fight for King and country.—The piece was written by Messrs. Horace Hodges and T. Wigney Percyval.

My father was unable to attend the first New York performance of that play, and his work on this Memoir prevented his seeing it until several weeks later. In his "Journal" he wrote:

[1917] "February 8. More damnable peace blather!— Belasco kindly invited us to visit his Theatre and sent his automobile for us, and 'Willy' and I went and saw performance of 'The Little Lady in Blue,'—a pleasing entertainment."

Two days afterward Mr..Winter wrote the following letter, which records his critical views of the production. —J. W.]

(*William Winter to David Belasco.*)

"New Brighton, Staten Island,
"February 10, 1917.

"Dear Belasco:—

"It was indeed a pleasure to see, at your theatre, the play of 'The Little Lady in Blue.' It is long since I have so much enjoyed anything. The rightly conducted Theatre still remains to me what it always was—the home of that magic art which cheers the loneliness of life and opens the portal into an ideal world. Alas, that it is not more generally conducted for such a purpose! 'The Little Lady' can hardly be considered *a play;* but, as you have presented it, it is a charming entertainment—a whimsical, almost grotesque, portrayal of eccentric characters and incredible incidents, which are made to *seem* real, for the moment by the glamour of the Stage. Since the plot is so frail, I was all the more surprised and delighted that so much interest could be excited and sustained and so much pleasure diffused by the histrionic treatment of a theme so slender. You have set the play on the stage in an exquisite manner, and it is acted throughout with a scrupulous care and zeal that, in recent years, I have seldom seen equalled. It is easy to ridicule such quaint, fantastic, almost dream-like pieces. As Frederick Locker wrote:

'We love the rare old days and rich
　　That poetry has painted;
We mourn that sacred age with which
　　We never were acquainted!'

"But they have a potent charm, a sort of mignonette and wild-thyme fragrance, a power to touch the gentler feelings and soothe the mind, and so they are precious.

"There is one blemish that should be removed—namely, the character of *A Girl of Portsmouth Town:* it adds nothing to the situation, and it is only a blot on the delicacy of the play.

"I am glad to know the production is prosperous: it deserves to be—and it ought to fill your theatre for months, and I hope it will.

"With kind regards,

"Faithfully yours,

"WILLIAM WINTER."

The cast of "The Little Lady in Blue" is appended:

Admiral Sir Anthony Addenbrooke	A. G. Andrews.
Anthony Addenbrooke	Jerome Patrick.
Captain Kent, R. N.	Frederick Graham.
Joe Porten	Horace Braham.
Baron von Loewe	Carl Sauerman.
John Speedwell	Charles Garry.
Cobbledick	George Giddens.
A Waiter	Adrian H. Rosley.
A Process Server	Harry Holiday.
Landlord of the Portsmouth Inn	Roland Rushton.
Anne Churchill	Frances Starr.
Miss Quick	Lucy Beaumont.
A Girl of Portsmouth Town	Eleanor Pendleton.

"THE VERY MINUTE"—A MEMORANDUM.

Memo.—David produced a new play called "The Very Minute" last Monday night [April 9, 1917], at his N. Y. theatre, with Mr. Arnold Daly in the principal part. All about bad effects of drinking too much liquor, &c. Novelty—striking! Good old Towse calls it "a shallow pretence of a serious play" and says it is a "nightmare." Commends D. B.'s "meticulous attention to the material and manner of production." Also commends A. D. for "moments of *powerful* acting." Well—he was there and I was not; but how A. D. must have changed! *I* never saw any more "power" in him than there is in a pennywhistle. Used to have a sort of *sonsy* quality that was pleasing. Competent in a commonplace way: unusual assurance—great conceit. Knows his business—generally *definite,* which is a merit. Disagreeable personality. Head turned with vanity. And nothing really IN him—that ever *I* could see.

This play written by John Meehan. Young man, said to be related to me by marriage. I never met him and do not know. Suppose I must see his play and write about it. Don't want to! "What, will the line stretch out to the crack of doom?" Where do they [plays] all come from, I wonder? Hope David has got another success, but surmise it's an awful frost,—as 'twere "the very *last* minute of the hour," I fear. Wish he would stop producing plays altogether until after I get through writing this "Life"!

["The Very Minute" was first acted at The Playhouse, Wilmington, Delaware, April 5, 1917: it was "an awful frost," as my father surmised, and it was withdrawn on May 7—the Belasco Theatre being then closed.—J. W.] This was the cast:

Horace Cramner	Forrest Robinson.
Mrs. Cramner	Marie Wainwright.
Francis Cramner	Arnold Daly.
Kathleen	Cathleen Nesbitt.
Philip Cramner	William Morris.

Mr. Husner...........................John W. Cope.
Dr. Monticou.......................Lester Lonergan.
Robert.............................Robert Vivian.
Bennett............................Leon E. Brown.

SUMMARY.

[The various passages in the following "Summary" of the character and career of Belasco were written disjointedly. They are here gathered and arranged in what appears to be their natural sequence,—as nearly as I can judge in the order in which Mr. Winter would have placed them. In two or three instances an unfinished sentence has been completed and here and there an essential word or two has been inserted or added. Otherwise the matter stands unrevised: I have not attempted to write connecting passages.—J. W.]

> *"Not fearing death nor shrinking for distress,*
> *But always resolute in most extremes."*
> —SHAKESPEARE.

The estimate that observation forms of a person still living cannot always be deemed conclusive: the person can invalidate it, in an instant, by some sudden action, some unexpected development, some surprising decadence; and, as a general rule, it should be remembered that no person is ever com-

DAVID BELASCO

Inscription:
"To my friend of many years, William Winter."

pletely comprehended by anybody. We have glimpses of each other; but, practically, each individual is *alone*. In the most favorable circumstances, accordingly, no life can be more than approximately summarized until the record is complete—perhaps not even then. It was perception of this fact that caused the old grave-digger of Drumtochty to declare that there is no real comfort in a marriage because nobody knows how it will turn out; whereas there is no room for solicitude about a funeral, because, at all events, the play is over. David Belasco, although he begins to see the shadow of the Psalmist's threescore years and ten, is still in the full vigor of life; he is, indeed, the most powerful, vital influence now [1917] operant in the English-speaking Theatre,—Herbert Beerbohm-Tree, in London, being his only competitor,—and (as I hope and believe) is approaching the highest achievements of his long, varied, and brilliant career, which there is reason to expect will continue for many years. . . .

Actors, it has been noted, who are actors only, often are remarkably long-lived. Men who attain eminence in theatrical management,—whether they be also actors or not,—seldom are so: Sir William Davenant died at sixty-two; Garrick at sixty-one; John Kemble at sixty-six; Thomas S. Hamblin at fifty-one; Charles Kean at fifty-seven; Benedict De Bar at sixty-three; John McCollough at fifty-three; Lester Wallack at sixty-eight; Lawrence Barrett at fifty-two; Edwin Booth at sixty; John T. Ford at sixty-five; Augustin Daly at sixty-one; A. M. Palmer at sixty-seven. Garrick had been three years in retirement when he died; Kemble, six; Kean, nearly one; Booth, more than two; Palmer, five. Belasco's career has already extended over a period of forty-six years and, excepting Wallack, he is now older than any of those men were when their professional labors ended,*—yet there is in him none of the dejection of age; none of the despondency of fatigue; no abatement of his ambitious purpose, resolute enterprise, and amazing energy; no sign of that forlorn loneliness which often settles on the mind as friends die, things alter and long familiar environment drifts away, the old order changing and giving place to new. On the contrary, his health is excellent, his mind virile,

---

*Lester Wallack's last appearance on the stage occurred May 29, 1886, at the Grand Opera House, New York, and Wallack's Company was then disbanded. He was born January 1, 1820, and died September 6, 1888. He surrendered his theatre into the hands of Theodore Moss in 1887, being then sixty-seven years old. Moss had a considerable part in the management of Wallack's Theatre for several years before that.

Beerbohm-Tree, referred to above as "Belasco's only competitor," died, July 2, 1917, in his sixty-fourth year. He was five months younger than Belasco was at that time.

his courage high, his spirit cheerful, and in every way he shows as indeed "strong in will to strive, to seek, to find, and not to yield." It is, therefore, a specially difficult and dubious task to attempt to make at this time a summary of his character, life, and labor. But if another of the abrupt and lamentable bereavements of the Stage which it has so often been my task to chronicle and estimate should befall at this time; if, suddenly, now, while all around seems bright and full of life and hope, mortality's strong hand should close upon Belasco and I should be required to write of him as of one whose work was finished and who had "bid the world good-night," I should write in these words:

From the beginning and until the end David Belasco was an embodiment of high ambition, zealous enterprise, resolute endeavor, and patient endurance. He did not drift into his career—he selected it. His natural proclivity for the Theatre was irresistible; in youth his aspiration was to reach a dominant place in that institution; all his early life was spent in arduous toil to equip himself for the eminence at which he aimed; through long years, in which he became well acquainted with bitter strife and grievous disappointment, he never lost hope or faltered in the purpose which at last he achieved,—supremacy in the American Theatre.

He was a rare and vivid personality; an extraordinary and many-sided man; the natural successor of Lester Wallack, Edwin Booth, and Augustin Daly as the leading theatrical manager of America; and, in the English-speaking world, he was absolutely the last of the managers who, personally, were important and interesting. His place will not be filled.

It has been said of David Belasco that he was a "posing and posturing charlatan." That harsh censure is the tribute of envy to merit and it is as unjust as it is mean. His nature was impetuous, his temperament was intensely dramatic, his sensibility was extreme, the tone of his mind was at times exuberant and florid, and, consequently, his language and his conduct were sometimes extravagant. He, also, understood the uses of advertising; he was occasionally over-solicitous as to public opinion; he possessed a full share of very human, almost childlike, vanity, and certainly he managed the public as well as the Theatre. But his devotion to the dramatic calling was true, passionate, and entire and to it he gave his life: he never desired retirement and never thought of it. The secret of his success—if any secret there be—was his inveterate determination, indefatigable labor, and profound sincerity of purpose. If the public poured great wealth into his hands (as it did), he

never spared wealth, labor, and time—toilsome days
and sleepless, care-full nights—to give the public in
return the very best there was in him and to make
that best as good as it could be made. He was a
master of every detail of his vocation and, alone
among American theatrical managers of the past
twenty years, he understood and practically recognized that Acting is a Fine Art and not merely a
business. The main result at which he aimed was
always good plays, correctly set and superbly acted.
If that result was not always attained by him, neither
has it always been attained by any other worker
of the Stage,—not since "Roscius was an actor in
Rome." While judgment and taste must deplore
his production of "Zaza" and "The Easiest Way"
justice and candor must concede his right to be
remembered by the best and most influential of his
works, which comprehend an amazing variety of
subjects and of merit, ranging, for example, from
"May Blossom" to "Peter Grimm," from "Men
and Women" to "Sweet Kitty Bellairs," from
"The Heart of Maryland" to "The Music Master,"
from "The Charity Ball" to "The Girl of the
Golden West," from "The Girl I Left Behind Me"
to "Adrea," from "Lord Chumley" to "Madame
Butterfly," from "The Darling of the Gods" to
"A Grand Army Man," and which, first and last,

deal with most of the great elemental experiences
of human life.

*   *   *   *   *   *   *

The sentiment of patriotism is a sublime and
lovely sentiment, but it cannot be nurtured by self-
deception, by vainglorious boasting and sycophantic
adulation. There is far too much talk about our
superiority as a people and far too little thought
about means of making that alleged superiority
actual. We are hearing much, and we shall hear
more, about the spiritual exaltation and the fine
idealism which has recently carried us into the Great
War,—but such talk is not honest. We had as
much reason to enter the War in 1915 as we had
in 1917. We have entered it, primarily, from self-
interest, for self-defence,—to fight now, in Europe,
in order that we need not fight, hereafter, in
America. Let us be honest and outspoken about our
course. It is idle to seek, as some of his "very articu-
late" political opponents and detractors do, to lay the
blame of our unworthy delay on Woodrow Wilson
(one of the great men of modern times) or on any
other man or group of men. The blame rests
squarely on the people of the United States as a
nation. The spirit of our country is and long has
been one of pagan Materialism, infecting all branches
of thought, and of unscrupulous Commercialism,

infecting all branches of action. Foreign elements, alien to our institutions and ideals as to our language and our thought,—seditious elements, ignorant, boisterous, treacherous, and dangerous,—have been introduced into our population in immense quantities, interpenetrating and contaminating it in many ways: in the face of self-evident peril and of iterated warnings and protests, immigration into the United States has been permitted during the last twenty years of about 15,000,000 persons—including vast numbers of the most undesirable order. We call ourselves a civilized nation—but civility is conspicuous in our country chiefly by its absence. Gentleness is despised. Good manners are practically extinct. Public decorum is almost unknown. We are notoriously a law-contemning people. The murder rate—the *unpunished* murder rate—in our country has long been a world scandal. Mob outrage is an incident of weekly occurrence among us. Our methods of business, approved and practised, are not only unscrupulous but predatory. Every public conveyance and place of resort bears witness to the general uncouthness by innumerable signs enjoining the most elemental decency—and by the almost universal disregard of the enjoinments! Slang and thieves' argot is the prevalent language of the people and there is scarcely a periodical or a newspaper in the land which does not exhibit and promote the corruption of good manners diffused by that evil communication,—while the publicist who dares to record the facts and censure the faults is generally stigmatized as a fool or ridiculed as a pedant. The tone of the public mind is to a woful extent sordid, selfish, greedy. In our great cities life is largely a semi-delirious fever of vapid purpose and paltry strife, and in their public vehicles of transportation the populace—men, women, and young girls—are herded together without the remotest observance of common decency,—mauled and jammed and packed one upon another in a manner which would not be tolerated in shipment of the helpless steer or the long-suffering swine. . . .

If true civilization is to develop and live in our country, such conditions, such a spirit, such ideals, manners, and customs as are widely prevalent among us to-day, must utterly pass and cease. The one rational hope that they will so disappear lies in disseminating EDUCATION,—not merely schooling, imperative as that is; but, far more, a truer and higher education imparted by the ministry of beauty; education which recognizes that material prosperity and marvellous discoveries of science are not ultimate goals of human pilgrimage but mere instruments to be used in spiritual advancement; the inspiration of noble ideals, gentleness, refinement, and the grace of manners; cheerful courage, resolute patience, and the calm of hope. For that education Society must look largely to the ministry of the arts and, in particular, to the rightly conducted Theatre,—an institution potentially of tremendous beneficence. . . .

Few managers have been able to take or to understand that view of the Stage. David Belasco was one of them. It is because his administration of his "great office" has been, in the main, conducted in the spirit of a zealous public servant; because for many years he maintained as a public resort a beautiful theatre, diffusive of the atmosphere of a pleasant, well-ordered home, placing before the public many fine plays, superbly acted, and set upon the stage in a perfection of environment never surpassed anywhere and equalled only by a few of an earlier race of managers of which he was the last, that David Belasco has, directly and indirectly, exerted an immense influence for good and is entitled to appreciative recognition, enduring celebration, and ever grateful remembrance. And, though on the two occasions when I differed with him I vigorously opposed his course, it is a comfort to reflect that nothing ever chilled our friendship and that all that could be done to sustain and aid his great and worthy purpose and to cheer his mind was done while he could benefit by it. . . .

* * * * * * *

Among American theatrical managers David Belasco was long unique,—the sole survivor, exemplar, and transmitter of an earlier and better theory and practice of theatrical management than is anywhere visible now. When he came to New York, to the Madison Square Theatre, representative theatre managers of our country were Lester Wallack, Augustin Daly, John T. Ford, Samuel Colville, Dion Boucicault, J. H. McVicker, R. M. Hooley, Henry E. Abbey, Montgomery Field, and A. M. Palmer, and our Stage was dominated and swayed by the influence of those men and of such players as John Gilbert, Joseph Jefferson, William Warren, Charles W. Couldock, Edwin Booth, Lawrence Barrett, W. J. Florence, Tommaso Salvini, Fanny Janauschek, Helena Modjeska, Ada Rehan, Mary Anderson, Henry Irving, and Ellen Terry. When, in 1895, Belasco first successfully struck out for himself, great changes had taken place and greater ones were impending. When, in 1902, he at last succeeded in establishing himself independently, in a theatre of his own, it was in almost a new world that he did so! Colville, Wallack, Ford, Bouci-

BELASCO AT ORIENTA POINT—SUMMER HOME OF
HIS DAUGHTER, MRS. GEST

cault, McVicker, Hooley, Abbey, Daly, Field, Gilbert, Barrett, Florence, Booth,—all were dead. Mansfield had made his ambitious venture in theatre management and had utterly failed in it: Irving had lost the Lyceum in London and was nearing the end of his life: Salvini and Mary Anderson had left the Stage: Jefferson retired within eighteen months and soon after died: Modjeska and Ada Rehan were in broken health, their careers practically closed. Fine actors were visible and, here and there, splendid things were being done: the histrionic fires have never yet been wholly extinguished. But actors and men truly comprehensive of, and sympathetic with, actors no longer controlled the Theatre: that institution had passed almost entirely into the hands of the so-called "business man,"—the speculative huckster and the rampant vulgarian,—and the prevalent ideal in its management was that of the soap chandler and the corner-grocery. The men who chiefly dominated the Theatre in the period of fifteen years since Belasco's establishment in the metropolis,—with many of whom he was long righteously and bitterly at variance,—were Charles Frohman, Al. Hayman, A. L. Erlanger, Marc Klaw, Samuel Nirdlinger, J. F. Zimmermann, William Harris, George C. Tyler, William A. Brady, Henry B. Harris, Lee Shubert,

J. J. Shubert, George M. Cohan, and Al. H. Woods.

There is not one of those men, his later contemporaries, with whom it is possible properly to compare Belasco. *He* was an artist, a dramatist, an authentic manager actuated by a high purpose and one who exerted a profound influence on the Theatre of his period. *The others*—though several of them have manifested various talents—all belong in the category of mere showmen,—speculators in theatrical business, and, save for the bad influence fluent from some of them, they are of no more interest or importance than so many "eminent brewers" or celebrated purveyors of tallow and pork.

One of the managers named, however, by reason of exceptional energy and shrewdness and by dint of incessant self-advertising, became and long continued to be the most conspicuous figure in the theatrical field. That manager was Charles Frohman, and because Belasco and he were personal friends and personal enemies, because they were professional associates and, in a business sense, professional rivals during many years, it is inevitable that the student of the theatrical period from 1885 to 1917 should attempt to make some comparison of them. That renders an estimate of Frohman desirable here. . . .

Charles Frohman was born at Sandusky, Ohio, June 17, 1860, and he lost his life in the sinking of the Lusitania, May 7, 1915. He entered the theatrical business, as an "advance agent," in January, 1877, and he remained in it until his death. He was honest in his dealings, amiable in his domestic and social relations, benevolent toward the poor, highly popular among his friends, able and energetic in business affairs, a gambler by temperament, and of a self-poised, resolute character. His management of the Theatre, however, was injurious, both to that institution and to society. He assisted to commercialize and thus to degrade the Stage. His policy was distinctly and unequivocally expressed by himself, in these words: "I keep a Department Store." That is precisely what he did, and that is precisely what no manager has a right to do,—while claiming *to exercise an intellectual power and foster a great art.* The man to whom Oofty Gooft and Edwin Booth, "Shenandoah" and "Hamlet," "Hattie" Williams and Helena Modjeska, "The Girl from Maxim's" and "Alabama," and so following, are all alike—mere theatrical commodities of commerce to be exploited as such—may be "a man of his word," an honest tradesman, a genial companion, a dutiful son, an affectionate brother, a loyal friend, generous in prosperity, unperturbed in adversity and expeditious in transaction of business,—but he is not and he never can be a true theatrical manager.

In the "Life" of Charles Frohman—by his brother Daniel (a man of far higher ability) and another writer—some informative utterances by him are quoted,— utterances which reveal and establish the quality of his mind more unmistakably than whole chapters of analysis could do. This is one of them, imparting his view of the greatest poet and dramatist that ever lived and of the consummate tragedy of youthful love, "Romeo and Juliet":

" 'Nonsense!' exclaimed Frohman. 'Who's Shakespeare? He was just a man. He won't hurt you. I don't see any Shakespeare. Just imagine you're looking at a soldier, home from the Cuban war, making love to a giggling schoolgirl on a balcony. That's all I see, and that's the way I want it played. Dismiss all idea of costume. Be modern.' "—The tragedy was acted in the manner he desired.

Charles Frohman was simply a wholesale dealer in theatrical produce. He "made" many "stars" —"stars" being a commodity requisite in his business and for the manufacture of which he expressed a strong liking. He never made an actor. There was nothing of importance accomplished in the Theatre through his activity that would not have been accomplished equally well if he had never been born. As far as the Art of the Theatre is concerned he stands in about the same relation to such men as Wallack, Daly, and Belasco as a maker of chromo-lithographs does to Corot or Inness.

* * * * * * *

Belasco was a good fighter—resourceful, courageous, pertinacious. He never forgot a kindness nor an injury,—yet bitter and, to a certain point vindictive, as his resentment of injury unquestionably was, he could easily be placated and he was instantly amenable to any appeal to his kindness of heart. I well remember one occasion on which I chanced to be with him and other friends (it was the last night of the run of "The Darling of the Gods," May 30, 1903) when he was called away by an urgent appeal. He presently returned and, speaking aside with me, informed me that the message had been from a person widely known among journalists and actors as one of the vilest creatures that ever scribbled slander about decent men and women for the blackguard section of the press and one who had done him great wrong and injury. "And now," Belasco said, "he comes to *me*—appealing for help!" "What have you done?" I asked. "What could I do?" he answered: "The man is in the gutter—friendless—penniless—starving. I couldn't refuse him—now, could I? I gave him what he asked for." That incident is significantly characteristic. . . .

* * * * * * *

Upon David Belasco's ability as an actor I can give no judgment, never having seen him act: he seldom appeared on the stage after 1880, and he did not come to New York until 1882. He played more than 170 parts between 1871 and 1880, and it is obvious that his early, continuous, and practical experience in acting and in observation of the dramatic methods and the stage business of many actors, of all kinds, as well as of the practice of some of the best stage managers ever known in America, must have largely contributed to the brilliant efficiency in direction for which he was remarkable. No more capable, resourceful mechanician has appeared in the modern Theatre. . . .

Belasco was a great stage manager because he possessed a comprehensive knowledge of human nature and human experience and an equally comprehensive knowledge alike of scenery (including stage lighting) and of acting; a dramatic temperament; clear insight; almost inexhaustible patience; ability to impart knowledge, and the rare and precious faculty of eliciting and developing the best that was in the actors whom he directed. It was

the latter attribute that made him unique among
stage managers of the last twenty years or so: the
general custom of that pestiferous animal "the stage
producer" is to thrust upon actors an arbitrary ideal
of character. . . .

Belasco possessed, moreover, exceptional understanding of the traits of actors: he knew their vanity
and sometimes almost intolerable conceit, their often
paltry purposes and petty ways; likewise he knew
and deeply sympathized with their fine and lovable
qualities,—the noble ambitions by which sometimes
they are actuated, their often forlorn hopefulness,
their courage under disappointment, their restless
impulse toward *expression,* their honest longing for
opportunity and recognition, their peculiarities,
foibles, and sensibility, and he possessed and exercised extraordinary judgment, consideration, and
tact in the control of them. . . .

* * * * * * *

Being human, Belasco possessed faults and made
mistakes: being successful, he never lacked for cen-
surers to point out the one or, with gleeful malice,
to celebrate the other. He was weak by reason of
an inordinate craving for approbation and by reason of an excessive amiability: rather than inflict the
pain of immediate disappointment he sometimes
foolishly temporized in dealing with importunate

persons, thus, at last, incurring their bitter resentment and enmity because of what they mistakenly
though naturally deemed his insincerity. But, in
every respect, his virtues far exceeded his faults, his
strength his weakness, and his rectitude his errors:
he was an extraordinary man, worthy of public
esteem and honor, and, in private, most loved by
those who knew him best. As the years speed away
and the great place he filled in the Theatre of his
time, and the great void which his passing must
make, become rightly appreciated, those whose
detraction followed David Belasco may admit their
injustice:

"They that reviled him may mourn to recover him,—
Knowing how gentle he was and how brave!
Nothing he'll reck, where the wind blowing over him
Ripples the grasses that dream on his grave!"

*   *   *   *   *   *   *

Much has been written, first and last, about
Belasco's utter absorption in artistic matters and
his ignorance of business affairs. It is true that,
first of all, he was an artist and that in his theory
of theatrical business the keystone of the arch was
the Art of Acting. But it cannot be too strongly
emphasized that he was one of the few managers
who united in himself a profound knowledge of the

drama, all the methods and expedients of histrionic art, the history of the Theatre and entire familiarity with its contemporary conditions. He was, in short, one of the most shrewd, sagacious, far-sighted, hard-headed managers that ever lived. He early saw the futility of trying to attend, himself, to every detail of a great and complex organization and so he employed capable and vigorous men, able and willing to work under his direction and to carry out his orders. But anybody who supposes that David Belasco was not perfectly well and intimately aware of everything that was going on around him and was not at all times the master of his own destiny in the Theatre is cherishing a delusion!

Most conspicuous among the men associated with Belasco throughout his long career in management was Benjamin Franklin Roeder, his general business representative and close personal friend, whose name is here fittingly linked with commemoration of the chief whom he so long and faithfully served. Mr. Roeder, originally, aspired to be a dramatist, and during the early days of Belasco's activity in New York, while connected with the Sargent School of Acting, he obtained an introduction to him from Franklin Sargent. Roeder had made a dramatization of the novel of "St. Elmo" (a subject which was successfully introduced on the stage many years later) and desired that Belasco should read his play with a view to its possible production. Belasco, pleased by the manner and address of the young writer, agreed to consider the matter and made an appointment to meet him and discuss it at the School office at one o'clock on the following Sunday afternoon. In the stress of business he forgot that appointment, but an urgent errand taking him to his office at eleven o'clock on the night of the specified day he found Roeder seated on the doorstep, asleep. He had been waiting there ten hours. "When I asked him why he had waited," said Belasco, telling me of this incident, "he answered, 'You said you might be late —and to wait.' I made up my mind then that there was surely a place for a boy so tenacious and that he was just the fellow for me. I took him on, at first as my secretary, and he has been my business assistant, sometimes my bulwark, always 'my friend, faithful and just to me,' ever since."

Members of the theatrical profession are almost without exception indiscreet and garrulous; secrecy, which often would be invaluable in that profession,— as in any calling in which success frequently depends on priority in exploitation of ideas which cannot be protected from imitation,—is almost unknown in it. Roeder unites in himself not only fidelity to his

BENJAMIN F. ROEDER, BELASCO'S GENERAL BUSINESS
MANAGER

employer, tenacity of purpose, familiarity with all
the commercial details of theatrical affairs, but also
excellent executive faculties, directness and celerity
in the despatch of business and, on all subjects, the
restful reticence of the reclusive clam. His services
were often invaluable to Belasco.

* * * * * * *

In person David Belasco was singular. His
height was only five feet, six inches, and in later
years he became rather stout, but in youth he was
slender and graceful. His raiment was, almost
invariably, black and in appearance much resembled
that worn by Roman Catholic priests of the present
day. His hair, originally black (not, as most hair
so designated is, dark brown, but *jet black*), became
first gray, then silver-white. His eyebrows were
remarkably heavy and black and so remained. His
eyes were extraordinarily fine—dark brown, large,
and luminous—and his gaze was attentive and direct.
I have not observed a countenance more singular,
mobile, and expressive. When he chose he could
make of it an inscrutable mask. But when indifferent or unaware of observation the changes of
expression—shadows of his thoughts—would flit
over his face with astonishing variety and rapidity,
so that I have watched him when he would appear
at one moment commonplace and dull—the next,

highly distinguished, then kind—gentle—thoughtful
—dreamy—ruminant—pensive—mischievous—pug-
nacious—alert—hard—cold—at   moments,   even
malignant—boyish—playful—tender.   On the rare
occasions when passion mastered him (or when he
chose to have it seem to do so—occasions always difficult to distinguish), his aspect became positively
Mephistophelian. . . .

*   *   *   *   *   *   *

One of the mental advantages possessed by
Belasco,—a qualification as precious as it is rare,—
was the faculty of absorbing knowledge without
effort. He learned all things with amazing ease.
When little more than thirteen years old he had
imbibed from an uncle, a visionary scholar, sufficient
knowledge of Hebrew to enable him to conduct a
religious service in that language, which he did,
"without the punctuation,"—an achievement the difficulty of which will be appreciated only by Hebrew
scholars. That faculty persisted in him always. . . .

Belasco early recognized the wisdom contained
in the old poet Prior's injunction as to the treatment
of woman,

"Be to her faults a little blind,
Be to her virtues very kind,"

and he consistently obeyed it. He possessed, furthermore, an intuitive knowledge of the nature of
women, a compassionate sympathy with them, and,
whether professionally or personally, exceptional skill
in pleasing and managing them: he was, in turn,
readily subservient to female influence. . . .

As a writer he manifested amazing vitality, persistent industry, lively fancy, considerable faculty
of imagination, keen observation, quick perception
of character but more of striking situation and
effect, and great knowledge of human nature. He
possessed more the sense of humor than the faculty
of it. . . .

Belasco all his life possessed the spirit of adventure. He was eagerly interested in the life of to-
day. His sensibility was extreme. He had great
goodness of heart. He was very generous, extremely
kind

* * * * * * *

A GREAT SHAKESPEAREAN PROJECT.

[Not long before my father died he broached to
Belasco the project of making a remarkable series
of Shakespearean productions. His suggestion was
eagerly adopted and, if he had lived, it would have

been put into effect during the theatrical season of
1918-'19. His death forced postponement of the
productions—but some preparatory work had been
accomplished and Belasco has not abandoned the
project, which is outlined in the following corre-
spondence, and which will, I believe, ultimately be
fulfilled.—J. W.]

(*William Winter to David Belasco.*)

"New Brighton, Staten Island,
"February 23, 1917.

"Dear David:—

"My work on your 'Life,' leading me into considerate
examination of what you have done and not done, the
scope of your experience, the difference between conditions,
past and present, has, incidentally, turned my mind toward
the future and what you might do, and I venture to make
a suggestion, which I hope you will not deem intrusive.
It would be a great thing for our Stage, and I think for
you, if you were to make a splendid production of a
Shakespeare play—and I believe that you could, with profit,
bring out 'King Henry IV.' It has not been acted in New
York since 1896, and then only for a few nights and in a
very inefficient way.* It had not been acted previous to
that for fifteen or twenty years. 'On the road' it is, practically, as little known. The Second Part has not been acted
in our city (except two or three performances at the Century [Theatre], by amateurs, signifying nothing) for more

*At Wallack's Theatre, March 19, 1896, by Mr. and Mrs. Robert
Taber (Julia Marlowe): see "Shakespeare on the Stage—Third Series,"
page 370.—J. W.

than half-a-century. A production of the First Part might be made; or, Daly's original scheme of combining the two parts might be fulfilled,—though I believe the former would be much the better venture.

"If the idea pleases you, I should be most happy to talk with you about it, in detail; to make suggestions, and to assist in any possible way. I hope you will consider this matter with care. If you do not bring out the play, before long somebody else will—and, if with proper care, gain reputation and money by it.

"I have been very sick, but am improving and the work goes on—though much slower than I would have it do. I hope to see you before long.

"With kind regards,
"Faithfully yours,
"WILLIAM WINTER."

(*David Belasco to William Winter.*)

"Belasco Theatre, New York,
"March 2, 1917.

"My dear Mr. Winter:—

"I received your letter and regret very much that you were so ill. I am glad, indeed, to learn that you are better. I think the weather is very depressing and debilitating.

"I have long wanted to do a Shakespearean play, and your suggestion gives me an idea. I think that 'King Henry IV.,' if well done and produced with simple dignity, would be most timely. Thank you very much for your suggestion.

"As soon as this hateful season is over (the spring season is always so hard on me—engaging actors, getting manuscripts together, etc.) do let me come over and talk over 'King Henry IV.': meanwhile, I must read it again, as parts of it are very faint in my memory. I do not believe in combining the two parts. I had thought of 'Julius Cæsar,' which I consider the greatest play in the world; but it is so well known that it invites comparison. It is much better to produce a Shakespearean play but little seen. . . .

"With many thanks, all good wishes—and looking forward to seeing you and talking over a Shakespearean production, I am,

"Faithfully yours,

"DAVID BELASCO."

(*William Winter to David Belasco.*)

"New Brighton, Staten Island,
"March 8, 1917.

"Dear David:—

"Your letter of March 2 has reached me.

"I was glad to hear from you, and I thank you for your kind wishes. I improve but slowly: still—I improve.

"The work goes on—but *not* well. It goes slowly. But still—it goes. I do not remember ever experiencing so much difficulty in putting biographical matter in order. . . .

"As soon as the weather settles, and the pressure of your business will permit, I shall be glad to have you come to see me here. We can then resume talks about your adventures; and we can confer about 'King Henry IV.' The more I have reflected on the subject the more I feel that you would do well to revive that play. It requires editing, of course,—but it is a superb work. Besides *Falstaff, King Henry the Fourth, Prince Henry* and *Hotspur* are all splendid characters (*I* prefer the *Prince* to *Hotspur:* actors usually do not), and several of the others are almost as good.

"The plan of combining the two Parts has some merits: but (in my judgment) to produce the First Part is the 'eftest scheme.' We will talk of it when you come. . . .

"Faithfully yours,
"WILLIAM WINTER."

(*William Winter to David Belasco.*)

"46 Winter Avenue, New Brighton,
"Staten Island, New York,
"May 18, 1917.

"My dear David:—

"In the course of my work on the 'Life' I have had occasion to examine and consider several forms of censure and disparagement which, first and last, have been a good deal circulated about you. One of these is the statement (which I, personally, have heard made by some who ought to have known better) that you have not 'produced Shakespeare' because you have been afraid the public would then 'find you out.' This has led me to make a very careful study of the subject and an exposition of the quality of your early experience and training as bearing upon competency to produce and direct Shakespeare in revivals. This, in turn, has kept the suggestion I ventured to make to you, some time ago, about 'King Henry IV.,' much in my mind. And turning over that subject and looking at it from many points, I have formulated a plan, fulfilment of which would give you an absolutely unique position among producers of Shakespeare, and I venture to lay it before you, in the hope that perhaps it may be of use, and that, at least, you will not think me presumptuous.

"It is as follows:

" 'King Henry IV.,' both parts, is a sequel to 'King Richard II.' The latter is one of the most eloquent and beautiful of all Shakespeare's plays. All three of the plays named could well and conveniently be acted *by the same company*. The actual expense of putting on all three of them would not be much more than that of putting on one. You could make an IMMENSE impression by bringing out those three plays as a 'Shakespeare Trilogy.' Thus:

"Mondays and Thursdays; 'King Richard II.'

"Tuesdays and Fridays; 'King Henry IV., Part One.'

"Wednesdays and Saturdays; 'King Henry IV., Part Two.'

"Thus, every week, you could give two full 'cycles' of the trilogy; and, on matinée days, the 'First Part of King Henry IV.,' or a modern play.

"In presenting such a thing you would undertake and accomplish a more distinctive, original, and impressive managerial enterprise than any single venture of any of the representative Shakespearean producers,—Garrick, Kemble, Macready, Phelps, Kean, Booth, Irving, Daly, or Beerbohm-Tree.

"*I* feel confident that, in a *business* way, it could be made profitable. If you got through even at cost, or at a small loss, it would (in *my* view) be, in a *business* way (wholly aside from the immense and incontestable service to art and the public), a profitable investment. And I *am sure* it would 'make money,' too.

"I would do anything and everything in my power to help so fine a scheme,—would arrange the plays, write notes, etc., etc., if you should desire it.

"Please do not think me intrusive with my suggestions. And please give this very careful consideration.

"It would be a special satisfaction to me to see you crown your career with such a wonderful, such an unparalleled, accomplishment. However much honest difference of opinion there may be regarding some of the productions you have made (as you know, you and I are hopelessly at variance about some of the plays you have brought out), there could be no room for cavil or honest censure of such a venture as the production of three of Shakespeare's greatest plays, which, practically speaking, are unknown, are *new*, to the American Stage, and which are peculiarly well suited to *your* purposes and treatment. And it would be all the more splendid that such production should not be made at the high-tide of general theatrical prosperity, but should be made when the whole world seems shattered, and the rest of theatrical managers are running about like ants that have been disturbed in their hill!

"Faithfully yours,
"WILLIAM WINTER."

(Telegram, David Belasco to William Winter.)

"New York, May 19, 1917.

"Dear William Winter, I [have] just read your letter. You are right, and I promise you and myself to do the plays as you suggest, counting upon your generous assistance, without which I could not do them. I shall come over as soon as I possibly can, to speak further of this. Thank you for your enthusiasm and your faith. God bless you!

"DAVID BELASCO."

CONCERNING SARAH BERNHARDT.

[It was part of my father's purpose in making this Memoir to devote a section in it to BELASCO'S CONTEMPORARIES. The notes which he made on the subject were not extensive. For that reason and for others I have decided not to attempt to supply the section. Before making the decision, however, I addressed to Belasco some inquiries bearing on the subject and especially one concerning his "favorite player." His reply to the latter embodies a notable tribute to a wonderful woman and is, I think, of exceptional interest. Among other things, it strikingly illustrates how radically doctors sometimes disagree. No person more admired the resolute courage shown by Sarah Bernhardt than Winter did, who wrote of her: "It is good to see upon the Stage—and everywhere else—indomitable endurance, the aspiring mind that nothing can daunt and the iron will that nothing can break." And no writer more justly appreciated than he did her artistic faculties, her supremacy as "an histrionic executant." His final estimate of her, however,—an estimate as exact as a chemist's analysis and one which will survive all disparagement,—is, in some respects, in such sharp disagreement with Belasco's that readers of the latter will find the former specially instructive. It is embodied, together with his studies of her acting, in his book entitled "The Wallet of Time."—J. W.]

(*David Belasco to Jefferson Winter.*)
"The Belasco Theatre, New York,
"May 31, 1918.

"My dear Jefferson Winter:—

"You ask me to tell you who, of all the players I have ever seen, is my favorite. My, but that is a hard question to answer! In fact, I don't think I *can* answer with just a name. I have so many favorites! It is a case of 'Not that I love Cæsar less but Rome more!' And then, too, I have seen and known so many players of so many different kinds—of *all* kinds—and our moods vary. As I look back into my memory and try to call up the actors and actresses of the Past it seems to me that John McCullough was the most *lovable* as a man and, in the great, heroic parts, the most satisfying as an actor. Barrett was the most *ambitious;* Booth was the most *powerful* and *interesting;* Owens was the *funniest* man I ever saw, and after him Raymond; Wallack was the most *polished* and *courtly;* Salvini was the most *imposing;* Irving the most *intellectual* and *dominating;* Mansfield the most *erratic*—and all of them were great actors and each of them, I think, was my special favorite! But if I could see only one more theatrical performance and had to choose which one of those actors I would see, I think I would choose Edwin Booth in *King Richard the Third.*

"Of the women—Adelaide Neilson was easily the most *winsome* and *passionate.* Modjeska was the most *romantic.* Mary Anderson was the *stateliest,* Ellen Terry the most *pathetic,* Ada Rehan the *greatest comedienne,* and Sarah

Bernhardt—ah, what shall I say of the Divine Sarah!

"If I were to have the choice of one last performance by the *one actress* I admire the most I am afraid I should quarrel with Fate and insist on choosing *two*—Adelaide Neilson in *Juliet* and Sarah Bernhardt in anything. To me, she is, in all seriousness, one of the everlasting wonders of art. Her voice was like liquid gold; her delivery was, and is, a supreme example for any man or woman that ever stepped on a stage. She added a language to all the others. French is beautiful; but French-as-spoken-by-Sarah-Bernhardt is sublime! As an actress I admired her most in the pre-Sardou plays; but she is great in everything. She has always practised one of the great truths your dear father taught—that the art of acting is the art of *expression* not *re*pression. I consider that she is the best *listener* I ever saw—and very few except stage managers know how difficult it is to seem to listen for the first times to speeches which have been heard over and over again, sometimes for many years. She is always mistress of the scene. It is a dramatic education just to watch her. She could play 'quiet' scenes as well as anybody else—if not better. But when it came to the great emotional outbursts Sarah Bernhardt could always make them and make them so that she brought her audience right up on their feet. A good deal of the so-called 'repressed school' of acting is not art but artifice—mere trickery. Many players of that school 'repress' because they haven't got anything to give out—they make a virtue of necessity and dodge what they cannot do. Sarah Bernhardt never tried to dodge anything and she never needed to, because she never undertook anything she could not do superbly. As to the secret of her wonderful success and great career that you hear people talk so much about, it is simply this: She loves her work.

SARAH BERNHARDT

A Belasco souvenir — tendre
Sarah Bernhardt. 1913 Sympathie

When man, woman, or child *loves* what they are doing, the doing of it is to them like God's sunlight to the flowers, it keeps them alive and makes them beautiful.

"Much as I admire Mme. Bernhardt as an actress I think I admire her most as a woman. She sets an example of pluck and perseverance for all of us, and I have always been very solicitous of her good opinion. She has come to see several of my productions and her approval has meant much to me. I once gave a special performance of 'Adrea' for her,* because that was the only way she could get to see it and her admiration and applause I regard as the highest honor.

"Last Christmas I sent her a telegram which I should like to give you. This is it:

" 'Dear and adored friend:—

" 'May God be good to you this coming year, may you have a bright and happy Christmas, and may your glorious spirit remain with us for many years to come. We all admire your courage and your genius and love to call you "The Great Woman" of our century!'

"Her reply is one of my most valued treasures:

" 'I cannot express to you sufficiently my appreciation of your adorable messages. I have long been an admirer and friend of yours. My one regret is that I have never played under your direction. That will be for another planet!

" 'All my heart devoted,

" 'SARAH BERNHARDT.'

* GRAND OPERA HOUSE, CHICAGO, THURSDAY MATINEE:—
April 19, 1906. A special performance in honor of Mme. Sarah Bernhardt. David Belasco presents Mrs. Leslie Carter in "Adrea."

"Yes, my dear Jefferson Winter, if I must have one, and *only one*, favorite player, I am quite sure it must be Mme. Sarah Bernhardt, in whom the Spirit of Courage, the Spirit of Youth, the Spirit of France, and the Spirit of Art are all united.

"Faithfully,

"DAVID BELASCO."

BRIEF EXTRACTS FROM MISCELLANEOUS CORRESPONDENCE OF BELASCO.

"In all my years of work in the Theatre I have never done anything with which I was wholly satisfied—and I never shall do so. It is the irony of Fate that we live only long enough to learn how, and then die before we can make use of the knowledge!"

"If I were asked what proportion of the aspirants for the Stage who apply to me for advice will ultimately become great artists, I should answer: 'One in two thousand.'"

"The good stage manager is born—like the good actor. It [stage management] is, in itself, a special gift and cannot be acquired by training."

"When I can think more with my head and less with my heart the world will think me wise—and I shall know myself a fool!"

"The eyes of the heart see quickly and judge rightly."

"I think Dreams are the only Realities of Life—and Love is their soul."

"My world is a small one, of my own making; a world of faith and dreams—and that's why there are so few people in it!"

"When we are not physically well, the thoughts follow the line of least resistance—if the Will allows them to; but the

Will is *Master*, and whatever we wish to be, whatever we wish to do, whatever we wish to get, we *can* get, we can *be* and *do*, by *willing* it. So it is that you will be happy; so it is that you will do wonderful things with your life; so it is that you will get into the Castle of your Dreams."

"For women, marriage is the greatest of all careers: therefore, do not try to mix any of the others with it!"

About Flaubert and de Maupassant: "Both of them are of the realistic school, and all students of human nature should read and reread them, for they are well worth thought and study. The joys and ills of life are so graphically portrayed that one may almost hear the souls of many women weep in their pages. Many of their women you will find frail and erring, but the light of love shines through nearly all their mistakes, hallowing them, and whether they be beautifully human, or just inhumanly beautiful, they are always women."

"Actors are prone to think too much of themselves and too much of the affairs of other people. Gossip and frivolity in the theatre have killed many a promising career. The first maxim I would teach all beginners on the stage is this, by Augustin Daly.

'A sure way to Success—Mind your business:
'A sure way to Happiness—Mind your own business!'

I read that on a sign in the waiting room of Daly's Theatre, more than thirty-five years ago, and I made up my mind if ever I had a theatre of my own I'd put it up where my actors could see it,—and I did. It's over the Call Board at my theatre now. The second maxim I would teach actors is this: 'Never fake on the stage. The public will always catch you and never forgive you!'"

"The day of the drunken actor, like that of the drunken statesman and the drunken doctor, has gone forever."

"Try with all your might to think sweet and happy thoughts—and in time you will come to have faith in real things and so will understand life."

"Life is very short, and happiness an elusive will-o'-the-wisp—a wraith of the night of Time who beckons and beckons, and when we try to follow him, escapes us very easily."

"The 'star' actors of to-day lack that careful schooling and full equipment conspicuous in all the great 'stars' of twenty-five, thirty, fifty years ago, and which is to be acquired only through the old-time stock system. According to the method of those days, it was never possible for the actor to play the same part many times in succession. He was obliged to demonstrate ability not only in many parts but through a period of many years, and thus to establish himself deservedly in the good opinion of the public. . . . I doubt whether any of the young 'stars' could play as many and as great a variety of parts and play them as well as the 'stars' of former days,—although striking successes are made repeatedly in characters especially written for some particular 'star.' . . ."

"In the old days we frequently produced plays with hardly anything at all to enhance them, either scenery or properties, but merely by a judicious use of clothes and lighting we made them effective: we did this because we did not have means to do them correctly. Nowadays, productions so made are hailed as novelties and the wonders of the age!"

"I maintain that the great thing, the essential thing, for a producer is to create *Illusion* and *Effect*. The supreme object in all my work has been to get near to nature; to

DAVID WARFIELD AS *VAN DER DECKEN*

make my atmosphere as *real* as possible, when I am dealing with a drama or a comedy of life. In mounting a fantastic play there is but one thing to do, and that is to be as fantastic as possible. And so, in a realist play to be as realistic as possible. And by this I mean to create the *illusion* of reality. To do that every scene must be treated as a separate, a new, problem,—and the setting of it so as to create illusion is a problem that will never be solved by the 'new art.' . . . When I set a scene representing a Child's Restaurant how can I expect to hold the *attention* of my audience unless I show them a scene that *looks* real? They see it, recognize it, accept it and then, if the actors do their part, the audience forgets that it isn't looking into a real place. In 'Marie-Odile' some benches, chairs, tables, a pot of carrots and a few other things, with the bare walls of the convent, were all we needed. But suppose I had tried to put 'Adrea' on in the same way? Let us cut our cloth to suit our pattern. Do not let us attempt to 'suggest' a Child's Restaurant by setting up a counter with a coffee cup and a toothpick on it, nor try to picture the court of a Roman emperor with the same bare simplicity that answers for a lonely convent in Alsace! . . ."

"After all, hard work, a little love, courage to go on, strength to fight the daily battle,—what more can a man ask?"

APPENDIX

(By J. W.)

Belasco's romantic drama of "Van Der Decken" was first produced at The Playhouse, Wilmington, Delaware, on December 12, 1915, with David Warfield in its central character, that of *The Flying Dutchman,* and it was acted during the balance of the season of 1915-'16 on a tour which embraced Washington, Baltimore, Pittsburgh, Cincinnati, and many other cities of the Middle-western States. It has not yet been presented in New York. Belasco esteems it as in some ways his best work. Mr. Winter did not see it. The following comments on "Van Der Decken" and its representation are quoted from an article by Charles M. Bregg, a respected journalist and dramatic critic of "The Pittsburgh Gazette":

"It is a play so delicate, so poetic in its inner meaning and so weird in its mystery and philosophy that one wonders at the artistic courage of David Belasco and the daring of this adventurous actor who has struck out into hitherto unsailed seas of dramatic endeavor. . . . The story, which has appeared in the folklore of nearly all the nations of Europe but which has found its most extensive expression in Holland—that of the rebellious seaman who was destined to an eternal roaming of the seas as a punishment for defying God—is not new in the literature of the stage. In Opera and in Drama it has appeared under various guises; but to David Belasco and to David Warfield has been left the task of giving the old myth a new setting. Under the title of 'Van Der Decken' Mr. Warfield appears as this Wandering Jew of the seas in a drama of intense emotional appeal tinged with a deep sense of the supernatural. In this new play *The Flying Dutchman* gains port and finds a peaceful ending as a reward for his self-sacrifice in surrendering the woman for whom he first sinned. This woman, according to the Belasco play, is a reincarnated image of the wife of the Dutchman left in Amsterdam nearly two centuries before, when he sailed away on that cruise around Cape Horn. Thus we find that the elements of mystery and of the supernatural are the main pivots of the dramatic action. To visualize them by stage investiture and amply to suggest them in action are tasks that few producers or actors would care to undertake. . . . There is [in the dramatic story] a romance, but it is so wrapped up in the mystery of other centuries, and perhaps is not always so clear in the philosophy of reincarnation, as to be appreciably understood. These are points about which there may be sound differences of opinion, but on a first hearing they seem, as a final result, to leave the play shorn of diverse interest and therefore somewhat monotonous in its appeal.

"But it is a weird and deeply interesting play in the compactness of the story and in its dramatic rendition. The fabric is so delicate that if it were not staged and played with the utmost care and good taste it might easily fall to pieces. . . . Mr. Warfield demonstrates afresh the fine, sympathetic quality of his acting. This

INA CLARE AS *POLLY SHANNON*, IN "POLLY WITH A PAST"

rôle is absolutely foreign to anything else he has ever done, and by the power of his personality and the care of his delineation he makes the part of the ill-fated sailor throb with sympathy and meaning. In makeup he emphasizes the poetic quality underlying the character. . . . In staging this play Belasco handles his lights as a great symphony conductor plays with instruments, bending them to his will and making them set the color of the entire play. The three acts are set with marvellous care. An old ship sail acts as the front drop curtain, and throughout the play the atmosphere is almost made to drip with salt water. One act is in a harbor; another, on board the ship of *The Flying Dutchman*, and the third is a beautiful little delph setting that is like some old picture of Hollandese ware. In the stage effects, such as wind, thunder, and lightning, Belasco can make old devices seem an echo of Nature herself. . . . The music of the stage is ghostly and haunting. . . ."

"Van Der Decken" was played with the following cast:

Van Der Decken........................David Warfield.
Nicholas Staats......................Ernest Stallard.
Mate Jacob Te Beckel..................William Boag.
Jansoon Kolp...........................Fritz Lieber.
Petie Vieck............................Fred Graham.
Raff Kloots.........................Harold Russell.
Rudie Schimmelpennick................Horace Braham.

SAILORS ABOARD THE FLYING DUTCHMAN'S SHIP "BATAVIA."
Kris...............................Arthur Fitzgerald.
Bram.................................Herbert Ayling.

Hein......................Worthington L. Romaine.
Hans...............................J. J. Williams.
Prinz.............................Lawrence Woods.
Klass.............................Edward L. Walton.
Jan Tanjes..............................Bert Hyde.
Pilot Krantz...........................Tony Bevan.
Boatman..............................Oren Roberts.
Trintie Staats.........................Jane Cooper.
Johanna................................Marie Bates.
A Little Boy....................Master MacComber.

"POLLY WITH A PAST."

"Polly with a Past" is a merry though thin piece of farcical fooling, which owes its exceptional success—it has already run nearly an entire season in New York—to the attractiveness of the setting provided for it by Belasco and to the earnestness and zest with which it is played. It was written by Messrs. George Middleton and Guy Bolton and then rewritten under the direction of Belasco. Its plot is conventional, though familiar stage figures and time-tried devices are handled in it with considerable breezy dexterity. *Polly Shannon,* an orphan, the daughter of a poor clergyman of East Gilead, Ohio, desires to study music in Paris. She makes her way as far as New York and there, having no money, she secures employment as cook and waitress in the service of two young bachelors, *Harry Rich-*

ardson and *Clay Collum.* A friend of theirs, *Rex
Van Zile,* is violently in love with a young woman,
Myrtle Davis, whose purpose in life is the reformation of the abandoned waifs of society. *Myrtle's*
attitude toward *Rex* is aloof and cool and he despairs
of winning her. *Harry* and *Clay,* who have heard
the story of their pretty little servant and become
interested in her, seek her counsel. *Polly,* premis-
ing that though a minister's daughter she is familiar
with French novels, suggests that the best way for
Rex to win *Myrtle's* love is for him to pretend to
become the helplessly fascinated victim of a notorious Parisian adventuress. Finally, after much per-
suasion, *Polly* agrees to assume the part of the
adventuress and, introduced into the ultra-respectable
Van Zile home, she does so with such entire success
that not only is *Myrtle* inspired with jealous interest
but that *Rex* is really charmed by her winning ways
and transfers his affections to her. Various complications occur, incident to the attainment of this
result—all of them amusing although transparently
artificial in contrivance—and as a whole the representation provides an unusually agreeable entertainment.

"Polly with a Past" was first acted at the Apollo
Theatre, Atlantic City, on June 11, 1917; and, after
a brief fall tour, it was produced at the Belasco

Theatre, New York, on September 6, with the following cast:

Harry Richardson	Cyril Scott.
Rex Van Zile	Herbert Yost.
Prentice Van Zile	H. Reeves-Smith.
Stiles	William Sampson.
Clay Collum	George Stewart Christie.
A Stranger	Robert Fischer.
Commodore "Bob" Barker	Thomas Reynolds.
Polly Shannon	Ina Claire.
Mrs. Martha Van Zile	Winifred Fraser.
Myrtle Davis	Anne Meredith.
Mrs. Clementine Davis	Louise Galloway.
Parker	Mildred Dean.

Excellent performances were given in this farce, especially by Cyril Scott,—a neat and skilful actor of pleasant personality, who bears himself with more breezy jauntiness than most men half his age,—H. Reeves-Smith and William Sampson, both experienced and accomplished players of the old school, and by Miss Ina Claire, a talented young actress, who, as *Polly Shannon,* made her first appearance on the legitimate stage in it. Belasco's attention was first directed to her during the season of 1915-'16 when, as one of the performers in a vaudeville, she sang a song called "Poor Little Marie-Odile" in which he was severely lampooned. He attended her performance, was favorably impressed by her singing and imitations, and engaged her. Miss Claire is pretty, extraordinarily self-poised, an expert mimic, has a good stage presence, is able to assume effectively a demure manner, and she played *Polly* with spirit, humor, and at least one touch of feeling.

"TIGER ROSE."

"Tiger Rose" was written by Willard Mack and then rewritten under Belasco's direction and with his assistance. It was first produced at the Shubert Theatre, Wilmington, Delaware, on April 30, 1917: on October 3, that year, it was produced at the Lyceum Theatre, New York, where it is still current (June, 1918) and where it bids fair to remain for many weeks. It is a picturesque and effective melodrama, in four acts (the third being presented as practically an undetached continuation of the second), the scene of which is a frontier post in the Canadian Northwest. The action of that play revolves around the love affair of a French-Canadian girl named *Rose Bocion.* She is an orphan and the ward of *Hector MacCollins,* a conventionally austere yet kindly Scotchman, a factor of the Hudson Bay Trading Company, in whose dwelling three of the acts take place. The girl, a lovely flower of the forest, is admired and courted by all the youth for many a mile around, including a capable but dissolute Irishman, *Constable Michael Devlin,* of the Royal North Western Mounted Police. *Rose,* however, will have none of them,— for she and *Bruce Norton,* a young civil engineer from a neighboring construction camp, have met by chance and have become lovers. *Norton,* in the camp where he is employed, unexpectedly encounters and kills a man who, years earlier, had first misled and then deserted his sister, a married woman, who in consequence committed suicide. *Norton* makes his escape into the wilderness and seeks to communicate with *Rose,* his only friend, hoping to obtain her help in getting clear of the region. An Indian squaw employed in the factor's household bears a message and eventually he succeeds in reaching the girl. But information of his crime has been transmitted to *MacCollins'* dwelling, by telephone, where it is received by *Devlin.* That blackguard, who has been made furious by *Rose's* bitterly contemptuous repulse of his dishonorable advances and who has surmised the identity of her lover with the fugitive, is vigilantly watchful, hoping to gratify his jealous hatred while in the performance of his duty. During the interview between *Norton* and *Rose* she detects the stealthy approach of *Devlin,* tracking him. After making a tryst with him at a remote

LENORE ULRIC AS *ROSE,* IN "TIGER ROSE"

and abandoned log cabin in the woods, she has
barely time to hide her lover in a huge old grandfather's clock, in the factor's house. From that
precarious concealment *Norton* escapes, down a
trapdoor in the floor, under cover of the dreadful
tumult of an appalling electrical storm (most realis-
tically and impressively managed in Belasco's presentment) and, eventually, makes his way to the
appointed meeting place. There, during the next
night, he is joined by *Rose* and a kindly physician,
Dr. Cusick, who has discovered her attachment and
who, somewhat unwillingly, has consented to assist
in the escape of her sweetheart. Various explana-
tions are exchanged and it is revealed that *Dr.
Cusick* (that being an assumed name) is actually
the wronged husband of *Norton's* sister and has been
for years seeking to find and kill the man slain by
him. After the family misfortunes have been discussed and an understanding arrived at and after
plans for the escape of *Norton* out of the Dominion
have been devised and arranged by the intrepid
Rose, the trio are about to separate when the
ubiquitous *Devlin,* who has divined their resort to
the ruined cabin, has concealed himself there and
listened to their conversation, suddenly emerges
from his hiding place and, "covering" the culprit
with a pistol, arrests him. *Rose,* however, abruptly

extinguishes the only light in the cabin, at the same instant shooting the weapon out of *Devlin's* hand and crying to her love to fly—which he does. *Devlin* makes an attempt to follow him, striking down and stunning *Cusick,* but, being unarmed, is stopped by *Rose* at the pistol point. Then, throughout the night she holds him there. With dawn, however, *Norton,* who has realized the predicament in which his escape will leave his sweetheart, returns, accompanied by a Jesuit priest whom he has met—and, as *Rose* will not submit to the removal of her lover to Edmonton, there to stand trial alone, but insists on an immediate marriage to him, the play ends with impending matrimony and the implication that *Dr. Cusick,* who, it appears has "done the State some service," will succeed in his declared intention of appealing to the legal authorities for lenient treatment of *Norton,*—an intention, by the way, which indicates a touching ignorance of the operation of criminal law in the region specified.

All this, if sometimes false to the probabilities of actual life, is always responsive to the purposes of acting, and, as presented by Belasco,—with scrupulous care to every aspect of the stage setting and to every detail of the stage management and with an unusually capable company,—the melodrama merits the success it has achieved. The central character is, of course, *Rose Bocion,*—who, with euphonious disregard of gender, is called *Tiger Rose.* This girl is headstrong, impulsive, and intense, she indulges with excessive freedom in violent expletives, and she fights hard for the man she loves. But there is nothing tiger-like in her conduct or her character. On the contrary, *Rose,* is winsome, brave, loyal, ardent, resourceful and utterly sincere, devoted and unselfish in her love. However, the name makes a striking title for the play. Miss Lenore Ulric, who acts the part, is possessed of exceptional natural advantages,—youth; a handsome face; abundant hair; expressive eyes, dark and beautiful; a slender, lithe figure; a sympathetic voice; strong, attractive personality, and an engaging manner. Her temperament is intense, her nature passionate, her style direct and simple. Her acting reveals force of character, experience, observation, thought, sensibility, ardor, definite purpose, and unusual command of the mechanics of art. It is, moreover, suffused with fervid, sometimes ungoverned feeling (which is a defect), and it is at all times sincere, individual, and interesting. She is an admirable listener, an excellent speaker,—articulating with great care,—and, at moments (as, for example, in a colloquy with *Father Tibault* as to belief in Diety), the disposition she exhibits in this performance seems altogether childlike and lovely. Under Belasco's sagacious direction she should go far.

CAST OF "TIGER ROSE."

Hector MacCollins....................Thomas Findlay.
Dan Cusick, M.D..................William Courtleigh.
Constable Michael Devlin, R.N.W.M.P......Willard Mack.
Bruce Norton.........................Calvin Thomas.
Father Thibault.......................Fuller Mellish.
Pierre La Bey......................Pedro De Cordoba.
George Lantry............................Edwin Holt.
Old Tom..............................Edward Mack.
Constable Haney......................Arthur J. Wood.
Mak-a-low...........................Chief Whitehawk.
Wa-Wa.................................Jean Ferrell.
Rose Bocion.............................Lenore Ulric.

DAVID BELASCO—HIS LATEST PORTRAIT, 1918

CHRONOLOGY

CHRONOLOGY OF THE LIFE OF
DAVID BELASCO

HUMPHREY ABRAHAM BELASCO,
BORN, LONDON, ENGLAND,
DECEMBER 26, 1830.

REINA MARTIN BELASCO,
BORN, LONDON, ENGLAND,
APRIL 24, 1830.

1853.

July.

25. DAVID BELASCO, eldest child of Humphrey Abraham, and Reina Martin, Belasco, was BORN, in a house in Howard Street, near Third Street, San Francisco, California.

1858. While David Belasco was a little child,— apparently about 1858,—his parents removed to Victoria, Island of Vancouver, B. C., taking him with them.

In the latter part of 185(8?) he was " carried on," at the Theatre Royal, Victoria, as *Cora's Child*, in "Pizarro,"—Julia Dean (Hayne) being the *Cora*. Later he played the child in "Metamora," when Edwin Forrest filled an engagement in Victoria.

186(2?). About 1862 he appeared with Julia Dean (Hayne), in "East Lynne," as *Little William*.

1864. In the latter part of 1864 he played the little *Duke of York*, in "King Richard III.,"

473

with Charles Kean, at the Theatre Royal,
Victoria.

1865-1871.　　In 1865 (March-April?) the elder Belasco
removed with his family to San Francisco,
California, and there established his permanent residence. As a boy, in that city, Belasco
attended several schools, chief among them the
Lincoln Grammar School. During part of
this period the Belasco home was in Louisa
Street, then in Bryant Street, afterward it
was in Clara Street.

1871.
March.
　　17.　　At the Metropolitan Theatre, San Francisco, Belasco appeared as an *Indian Chief*
in Professor Hager's "Great Historical Alle-
gory, 'The Great Republic,' "—which was
several times repeated, for the benefit of the
schools whose pupils participated in the
performance: in the Second Part thereof he
personated *War*.

April.
　　15.　　He appeared, in Hager's "The Great
Republic," at Sacramento, California.

June.
　　2.　　(Friday Evening.) He took part in a
series of public "competitive declamations"
(reciting "The Maniac"), by pupils of the
Lincoln Grammar School, at Platt's Hall,
San Francisco. On same occasion he

appeared as *Highflyer Nightshade*, in "The Freedom of the Press."

7. At the Metropolitan Theatre, revival of Hager's "The Great Republic," in which he again appeared as an *Indian Chief*, and as *War*.

22. He appeared as *Fornechet, Minister of Finance*, in a presentment of Sutter's "Life's Revenge," by the Fire-Fly Social and Dramatic Club, at Turnverein Hall, Bush Street, near Powell, San Francisco.

July.

10. BELASCO'S FIRST REGULAR APPEARANCE on the professional stage,—as a super, with Joseph Murphy, in "Help," at the Metropolitan Theatre. Subsequently he was given a small part, a few words to speak, in this play. "Help" was played till July 16, Sunday night.

19. "Help" revived at Metropolitan Theatre.

22. End of Murphy's engagement in "Help."

1872.

July.

22. He played *Bloater*, in "Maum Cre" (then first acted in San Francisco), with Joseph Murphy, at the Metropolitan Theatre.

December.

16. He appeared at the Metropolitan Theatre, San Francisco, with Minnie Wells (not Mary Wells), in "The Lion of Nubia" (not Lioness), as *Lieutenant Victor:* on this occasion he was billed as Walter Kingsley.

1873.

February.

23   He played *Peter Bowbells* in "The Illustrious Stranger," in a Benefit Performance, for Marion Mordaunt, at the Metropolitan Theatre.

March.

.5.   "Grand Reopening of the Metropolitan Theatre," under direction of John R. Woodard: cheap prices: The Chapman Sisters, in H. J. Byron's "Little Don Giovanni." Belasco played the *First Policeman*.

18.   He played *Prince Saucilita* (giving burlesque of a local character known as "Emperor" Norton), in "The Gold Demon," with the Chapman Sisters, at the Metropolitan Theatre.

21.   He played *Strale*, in "Checkmate," with the Chapmans, at the Metropolitan.

April.

2.   (One night only.) He played *Reuben*, in "Schermerhorn's Boy," and *Strale*, in "Checkmate," with the Chapmans, at the Academy of Music, Oakland, California.

3.   At the Metropolitan, San Francisco, he appeared, with the Chapmans, as the *Genius of the Ring*, in "The Wonderful Scamp; or, Aladdin No. 2," and as *Peter True*, in "The Statue Lover."

9.   He played the *First Fury*, in "Pluto," with the Chapmans, at the Metropolitan.

18.   Revival of "Little Don Giovanni" at the

BELASCO LEADING THE PARADE OF "THE LAMBS" UP PENNSYLVANIA AVENUE, WASHINGTON, D. C.

INSCRIPTION:

"The first time I 'paraded' into town since my old days in the West, when I used to bang the cymbals and pound the drum!"—D. B.

Metropolitan: Belasco as the *First Police-man*.

28. Last regular performance at the Metropolitan Theatre, San Francisco. The Chapman Sisters in "Cinderella,"—produced 23.

May.

3. He played with the Chapman Sisters, in "Little Don Giovanni," in Sacramento. Later he appeared, with the Chapman Sisters, in several California towns.

August.

18. He played *Bloater*, in "Maum Cre," with Joseph Murphy, at Shiels' Opera House, San Francisco.

25. He played *Bob Rackett*, in "Help," with Murphy, at Shiels'.

26. At the home of his parents, No. 174 Clara Street, San Francisco, California, David Belasco and Cecilia Loverich were married.

September.

1. At Shiels' Opera House he played *Baldwin*, with Murphy, in "Ireland and America": Same bill, September 2, 6, and 7. "Maum Cre" 3, 4, and 5.

10. He played *Harvey*, in "Out at Sea," with Laura Alberta, at Shiels' Opera House.

20. He played *Sambo*, in "Uncle Tom's Cabin," to the *Topsy* of Laura Alberta, at Shiels'.

25. "Twice Saved; or, Bertha the Midget," was acted at the Opera House (formerly Shiels', subsequently Gray's) and Belasco played *Major Hershner*.

29.   He acted *Spada*, in Stirling Coyne's "The
Woman in Red," with Fanny Cathcart, at
the Opera House. (That house was first
billed as Gray's Opera House, on October 3,
and "The Woman in Red" was played there
till October 5.)

October.

6.   Belasco played at Gray's Opera House, as
Darley, with Fanny Cathcart and George
Darrell, in "Dark Deeds."

18.   Benefit performance, at Gray's Opera
House, to James Dunbar: Belasco acted
Mons. Voyage, in Third Act of "Ireland as
It Was."

October-November, *et seq.*

He went to Virginia City, Nevada, where he
became a member of the stock company at
Piper's Opera House.

1874.

March.

1-7?   Belasco returned to San Francisco from
Virginia City.

10.   Engagement of Adelaide Neilson in San
Francisco began at the California Theatre,—
Miss Neilson making her first appearance
there in "Romeo and Juliet." Belasco participated in all the performances given during that engagement,—which ended on March
30,—as a super and helper about the stage.

May.

4.   Grand Opening of Maguire's New Theatre,
San Francisco, (the old Alhambra, rebuilt and

altered),—"The Entire Lingard Combination," Wiliam Horace Lingard, Dicky Dunning, Alice Lingard, etc., appearing in "Creatures of Impulse," "Mr. and Mrs. Peter White," and a miscellaneous entertainment.

June-September.

Belasco worked as a copyist, etc., for Barton Hill, at the California Theatre and played minor parts (not recorded) at Maguire's New Theatre. Also, he made several brief excursions as a "barnstormer" to small towns of California and Nevada.

September.
(14?).   Belasco became attached to Maguire's New Theatre as assistant stage manager and prompter, actor of small parts, hack playwright, and secretary and messenger to Thomas Maguire. In this employment he came into association with James A. Herne, Thomas Whiffen, Annette Ince, Ella Kemble, Sydney Cowell, etc. He remained there for about four months.

October.
12.   He played the *Dwarf* in "Rip Van Winkle" at Maguire's,—Herne being *Rip*.

December.
24.   Belasco played *Pietro* and *Galeas*, in the prologue and drama of "The Enchantress," at Maguire's New Theatre.

1875.

January to (May?).

Belasco was "barnstorming" with a Miss Rogers, originally a school teacher, who obtained financial support and starred in a repertory including "East Lynne," "Camille," "Frou Frou," and "Robert Macaire." Miss Rogers' tour began in Portland, Oregon, and continued through small towns along the Big Bear and Little Bear rivers. It proved a failure and the company was disbanded,— Miss Rogers and Belasco, however, continued to appear together for several weeks, presenting one-act plays such as "A Happy Pair" and "A Conjugal Lesson."

June.

—.   He was in San Francisco.

July.

4.   He participated, as assistant to James H. Le Roy, in stage management of a benefit performance, for Frank Rea, at Maguire's New Opera House.

August.

4.   He assisted, in various ways, in a presentation at the California Theatre of "The Bohemian," in which George Ceprico (amateur) appeared as *Edmund Kean*.

7.   Production at the California Theatre of [a variant, by Belasco?] Le Roy's version of "The New Magdalen,"—Ellie Wilton playing *Mercy Merrick*.

8.   "Lost in London" was presented at Maguire's New Theatre, at Belasco's sug-

gestion [acted according to a prompt book or "version" prepared by him?].

November.

17. Benefit, to "Sam" Wetherill, at Maguire's New Theatre,—stage management of Belasco.

December.

6. Belasco played a subsidiary part in "The Jealous Wife," in a performance ("last night of the season") at Maguire's, for the benefit of Katy Mayhew.

13. C. R. Thorne's Palace Theatre (formerly Wilson's Amphitheatre), corner Montgomery and Mission streets, San Francisco, was opened, with "Gaspardo; or, The Three Banished Men of Milan," and Belasco appeared in it as *Santo, a Monk.*

21. He played *Signor Mateo,* in "The Miser's Daughter."

24. He played *Selim,* in "The Forty Thieves," at Thorne's Palace Theatre.

30. He played *Gilbert Gates,* in "The Dawn of Freedom," at the same house. Thorne closed his theatre, suddenly, December 31.

1876.

January.

7. The Palace Theatre was reopened, as the Palace Opera House, under management of Colonel J. H. Wood, presenting Frank Jones in "The Black Hand; or, The Lost Will," in which Belasco played *Bob, a Policeman.* That engagement lasted for about three

weeks, at the end of which time, apparently, he went back to Maguire's New Theatre.

March.

6. Opening of Baldwin's Academy of Music, San Francisco. Thomas Maguire, proprietor. James A. Herne, stage manager. David Belasco, assistant stage manager and prompter. Bill: Barry Sullivan, in "King Richard III.,"—Belasco played *Ratcliff*.

11. Sullivan revived "The Wonder," at Baldwin's, and Belasco played in it as *Vasquez*.

13. Sullivan acted in "Hamlet," at Baldwin's: Belasco played *Bernardo* and the *Second Actor*.

16. Sullivan presented "Richelieu," at Baldwin's, and Belasco appeared as one of the *Secretaries*.

20. Played the *First Officer*, in "Macbeth," with Sullivan, at Baldwin's.

23. Played the *Waiter*, in "The Gamester," with Sullivan as *Beverley*.

27. Played the *Duke of Burgundy*, in "King Lear," with Sullivan, at Baldwin's.

29. Played a *Messenger*, in "Othello," with Sullivan, at Baldwin's.

31. Played *Salarino*, in "The Merchant of Venice," with Sullivan, at Baldwin's.

April.

5. Played the *Lieutenant*, in "Don Cæsar de Bazan," with Sullivan, at Baldwin's.

7. Played *Furnace*, in "A New Way to Pay Old Debts."

10. Played *Marco*, in "The Wife."

16. End of Barry Sullivan's engagement at Baldwin's Academy of Music, "King Richard III." Belasco played *Ratcliff*.

18. Mrs. James A. Oates began an engagement in Opera at Baldwin's, and Belasco, with other members of the dramatic stock company, returned to Maguire's New Theatre (whence they had come to Baldwin's), where they supported Baker and Farron, in "Heinrich and Hettie."

May-June—part of July.
Belasco went "barnstorming."

July.

23. He played *DeMilt*, in "Under the Gas-Light," in a benefit, by John McCullough and others, for E. J. Buckley, at the California Theatre.

September.

4. Edwin Booth began an eight weeks' engagement in San Francisco (the first in twenty years), at the California Theatre, in "Hamlet," "Richelieu," "Othello," etc., and Belasco was employed as a supernumerary in his company.

October.

—. Belasco was employed by James M. Ward as stage manager and playwright, at the Grand Opera House.

16. He appeared with Ward and Winnetta Montague, at the Grand Opera House, in "The Willing Hand."

22. He appeared at Baldwin's, as *Doctor of the*

Hospital, in "The Two Orphans," for benefit of Katy Mayhew.

1877.

February.

16.   He appeared at Egyptian Hall (No. 22 Geary Street, near Kearny), in association with Frank Gardner and his wife (Carrie Swan), acting *The Destroyer,* in "The Haunted House,"—a play written by himself,—*Valentine,* in an abridgment of "Faust," and *Mr. Trimeo,* in "The Mysterious Inn."

The presentments at Egyptian Hall were all built around a variant of the "Pepper's Ghost" illusion.

17.   At Egyptian Hall he appeared as *Avica, Spirit of Avarice,* in "A Storm of Thoughts"; *Phil Bouncer,* in "The Persecuted Traveller," and as *The Destroyer,* in "The Haunted House."

20.   At Egyptian Hall "Our Mysterious Boarding House" was presented, in which he played *Our Guest,* replacing "The Persecuted Traveller," in bill as on 17.

April.

2.   Same place, he played *Mark,* in "The Prodigal's Return," as well as *Avica* and *Our Guest,* as above.

The engagement of the Gardners and Belasco at Egyptian Hall continued for eight weeks.

Other plays which Belasco recalls having written for presentation there are "Wine,

Women, and Cards" and "The Christmas Night; or, The Convict's Return." I have not, however, found *record* of the presentation of them. During that engagement at Egyptian Hall, Belasco also gave several recitations, including "The Maiden's Prayer," with musical accompaniment, and "Little Jim."

May-July.

Belasco acted with Gardiner and his wife, in various cities and towns of California and the Pacific Slope, in the plays above mentioned.

August.

18. Belasco played *John O'Bibs*, in Boucicault's "The Long Strike" (billed as "The Great Strike"), and the *Earl of Oxford*, in the Fifth Act of "King Richard III.," in a benefit for A. D. Billings, at the California Theatre, San Francisco.

September.

24. A theatrical company, from the California Theatre, San Francisco, under the management of Thomas W. Keene, of which Belasco was stage manager, began a "Fair week" engagement at the Petaluma Theatre, Petaluma, California. Bill: "The Lady of Lyons," in which Belasco played *Monsieur Deschapelles*; and "The Young Widow," in which he played *Mandeville*.

25. Same engagement: "The Hidden Hand," Belasco playing *Craven Lenoir*; and "Robert Macaire," in which he played *Pierre*.

26. Same. "The Wife," Belasco as *Lorenzo;* and "My Turn Next," Belasco as *Tom Bolus.*

27. Same. "The Streets of New York," Belasco as *Dan;* and "The Rough Diamond," Belasco as *Captain Blenham.*

28. Same. "Deborah," Belasco as *Peter;* and "Solon Shingle" ("The People's Lawyer"), Belasco as *Lawyer Tripper.*

Same. Benefit of Keene. "The Ticket-of-Leave Man," Belasco acted one of the subsidiary parts.

October.

—. Belasco joined the Frayne Troupe, at Humboldt, Oregon, opening as *Mrs. Willoughby,* in "The Ticket-of-Leave Man." This engagement lasted about three months.

1878.

January.

4. He played at the Opera House, San José, as a member of the Frayne Troupe (Frank I. Frayne, manager), comprising also M. B. Curtis, H. M. Brown, E. N. Thayer, Mrs. Harry Courtaine, Gertrude Granville, and Miss Fletcher.

He played in many Pacific Slope towns and cities with this company.

January-March.

He returned to San Francisco and performed miscellaneous theatrical drudgery.

March.

4. Belasco played *James Callin,* and *Pablo,*

an Italian Harpist, in the prologue and drama of "Across the Continent," with Oliver Doud Byron, at the Bush Street Theatre, San Francisco. (Six nights: revival, March 18 to 23.)

26.   The New York Union Square Company acted at the Baldwin Theatre, San Francisco, in "Agnes," and Belasco appeared with it, as the valet, *Rudolphe.*

April.

8.   "One Hundred Years Old" was acted at the Baldwin Theatre, Belasco playing the servant, *Louis.*

15.   "Saratoga" was acted at the Baldwin, Belasco playing *Gyp.*

25.   "A Celebrated Case" was revived at the Baldwin, Belasco playing a subsidiary part.

May, *et seq.*

Belasco travelled with the Union Square Theatre Company, as stage manager, during a tour of towns and cities of California, Oregon, etc. At the end of that tour he received a memorable tribute from the members of the company: see page 106.

July.

8.   Boucicault's "The Octoroon," "retouched and rearranged" by Belasco, was revived at the Baldwin Theatre.

September.

2.   Belasco's version of "The Vicar of Wakefield," entitled (like Wills' version) "Olivia," was produced for the first time at the Baldwin Theatre, San Francisco, Rose Wood

acting *Olivia*, A. D. Bradley *Dr. Primrose*, James O'Neill *Mr. Barchell*, and Lewis Morrison *Squire Thornhill*.

October.

14. An alteration by Belasco of Wills' "A Woman of the People" was acted at the Baldwin.

28. Belasco's "Proof Positive" was acted at the Baldwin.

November.

4. Clara Morris began her first San Francisco engagement at the Baldwin, Belasco being the stage manager.

December.

23. "Not Guilty," by Watts Phillips, revised by Belasco, and produced under his direction, was acted for the first time in San Francisco, at the Baldwin Theatre: notable success.

1879.

January.

—. Belasco resigned his position at the Baldwin Theatre and rewrote his play of "The Lone Pine" for Denman Thompson. He disagreed with Thompson and his manager, J. M. Hill, and his play was not produced.

February.

—. Belasco was re-employed as stage manager, etc., at the Baldwin.

6. He played *Colonel Dent*, in "The Governess," with Clara Morris, at the Baldwin Theatre (one night only: farewell of Miss Morris).

17. Belasco's dramatization of Gaboriau's "Within an Inch of His Life" was acted for the first time at the Grand Opera House: notable success.

March.

1. "Within an Inch of His Life" was withdrawn.

3. The first presentation of Salmi Morse's "The Passion Play" was made at the Grand Opera House, San Francisco, under the stage management of Belasco and "Harry" Brown, —James O'Neill appearing in it as *Jesus Christ.*

11. "The Passion Play" was withdrawn at the Grand Opera House.

April.

15. Revival of "The Passion Play" at the Grand Opera House.

20-21, An injunction prohibiting further presentation of "The Passion Play" was issued, and, that being disregarded, O'Neill and his associates were arrested (21st): O'Neill was imprisoned, and later he was fined $50 and his associates $5 each, for contempt of court.

May.

5. An adaptation of Sardou's "La Famille Benoiton!" entitled "A Fast Family," made by Belasco, was played at the Baldwin.

19. At the Baldwin Belasco acted the old man, *Timothy Tubbs,* in his play of "The Millionaire's Daughter," which was then first presented,—five nights: revival May 26 to 31.

June.

2. Rose Coghlan, engaged at Belasco's request,
began her first engagement in San Francisco,
at the Baldwin, playing *Lady Gay*, in "London Assurance."

30. First performance of "Marriage by Moonlight" (afterward renamed "The Moonlight
Marriage"), by Belasco and James A.
Herne, occurred at the Baldwin Theatre.

July.

13. (Sunday night.) Special benefit for Belasco and James A. Herne, at the Baldwin:
"The Moonlight Marriage" and "Rip Van
Winkle."

15. First performance of Belasco's version of
"L'Assommoir," based on Zola's novel, was
made at the Baldwin, with an "all-star company,"—Rose Coghlan, Lillian Andrews, Jean
Clara Walters, O'Neill, Morrison, Herne, etc.,
being in the cast.

September.

9. At Baldwin's Theatre, San Francisco, first
production of "Chums" ("Hearts of Oak"),
by David Belasco and James A. Herne.

21. (Sunday.) Last performance of "Chums"
at Baldwin's. Failure.

October.

6. Herne-Belasco partnership presented
"Chums" at Salt Lake City.

Other places were visited. The business was
bad. Failure. "Chums" was closed, and company disbanded.

Belasco, Herne and his wife (Katharine

Corcoran) went to Chicago and lodged at the old Sherman House.

November.

17. First performance in Chicago, at Hamlin's Theatre (formerly the Coliseum?), of "Hearts of Oak" ("Chums"). Notable success.

30. "Hearts of Oak" closed at Hamlin's.

December.

1. Belasco-Herne Company appeared in Cincinnati.

20. (About) Belasco-Herne Company was playing "Hearts of Oak" in Indianapolis.

A version of "The Mariner's Compass" (on which "Hearts of Oak" was built) was presented in cities of the Middle West, under the name of "Oaken Hearts," to trade on the success of the Belasco-Herne title: unauthorized use of that title was stopped by legal action taken by Herne in courts of Michigan in May, 1880.

1880.

March.

15. "Hearts of Oak" was acted at Hooley's Theatre, return engagement, till March 27.

29. "Hearts of Oak" was performed for first time in New York, at the New Fifth Avenue Theatre—untruthfully announced as "by James A. Herne." Failure. During this engagement Herne was several times incapacitated to perform and Belasco appeared in his place as *Terry Dennison*.

April.

16.   Last performance of first "Hearts of Oak" engagement in New York.

Belasco and Herne took their play to the Arch Street Theatre, Philadelphia. There Herne quarrelled with Belasco and bought his half-interest in the play for $1500, which he did not pay till several years later.

Belasco returned to New York, seeking employment, but could not obtain it. He then made his way, by various shifts, across the continent, to his home in San Francisco.

June.

16.   Belasco reached San Francisco, after his disastrous experience with Herne and "Hearts of Oak."

He obtained immediate employment at the Baldwin Theatre, where Adelaide Neilson was then playing her farewell engagement (it began on June 8). James H. Vinson and Robert M. Eberle were, officially, the stage managers: Belasco officiated as assistant stage manager and as prompter, and, on July 17, he "rang down" the curtain on *the last performance ever given* by Miss Neilson:—*Juliet*, in Balcony Scene from "Romeo and Juliet," and *Amy Robsart*, in the play of that name.

During this engagement at the Baldwin, though actually he performed much important labor, both as stage manager and as writer and adapter of plays, Belasco's acknowledged position was wholly subsidiary: for reasons of business expediency he again assumed, for a time, use of the name Walter Kingsley.

July.

19. His play of "Paul Arniff" was produced, for the first time, at the Baldwin Theatre: it is founded in part on "The Black Doctor."

August.

16. John T. Malone made his first appearance on the stage, acting *Richelieu*, at the Baldwin, under the direction of Belasco.

30. A new version, by Belasco, of T. P. Cooke's "True to the Core" was acted at the Baldwin.

November.

15. William E. Sheridan began his first San Francisco engagement, at the Baldwin, during which, under stage direction of Belasco, he appeared in "King Louis XI.," "Wild Oats," "The Lady of Lyons," "The Merchant of Venice," etc., etc.

December.

28. First production in America of the once famous melodrama of "The World" was made, under Belasco's direction, at the Baldwin Theatre, San Francisco.

1881.

January.

17. Belasco's "The Creole" (based on "Article 47") was acted for the first time in New York, at the Union Square Theatre,—Eleanor Carey appearing in it as *Diana*.

February.

6(?).   Last performance of "The Creole" at the
Union Square Theatre.

March.

27.   Belasco left San Francisco, with the Baldwin Theatre stock company, for Portland,
Oregon.

April.

15.   He returned from Portland and resumed
employment at the Baldwin Theatre.

July.

18.   Belasco's play of "La Belle Russe" was
anonymously produced, under his stage
direction, at the Baldwin Theatre, San
Francisco (first time anywhere), Miss
Jeffreys-Lewis, Osmond Tearle, and Gerald
Eyre acting the chief parts in it. Exceptional success.

26.   Belasco's authorship of "La Belle Russe"
was announced, in advertisements of that
play.

30.   Final performance, original run, of "La
Belle Russe," at the Baldwin.

August.

15.   At the Baldwin occurred the first performance of Belasco's dramatic epitome of
Adolphe Belot's story, "The Stranglers of
Paris," Osmond Tearle acting *Jagon:*
Belasco's name was not made known at
this time as the stage-adapter of the
story.

September.

25.   Belasco left San Francisco, with Maguire,

for the East, to arrange for the sale of his play of "La Belle Russe."

During his stay in New York, October-December, this year, Belasco negotiated regarding presentment of "La Belle Russe" with Augustin Daly, John Stetson, A. M. Palmer, and Lester Wallack. He finally sold his interest in that play outright, to Frank L. Goodwin, for $1500, a return ticket to San Francisco, and $100 for travelling expenses.

December.
25.   Belasco reached San Francisco from New York.

1882.
March.
7.   First performance of Belasco's spectacle melodrama of "The Curse of Cain" occurred at the Baldwin.

April.
16.   End of Thomas Maguire's control of the Baldwin Theatre, San Francisco.

May.
8.   First production in New York of Belasco's play of "La Belle Russe" was made at Wallack's Theatre,—Osmond Tearle and Rose Coghlan playing the chief parts.

June.
12.   A "sensation revival" of Belasco's "retouched and re-arranged" version of Boucicault's "The Octoroon," introducing Callender's Colored Minstrels, was effected at the

Baldwin, under the stage direction of Belasco and the management of Gustave Frohman: notable success.

July

10. Belasco's "American Born" was acted, for the first time, at the Baldwin Theatre, San Francisco,—Edward N. Marble being then the lessee of that house.

—. First meeting of Belasco and Charles Frohman.

18(?). Belasco left San Francisco, travelling, as stage manager, with the [Gustave] Frohman Dramatic Company.

31. That company began an engagement in Denver, Colo.,—at the end of which, apparently, it was disbanded.

August.

16. Belasco's "American Born" was successfully produced, at the Grand Opera House, Chicago, under the joint management of Gustave and Charles Frohman.

October.

9. First production of "Young Mrs. Winthrop," by Bronson Howard, at the Madison Square Theatre. This was the first play produced at that theatre under the stage management of Belasco, and the incident marks his establishment in the Theatre of New York.

The 100th performance of "Young Mrs. Winthrop" occurred January 12, 1883: the 150th, March 5.

1883.

April.

7. Last performance (original "run") of "Young Mrs. Winthrop" at the Madison Square Theatre.

9. First performance, by professional actors, Madison Square Theatre, of "A Russian Honeymoon," by Mrs. Burton N. Harrison, produced under stage management of Belasco.

June.

4. Last performance of "A Russian Honeymoon" and end of "the regular season" at the Madison Square.

5. Beginning of the "summer season" at the Madison Square, with first production of "The Rajah; or, Wyncot's Ward," by William N. Young, revised by Belasco, and produced under his stage direction.

September.

11. 100th performance of "The Rajah" at the Madison Square.

October.

31. 150th performance of "The Rajah."

November.

12. At the New Park Theatre occurred the first performance in New York of Belasco's melodrama (revised for the occasion) of "The Stranglers of Paris," which was produced under the stage direction of the author and the management of Charles Frohman: Henry Lee appeared as *Jagon*.

December.

8. "The Rajah" was withdrawn at the Madison Square.

10. At the Madison Square first production of "Delmar's Daughter; or, Duty"; by Henry C. De Mille, under Belasco's direction. It was a failure and was withdrawn on the 15th.

17. "The Rajah" was revived at the Madison Square.

1884.

January.

29. Last performance of "The Rajah."

31. First New York performance, Madison Square Theatre, of "Alpine Roses," by H. H. Boyesen; stage direction of Belasco. Georgia Cayvan, Marie Burroughs, Eben Plympton, and Richard Mansfield played the chief parts in this drama.

April.

10. Last performance of "Alpine Roses."

12. At the Madison Square Theatre, first production, on any stage, of Belasco's drama of "May Blossom," founded in part on his earlier play of "Sylvia's Lovers": produced under the stage direction of the author.

July.

5. Belasco sailed for England, on board the SS. Alaska, to witness performances of "Called Back," at the Haymarket Theatre, London,—that play having been purchased for production in America by the Mallory

brothers. First meeting of Belasco and author occurred on this voyage.

19. He sailed for New York, on board the SS. Alaska.

27. He arrived in New York.

August.

27. Public announcement by the Mallory brothers that Albert Marshall Palmer had become a partner in the management of the Madison Square Theatre. Friction between Belasco and Palmer, relative to management of the stage, had arisen some time earlier.

September.

1. First production in America of "Called Back," made by the Mallory brothers at the Fifth Avenue Theatre, under the stage direction of Belasco.

9. 150th performance of "May Blossom" at the Madison Square Theatre.

27. Last performance of "May Blossom" at the Madison Square Theatre.

29. A new policy was put into effect at the Madison Square Theatre, under the influence of Palmer, marked by the presentation, on this date, of "The Private Secretary." This farce was placed on the stage almost entirely under the direction of Frank Thornton.

After the successful production of "Called Back" at the Fifth Avenue Belasco resigned his position as stage-manager of the Madison Square Theatre company.

1885.

> Belasco contemplated abandoning stage direction and reverting to acting,—it being his plan to appear at the head of a company managed by himself as *Hamlet* and in the central part of a play he wished to write for his own use.
>
> He became acquainted with Steele Mackaye.

1886.

   February.

     15.   At Wallack's Theatre, New York, occurred the first production on any stage of "Valerie," a play in three acts altered by Belasco from Sardou's "Fernande."

   March.

     13.   "Valerie" was withdrawn at Wallack's.

   May.

     —.   Belasco returned to San Francisco as stage manager of Al. Hayman's "all-star stock company."

     31.   That company appeared, under his direction, at the Baldwin Theatre, in a dramatization of the novel of "Moths."

   June.

> Hayman's company acted at the Baldwin under Belasco's direction as follows:

     7.   In Belasco's "Valerie."

     14.   "The Marble Heart."

     21.   "Anselma."

     24.   "The Lady of Lyons."

     28.   "Alone in London."

July.

18.   (Sunday night.) Belasco took a benefit at the Baldwin Theatre, San Francisco: extraordinary programme and great public enthusiasm.

26.   He left San Francisco for New York, to take up work there in connection with the Lyceum Theatre.

September.

Belasco revised A. C. Gunter's "A Wall Street Bandit,"—which was produced at the Standard Theatre, September 20.

18.   Henry C. De Mille's play of "The Main Line; or, Rawson's Y" was produced at the Lyceum Theatre, under Belasco's stage direction.

October.

18.   May Fortesque (Finney) began an engagement at the Lyceum, acting *Gretchen*, in Gilbert's "Faust": Belasco officiated as stage director throughout that engagement, during which Miss Fortesque also acted as *Gilberte*, in "Frou-Frou"; *Iolanthe*, in "King Rene's Daughter," and *Jenny Northcott* in "Sweethearts."

1887.

March.

23.   Under Belasco's direction, pupils of the Lyceum Theatre School of Acting gave a performance, at the Lyceum, of an English translation of Molière's "Les Précieuses Ridicules."

May.

3. First production, at the Lyceum Theatre, of "The Highest Bidder," made by Belasco on the basis of a play called "Trade,"— which was written by John Maddison Morton and Robert Reece, for the elder Sothern. Notable success.

July.

16. End of the original "run" of "The Highest Bidder," and close of the season at the Lyceum Theatre.

August.

22. Revival of "The Highest Bidder" at the Lyceum.

September.

12. "Pawn Ticket 210," by Belasco and Clay M. Greene, was produced by Lotta, at Mc-Vicker's Theatre, Chicago.

19. Cecil Raleigh's farce, "The Great Pink Pearl," and Augustus Thomas' one-act drama, "Editha's Burglar," were produced, under Belasco's stage direction, at the Lyceum.

October.

24. At the Fourteenth Street Theatre "Baron Rudolph,"—originally entitled "Only a Tramp,"—by Bronson Howard, first rewritten as well as renamed by Howard; then, at Howard's request, altered and improved by Belasco, was produced, for the first time in New York, by George S. Knight, —Charles Frohman representing Knight in the business management and Belasco stage directing the performance. Failure: the

play was kept on the stage four weeks, to bad business. (In its original form Knight first presented "Baron Rudolph" in New York, at the Windsor Theatre, October 17, 1881.)

November.

1. At the Lyceum occurred the first performance on any stage of "The Wife," by Belasco and Henry C. DeMille.

19. "Baron Rudolph" was withdrawn at the Fourteenth Street Theatre.

December.

—. During this month Belasco revised and rectified William Gillette's dramatization of Haggard's "She,"—which had been produced at Niblo's Garden on November 29. His work, for which he received $1,000, made a popular success of that spectacle.

1888.

June.

16. 239th consecutive performance of "The Wife," and close of the Lyceum Theatre.

August.

21. The Lyceum was reopened for the season with first performance anywhere of Belasco and De Mille's "Lord Chumley."

September.

11. Belasco's revision of E. J. Schwartz's "The Kaffir Diamond" was produced at the Broadway Theatre, New York, with Louis Aldrich in the chief part. (Belasco was paid $300 for his work on this play.)

November.

11.   —th and last performance at the Lyceum of "Lord Chumley."

1889.

March.

11.   The fifth annual performance of the Academy of Dramatic Art (formerly the New York School of Acting) occurred at the Lyceum Theatre, under the direction of Belasco, Franklin H. Sargent, and Henry C. De Mille,—pupils of that school appearing in an English version of Sophocles' "Electra."

18.   "The Marquis," a version of Sardou's "Ferréol," prepared by Belasco, was produced under his stage direction at the Lyceum. Failure.

29.   Revival of Belasco-De Mille drama of "The Wife," at the Lyceum.

April.

29.   A play by William Gillette, based on Mrs. Humphry Ward's novel of "Robert Elsmere" and bearing the same name, was produced at the Union Square Theatre under the stage direction of Belasco—by special arrangement with the directorate of the Lyceum Theatre: Belasco received $500 for his labor on this production.

May.

6.   James Albery's play of "Featherbrain" (adapted from a French farce called "Tête de Linotte") was produced, under stage management of Belasco, at the Madison Square Thea-

tre—a special company organized by Daniel Frohman appearing in it.

18.   Close of the season at the Lyceum.

(Month, date?)   Belasco and De Mille were commissioned to write a new play for the season of 1889-'90, at the Lyceum.

—.   First meeting of David Belasco and Mrs. Leslie Carter.

September.

—.   Mrs. Leslie Carter sought Belasco at Echo Lake, New Jersey, and obtained his promise to undertake her training for the stage.

November.

19.   First performance anywhere of "The Charity Ball," by Belasco and De Mille, stage direction of the former.

This was the last play for the Lyceum with which Belasco was concerned.

December.

—.   Belasco, being in need of the use of a stage for rehearsals of Mrs. Carter, agreed to revise a play by Mrs. Abby Sage Richardson, based on Mark Twain's "The Prince and the Pauper," and to rehearse a company in it, on the understanding that, as payment, he should be permitted to rehearse Mrs. Carter on the stage of the Lyceum Theatre.

1890.

January.

20.   Belasco's revision of "The Prince and the Pauper" was acted at the Broadway Theatre,

Elsie Leslie appearing in it as *Tom Canty*
and as *Prince Edward of Wales.*

January-February.

Belasco was active in planning a play for
Mrs. Carter, called "The Heart of Maryland," in negotiation for its production under
the management of A. M. Palmer, and in
training of Mrs. Carter.

February.

26.   The bargain between Daniel Frohman and
Belasco, for the latter to use the stage of
the Lyceum Theatre, was wrongfully abrogated by the directors of that institution.
Belasco soon afterward resigned his place at
the Lyceum.

March.

27.   Belasco ended his association with the
Lyceum Theatre.

May.

24.   200th performance of "The Charity Ball,"
and close of the Lyceum Theatre.

October.

21.   A melodrama entitled "Men and Women,"
by Belasco and De Mille, was produced at
Proctor's Twenty-third Street Theatre, by
Charles Frohman, under the stage direction
of Belasco: and, to accommodate Miss Annie
A. Adams, an old friend, Belasco wrote in
this play a small part for Miss Maude
Adams.

November.

10.   Belasco, with E. D. Price as business manager (the financial capital having been pro-

vided by Mr. N. K. Fairbank, of Chicago), presented Mrs. Leslie Carter, at the Broadway Theatre, as a star, in a play by Mr. Paul M. Potter, called "The Ugly Duckling"; that was *Mrs. Carter's first appearance on the stage.*

1891.

March.

14.　End of tour of Mrs. Carter in "The Ugly Duckling," and of career of that play, in Kansas City, Mo.

25.　200th consecutive performance of "Men and Women" at Proctor's Twenty-third Street Theatre.

28.　Last performance of "Men and Women,"— original production.

April.

15.　Belasco, Mrs. Carter, and Mrs. Dudley, her mother, sailed for England, on board SS. City of New York, and proceeded to Paris, to see the French play with music afterward presented in America as "Miss Helyett."

November.

3.　"Miss Helyett," a farce with music, adapted from the French by Belasco, was, by him, in association with Charles Frohman, produced at the Star Theatre, New York,— Mrs. Carter appearing in it as *Miss Helyett.*

December.

17.　50th performance of "Miss Helyett" at the Star.

1892.

> January.
>> 10.   Last performance of "Miss Helyett" at the Star.
>> 11.   "Miss Helyett" was transferred from the Star to the Standard Theatre.
>> 29.   100th performance of "Miss Helyett."

> February.
>> 13.   Close of the New York engagement of Mrs. Carter in "Miss Helyett": she then went on a tour in that play, under the management of Frohman and Belasco, which lasted until the end of the theatrical season of 1891-'92.
>>
>> During the greater part of the remainder of 1892 Belasco's attention was bestowed principally on the writing of "The Girl I Left Behind Me."

1893.

> January.
>> 16.   "The Girl I Left Behind Me," by Belasco and Franklyn Fyles, was produced, by Charles Frohman, for the first time anywhere, at the New National Theatre, Washington, D. C.,— under the stage management of Belasco.
>> 25.   The Empire Theatre, New York, was opened, under the management of Charles Frohman, with a performance of "The Girl I Left Behind Me."

> March.
>> 29.   "The Girl I Left Behind Me" was played at the Empire with an entirely new cast—the original company, with one or two exceptions,

going to Chicago, where, during the World's Columbian Exposition, it was presented in that drama, at the Schiller (now, 1917, the Garrick) Theatre, for many weeks.

June.

24. 288th consecutive performance of "The Girl I Left Behind Me," at the Empire, and close of the first season at that theatre.

October.

24. First performance in New York, at the Empire Theatre, of "The Younger Son," adapted by Belasco from a German play called "Schlimme Saat" ("Evil Seeds"). Failure: it was withdrawn after four performances.

1894.

August.

22. Belasco left New York, taking his brother Frederick with him, for San Francisco,— called there by the illness of his mother, who was thought to be dying.

1895.

October.

9. Belasco's play of "The Heart of Maryland" was presented, by the author, in association with Mr. Max Bleiman, of New York, for the first time anywhere, at the Grand Opera House, Washington, D. C.

22. "The Heart of Maryland" was acted for the first time in New York, at the Herald Square Theatre: notable success.

1896.

  March.

   3.   150th performance of "The Heart of Maryland."

   31.   An extra performance of "The Heart of Maryland" was given at the Herald Square Theatre, for the benefit of the Hebrew Infant Asylum.

  April.

   18.   200th performance of "The Heart of Maryland," and distribution of souvenirs at the Herald Square.

  May.

   16.   End of the "run" of "The Heart of Maryland," and close of the season at the Herald Square Theatre: 229 consecutive performances had been given of this fine melodrama.

  June.

   3.   Trial of Belasco's suit against N. K. Fairbank, to recover $65,000, losses, expenses, etc., incidental to instruction of Mrs. Carter and her tour in "The Ugly Duckling," was begun before Justice Leonard Giegerich and a jury, in Part V., Supreme Court, State of New York. This suit was fought with extreme acrimony at every point.

   23.   The jury in Belasco's suit against Fairbank returned a verdict for the Plaintiff, awarding him $16,000 and interest, for five years, at 5 per cent.

August.

20. "Under the Polar Star," revision by Belasco of play by Clay M. Greene, was produced at the Academy of Music, New York.

1897.

August.

16. Belasco presented "The Heart of Maryland" at the Baldwin Theatre, San Francisco.

October.

5. At the Manhattan (previously the Standard) Theatre Belasco, in partnership with Charles Frohman, presented, for the first time in New York, a tragedy of Chinese character entitled "The First Born," by Francis Powers. It was produced under the stage management of Belasco, and Powers appeared in its principal part, *Chan Wang:* notable success. The tragedy was acted in association with a farce called "A Night Session," derived from a French original by Georges Feydeau.

23. The theatrical company that acted "The First Born" in New York sailed for England,—a new company taking its place at the Manhattan.

November.

6. "The First Born" was acted at the Duke of York's Theatre, London,—where it failed and was withdrawn after one week.

Last performance of "The First Born" at the Manhattan Theatre. Nov. 29.—Transferred to Garden Theatre, where it was acted until December 11.

1898.

—. Close of the third season of "The Heart of Maryland" at Springfield, Mass.

March.

30. Belasco, Mrs. Carter, and the company which had been acting in "The Heart of Maryland" sailed for England on SS. St. Paul.

April.

8. Belasco, in partnership with Charles Frohman, presented Mrs. Carter, at the Adelphi Theatre, London (her first appearance abroad), as *Maryland Calvert*, in "The Heart of Maryland."

June.

25. End of the season of "The Heart of Maryland" in London.

September.

7. Belasco arrived in New York, from England, on board SS. Majestic.

December.

25. Belasco's adaptation of "Zaza," from a French play of that name, by MM. Pierre Berton and Charles Simon, was acted for the first time, at the Lafayette Square Opera House (now, 1917, the Belasco Theatre), Washington, D. C., Mrs. Leslie Carter appearing in its central part.

1899.

January.

9. "Zaza" was acted for the first time in New York, at the Garrick Theatre.

11. Death of Mrs. Humphrey Abraham Belasco, at 174 Clara Street, San Francisco, in her 69th year. Mrs. Belasco was buried at Hills of Eternity Cemetery, San Mateo, California.

June.

5. 150th performance of "Zaza," observed by distribution of souvenirs during the evening.

17. End of "run" of "Zaza," and close of the season at the Garrick: 164 performances had been given.

December.

25. Belasco's "Naughty Anthony" was produced, first time, at the Columbia Theatre, Washington, D. C., with Blanche Bates and Frank Worthing in its principal parts.

1900.

January.

8. Belasco presented his farce of "Naughty Anthony," for the first time in New York, at the Herald Square Theatre.

March.

5. At the Herald Square, first performance anywhere of the tragedy, in one act, by Belasco, entitled "Madame Butterfly,"— founded on a story of the same name by John Luther Long,—Blanche Bates acting in it as *Cho-Cho-San* and Frank Worthing as *Lieutenant B. F. Pinkerton.*

21. Close of the Belasco season ("Naughty Anthony" and "Madame Butterfly") at the Herald Square Theatre.

April.

5. Belasco, Mrs. Carter, and the theatrical company to act "Zaza" sailed for England on SS. St. Paul.

16. Belasco, in partnership with Charles Frohman, presented Mrs. Carter in his play of "Zaza," at the Garrick Theatre, London.

28. In association with Charles Frohman, Belasco presented "Madame Butterfly" at the Duke of York's Theatre, London: memorable triumph.

May.

—. Belasco fell on stairs of the Garrick Theatre, London, and was seriously injured.

July.

28. End of the London engagement of Mrs. Carter, in Belasco's "Zaza."

August.

—. Belasco and Mrs. Carter sailed for New York on board SS. ———.

—. They landed in New York.

1901.

February.

5. Belasco, in partnership with Charles Frohman, presented at the Garden Theatre, for the first time on any stage, a dramatization of Ouida's novel, "Under Two Flags," by Mr. Paul M. Potter,—revised by Belasco. Blanche Bates, making her first appearance in New York as a star, acted in it as *Cigarette.* Stage direction of Belasco.

June.

1. 133rd performance of "Under Two Flags" at the Garden Theatre, and close of the season there.

September.

9. At the Hyperion Theatre, New Haven, Conn., Belasco presented David Warfield as a star, in "The Auctioneer,"—then first acted on any stage,—a play built on suggestions by Belasco, by Charles Klein and Lee Arthur, and amended by Belasco.

23. Belasco presented Warfield in "The Auctioneer," for the first time in New York, at the Bijou Theatre.

December.

12. At the New National Theatre, Washington, D. C., Belasco, for the first time anywhere, presented his play of "Du Barry," with Mrs. Carter in the central part.

"Du Barry" was to have been given on Monday, the 9th inst., but difficulty in handling the elaborate and heavy stage settings and the need of additional rehearsals delayed it till the 12th.

25. First performance of "Du Barry" in New York occurred, at the Criterion Theatre.

1902.

January.

1. A silver loving cup was presented to Belasco, on the stage of the Criterion Theatre, by Mrs. Carter and all the other members of the "Du Barry" company: Mr.

Charles A. Stevenson made the presentation speech, and Mr. Belasco replied.

14. Belasco, by lease, secured control of the Republic Theatre, New York.

25. Belasco was sued by M. Jean Richepin, demanding an accounting for the receipts from representations of "Du Barry,"—on the ground, as alleged, that Belasco's "Du Barry" is, in fact, Richepin's play of the same name.

March.

13. Judge John J. Freedman, in the Supreme Court, New York, denied a motion by attorneys of M. Jean Richepin to strike out essential clauses from Belasco's answer in Richepin's suit against him, alleging plagiarism in the play of "Du Barry."

The Plaintiff never proceeded in this case, and it was formally discontinued, in January, 1908.

17. Belasco was severely injured by the fall of a heavy piece of scenery, during representation of "Du Barry," at the Criterion Theatre: he was struck on the head, badly cut, and rendered unconscious for a quarter of an hour.

April.

19. Work of reconstruction of the Republic Theatre was begun: the whole interior of that theatre was torn out and rebuilt,—a sub-stage chamber, twenty-five feet deep, being excavated (which entailed much blasting of solid rock), a perpetual spring of water

being incidentally tapped, which it was extremely difficult to dam.

May.

31. 165th performance of "Du Barry" at the Criterion, and close of that theatre for the season.

September.

29. Belasco opened the first Belasco Theatre, New York (previously the Republic), presenting Mrs. Carter, in a revival of "Du Barry."

November.

17. The first performance, anywhere, of "The Darling of the Gods," a tragedy of Japanese life by Belasco and John Luther Long, occurred at the National Theatre, Washington, D. C., under the management and stage direction of Belasco: Blanche Bates, George Arliss, and Robert Haines acted the chief parts in it.

December.

2. Suit for $20,000 damages for malicious libel was entered by Belasco against the writer known as Onoto Watanna (Mrs. Bertrand W. Babcock), in the Supreme Court, New York, before Judge James J. Fitzgerald.

3. First New York presentment of "The Darling of the Gods," at the first Belasco Theatre.

1903.

January.

—. Belasco entered into a contract with Hen-

rietta Crosman for her appearance as a star
in a dramatization of the novel by Agnes and
Egerton Castle, called "The Bath Comedy."

February.

  6.   Order for the arrest of Onoto Watanna
        (Mrs. Babcock), obtained by Belasco, in his
        suit against her claiming $20,000 damage
        for malicious libel, was vacated by Judge
        David Leventritt,—defendant, in effect, with-
        drawing the libel: appeal against vacation of
        the order of arrest entered by Belasco's
        lawyers.

May.

  30.   "The Darling of the Gods" was withdrawn
        at the Belasco Theatre and that house was
        closed for the season,—186 performances hav-
        ing been given.

June.

  6.   End of tour, under Belasco's direction, of
        Mrs. Carter and a company of 147 other
        players, presenting "Du Barry," at Minne-
        apolis, Minn.: it had lasted thirty-eight weeks.

  10.   Belasco gave a brilliant reception in honor
        of Mrs. Carter, on the stage of the Belasco
        Theatre, New York,—which was attended by
        several hundred persons of varied social and
        artistic distinction.

September.

  16.   The Belasco Theatre was reopened with
        a revival of "The Darling of the Gods."

  28.   Beginning of Warfield's third tour in "The
        Auctioneer," at the Harlem Opera House,
        New York.

November.

14. Last performance of "The Darling of the Gods" at the Belasco Theatre.

16. A contemptible outrage was perpetrated at the Belasco Theatre, New York, when, during representation of the First Act of "Zaza," a process server, employed and instructed by Mr. A. Hummel, leaped upon the stage and handed to *Mrs. Leslie Carter* notice of an action brought by Miss Eugenie Blair and Mr. Henry Gressit, against *David Belasco*, praying for an injunction to stop the latter presenting "Zaza"! The plaintiffs alleged rights of ownership of the play by Charles Frohman. Hummel (firm of Howe & Hummel) was attorney for C. Frohman as well as for Miss Blair and Gressit.

23. Belasco produced, for the first time anywhere, at the Lafayette Square Opera House (now, 1917, Belasco Theatre), Washington, D. C., his stage version of "The Bath Comedy," entitled "Sweet Kitty Bellairs."

24. Suit was brought by Joseph Brooks, in the Supreme Court, New York, against Belasco, in an endeavor to establish that he, Brooks, was a copartner with Belasco in management and presentation of David Warfield, in the play of "The Auctioneer."

December.

8. First performance of "Sweet Kitty Bellairs" in New York,—at the first Belasco Theatre.

11. Judge Scott denied application, by Miss

Blair and Mr. Gressit, for an injunction to stop Belasco's presentation of "Zaza."

23. By arrangement with Belasco Herbert Beerbohm-Tree presented "The Darling of the Gods" at His Majesty's Theatre, London, appearing in it as *Zakkuri*, with George Relph as *Kara* and Miss Marie Löhr as *Yo-San*.

1904.

January.

8. Publication, in the newspaper press, of letter by David Warfield repudiating Joseph Brooks' assertion of partnership with Belasco in the management and presentation of Warfield, in "The Auctioneer."

10. Warfield's tour in "The Auctioneer" was abruptly ended at New Orleans.

25. Judge David Leventritt, in the Supreme Court, New York (First District), refused to issue a mandatory order, prayed for by Joseph Brooks, directing David Warfield to continue to act in "The Auctioneer."

February.

3. Legal action was brought in the Circuit Court of the United States for the Southern District of New York by Grace B. Hughes (otherwise known as Mary Montagu) to restrain Belasco, Maurice Campbell, and Henrietta Crosman from further presenting Belasco's play of "Sweet Kitty Bellairs,"— Plaintiff alleging that Belasco's play was, in fact, an infringement of one by her, entitled "Sweet Jasmine."

February.

14. Hon. W. M. K. Olcott was appointed as Receiver for the play of "The Auctioneer" (as represented with Warfield in the central part), in the Brooks-Belasco "partnership" suit.

March.

18. The application by Grace B. Hughes for an injunction against Belasco, *et al.*, as above, was argued before Judge E. Henry Lacombe.

26. Judge Lacombe denied the motion for an injunction as prayed for by Grace B. Hughes, holding that there was *no plagiarism* by Belasco. This case was finally stricken from the Calendar, without trial, March 3, 1913.

June.

4. End of the first New York run of "Sweet Kitty Bellairs," at the Belasco Theatre.

July.

31. Belasco presented "The Darling of the Gods," with Blanche Bates and the original New York company, at the Imperial Theatre, St. Louis, thus incurring the bitter, active animosity of the Theatrical Syndicate,—the Imperial Theatre not being under the control of that organization.

September.

12. Belasco produced, for the first time anywhere, at the Young's Pier Theatre, Atlantic City, N. J., Charles Klein's play of "The Music Master," revised by Belasco—David Warfield acting in it, as *Herr Anton von Barwig*.

September.

16.   The Belasco Theatre was reopened with a
revival of "The Darling of the Gods."

28.   At the Montauk Theatre, Brooklyn, Mrs.
Carter's "Farewell Tour" in "Du Barry"
began, under Belasco's direction.

26.   First presentation of "The Music Master"
in New York,—at the first Belasco Theatre.

December.

26.   In Convention Hall (which, having been
shut out of all theatres by the iniquitous
Theatrical Syndicate, he had hired and converted into a theatre, for one week's engagement) Belasco produced, for the first time
anywhere, the tragedy, written by him in
collaboration with John Luther Long, entitled
"Adrea,"—Mrs. Leslie Carter acting the principal part in it.

1905.

January.

11.   First performance of "Adrea" in New
York, at the first Belasco Theatre.

May.

4.   End of the first run of "Adrea" and close
of the Belasco Theatre for the season.

June.

—.   Belasco went to London.

September.

20.   Belasco reopened the Belasco Theatre with
a revival of "Adrea."

October.

3.   At the new Belasco Theatre, Pittsburgh,

Pa., Belasco produced, for the first time anywhere, his play of "The Girl of the Golden
West,"—Blanche Bates acting the central
character and Frank Keenan and Robert
Hilliard playing the chief supporting
parts.

November.

14. First performance in New York of "The
Girl of the Golden West,"—at the first
Belasco Theatre.

1906.

June.

23. End of Mrs. Carter's tour at Williamsport,
Pa.,—in "Zaza"; her last performance under
Belasco's management.

November.

12. Belasco produced his play "The Rose of the
Rancho,"—based, in part, on an earlier one
by Richard Walton Tully, called "Juanita,"—
at the Majestic Theatre, Boston, Mass. (first
time in this form), Frances Starr appearing
in it as *Juanita*, that being her first venture
as a star.

27. First New York presentation of "The
Rose of the Rancho" occurred at the first
Belasco Theatre.

December.

5. The corner-stone of Belasco's Stuyvesant
Theatre (1917, the Belasco) was laid by
Blanche Bates. Bronson Howard made a
brief address.

1907.

September.

23.   Belasco produced, at the Hyperion Theatre, New Haven, Conn., for the first time anywhere, a play written by himself in conjunc-
tion with Misses Pauline Phelps and Marion
Short, entitled "A Grand Army Man,"—
David Warfield appearing in it as *Wes'
Bigelow.*

October.

16.   Belasco opened his Stuyvesant Theatre,
New York,—now, 1917, the second Belasco
Theatre,—presenting Warfield in "A Grand
Army Man."

November.

18.   He presented Mr. William De Mille's "The
Warrens of Virginia," first time, at the Lyric
Theatre, Philadelphia.

December.

—.   First New York performance of "The Warrens of Virginia," Belasco Theatre.

1908.

February.

24.   Belasco revived "The Music Master" at the
Stuyvesant Theatre.

May.

2.   Close of the season at the Stuyvesant,—
performance of "A Grand Army Man."

September.

7.   William J. Hurlbut's play of "The Fighting Hope" was produced by Belasco and
under his stage direction (first time anywhere) at the Belasco Theatre, Washington,

D. C., Blanche Bates and Charles Richman acting the principal parts.

22.   First New York presentation of "The Fighting Hope,"—at the Stuyvesant Theatre.

December.

31.   At the Parsons Theatre, Hartford, Conn., Belasco produced, for the first time anywhere, the repulsive play of "The Easiest Way," by Mr. Eugene Walter—Miss Frances Starr playing the central part in it.

1909.
January.

19.   Belasco presented "The Easiest Way," for the first time in New York, at the Stuyvesant Theatre,—"The Fighting Hope" being transferred to the Belasco.

February.

7.   Belasco left New York for San Francisco, to visit his father.

12.   Arrived in San Francisco.

24.   A dinner in honor of Belasco was given at Bismarck Café (now, 1917, the Hofbrau Café), San Francisco, by former schoolmates of his at the old Lincoln Grammar School of that city.

27.   Festival at the Bohemian Club, San Francisco, in honor of Belasco.

March.

2.   He left San Francisco.

7.   He arrived in New York.

April.

29.   Announcement made that H. G. Fiske and Belasco and the Theatrical Syndicate "will

book in each others' theatres when mutually agreeable."

June.

1. Marriage of Belasco's elder daughter, Reina Victoria Belasco, and Morris Gest, theatrical manager, at Sherry's, New York.

August.

16. At the Savoy Theatre, Atlantic City, for the first time anywhere, Belasco produced "Is Matrimony a Failure?" (adapted by Leo Ditrichstein from "Die Thur Ins Frei" by Oscar Blumenthal and Gustav Kadelburg), Frank Worthing and Jane Cowl acting the chief parts.

23. First New York performance of "Is Matrimony a Failure?" at the first Belasco Theatre.

December.

6. First presentation of "The Lily" (adapted by Belasco from a French original by MM. Pierre Wolff and Gaston Leroux) was effected at the Belasco Theatre, Washington, D. C., Nance O'Neil and Charles Cartwright playing the principal parts.

23. Belasco presented "The Lily," for the first time in New York, at the Stuyvesant Theatre.

1910.

January.

17. Belasco produced Mr. E. Walter's play of "Just a Wife," at the Colonial Theatre, Cleveland, Ohio.

January.

31. First New York performance of "Just a Wife,"—at the first Belasco Theatre.

July.

—. It was decided to restore to the theatre known since 1902 as the Belasco its former name of the Republic Theatre, and to change the name of Belasco's Stuyvesant Theatre to the Belasco Theatre.

August.

22. The Republic Theatre was reopened, under that name, with the first performance of Winchell Smith's dramatization of the story of "Bobby Burnitt."

September.

19. Under the management and stage direction of Belasco the first presentation in America was effected, at the Nixon Theatre, Pittsburgh, Pa., of "The Concert," adapted by Leo Ditrichstein from a German original by Herman Bahr,—Mr. Ditrichstein appearing in it as a star.

October.

10. First New York performance of "The Concert" occurred at the (second) Belasco Theatre.

24. Belasco produced Mr. Avery Hopwood's farce of "Nobody's Widow" (first time anywhere) at the Euclid Avenue Opera House, Cleveland, Ohio,—Blanche Bates acting the chief part in it.

November.

14. First New York presentation of "Nobody's Widow" at the Hudson Theatre.

1911.

January.

2. First performance of Belasco's play of "The Return of Peter Grimm," at the Hollis Street Theatre, Boston. David Warfield appeared in its principal part.

27. Marriage of Belasco's younger daughter, Augusta Belasco, to William Elliott, actor, at the Hotel Marie Antoinette, New York.

February.

24. Mrs. Elliott, dangerously ill, taken by Belasco to Asheville, N. C.

April.

11. Death of Humphrey Abraham Belasco, at 1704 Sutter Street, San Francisco, California, in the 81st year of his age. Buried at Hills of Eternity Cemetery, San Mateo, California.

17. Belasco produced William C. De Mille's play of "The Woman" (first time anywhere) at the New National Theatre, Washington, D. C.,—Helen Ware and William Courtleigh acting the principal parts in it.

May.

1. Belasco takes his daughter, Mrs. Elliott, to Colorado Springs, Col.

June.

5. Death of Augusta Belasco, Mrs. William Elliott, at Broadmoor, Colorado Springs.

9. Funeral of Mrs. Elliott at Temple Aha-

wath Chesed, New York. Buried at Ahawath Chesed Cemetery, Linden Hills, Long Island.

September.

19. First New York performance of "The Woman" occurred at the present (1917) Republic Theatre.

October.

18. "The Return of Peter Grimm" was first presented in New York,—at the second Belasco Theatre.

30. Belasco presented Edward Locke's play of "The Case of Becky," for the first time anywhere, at the New National Theatre, Washington, D. C.,—Miss Frances Starr acting the central character.

December.

10. First performance on any stage of Puccini's "La Fanciulla del West,"—opera on Belasco's play "The Girl of the Golden West," —at the Metropolitan Opera House, New York,—stage direction of Belasco.

1912.

February.

19. Legal action was begun in the United States District Court for the Southern District of New York, by Abraham Goldknopf, praying for an injunction to restrain Belasco and William C. De Mille from further presentment of their play of "The Woman," alleging that play to be, in fact, an infringement of Plaintiff's play of "Tainted Philanthropy." (See November, *et seq.*)

April.

20.　254th performance of "The Woman" at the Republic Theatre, and close of the season at that house.

29.　Belasco produced (first time anywhere) "The Governor's Lady," written by himself in collaboration with Miss Alice Bradley, at the Broad Street Theatre, Philadelphia, Pa.

May.

4.　End of the run of "The Return of Peter Grimm" in New York, and close of the Belasco Theatre for the season.

June.

25.　Legal action was brought against Belasco by Amelia Bachman and George L. McKay, alleging plagiarism by him, in "The Case of Becky," from their play of "Etelle." (See May 13, 1913.)

July.

31.　Trial of Goldknopf suit against Belasco was begun before Commissioner Gilchrist: continued, August 5, before Judge George C. Holt, in United States Circuit Court.

September.

9.　First New York performance of "The Governor's Lady" occurred at the present (1917) Republic Theatre.

October.

1.　Belasco presented "The Case of Becky," for the first time in New York, at the second Belasco Theatre.

November.

1.　At the Empire, Syracuse, New York, Belasco produced (first time anywhere) the

play by Frederick Hatton and Fanny Locke
Hatton, entitled "Years of Discretion."

26. By permission of the Court Belasco presented, at the Belasco Theatre, for one
performance only, in the morning, De Mille's
play of "The Woman" (then filling an engagement at the Grand Opera House), and in
the afternoon, Mr. Goldknopf's play of
"Tainted Philanthropy": Judge Holt adjourned Court to the Belasco and witnessed
both performances.

29. Judge Holt rendered decision in suit by
Mr. Goldknopf against Belasco in favor of
the Defendant,—holding that there is *no
plagiarism* by Belasco of Goldknopf's play.

December.

10. At the Broad Street Theatre, Philadelphia,
Pa., Belasco presented (first time anywhere
in America) the fairy play of "A Good Little
Devil," adapted by Austin Strong from
original by Rosemonde Gerard and Maurice
Rostand,—Ernest Lawford and Mary Pickford acting the principal parts.

12. First New York production of "Years of
Discretion" occurred at the Belasco Theatre.

1913.

January.

8. The first New York performance of "A
Good Little Devil" was given at the present
(1917) Republic Theatre.

March.

3. Grace B. Hughes' suit against Belasco,
alleging plagiarism in his "Sweet Kitty Bel-

lairs" from her play of "Sweet Jasmine," was stricken from the Calendar of the Circuit Court of the United States, Southern District of New York.

(Same date.) In the suit of A. Goldknopf against Belasco, as above, final judgment was entered, dismissing Plaintiff's complaint upon the merits.

May.

13-14. Suit by Amelia Bachman and George L. McKay, against Belasco, alleging plagiarism by him, in his "The Case of Becky," from their play of "Etelle," was tried before Judge Julius M. Mayer, in the United States District Court.

June.

18. Belasco sailed on board SS. Campania, for Paris, *via* Fishguard, Great Britain, *re* purchase of Henri Bernstein's play of "The Secret."

July.

9. Judge Mayer rendered decision in the suit of Amelia Bachman and George L. McKay against Belasco, in favor of the Defendant, holding that there is *no plagiarism* in the play of "The Case of Becky," and dismissing Plaintiffs' complaint upon the merits.

15. Final judgment was entered against Amelia Bachman and George L. McKay, in their suit as above. This case was appealed: see April 6, 1914.

August.

28. At the Lyceum Theatre, Rochester,

N. Y., Belasco produced (first time anywhere) the adaptation made by Leo Ditrichstein of the comedy "Pour Vivre Heureux,"
by MM. André Rivoire and Yves Mirande,
and entitled "The Temperamental Journey,"
—Mr. Ditrichstein appearing in it as a star.

September.

4. First New York performance of "The
Temperamental Journey" occurred at the
present (1917) Belasco Theatre.

October.

27. Belasco produced (first time anywhere),
at the Euclid Avenue Opera House, Cleveland, Ohio, a play by Roland B. Molineux,
called "The Man Inside."

November.

11. At the Criterion Theatre the first performance was given in New York of "The
Man Inside."

December.

8. At the Detroit Opera House, Detroit,
Mich., for the first time anywhere, Belasco
produced his English adaptation of Henri
Bernstein's French play of "The Secret,"
Miss Frances Starr appearing in the prin-
cipal part.

23. First New York performance of "The
Secret" at the second Belasco Theatre.

1914.

April.

6. The appeal of Amelia Bachman and George
L. McKay, in suit against Belasco, alleging
plagiarism, was argued before the United

States Circuit Court of Appeals for the Second Circuit. Decision on this appeal was in favor of Belasco,—affirming Judge Mayer's decision, in dismissing Plaintiffs' case that there is *no plagiarism.* Opinion by Lacombe, J., 224 Fed. Rep., page 817.

N.B. This is the only case against Belasco which was ever carried to an appeal.

May.

4. Belasco presented Frederick Ballard's play of "What's Wrong" (first time anywhere) at the New National Theatre, Washington, D. C.

July.

27. He produced (first time anywhere) "The Vanishing Bride," a farce adapted by Sydney Rosenfeld from a German original by Leo Kastner and Ralph Tesmar, entitled "Tantalus." Mr. Thomas A. Wise and Miss Janet Beecher played the principal parts.

September.

28. At Ford's Opera House, Baltimore, Md., he presented (first time anywhere) the English version by Leo Ditrichstein of "The Phantom Rival," by Ferenc Molnar, Mr. Ditrichstein appearing in it as a star. (This English version was, originally, called "Sascha Comes Back.")

October.

6. First New York presentment of "The Phantom Rival" was effected at the present (1917) Belasco Theatre.

1915.

January.

18.   For the first time in America, Belasco pre-
sented, at the Belasco Theatre, Washington,
D. C., Edward Knoblauch's play of "Marie-
Odile," Frances Starr acting the central part.

26.   First New York performance of "Marie-
Odile," at the Belasco Theatre.

March.

29.   Belasco, in association with Charles Frohman, revived "A Celebrated Case" in
Boston.

April.

5.   At the Playhouse Theatre, Wilmington,
Del., Belasco presented (first time anywhere)
the farce of "The Boomerang," by Winchell
Smith and Victor Mapes.

7.   Belasco and Frohman presented "A Celebrated Case" at the Empire Theatre, New
York.

26.   At the Parsons Theatre, Hartford,
Conn., he produced a play by Henry Irving
Dodge, called "The Love Thought,"—Miss
Janet Beecher and Hardee Kirkland playing
the principal parts in it.

June.

28.   At the Apollo Theatre, Atlantic City,
N. J., he presented (first time anywhere) a
play called "The Girl," by George Scarborough. (This was afterward renamed "Oklahoma," and, again, "The Heart of Wetona":
see January 22 and February 29, 1916.)
Lenore Ulric played *Wetona*, the chief part.

August.

10. First New York performance of "The Boomerang" was given at the present Belasco Theatre.

December.

12. At the Playhouse, Wilmington, Delaware, Belasco first produced his drama of "Van Der Decken," with David Warfield in the character of that name.

1916.

January.

14. Lila Longson began an action at law against Belasco, Winchell Smith, and Victor Mapes, in the District Court of the United States for the Southern District of New York, alleging that their play of "The Boomerang" is an infringement of her play of "The Choice."

20. Belasco presented "Oklahoma" (first called "The Girl," later renamed "The Heart of Wetona") at the Stamford Theatre, Stamford, Conn.

February.

29. In association with "Charles Frohman" (Company), he presented "The Heart of Wetona" at the Lyceum Theatre, for the first time in New York.

April.

17. Belasco produced (first time anywhere) a farce by Roi Cooper Megrue called "The Lucky Fellow" (afterward renamed "Seven Chances"), at the Apollo Theatre, Atlantic City, N. J.

May.

At the Apollo Theatre, Atlantic City, he produced (first time anywhere) a play called "The Treadmill" (later renamed "Alias"), made by Willard Mack on the basis of a story by John A. Moroso entitled "Alias Santa Claus."

August.

7. "Seven Chances" was produced for the first time in New York, at the Cohan Theatre.

September.

19-21. Suit of Lila Longson against Belasco *et al.* was tried before Judge William B. Sheppard, who held that there was no infringement and dismissed the complaint.

25. Entry of final judgment against Lila Longson and dismissal of her complaint, upon the merits.

October.

16. Belasco produced, for the first time anywhere, "The Little Lady in Blue," by Horace Hodges and T. Wigney Percyval, at the Belasco Theatre, Washington, D. C.

28. Belasco planted two juniper trees, in the Shakespeare Garden, Cleveland, Ohio, with public ceremonies.

December.

22. First New York performance was given of "The Little Lady in Blue," at the Belasco Theatre.

1917.

February.

5. Belasco presented "Alias" (formerly "The

Treadmill") at the Belasco Theatre, Washington, D. C.

March.

31. —th and last New York performance of "The Little Lady in Blue" occurred at the Belasco Theatre.

April.

5. Belasco presented (first time anywhere) a play by John Meehan, called "The Very Minute," at the Playhouse, Wilmington, Del., Mr. Arnold Daly then first appearing under his management as a star.

9. "The Very Minute" was acted for the first time in New York, at the Belasco Theatre. Failure.

May.

ADDED BY J. W.

7. Last performance of "The Very Minute," and close of the Belasco Theatre, for the 1916-'17 season.

July.

3. Belasco officiated as one of the pallbearers at the funeral of William Winter.

August.

25. Belasco produced a play entitled "Polly With a Past," written by George Middleton and Guy Bolton and revised by himself, at the Stamford Theatre, Stamford, Conn.,—presenting Miss Ina Claire in the central part.— A trial performance of this play was given at Atlantic City, N. J., June 11.

September.

6. The first New York performance of "Polly
With a Past" occurred at the Belasco Theatre.

October.

3. Belasco produced the melodrama called
"Tiger Rose," by Willard Mack, at the
Lyceum Theatre, New York: trial performance of this play was given at the Shubert
Theatre, Wilmington, Delaware, April 30,
1917. Preliminary tour began, September
21, at

INDEX TO VOLUME TWO

INDEX TO VOLUME TWO

B.= David Belasco.

C

Caldwell, James H. (Am. th. man.: 1793-1863): 150.

California Th., S. F.: first attempt in Am. to light stage by electricity made at, 245.

Campbell, Maurice (Am. th. agent): 321.

"Campdown Races" (song): 206.

Cannon, Hon. Joseph Gurney (Congressman: 1836-19—): helps B., 178.

"Caprice" (play): 320.

Carabiniere," "Il (play—It.): 71.

Carbineer," "The (play—B.'s): 71.

Carpenter, E. C.: 68.

CARTER, MRS. LESLIE (Caroline Louise Dudley—Mrs. William Louis Payne: Am. actress: 186[4?]-19—): 1; 6; 29; 30; 31; her performance of *du Barry*, 37; her method—developed by B., 38; B.'s reason for not taking her to London in "Du B.," 44; 45; 48; 50; 51; B.'s tribute to, 61; production of "Kassa" by, 68; 69; 70; end of extraordinary tour of, under B.'s direction, 90; 91; 112; 114; 126; her impersonation of *Adrea* critically considered and qualities of specified, 148, *et seq.;* 182; 184; 185; 184; marriage of—professional association of, and B. ended— *Adrea* her best performance— and qualities of it, 185; 186; 187; 277.

Caruso, Enrico (It. singer: 1874-19—): 214.

CASE OF BECKY," "THE (play): 320; 322; produced—and writing of, 343; described and considered, 344; B.'s recollections *re*, 345; cast of—unexpected success of—plagiarism charged in, 346; B. vindicated *re* same—decision quoted, 347.

Castle, Agnes (Mrs. Egerton Castle): 94.

Castle, Egerton (Eng. novelist and newspaper man: 1858-19—): 94; B.'s letters to, *re* "Sweet Kitty Bellairs," 106, *et seq.*

"Cataract of the Ganges" ("The Ganges"): 82.

"Catherine" (play): burlesque of, 10.

Catherine the Second, Empress of Russia (1729-1796): 29.

Celebrated Case," "A: 363; first produced, 363; considered, 364; revived by B. and C. Frohman— cast of, 365.

"Charles I." (drama): 264.

Children of the Ghetto," "The (play): 87.

Chimney Corner," "The (play): 249.

Chester, George Randolph (Am. writer: 1869-19—): 289.

Choice," "The (play): 323.

Chronicle," "The S. F. (newspaper): 133.

Cid," "Le (play—Fr.): 317.

City Directory," "The (farce): 9.

Civinni, C. (It. librettist): 213.

Claire, Ina (Am. actress and mimic): B.'s attention directed to—and first appearance under, 464; quality of, revealed in *Polly Shannon*, 465.

Clarke, John Sleeper (Am.-Eng. actor and th. man.: 1833-1899): 153.

Clemens, Samuel Langhorne (Mark Twain: Am. author: 1835-1910): 67.

"Coal Oil Tommy" (song): 206.

Cohan, George M. (Am. actor, th. man., and playwright: 1878-19—): 430.

Cohan & Harris (Am. th. mang's.): 289.

Collins, William Wilkie (Eng. novelist and dramatist: 1824-1889): 164; 234; comment on his "No Name," 286.

Colman, John (Eng. th. man. and dram.: 1732-1794): 313.

Comedy of Errors," "The: 317.

CONCERT," "THE (farcical comedy): adapted by L. Ditrichstein and produced by B., 289; theme of—and critically considered, 290, *et seq.;* cast of, 290.

Congreve, William (Eng. dramatist: 1670-1729): 313.